An Accidental Manager

ROGER COLLIS

An Accidental Manager

Tales from the Corporate Jungle

GROVE STREET BOOKS

2014

ISBN 978-1-941934-00-5
Library of Congress Control Number: 2014946418

Grove Street Books
PO Box 117
Peterborough, New Hampshire 03458
www.grovestreetbooks.com

GROVE
STREET
B O O K S

Designed by Kirsty Anderson
Printed by Kase Printers, Hudson, New Hampshire

Cover illustration by Sax from
Chief Executive magazine, April 1983

I could not tread these perilous paths in safety,
if I did not keep a saving sense of humor. HORATIO NELSON

Capitalism is a conspiracy, not for the free market
but against it. KARL MARX

Mon vieux, les promesses n'engagent que
ceux qui les croient! JACQUES CHIRAC

These are my principles. And if you don't like them,
I have others. GROUCHO MARX

It's a wise man who knows how to quit when he's behind.

Contents

Part 2

Part 3

Part 4

Introduction

This is a collection of the columns that I would most like to remember (and be remembered by) from the hundreds I have published over five decades in newspapers and magazines around the world.

The stories reflect the evolution of management style and company life and business travel from the telex and typewriter age of the 1960's and 1970's to cyberspace and the digital age of today.

They are based on my own roller-coaster business career – from copywriter at a 'creative boutique' in Lausanne for British international advertising agency Colman Prentis & Varley for mostly U.S. clients in Geneva; to become head of European marketing for Miles Laboratories, an emerging U.S. multinational; and group vice president responsible for business development for a Swedish health care company in Geneva; and finally headhunted as marketing and sales director for the British subsidiary of pharmaceuticals giant Merck Inc. of Rahway, New Jersey.

I became an accidental manager, I suppose, by default, by inertia, going with the flow, until I resigned from my last corporate job and moved to the South of France with the vainglorious notion of reinventing myself as a professional writer and broadcaster. I may have left a promising career behind me.

Arriving in Lausanne on that fateful day in September, 1961, I still thought I was destined somehow to fulfill my dreams of being a poet and actor – both precarious occupations even in the heady 1960's. And believe it or not, it was a slim volume of poetry that got me the job at CPV, then the largest and most prestigious British international advertising agency, without any experience as a hidden persuader.

Some of these stories are earnest disquisitions on management, though usually with a satirical spin; others are thinly disguised fictional vignettes from my checkered career where you will meet a cast of characters: the Chairman; the Welshman; Guratsky; the bitch-goddess Helen, my secretary; Sammy Kalbfleisch; Mel Geist; and Stanley Zilch, the crazed soothsayer of Blue Skies Research in Broken Springs, Colorado.

Roger Collis

Satire is a serious business – not least because good satire is almost indistinguishable from reality. This is why satirists are always in danger of being overtaken by real life. Imagination is reality. You could never imagine how many cracks my crystal ball has sustained over the years.

Writing satire is a dangerous game too, especially if you are an executive in a multi-national company, 'fouling your own nest' as one colleague pointed out with a touch of Schadenfreude.

And indeed, I was always treading what Graham Greene described as 'the dangerous edge of things.' I came close to a heresy trial and execution on several occasions. Some of my more subversive pieces were published when I was safely ensconced in the South of France.

Whether managers are more fulfilled, more secure, more effective, than they were in the 1960s and 1970s is an open question. Have relationships within organizations improved or become more stressful?

Much has changed, of course: technology not only enables, but requires managers to be totally wired at all times, so that business travelers now have two jobs, one on the road and one fighting their corner back in the office. Thanks to the U.S.-led post-9/11 'War on Terror' and the age of mass tourism, business travel has become more onerous and less fun. Airports have become the slowest common denominator of air travel.

Instant communications in the form of smart phones, iPads and a raft of 'mobile devices' have brought new challenges. It is impossible these days, or at least stubbornly eccentric, to be plausibly out of touch on the road. The old lament, 'I'm sorry, I couldn't get to a phone' or: 'The hotel didn't give me the message,' would meet these days with bemused incredulity.

It is hard to imagine today the appalling frustration at being incommunicado at airports and during trans-Atlantic flights. I still shudder when I recall a delayed flight with fellow execs milling around the transit desk, silently screaming, 'A phone, a phone, my kingdom for a phone!'

Thanks to the Internet, even a small local company can market its products and services worldwide. 'Viral marketing,' diffusing awareness through 'social media' is a new buzzword. Who remembers old buzzwords and the 'how to' books: the 'Three-minute manager;' 'In search of excellence'..?

Organizations have changed over the years. Job security has disappeared, even in the so-called 'blue-chip' companies. The executive proletariat is learning to adapt by exploiting new 'portable' skills and seeking fulfillment in 'portfolio careers.' Loyalty is a delusion; no longer a two-way street.

'Globalization' has seen the transformation of companies from the old export-led by the so-called 'international' divisions of U.S. companies to 'domesticated' companies in several countries, often losing their original national identities.

Back in 1970, I wrote a teaching 'case study' for Harvard Business School, 'Chameleon Corporation' describing the evolution of a medium-size family company in the Mid-West of the United States from exporting through local distributors around the world to being a truly international corporation with 'domesticated' operations in major markets. This led to a so-called 'matrix' management involving 'shared responsibility' between local or regional, general managers, with P&L responsibility within their legal entities, and reporting to the international vice-president president; and area-based international product line managers, with P&L responsibility for the fortunes of their divisions, reporting to division vice presidents back at the corporate Kremlin: A recipe for bedlam and strife, not to mention fear and loathing throughout the organization.

'Kinetic equilibrium' is how my erstwhile chairman described it.

But it illustrates a crucial reality of management today: typically managers in most organizations have more responsibility than authority. They have to get things done through other people who do not report directly to them.

Management is always re-inventing the wheel. The IT revolution has helped to strip out layers of middle-management to create 'flatter' hierarchies, with 'business units' as semi-autonomous 'profit centres' and a stripped down 'headquarters unit.' Entrepreneurship, or rather 'intrapreneurship,' was the name of the game. As management gurus came and went, corporations centralized and decentralized every so often in seismic 'restructuring.'

The earliest of these pieces appeared in German translation in *Werbung/ Publicite*, the bilingual monthly magazine of the Swiss Advertising Association, in German and subsequently, as a monthly page in English. A few early whimsical pieces were published in the old miscellany page in *The Guardian* in the 1960's.

Others were published in *Chief Executive*; five notoriously appeared on the op-ed page of the *Wall Street Journal* in 1984; some first appeared in my weekly column *The Frequent Traveler*, which ran for 23 years (1985 to 2008) in the *International Herald Tribune*; some I voiced for *Business Matters* on the BBC World Service. Thirty-nine stories were collected in my first book, *If My Boss Calls, Make Sure You Get his Name*, published in 1984; many of them are republished here.

Several stories are taken from my 'Roger & Out' column in *Business World* magazine; others first appeared in 'The Professional Expatriate' column in *Resident Abroad* magazine, published by the *Financial Times*, and have subsequently appeared in various guises in publications around the world.

I have arranged the pieces in more less arbitrary order, early pieces cheek by jowl with later ones; all are dated (though not too dated, I hope) along with the publications in which they first appeared, which puts them in some sort of context. I have tried not to include specific travel pieces from my IHT column, but some have inevitably asked to 'cross-over' as travel reflects an abiding concern of management life.

The Anxiety Game

1974 Werbung Publicite; 1982 'Business Matters,' BBC World Service; 1984 'If my boss calls, make sure you get his name.' 1983 Wall Street Journal – Europe

As every successful executive knows, the real purpose of communications within a company is not to opine or inform but to generate and transfer anxiety. For of all the games that managers play, the most subtle and rewarding is the 'anxiety game.'

Ever since big corporations lost their entrepreneurial zeal and became preoccupied with running the machine for its own sake, it is how you appear rather than what you achieve which really gets you to the top. The adroit manager knows how to pass the buck without really seeming to by transferring his anxiety to some other hapless executive. It's rather like a sinister game of musical chairs. You want to make sure you've got your seat-belt fastened when the music stops.

There are three principal anxiety routes. First we have the 'lateral transfer.' Here the idea is to get a peer (preferably a specialist staff man) assigned to a project that's going sour. ('You know, Charles, this problem is really research-oriented. I recommend that we make use of Guratsky's expertise.') When the time-bomb explodes, Guratsky has to be pretty nimble to escape absorbing the blame. ('Charles, I know you share my disappointment with Guratsky...')

If by any chance everything turns out well, you can take the credit. ('I'm glad old Guratsky was able to follow my brief.') Either way, you have passed on anxiety and responsibility while appearing to be managerial yourself.

Next is the 'upward transfer.' This can take several forms. The one I like best is the 'smorgasbord gambit.' Here you present your boss with a number of options. Well handled, this can make you look highly resourceful. You flatter the guy by taking his professional advice on such and such. (Advertising is a good example. Everyone is an expert here.) If the project is sensitive, his anxiety will become acute. But if he's astute, he will start working on a 'lateral' or 'upward' transfer.

Then, of course, there is the 'downward transfer.' This is often a countermove to an 'upward transfer,' when it is known as the 'Harvard Defense.' Under the guise of good delegation, you assume a specious guiding manner and push your responsibility for something nasty down to the insecure peon who reports to you. (Now look, Howard, I want to make you look good when you present to the Executive Committee. You know, with my travel load, you're so much closer to the problem than I am. Anyway, it's good for you to have the exposure. Use that idea of mine if you like. It's up to you. But don't worry if people start throwing rocks. I'll be there to field for you.')

You bet you'll be there. With plenty of Delphic eyebrow movement. Thus if Howard joins the walking wounded, you can share exasperated grimaces with his tormentors. And if he pulls off the presentation, you can smile expansively and take the applause.

Professional anxiety-game players are sedulous practitioners of the planned crisis. The idea is to create a diversion under cover of which anxiety for a real problem can be transferred.

For example, an impending sales crisis in France can be camouflaged by dramatizing a United Nations' lucubration on the plight of the grape harvest. Or by inventing a crisis in the Balkans. You announce that the ministry has rejected advertising claims. You invent some spurious contact with the government and get the first plane out. Before leaving, you address a memo to the company media specialist, asking him to make a 'detailed evaluation of the television and radio mix' in France. The trick is that he never gets the memo. You only actually send it to the extensive copy list. Later, if the French problem erupts, nobody will believe that he hasn't been sitting idly by. Obloquy is neatly transferred as you manifest indignant concern. (My God, Charles, it's unbelievable! After the trouble I took to identify the major action points, why the hell didn't Guratsky...') Just to provide additional cover, you refurbish several ancient and voluminous reports to give credence to a fertile but overwhelmingly harassed mind.

Virtually every piece of paper circulating in a company has an 'anxiety value.' The expert knows how to exploit this by creating an 'anxiety gap' between him and his colleague. Anything from a nagging, ulcer-tugging worry to raging paranoia.

Connoisseurs find the Telex an ideal anxiety vehicle. Imagine getting back to the hotel on a Friday evening after a hard day with the local distributor to find a Telex: 'Please call me at 5.30AM your time Monday. Charles requires you brief... garbled... garbled... your markets. Regards, Greenwald.

There's nothing like a quiet weekend away from home for updating the resumé.

The consultant explosion

1983 Wall Street Journal – Europe; 1984 'If my boss calls' ... 1982 'Business Matters,' BBC World Service; 1993 'Roger and Out,' Business Life

Have you noticed that nearly everyone you meet nowadays is a consultant, or at least pretends to be? Top theologians at the Harvard Business School (that august seminary for the corporate priesthood) are predicting that in a few years time the entire business world will consist of consultants. With characteristic prescience they are preparing graduates for the fast track in consultancy with special courses in apologetics and cigar handling.

One pundit of my acquaintance (a high-caste consultant from Bangalore) attributes what he calls the 'consultant explosion' to some sort of arcane synergism wrought by the world recession and the warm weather. Some behavioral scientists theorize that consultancy is the modern executive's way of 'dropping out' – of exercising what psychologists call a 'sense of primary retroactive deprivation' as a way of compensating for the lavish self-determination of the younger generation: the new leisured class.

Others talk of a primeval yearning in Corporate Man for authority without responsibility, a state of grace best achieved either in a top staff job at the corporate Kremlin, politics, investment banking – or as a consultant. (See Guratsky's seminal *Zen and the Art of Strategic Forecasting*.) It's safer to be a guru than an entrepreneur.

Or it used to be. Nowadays, many companies are changing from centralized functional organizations into decentralized, divisional ones made up of profit centers or business units. There is today a discomforting emphasis on 'entrepreneurship,' and up to 50 percent of staff people can suddenly find themselves casualties of a major reorganization.

But, whatever the reason, there's no doubt that if the trend continues, the company as we know it today will disappear, as more and more spent or superfluous executives take refuge in consultancy.

Of course, the best way to become a consultant is to be fired. (I recommend Stanley Zilch's seminal handbook, *The Art of Getting Fired*. Or for the more philosophically minded, Arnold Fishmouth's *Beyond the Peter Principle*.)

Time was when the firing maneuver used to be quite a pageant, with a brass band playing slow, martial airs, a 12-gun salute and press releases unleashed with thousands of multicolored balloons. A freshly fired vice president would gather up the 22-carat shards of his career and depart gratefully to his tastefully furnished consultant's suite. In these democratic times one can dispense with a good deal of the ceremony. Nowadays, any executive with a reasonable sense of occasion, a severance check, a little black book and a Gold Card can become a consultant.

In fact, it's sometimes hard to tell the difference between a consultant and an unemployed executive.

[That's not quite as cynical as it sounds. A recent symposium on 'Putting Grey Power Back to Work' was all about the re-deployment of redundant executives as internal consultants with companies to take on specific assignments, such as gearing up a new factory, helping to relocate offices or choosing a new cactus plant for reception. (Often they are re-hired for a higher salary by the company that 'let them go' – the irony being that they are now self-employed.) Says a head-hunter in Monaco: 'We're building up a centralized CV file of top executives who would like to do just that.']

There's a certain poignancy in the sight of a recently-fired tycoon at a dinner party, ill at ease in his new social role. Take the other evening, for example. I was sitting next to a turkey-necked crone who was the owner of the ex-tycoon in question. Reacting to a snide rejoinder from her neighbor, she sprang to her husband's defense, knocking over several wine glasses as she landed on the other side of the table.

'Of course, George always felt he could make so much more of a contribution if he went on his own, didn't you, George? And then after we turned down the presidency and they made this wonderful offer of early retirement we just had to take it, didn't we, George? No, he's still evaluating potential clients. One has to be so selective. It's a question of values, isn't it George?'

There's no doubt that the proliferation of consultants is getting out of hand. The trouble is that consultant's beget consultants. This results in a daisy-chain of primary, secondary and tertiary consultants. (A useful guide here is Mel Silverman's *Who Consults Whom?*)

Few consultants these days have any direct contact with the client, who is becoming an endangered species as more and more clients become consultants.

This is seriously upsetting the ecological balance of international business. And I wouldn't be at all surprised if any day now the United Nations sponsored 'International Client's Year' as a way of drawing attention to the consultant explosion in the over-developed countries of the world.

Selling the sizzle

1995 Business Life

Some years ago, I was having a drink with the chairman – I'll call him Gerald – of a famous London advertising agency. Gerald had picked up a chunk of new business and brought his wife along to celebrate.

'Gerald, you're the best salesman I ever met.' I meant it as a compliment (after all it was his treat!) But his wife rounded on me. 'Gerald is not a salesman: he is an advertising man,' she snarled.

Sorry I spoke. But in business, or indeed, life, we are all salesmen in one way or another. We sell products, services, sentiments, ideas – or simply ourselves. Every successful executive knows, whatever his or her job title, that selling is an integral part of their personality, their management style.

The first step towards salesmanship is selling yourself on yourself. If you don't believe in yourself, you'll never be able to sell to others. That's the key:

the 'product' is you. Selling is nothing more than a transfer of enthusiasm. Not that I've found myself to be a pushover on those recurring days when my level of self-esteem would make Kafka come on like an optimist.

Still, optimism – a vital precursor to self-confidence – can be acquired in several spurious ways – which doesn't necessarily make it less authentic. There's nothing to match the euphoria of going into a budget meeting with a job offer in your pocket. Even an exploratory call from a headhunter can inspire you to put across the Big Idea to the board.

Sometimes there can be merit in being passive.

'You'd better go and see Tom. He's sure to have an idea for us.' This may involve selling Tom your need for an idea. The selling process can thus be turned upside down, to your advantage. It can also be a subtle way of getting your idea adopted.

Talking of adoption; the best ideas have many parents; bad ideas are orphans. Throwing ideas around is like musical chairs: make sure you are not left holding the dummy when the music stops.

On the other hand, a great idea can all too easily be appropriated by someone else. Of course, this may be what you want. But how many times have you made a suggestion only to have it taken up, and refined, by your best enemy? Whatever the circumstances, it usually pays to keep residual rights of authorship for eventual glory. This can be done by 'banking' your idea with the boss's boss – or one of his peers.

You may also want to protect the provenance of an idea that you have sold to a subordinate – insurance in case he or she sells it to your boss; at its most dangerous on your open flank in a group discussion. (This is the flip-side of Management by Persuasion, called Management by Pre-Emption.)

Lateral selling – to peer groups in other departments and subsidiaries – is even more tricky. You obviously want to stay on good terms (you may become a victim of a 'lateral arabesque' to the Zambian subsidiary in a future reorganization). But in selling an idea you're sure to come across the Not Invented Here syndrome. So here again, you have to make them believe that it's their own idea. This is crucial when selling a bad idea, or an Idea Whose Time Has Not Yet Come. Don't miss the 'sell-by' date.

Every good salesman knows that you don't sell a product, or a service, you sell its benefits. Sell the sizzle, not the steak; an old adage, but a good one. It's the sizzle that makes people's mouths water, makes them suddenly, excruciatingly conscious of their needs, desires, aspirations... You have to think about the 'what's in it for me' syndrome. Your boss has to see an inside track for his or herself in your new plan for decentralization; if you are selling software, talk in terms of functionality and better service to customers; if you are selling the idea of maintaining advertising in the recession, point out how crucial it is to keep market share, even at the expense of third-quarter earnings, and how to sell this eventuality to the shareholders. And so it goes.

How, where and when to sell ideas depends on circumstance. You may find the right time to strike is just before the chairman goes on holiday so that he has plenty of time to assimilate the idea and make it his own. Or, just before the shareholders' meeting when he's wound up (Management by Terror, or Management by Grasping at Straws).

These days, I am usually selling the idea of taking up someone else's time; not always to their advantage. (As Joan Didion wrote: 'Writers are always selling somebody out.') One advantage of selling on the phone is that you don't have to buy lunch (not that day anyway). Another is that you can usually keep the chat short, if not sweet.

This brings me to the last maxim in the salesman's lexicon: You run the risk of losing a sale if you keep on talking after a commitment has been made. Once you've sold, shut up.

I'm sure you'll buy that.

Roger Collis

Vocation Vacations

2005 International Herald Tribune

Do I want to take the office with me when I go on vacation? Or do I steal a few days at either end of a business trip for rest and recreation?

It often amounts to the same thing. These days, we are all faced with the ability (and obligation) to keep in touch with anyone anywhere in the world, and, perhaps more ominously, for anyone to be able to keep in touch with you, although anybody calling your office or mobile number can reach you without needing to know whether you are actually at your desk or on the other side of the world. It is quite a challenge for anyone's management style to go convincingly missing – although I have been known to check out of a hotel with the red message light still blinking.

There are varying degrees of staying in touch, from being loosely tethered to the center of the universe, via phone, e-mail or fax, and only reacting to crises, to actually doing your job as if you were there. That is why vacations can be more stressful than staying at home.

One does not have to be a workaholic to know that the compulsion to stay in touch sometimes stems more from a need for reassurance than from a devotion to duty.

They say it takes the first few days of a vacation to unwind, the next few days to relax and the last few days to worry about what you might find (or may not find) when you get back to the office.

Relaxation is the mother of anxiety.

Better to have a problem screaming down the phone than screaming in the mind. On vacation, F. Scott Fitzgerald's 'dark three o'clock in the morning of the soul' can hit you at any time of the day or night.

Better to live with the devil you know.

All it takes is a mobile phone, a Blackberry and a Wi-Fi enabled laptop to stay on top of holiday stress.

An American Management Association survey found that one quarter of executives claim to be in daily contact with their offices during vacation; 40 percent plan to conduct some office-related work; and 44 percent are required to provide their office with their itineraries and contact numbers. According to the YPB&R/Yankelovich Partners National Business Travel Monitor, over 60 percent of travelers take time out for leisure on business trips. A professional 'extender' will typically stop over somewhere on the way (or make a side trip), take off the middle weekend, or add two days to either side of a 10-day trip. There is also a trend toward frequent shorter breaks, replacing a traditional summer vacation – except, of course, for the French, who take off with ritualistic insouciance for a whole month in August.

An ideal weekend escape is a change of lifestyle. This can mean sharing a new adventure with your partner away from the routines of a domestic weekend at home; or becoming a tourist in a city that you know only from the superficial perspective of business trips.

The company Worldwide Escapes (www.worldwideescapes.com) offers customized weekend trips for business travelers in countries in Asia and South America. Trips usually depart from major business cities on Fridays and return Sunday night, enabling a business traveler who visits Hong Kong to get away for two days, exploring, say, the Guilin mountains in southern China, two hours away by plane.

Or to take off from Santiago for a weekend exploring the Cajón del Maipo area in the foothills of the Chilean Andes, by hiking, horseback or rafting.

Vocation Vacations (www.vocationvacations.com) offers a novel twist to the notion of the 'working holiday.' The idea is that you unwind by going to work – in an entirely different job! Two- to three-day packages give you the chance to 'test-drive a dream job by shadowing someone who does it for a living.' So if you are jaded from your daily grind as accountant, you might find transient fulfillment as an auctioneer, golf instructor, radio personality, winemaker or landscape designer.

These are among the 48 'vocational vacations' available in the United States and Britain, with 34 more to come, including cruise ship host, music producer, restaurateur, marine biologist, park ranger, zookeeper and fashion model.

Brian Kurth, a former marketing director who dreamed up the idea for the Web site while stuck in traffic and then created it in March 2004, says, 'We focus on dream jobs and careers that people can actually pursue.

We've already seen people making huge shifts.

One guy in Texas opted out of his technology job to study winemaking after a successful Vocation Vacation. And an attorney in Los Angeles left her job to open a dog day care center.' I thought of making a late late career change by starting a similar site, WalterMitty.com. But it has, of course, been snapped up (check it out if you are into home cinema.)

How about Dream-job-vacations.com? Perhaps that could be my belated ticket to fame and fortune.

Mammon & the muse

1980 Werbung/Publicite; 1984 'If my boss calls…' 1995 The Author, Society of Authors.

After slaving for weeks in the hardboard jungle behind the plush front offices, we had hauled our layouts through the rain to the vivisection room in the Du Pont de Nemours building.

I was immoderately proud of my headline: '*Worried About Your Wells, Mr. Harper?*' A seductive introduction, I thought to a disquisition on abstruse chemicals.

The product managers were politely non-committal, preferring to defer to Mr. Big, who delivered the coup de grace in the manner of a famous surgeon performing for his students.

Mr. Big dropped cigar ash on the precious layout. 'Who the hell is this Harper guy?' he said. 'We're paying for advertising, not for poetry.'

It was a bitter pill. Especially as Mammon had momentarily usurped the Muse as my mentor. And my new job was on the line.

They gave me the Du Pont advertising bible, from which I discovered that you can write any headline you like, provided it contains three elements: the name of the product, the name Du Pont and a 'major product benefit.'

A week later my faltering career was reprieved when I returned with the immortal headline: '*Du Pont Nugreen Feeds Through the Leaves.*'

I was working for Colman, Prentis & Varley, who billed themselves back in the 1960s as the 'largest British international advertising agency.' The managing director, Leslie Cort, was a daunting Yorkshireman who had taken me under his wing. 'Roger,' he would mischievously intone at cocktail parties, 'is a poet.'

I used to feel like a small boy who has been summoned by proud parents to recite *The Wreck of the Hesperus* in front of their friends.

'Leslie,' I would silently implore, 'can't you introduce me as one of your bright young creative men?'

Mind you, that depended on how my poetry was going.

I tended to alternate between being a poet and a copywriter, according to how many rejection slips I was getting at the time from the small magazines. Nowadays, alas, I have most of my eggs and none of my illusions in the commercial basket.

I met quite a few fellow poets in the copywriting stables. Many of them were good copywriters as well as good poets. Of course, we had a sprinkling of novelists manqué. But it was the poets who seemed to find the art of writing selling copy particularly compatible with their literary vocation.

And if you think about it there are many similarities: the need to weigh the value of each word, compactness and brevity; the deployment of imagery and metaphor; the zapping title or headline that explodes the meaning and the need for the text to wear well after repeated readings. You can always spot a lazy line.

Good advertising copy, like poetry, is hewn out of granite. The message, like Michelangelo's sculpture, is liberated from the natural stone.

There is satisfaction (not untinged with irony) for a poet with a slim volume to his credit (circulation circa 300) to think that a margarine commercial is reaching millions. Ah, but if only he could sign his masterpiece. With what mixed emotions does he hear his anonymous slogans retailed by the public.

His only chance for an ego trip is when the industry feasts his fecundity at the annual advertising awards – or when the agency down the street offers him a better job! What poet's heart is not gladdened by such appreciation. You can see him at the celebratory lunch as, with champagne glass raised, he smiles his simple thanks through the racing bubbles.

And yet, and yet. I wonder how many margarine commercials have buried in them a cry for help ('I am a prisoner in a blacking factory.') A way of saying, 'Hey, you out there! Listen to me. I'm working in advertising but I'm really a poet trying to get out.'

And that's the rub. The poet may perpetuate his own message rather than his client's, which gets lost in the execution. Good copy (and perhaps good poetry) is the perfect synthesis of content and style. And, like poetry, can sometimes communicate without being consciously understood.

But I guess in the final analysis the poet/copywriter must reconcile himself with the fact that advertising is not an art form but a selling mechanism.

'It's not creative unless it sells.' A truth from which it would take a semantic Houdini to escape.

Decisions, decisions

1994 Business Life

'Any idea that the buck stops here is bravado, mythology, total nonsense,' a senior colleague said as I started my last corporate incarnation.

He nodded towards the appalling pile of paper his secretary had just brought in. 'That's stuff waiting for decisions of some kind. What I do is make the quick and obvious ones, delegate some to my staff, and chuck the rest out. You can be sure that anything really important is going to come screaming down the phone sooner or later. But you'll find most things either resolve themselves or get overtaken by events.'

What you might call a balanced view of decision-making. And one which brought Bill an enviable reputation as the most decisive executive in the company (It also brought him a 22-carat handshake – one of the best involuntary decisions he never made.)

Putting Bill's practice into theory, there are three essential approaches to decision-making.

1. First, tackle the 'quick 'n easy' decisions – ranging from fixing a date

for an agency lunch to deciding, on principle, that we must cut variable costs to protect bottom-line profit. (This is an example of a 'motherhood' statement, or 'phantom' decision,' begging the question of how it can actually be achieved! Which, of course, requires a much more difficult decision, or unending series of decisions.)

2. Delegation. This means transferring your responsibility for a tricky decision to someone else – preferably someone who is after your job. All decisions in an organization have an 'anxiety value.' The decisive manager knows how to exploit this by creating an 'anxiety gap,' sometimes known as a 'decision quotient,' between him or herself and colleagues.

There are often times when you need to convince someone that your decision is theirs. You can do this with a good, bad, or unpopular decision, depending on the circumstances. But never allow anyone else to make an 'obvious' decision, which should emanate from you. And, in all cases, make sure you retain the option of second-guessing the outcome.

Collective, or consensus, decisions are a useful form of delegation. Get everybody on board and you sink or swim together. In Japan, this is part of the corporate culture. With us it's a bit different. 'So we're decided on the need for a radical review of our computer software. I'd like to ask Howard to form a task force to recommend what system we should install across the company.' This shows how a simple, unthreatening, 'open-ended' decision can lead to a stressful 'forced-choice' decision, especially when it's made by specialist staff – top management, of course, being unable to understand the pros and cons of the recommendation, which becomes by default, a decision made by Howard's task force.

3. Procrastination. As everyone knows, it's how you appear, rather than what you accomplish which gets you to the top. Decisiveness is in the eye of the shareholder, or the beholder. Sometimes, the best decision is no decision. To paraphrase Franklin D. Roosevelt: 'The only thing we have to fear about decisions are the decisions themselves.' (See Stanley Zilch's: *The Art of Procrastination*, or Arnold Fishmouth's *Farting Around in Organizations*.)

There's more to procrastination than a simple Micawber-like propensity for waiting for the right decision to turn up. The professional procrastinator will avoid a decision by convening yet another meeting, a fact-finding trip, or more market research, the results of which can be discussed at another meeting safely in the future – preferably when you have moved on and upwards. Advertising agencies are expert at this game. 'We sincerely believe that at this point a formal proposal would be premature,' the new account director prevaricates. 'We recommend running the concept once again through another set of focus groups, but this time of very frequent users of the product… to gather more attitudinal data which we can then run past the creative boys and girls… develop a new set of storyboards which we can then test…'

'I've made a decision, don't confuse me with the facts,' is not quite as flippant as it sounds. For one thing, you may not have the facts – and what's more important, neither may anyone else. And too many facts can lead to 'information overload' – a fatally costive condition. Some of the best decisions are made with too little information.

Some people make a meal of the simplest decisions. There was *The New Yorker* cartoon with a waitress asking a group of suits engrossed in their menus: 'Have you gentlemen finished the decision-making process?'

Mind you, I've known occasions when a decision to have a third pre-prandial martini (at a two-martini lunch) had awesome outcomes. But by and large, we normally never give a second thought in deciding between steak or chicken breast, or which suit to wear. We probably make a thousand involuntary decisions every day, and nothing goes horribly wrong as a result.

Some people subscribe to the random theory of decision-making – let the chips fall as they may. Others believe that the best decisions are not the ones that you consciously make, but the ones you feel are right. Assuming that you have delegated decision-making to the subconscious.

Gary Kasparov, the chess master, has said that some moves in chess should be played by instinct – without hesitation. 'There's a danger in thinking too much. A chess player must trust himself in the same way that a concert pianist trusts his fingers.'

My only problem is that I'm the last person I'd trust to make a decision.

Meetingmanship

1984 Business Life; 1985 International Herald Tribune

Try to phone anybody these days and the chances are (once you've gone around the houses with 'dial one if you know the extension number...') you'll get an earful of the xylophone version of Greensleeves, or a low-fi rendering of The Four Seasons by the Muzak Symphony Orchestra. Then the doom-laden words: 'He's in a meeting.' Or the pompous: 'He's in conference.' Yes, yes, our cheque is in the mail.

Of course, it all depends what you mean by 'meeting' or 'conference.' Some executives are perpetually in meetings, it seems, when you want to get hold of them. This can mean almost anything: Either they are nattering with their secretary, or someone else's secretary, on another line, in with the boss, gone for lunch, not back from lunch, gone for the day, trying out their new water wings in the company think tank or truly engaged in motivating the troops at a cost-effective little resort on the Costa Extravaganza. You may be passed from one voice mail to another or else patched through to a mobile. Even if you do manage to speak in person and in real time, you may find that the guy you want is sitting across the aisle from you in business class, on the way to the same conference.

Meetingmanship requires a strategic and tactical approach, depending on whether you're talking conferences or meetings. Conferences differ from meetings, mainly because they are occasions when you are talked at rather than talking among, if you follow. They come in several guises: from management development seminars, new product launches and sales meetings to association jamborees. (You even get conferences for conference organizers.) Conferences are a way of wasting everybody's time away from the office and form an integral part of 'Management by Absence'; while meetings are great way of wasting other people's time when in the office ('Management by Pre-emption'). Successful conferences and meetings are an end in themselves, rather than a means to an end. 'We are, therefore we meet.' Or vice versa.

They are also a good excuse for holding impromptu board meetings in the absence of a fellow director who wasn't able to make it to the conference, poor chap. ('Howard, we're sorry you weren't able to join us in Mogadishu.')

This is an egregious example of the 'invisible agenda' (somewhat similar to the 'invisible organization' within the company) whereby executives are able to meet and conspire in those invigorating after-hours sessions far from the daily pressures of the office.

Meanwhile, back in the office, there are many variations to this gambit. You have 'shadow meetings' (meetings within meetings) when a caucus, or a breakaway group, has its own meeting and subverts the official one ('Management by Destabilization'). A related gambit is to invite as many people as you can who have no interest whatsoever, nor any conceivable contribution to make, while excluding people you don't want, either by calling the meeting in their absence or simply forgetting to circulate their copy of the agenda.

The same goes for minutes. Minutes are best written before the meeting and circulated to a select few. They reflect what you have decided, rather than what the participants said. In a refined form, this involves distributing 'minutes' to folk who thought they'd simply been chatting in your office, or while traveling. You can formalise any kind of discussion by calling it a meeting. ('Come in, Howard, we're having a meeting.' Or, 'You remember that meeting we had on the flight from Paris the other day?')

Keeping the initiative is the essence of meetingmanship. You need to consider where you're going to meet. ('The venue is the message,' as Marshall McLuhan might have said.) The approach might be casual: 'Your office or mine?' Or, 'I've managed to get the boardroom.' Or more authoritative: 'I've decided we ought to join the others in Cleveland.'

You also need to decide whether to turn up early - which may or may not involve changing the time at the last moment ('I thought we'd start early, Howard; I'll fill you in later.' Or late ('Sorry I'm late, Howard, would you quickly recap?') Or not turn up at all.

Which tactic you use will depend on who is in the chair. Some meetings are leaderless when they start - a chairman emerging by dint of rank or strength of personality. A useful role is that of 'shadow chairman,' speaking, as it were, from the back benches. This is often done as a prelude to a meeting within a meeting. But perhaps the ultimate ploy is to chair a meeting consisting of your boss and other heavy hitters. Do this through a 'planned crisis,' for which, of course, you provide a miraculous solution.

You may also need to decide whether to make your presentation on slides, an overhead projector or a flip-chart (this works well for brainstorming, when you control the meeting by selectively writing down what people say) or with your new Banana 2 laptop with split-screen color graphics.

Whether you decide to take notes - or ostentatiously not to take notes - may depend on the kind of 'statement' you want to make. A similar effect can be achieved at an international conference by using or not using the earphones for simultaneous translation. Or you might want to plug in your Walkman.

You must consider too whether to hand out copies of your presentation before, during, or after the meeting or conference, and to whom. Tactics may dictate whether you adjourn for lunch, work right through, or send out for sandwiches.

Lunch meetings are still popular in countries like Britain, Spain and France. But in the United States, any hint of hedonism these days is likely to invoke the combined wrath of Mammon and the shareholders: strictly a matter of putting the guilt on the gingerbread and avoiding gilt by association. I rang a business friend in New York on a recent trip. 'Let's do lunch,' he said. 'We don't need to eat.'

The ultimate conference style is to teleconference from a yacht cruising in the Caribbean. But telephone meetings have a unique sense of urgency and putative fulfillment, especially from an overseas subsidiary. (The number one rule for business travelers is never to do business in the country you are visiting, but always be on the phone to somewhere else.) You don't have to buy lunch. And you can always get somebody to say you are in a meeting or at a conference.

Roger Collis

The Medium is the Merchandise

1977 Werbung/Publicite

'I want you to think of this supermarket as a magazine,' Guratsky said. We'd entered The Emporium – 'A unique concept in retail marketing,' the notice said – in the heart of Bermondsey.

'I'm sorry, Tom, it's too early in the morning,' I said.

Guratsky smiled patronizingly and snapped on a green eyeshade in the time-honored editorial manner. 'I'll explain.'

We sat down at the marble-topped counter of what seemed to be like an old-fashioned soda fountain and ordered strawberry milk shakes with ice-water chasers.

'The trouble with supermarkets is that they only carry top-selling brands – the manufacturer is at the mercy of the computer. He can lose distribution overnight if his share of the market drops a couple of percentage points; if he's not spending enough money above or below-the-line, or fails to deliver an additional discount. At the same time, the consumer has fewer brands to choose from. The business initiative has passed from the manufacturer to the distributor and retailer. I believe the supermarket would be a worthier institution if it didn't have such dictatorial powers.'

'You may be right. But what's this got to do with magazines?'

'I'll tell you. The difference between The Emporium and conventional supermarkets is that we sell shelf-space in the same way as a magazine sells page space to advertisers. This means, of course, that manufacturers decide for themselves how much shelf space they want to allocate and to which brands. They are also free to merchandise and set up their own in-store displays for an agreed price, which is virtually impossible in most supermarkets. This enables them to have a real dialogue with the consumer at the point of sale. We are simply providing a medium, an interface, if you will, for introducing the manufacturer to the customer. Holistic marketing we call it.'

'I get it: the medium is the merchandise. But tell me, Tom, how do you go about negotiating the shelf rates, sorry, page rates, with the advertiser?'

'The same as any other magazine. The Emporium is a monthly and the page rate depends on circulation, which is the number of people circulating in the store. Good page positions correspond with high-traffic points. For instance, we're sitting right now on the inside of the back cover.'

'Fascinating. But to extend the magazine analogy, wouldn't you have to have some kind of editorial?'

'That's exactly what we do have,' Guratsky said, adjusting his eyeshade and filling his pipe with Acapulco Gold. 'I produce a theme issue each month. In January, we had a son-et-lumiere of a Bohemian hunting weekend in the 1920s to celebrate the game season. This month, we're planning to highlight our new fish boutique with a marine exhibition. We hope to have a live shark on display – a joint promotion with Jaws 5 at the local cinema. And the air-conditioning will pipe in authentic seashore smells, like fried scampi and exhaust smoke, with wrap-around sound of traffic over a background of waves breaking on the sea-shore. That's the responsibility of our environment editor Joe Slocum.

'We have a full editorial staff – the mast-head is over the door – consumer affairs, health and beauty. We even have a nostalgia editor, Sandra Smith, who's responsible for simulating the personal touch that used to be such an attractive feature of the old corner store. You're old enough to know what I mean. It sold everything from ice-cream and toothpowder to vintage sardines and fly-papers. You passed the time of day with the proprietor while he weighed out the cheese and bacon. Maybe you sampled the dill pickle from the brine counter below the counter. The essence of the corner store was variety and a human touch.'

'Nostalgia is all very well, Tom. Friendliness, yes the personal touch, but nobody has the time to spend, not to mention putting up with the clutter and confusion of the old Ma and Pa store; you can't go back 100 years with a modern supermarket. You'll be out of business in no time.'

Guratsky shook his head and smiled. 'You miss the point; we're simply trying to translate that old-fashioned atmosphere into the modern idiom. We found a genuine old barrel that was being used at an antique cheese auction at Sotheby's, and had it put up here. Our chemists have even recreated the smell of freshly roasted coffee. You remember fresh coffee? Along with floor polish, with a touch of mice droppings. People love to come in and chat with our psychologist: some of the tapes are fascinating.'

'That's all very well. But what people want these days is service, which is what the supermarket provides.'

'Modern supermarkets are supremely efficient shopping machines. But they've become dehumanized. There's a reaction today against slick merchandising. The modern consumer yearns for a return to the more wholesome values of yesterday – even if they don't quite realize what it is they're missing. You see how we've broken up the somewhat bleak interior of the store into more intimate boutique sections? This soda fountain, for example. This is the age of the environment. And we believe we have created a new medium reflecting the new consumer values.'

'It certainly sounds very uplifting, Tom. I suppose it depends on whether you like your medium hot or cold; which assumes that this checks out, if you'll pardon the pun, with Marshall McLuhan – as well as your bank manager.'

Making your presents felt

1993 Business Life; Executive Travel

I think it was Picasso who described his early days as a struggling artist in Paris as a time when the difference between a sale and a gift was negligible. Paraphrase that slightly and you've hit the nail on the thumb as far as business gifts are concerned – there's a very fine line between a bribe and a genuine business gift. It's the kind of 'now you see it, now you don't' distinction that has proved to be an ethical minefield for unwary executives, both on the giving and receiving end. An ill-considered gift can easily turn out to be an exploding cigar. Remember that gift giving is a form of communication; it says as much about the giver as the receiver.

Take the case of the hapless executive who destroyed a carefully nurtured relationship in China by giving a clock, a symbol of death, as a New Year present. On the other hand, get it right, and you may come home with a contract: that happened to the smart lad who offered his Saudi contact a sounding device for calling back falcons.

When is a business gift a bribe? This is often the kind of 'now you see it, now you don't' that has proved an ethical minefield for executives on both the giving and receiving end -not to mention those in the middle. You might say that a bribe is open persuasion done covertly ('Give us the Fingelstein contract and we'll open a holiday fund for you at the Schweizerische Bankgesellschaft in Zurich') and a gift is hidden persuasion done openly ('Please accept this Picasso lithograph for your boardroom as a small token...')

More cynically perhaps, a bribe is a gift that you wouldn't want to be discovered. (It's fear of the consequences that keeps most people honest.) But get it wrong and you may end up in court with the organ softly playing *Here Comes the Bribe* as you step inside the witness box, or worse. The fact that the law hasn't quite caught up with business practice isn't going to help you very much.

A genuine gift – as distinct from a bribe – is a gesture of friendship. The personal touch is more important than monetary value. It can help avoid one of the pitfalls of gift-giving called 'escalation,' a kind of arms race in which the recipient feels obliged to reciprocate with a more lavish gift. This is what the economists call 'gift-push' inflation. Try to make sure you get something that the other person wouldn't think of buying for him or herself.

Most people would recognise a Gucci attaché case stuffed with crisp treasury bills as a bribe rather than a gift, but what about an empty Gucci attaché case? Or the offer of a free holiday in the Caribbean? Or if somebody picks up your hotel expenses when you visit them? Or a press trip to Miami? My paper doesn't allow me to go on press trips, although many journalists do. In which case, are they being bribed? Am I being bribed if I accept lunch from that nice PR lady? Or is that simply lubricating the larynx of trade?

Of course, in some parts of the world, Africa for example, bribery and corruption are a way of life and the only sure-fire way to do business. A former colleague of mine, who dashes around Africa selling pharmaceuticals, describes a bribe as being 'direct results related and dished out before, rather than after, the favour is granted.'

Before leaving on a trip he stocks up with gifts (or bribes) for every hierarchical contingency - from plastic ball points ('for anyone you meet') and imitation marble desk sets to gold Waterman fountain pens. He tells me that in one African republic the head of government medical stores, before processing an order, requires five per cent of its value deposited in his bank in Finsbury Park. But before getting in to see this gentleman, you first have to bribe the chief store keeper with three Marks and Spencer shirts. (Size 17 collar if you're thinking of going out there.) And so it goes.

Closer to home, we like to think we do things with a bit more style. But let's face it, gift giving, however gracefully handled, is rarely an act of disinterested generosity; it's intended to acquire goodwill and to create a sense of obligation. The subtle art of giving a business gift (as distinct from a bribe) consists of wrapping that obligation (wrapping is important, as we'll see later) in a form of personal expression which compliments the intelligence and sensibility of the recipient. The idea should be to create an 'obligation gap' which is within the limits of a person's capacity for self-deception. If the obligation gap is too wide, or the motive too glaringly obvious, it can produce embarrassment or even hostility rather than gratitude. Like politics, gift giving (and you can include bribes) is the art of the possible; in other words, what you can get away with. I'll try to show what I mean with three examples from my own chequered career.

About 100 years ago, when I was a corporate executive, I had to recommend a new distributor for our market in Greece. My prime candidate, let's call him Costas Obstreperous, was in my office for the crunch meeting when he took me aside and said he'd like to offer my wife a small car. It was a crude thing to do and I was suitably appalled. The irony was that I was going to recommend him anyway, and I did, in spite of the bribe. He got the business. I've always wondered if somebody else's wife got the car.

Another occasion was a meeting I'd set up a few days before Christmas between my chairman and the chairman of our advertising agency. Our visitor was waiting in reception with the couple of cohorts. 'Can you find a cool place for this?' he said, handing me a long parcel. 'It's a side of smoked salmon.' Acute embarrassment, especially with the chairman hovering. 'Look,' I said, 'here are my car keys; can you put it on the back seat?' During the meeting, I found myself holding back from a blistering attack on the agency's presentation, my embarrassment metamorphosing to hostility. (It took three sessions with my analyst to come to terms with a side of smoked salmon.) How could such a smooth operator be so crass? If only he'd taken the trouble to mail it to me with a personal note whacked out on his Banana PC, it might have seemed more of a gift than a bribe.

In pleasant contrast was a gift I subsequently received from another ad agency executive. The guy had taken the trouble to find out that I am an Eric Von Stroheim buff, presenting me with a new Thomas Quinn Curtiss biography, suitably inscribed and a marvellous archive photograph of Stroheim in *La Grande Illusion*, which still adorns my office. I'm ashamed to say I've forgotten the executive's name, which puts me almost in the same category of the American tycoon who called across to his wife at a cocktail party, 'Hon, what's the name of those close personal friends of ours in Broken Springs?' Ah, the transience of business friendships!

On the other hand, business gifts (and what ultimately distinguishes them from bribes) should be made as a gesture of friendship; a gift is an investment in a relationship. Clichés such as 'It's the thought that counts' and 'It's not what you do, it's the way you do it' are worth brushing off and taking to heart, especially at this time of year. If you can't make a personal effort, you shouldn't bother with a gift; it may do more harm than good. So do your homework. Time spent in reconnaissance is seldom wasted, goes the old military maxim.

It's not hard to find out someone's particular interest or hobby. Secretaries or colleagues are an obvious source of ideas. I once had a chairman who was a world authority and collector of Samurai swords. I couldn't afford to buy him one – they cost thousands – and it would have been grossly inappropriate anyway, but he was delighted when I sent him a lavishly illustrated auction catalogue which he hadn't seen. If someone enjoys

Scotch whisky, a case is always welcome (provided it isn't just shipped from the supplier with a printed card), but a better idea might be to select half a dozen obscure malts, perhaps with a copy of David Daiches' classic book on the history of Scotch whisky.

Another thing to consider is how to reach the right recipient in an organization. This is often a matter of knowing your way around the invisible hierarchy. For example, the chairman's PA may be much more useful to you than the boss. A warehouse dispatcher may be able to do more for you than the production director, and so on. What's more, such people are less likely to be highly gifted (this has nothing to do with talent) than the chairman, who is so flooded with gifts that he may not notice yet another desk diary.

You may find original ideas stalking the pages of the glossy magazines. 'Now it's easier than ever to give your loved one, a valued business associate [sic] or yourself the kind of gift that creates truly memorable dining... Klipstein's gourmet steaks. Their mouth-watering taste...' Or perhaps a Feinschmecker ham from the Black Forest or an Ansel Adams print of Yosemite or one of your company's products. Candied fruits are likely to go down better than fan belts, but you never know. Or how about 'Model 1800 British twelve-pounder cannons in valuable brass - a life-long talking point'? Or 'Sterling silver bicycle chains, the real McCoy at only $160'? Well, yes. Personally, I feel you can't go wrong with a well-chosen book or a magazine subscription. But whatever you choose, try to make sure it is something that the recipient wouldn't normally think of buying for him or herself.

Creativity, thoughtfulness and the personal touch are more important than the monetary value of a gift. It can help avoid one of the pitfalls of gift giving called 'escalation' - a kind of arms race in which the recipient feels obligated to reciprocate with a more lavish gift. (Economists call this 'gift push inflation'.) The perception of equality is important for a relationship to survive ('Balance of Power'). On the other hand, a highly gifted person (this has nothing necessarily to do with talent) has a certain 'expectation threshold' which needs to be carefully measured. It depends on who is doing the giving.

A peon may make just the right impression with a first day stamp cover of the Vancouver Games, but a chairman-to-chairman gift requires a more lavish approach, say the use of your yacht for a fortnight cruising the Mediterranean. Nothing offends people more than the impression that they can be bought cheaply. I'm sure you know the story of the gorgeous creature who was enchanted at her table companion's proposition that they share a stateroom on the QE2, but was aghast when he asked how much it would cost to sleep with her for one night. 'What do you think I am; a prostitute?' she bridled. 'Madame, we've already established that,' he replied. 'I'm now discussing the price.'

Buying a gift for a foreign business contact needs special care, although thoughtfulness is appreciated by everyone. The Japanese, a ceremonious people who set great store by long-term relationships and human values, have developed gift giving into an art form. Don't try to out-gift them and never surprise them with a gift, they may be embarrassed by not having one for you at the time. Wrapping is important - try to make it rice paper and avoid ribbons, bold colours and black and white combinations, which are reserved for funerals. I could go on, but the best guide, if you can hold of it, is Stanley Zilch's *Japan on Two Faux Pas a Day*.

The French, as everyone knows, can be tricky. To offer a gift at the first encounter is likely to be considered gauche (although this may change at the next elections.) Avoid home decoration gifts (your taste may be on the line) or anything which is too personal; when invited home for a meal, send flowers beforehand (avoid chrysanthemums) rather than afterwards or the gift may be interpreted as a reward rather than a thoughtful gesture; never give a French businesswoman perfume, it is far too intimate a gift for a business relationship.

In Germany, avoid red roses (they are reserved for lovers), the number 13, and get local advice on wrapping a gift. Germans appreciate entertainment, but it should be well-planned and somewhat formal.

Arabs are magnanimous and appreciate generous people. If you're well off, it's best to be generous or they'll have no respect for you. Watch out for the 'escalation. syndrome.' Never offer a gift to a wife (or wives) and do not admire an object openly: you may find it's yours!

In Latin America, never give a knife (it implies cutting off a relationship) or a handkerchief (it's associated with tears). Never go empty-handed to visit a home but otherwise do not give a gift until you have developed a personal relationship with a business contact.

Yes, it's all very difficult; especially so for Anglo-Saxons who tend to be caught up in the undemonstrative Puritan Ethic which makes them feel that to give is better than to receive. Certainly, they feel more comfortable giving, especially Americans. But it's a mistake: the one who gives must allow the recipient to repay. I'm surprised that the Harvard Business School – that august seminary for the corporate priesthood – hasn't got (gotten?) around (as far as I know) to teaching the principles of international gift giving. One can envisage a new breed of gift consultants to advise on strategic and tactical gift planning for companies.

All is fair in gifts and war. You may even want to send an anonymous gift to someone you don't like. My old friend Sammy Kalbfleisch was telling me about a new service called 'Unsolicited Gifts Incorporated'. For a fee you can have cheese, kippers and whatever sent by surface mail. The full persecution package is a carefully orchestrated mailing of perishable foods. The victims aren't even safe away from their office. A special hotel division arranges to switch breakfast cards that people hang outside their doors when they go to bed. Imagine a competitor, who has a sensitive meeting first thing in the morning, being woken up at five o'clock with a breakfast trolley replete with Boeuf Stroganoff and Champagne.

Now that really is using business gifts as a management tool.

Meanwhile, back at the conference

1984 International Herald Tribune; 1988 Airport magazine.

On any given working day as many as 50 percent of all executives are likely to be away from their desks attending a conference or seminar of some kind, according to a report published by the Blue Skies Research Institute in Broken Springs Colorado. If attendance at internal company meetings and time spent logged on to the Internet or gazing into space is taken into account, this figure may approach 100 percent, especially among senior executives.

Stanley Zilch, a Brussels-based consultant in time management, says that one measure of an executive's success is how much time he or she manages to spend away from the office. 'Management by Absence' (MBA) is replacing 'Management by Rumor' (MBR) as the fashionable tenet in executive behavior.

The title 'Conference Delegate of the Year' is being awarded for the first time this year. The judges will take into account not only the total number of conferences attended but also expense-account miles traveled and time spent on the road. There is a points system based upon a 'conference basket' of management development seminars, trade fairs, sales conferences, incentive meetings, new product launches and so on.

Companies themselves record points and award conferences and holidays (often much the same thing) to high-scoring employees. This is called 'incentive travel.'

During the last economic recession, the conference business became one of the few growth industries. To be sure, many companies cut back on business travel and conference expenses. But there is widespread recognition that conferences are making a major contribution towards full executive employment. There are hundreds and thousands of executives attending conferences who might otherwise be queuing at job centers and management soup kitchens. Many a manager has been saved from becoming a consultant by a well-chosen conference.

As yet more companies change from centralized, functional types of organizations into decentralized divisional profit centers with flatter hierarchies, they may be shedding up to 30 percent of their staff. In fact, up to 50 percent of personnel can be casualties in a major reorganization. Instead of firing these people, many companies find it more cost-effective to send them out on the conference circuit. It's really a question of balancing conference costs against the expense of golden handshakes.

Moreover, companies are finding that they can cut overhead costs by allocating one office to several executives. There are special computer programs for doing this: inventory control software has been found useful in predicting the probability of any one executive needing the communal office on any particular day.

Some companies also find that they can more than double-up executives for a given job function. A 'conference-intensive' company, for example, may find that it needs half-a-dozen sales and marketing directors, three times the number of vice presidents and a score or more of CEOs.

The conference year for a typical executive might start in London with 'Globalize or Die' at the Savoy Hotel or 'Megatrends for Corporate Planners' at the Hilton. Then on to Paris for 'Meeting the Asian Challenge' at the Crillon and then down to the Cote d'Azur for the popular three-month 'Currency Futures' conference at the Monte Carlo Business School. Then perhaps to Florence for the 'Cash Flow Festival,' and moving to Davos for winter-sports deliberations in the snow with business leaders and politicians. Any remaining gaps in a schedule can easily be filled at one of the nonstop seminars on offer at the Management Center Europe in Brussels.

With the emergence of conferences as an end in themselves rather than a means to an end, there is a new freedom from traditional hierarchical roles and behavior. This is changing national mores. One is even beginning to detect, especially at the more relentlessly international gatherings, a merging of national characteristics into a distinct 'conference style.'

Of course, one still recognizes the braying of the public school type or the ineffable resignation of the Gallic shrug. But the ultimate in conference chic is a suave mid-Atlantic 'guess-where-I-come-from?' style.

Everyone comes to a conference pretending to be someone else. The British try to look like Americans and the Americans try to look British (dress British, think Yiddish is the watchword here). The Italians masquerade in impeccable Savile Row tailoring while the Germans have a penchant for designer moustaches, which make them look like Mexican desperadoes. Only the French preserve a tenuous individuality. All in all it's harmless Freudian fun.

There are many motives for attending a conference. For example, escapism, selling, buying, looking for a client, keeping an eye on a client, looking for a job, looking for someone to fill a job, or just plain honest-to-goodness self-aggrandizement. The theme of a conference is simply a convenient and plausible matrix to act out personal needs and fantasies. They are also a good excuse for holding impromptu board meetings in the absence of a fellow director who couldn't make it to the conference. Poor chap.

Any executive can rationalize by saying that his or her really important work is done at conferences networking during those invigorating after-hours sessions, far from the daily pressures of the office. But we know that the growth of the conference business is really a self-fulfilling prophesy.

Fear and loathing at Doberman & Pinscher

1979 Werbung/Publicite; 1985 Chief Executive

'The way they fired me was to offer me a job in Chicago. I'd had this mysterious phone call when I was in Germany asking me to go to the Ritz in Paris for a 9 o'clock meeting.

A very hung over and nervous Patillo was standing in the room smoking, with the Dwarf sitting on the bed; I think they'd been on a plane all night drinking themselves sick, no doubt.

Patillo said: 'It's not working out between you two; it's a matter of chemistry.'

I said I was amazed to hear something like that, having worked 18 years in the same company.

'Anyway,' Patillo said, 'it's not working out and the solution is for you to go to Chicago in a senior international position.'

My answer was that surely it would be more sane, more logical to leave me in Europe and send the Dwarf back to the United States.

Whereupon, the Dwarf said: 'So you're refusing a transfer?'

Then I said to Patillo: 'Look, we're both adults. I know exactly what's happening. That new broom sitting over there is trying to sweep the whole thing clean. This is not a serious offer. Why don't you come downstairs; I'll buy you a cup of coffee and we can talk it over quietly.'

Patillo said, no, he was too embarrassed to come down and have coffee with me; he didn't know what to say; he was going to have to think about it.

The Dwarf's parting shot was: 'Well, then, it's going to be the lawyers.'

Shortly afterwards the lawyers started and a few months later, management in Chicago realized that the Dwarf was totally incompetent and shipped him back to the United States. The dreadful irony is that the whole trauma could have been avoided if they'd learned from the experience of others. If someone had just phoned McCann, or Benton & Bowles, or BBD&O, you name it. I'd told them this was no way to run an advertising agency. Because you in Chicago don't understand Europe doesn't mean that putting an American over here who *you* can understand will solve anything.

The Ritz meeting was November 1978. It was about mid-1977 that Patillo had told me they were thinking of appointing one person to run the whole of Europe and would I be interested in the job? I said, I certainly would; I'd be most flattered, but I wanted it understood that the request was coming from Chicago, not from me.

At that time, Europe was split into three operating units, each reporting direct to Chicago. I was sitting in Paris as managing director of so-called Southern Europe, comprising France, Italy and Spain. I'd been promoted to that job in July 1976 from managing director in Italy.

A few months later, in April 1978, Patillo came over to say that they'd finally made the decision to form a Doberman & Pinscher European entity; that I would now report to someone I'd never heard of and that he would come and live in Paris. Also that he was a creative guy. Nothing wrong with that, of course, but he had no management experience and had never been outside the United States.

Without wanting to prejudge the man, I did say to Patillo that in my opinion it was unlikely to work out. Other agencies had tried it, sending over Americans who knew nothing about the local scene, and that this error would be compounded by the fact that this man had no proven management skills. I did say, however, that I would do all I could to help the guy. At which, to my utter amazement, Patillo actually asked me if I would train him. Imagine, having put him over me, I was being asked to train him!

My title was now director of marketing and client services for Europe, an escalation in the geographical sense, but in fact a demotion, because I'd been pushed from a line to a staff position. But I went along with this on the assumption that things would work out. And because Patillo had told me the new man was only going to be around for two to three years. I told Patillo I didn't think the man could possibly last longer than two years. I was wrong. As it turned out, he only needed nine months to wreck the whole European structure.

The Dwarf duly arrived in Paris and my misgivings were soon confirmed. Having been told to train the guy, I don't think I ever had a single meeting with him. He would never say good morning, and never came into the office before noon. I suppose he rationalized that nobody in Chicago would be up at that time. He fired the managing director of the French agency, who was an excellent man, and generally upset everyone else. He even resented us speaking French in the office, and decreed that July 14 should be celebrated on July 4. Ludicrous. The business was slowly going downhill because the Dwarf was not communicating – I don't mean in the literal, linguistic sense, but in the mental sense – with anyone who wasn't an American. So he confined his contacts to our one major U.S. client in Europe.

The mistake of Doberman Chicago was that anything they did not understand they tried to Americanize. Like the British thinking all foreigners are deaf because they don't understand English. Unless you have a strong base of U.S. clients, like JWT and McCann, you can't afford to behave like an American agency if you want to pick up European business.

I ended up with a reasonable settlement because I became a client myself, having joined the Italian liqueur company whose account I'd handled for 15 years at Doberman. I've already fired Doberman in the UK and I'm looking forward to firing them in other markets soon.'

[This is a first person account (disguised at the time) by my friend the late Dr Ronald Beatson who had a distinguished career with the London Press Exchange (LPE), The Leo Burnett agency and as Director General of the European Association of Communication Agencies. He died in 2002.]

Harry Toombs' Apocalypse

1985 Chief Executive

Harry Toombs, managing director of Diamond Laboratories, lifted his huge swollen hands from the desk and moved them slowly in front of his face like a punch-drunk boxer. Rheumatoid arthritis. He had woken up with it one morning about a year ago. Ironic that he should fall victim to one of Diamond's most profitable diseases just six months after he joined the company. He was washed up. They had hit him with the news yesterday. The handshake was 22-carat, but his pride was shattered.

It was Guratsky's first day with the British company. He had arrived that morning from New Jersey, where he had spent three months on an 'induction' program with the parent company. He was also shattered, but for a different reason. Toombs was supposed to be his boss.

'I'm afraid it's going to be rather difficult for you, Tom,' Toombs said. 'You'll find that the Chairman will continually go behind your back with your own people, and second-guess you on pretty well everything. And you never hear anything directly. It's strictly management by rumor. I suppose you'll be reporting to the Chairman now until they find a replacement for me.' A shrug; Toombs had his own problems to think about.'

Toombs was a big, bluff man of 59, who like many British managers, reveled in the trappings of his position; the Daimler Sovereign in the director's parking lot, expense-account living in a manner to which he had become accustomed, the imitation Queen Anne furnishings of his office suite, which looked like the waiting room in a high-class brothel. Like many executives in the industry, he had served as a salesman, and risen through the ranks in a thirty-year career. He was a genial bully; but an effective businessman for all that.

Guratsky would have felt sorry for Toombs had he not dissembled over the last several months, both when Guratsky was interviewing for the job, and after he had been hired. He had been hired as marketing director of the UK company, and on the understanding that he would be a prime candidate for managing director when Toombs took early retirement in a couple of years' time for health reasons. A nice carrot, and just enough time to build a solid reputation at Diamond in a key job.

But the moment he had signed up with Diamond, Guratsky learned from Toombs that the company was scheduled to be split into two separate marketing divisions. Both Toombs and the Chairman had lied to him during his several interviews with the company.

Okay, so he had half the job he was hired for. Better settle for that. Tom, when you've just burned some pretty valuable boats. No sweat; Guratsky was a big boy.

But there was more to come. With Toombs conveniently out of the way, the Chairman would further cut down Guratsky's job by putting him in charge of a so-called marketing services division, which was eventually intended to disappear. At the same time, the Chairman would bring in two long service Diamond executives to head up the two new marketing divisions. One of these two men would later be thrown out, and the chairman's anointed man would be triumphantly appointed to head up a newly consolidated marketing and sales operation – for which Guratsky had been hired in the first place. It's strictly a matter of re-inventing the wheel in these large corporations.

So Guratsky, it transpired, had been hired as a very short-term caretaker; the fact that his entry into Diamond coincided to the day with the exit of Toombs, was not entirely coincidental.

Harry Toombs had also been nicely duped. As former marketing director of Merton Drugs, Toombs had masterminded a highly successful promotion strategy for an anti-inflammatory product for rheumatoid arthritis. Diamond, market leader in this category, and with sixty percent of its turnover in three products, was extremely vulnerable to this aggressive competition. If you can't beat them, get them to join you.

Toombs, fearful of losing a top-management power struggle at Merton, was delighted at the opportunity to escape to Diamond when a mysterious offer came from the president of Diamond International in New Jersey. They had met in a bar in Nairobi. By design, or accident, we shall probably never know.

Toombs was kept on ice in New Jersey for a few months, like a defecting spy, and then shipped over to Diamond Ltd. as managing director of that benighted subsidiary.

This did not entirely suit the Chairman's plans. The last thing he wanted was a managing director as a chief executive. He had had that job himself before being elevated to his present position, which included responsibility for the UK, Ireland, and Scandinavia. But this was not a large enough area for him to afford to relinquish his power base in the UK, especially to an aggressive, take-charge guy like Harry Toombs. The Chairman was manoeuvring to become vice president for the whole of Europe. Then, of course, he would need a chief executive for the UK, but one of his own hand-picked acolytes.

So Toombs would have to go. Meanwhile, he was effectually neutralized. As Toombs had said to one of his friends: 'This is a managing director's office; if you look outside, you'll see a managing director's car; and I assure you I have a managing director's salary; but I am not managing director of this company.'

Guratsky shook out a Gauloise and crumpled the empty pack in his hand. He stared at Toombs through a cloud of smoke. Half an hour later they went out to lunch together. At least let Diamond pay for that.

An hour later, both men realized the extent to which they had been sacrificial pawns in the Chairman's nefarious master-plan.

Management by rumour

1983 Chief Executive; 1984 'If my boss calls...'

The Welshman is cock-a-hoop. He must have an inside track on something or somebody. 'Morning, squire.' He comes in and shuts the door. In his Monday-go-to-meeting suit he has the deeply satisfied air of a trade union official who has just turned down a new pay offer. 'Can't stay long, squire, I've got to get my slides ready for the board meeting.' He sinks into the visitor's chair and flexes his fingers like a concert pianist. 'So, when are we off to France then?' He plays a few practice chords.

I am appalled by this affront to my cool. The Paris assignment, sabbatical, exile, training program, whenever and however it is finally packaged, was only broached to me by the Chairman ('Of course, Tom, this is just within these four walls') late on Friday afternoon. None of my people, not even Helen, knows. Or knew. At her desk outside my door Helen is suspiciously quiet. Clearly she is withholding coffee until I come clean with the news.

Bluff it out. 'Joe, the French thing's just a trial balloon. Obviously, I can't leave this operation with the profit plans coming up. There's just nobody I can delegate to.'

'Well, trial balloon or not, all I can say, squire, is the Chairman was talking to the States over the weekend to organize a replacement for you. I understand that Mel Geist is coming over.' The Welshman blows on his finger nails. 'You're supposed to be out of here by early next week.' He smiles sickeningly.

Blast the Welshman. 'Knock it off, Joe. 'I wouldn't have time to hand over the department.'

I fall right into this one.

'Maybe that's what the Chairman has in mind. I wouldn't be surprised if he's getting Mel Geist over here to do a bit of mucking out so you can have a nice clean marketing department when you get back. Not bad in a way. At least you'll have someone to blame if it doesn't work out.' A leer. 'I'll tell you what the Chairman said if you like.'

I am nettled as hell. 'Get lost, Joe. Go back to your tablet punching.'

'If that's how you want to play it, squire. I was just trying to keep you in the picture. Don't say I'm not communicating.' A final cadenza and back to water the grapevine.

The grapevine vibrates with activity all morning. By lunchtime it's clear that a major reorganization is underway. In the manner of a general plotting the course of a battle, I pencil in names on a blank organization chart. It's a scissors-and-paste job. Sometimes the little boxes get shunted to other departments as the day proceeds. Empires wax and wane. Names disappear and new names emerge.

Helen has two phones going. The grapevine is shooting out hundreds of tendrils. My peers all pass by with conflicting stories of gloom and exaltation. The personnel director is in tears because she has heard from the head of word processing that she will now be reporting to the Welshman instead of direct to the Chairman. I lose, regain and lose once more the sales training department. All in the space of an hour. A couple of entrepreneurial souls are running a book on the executive sweepstakes. My odds are lengthening.

At one o'clock I repair to the canteen. The lady on the salad counter is usually reliable on management movements.

It transpires that the Chairman has read an article called 'Management by Rumour' in the *Harvard Business Review*. Photocopies are whipped around in a desperate attempt to predict what will happen. The Chairman is addicted to the more fanciful tenets of the management gurus. I recall with a shudder such titles as 'Management by Conflict', 'The Invisible Hierarchy' and other essays in bedlam and strife.

By mid-afternoon nobody knows who is reporting to whom. This is something of a challenge to the ambitious and a solace to the shiftless who prowl the corridors in search of rumours. Everyone is talking about the 'new organization' but nobody knows what it is, except the Chairman, who seems to be making it up as he goes along. The Xerox is choked with resumes.

I'm working on my French irregular verbs when the Welshman calls.

'I thought you might like to learn something to your advantage.'

'What's that? You off to run the Australian factory?'

'Listen squire, do you want to hear or don't you? We're splitting your department into three entities. You're being offered one of these when you come back from France.'

'Fahcrissake, Joe. What are these entities?'

'Not my area, squire. All I know is we're pulling out marketing services and forming two sales groups. You have to decide which of the three you want. Can you let me know by five-thirty?'

'Joe, this is ridiculous. We have to discuss this. And some sort of announcement's got to be made.'

'Plenty of time to discuss when you get back from France, squire. And the Chairman doesn't want an announcement. I'm quoting him now. He said, "I want this circulated as a controlled leak."'

Say, 'Shalom' to Mr Yitz

1984 Chief Executive; 1984 'If my boss calls...'

All you need for survival in New York City, I had decided, are nerves of tungsten carbide and a working knowledge of colloquial Yiddish. Having long despaired of a genetic miracle, I was bolstering my courage with Beefeater martinis and an ample supply of rocks. And for the second prerequisite, I was working my way through Leo Rosten's erudite and witty lexicon, *The Joys of Yiddish*. Already, in spite of jet-lag protracted by a subliminal hangover, I had introduced several new words, like *shlep, shmalz, megillah* and *yenta* into my conversation. The next step would be to learn the meanings of these words.

I'd had a little help from my friends. Sammy Kalbfleisch, a half-generation American who had wisely refrained from anglicizing his name to Vealsteak, had guided me around this adventure playground. He had taught me the rudiments of pronunciation. For example, saying the word chutzpah with the chu as in 'choo-choo' could give the game away altogether. I'd learned how to rattle the kh of khoots-pah around my throat like a professional.

Sammy had also taught me how to invert sentences and how to invest a simple question like, 'You want that I review the television schedules?' with six different meanings (sarcastic, mock-subservient, incredulous, indulgent, offended or scornful) merely by placing the emphasis on a different word. I was learning to wield my own language with a new astringent force.

In fact I was becoming so confident that I'd almost lost my fear of taxi-drivers. A riposte like, 'Listen, Mac, you think I've got all day?' would invite the devastating reply, 'You want I should sing, too?' Or more to the point, 'Go hit your head against the wheel.' Of course, in business one had to be a bit careful. I was conscious of this as I made my semantic dispositions for tomorrow's meeting at the advertising agency.

The curtain rises on the conference room at Doberman & Pinscher Advertising. After-lunch cigar smoke and uneasy somnolence. Our top management, the account team, jesters, concubines and slaves are gathered in caballistic groups. Sound effects men are releasing electronic applause as Dave Weinglass finishes a marathon presentation.

Myself: (wagging forefinger) Dave, fantastic. I loved the color slides. But I have to tell you your explanation for the first quarter sales decline was *farblondjet* (pronounced farblawn-jit). I mean you were way off track. Whatever the real reason, questionable television scheduling it was not.

Weinglass: (blinking at this coded message) I'm not sure I get your point, Tom. I thought that I had stressed the, ah, major reason for the, shortfall – which incidentally we've protected at the bottom line – was the way the creative was perceived by the prime target viewers. I never meant to suggest that it was, ah, in any way, ah, a lack of expertise, of ability in buying demographics. Of course, in terms of, ah, gross rating points…

Myself: Play it straight, Dave, no *shtiklech*. An explanation that is not. That we should have such a diagnosis!

Weinglass: Okay, Tom, but did you attend the creative briefing sessions?

Myself: Did I attend the creative briefing sessions! Did you write your mother?

Weinglass (rattled) Well maybe we could have let the creative guys run through the tapes of the call-back interviews before we produced the commercial.

Myself: Aha!

Sammy Kalbfleish would be proud. Correction: Would Sammy Kalbfleisch be proud!

The scene of these meditations was Yitz's on Seventh Avenue where I was taking a total immersion course in delicatessen eating. It was lunchtime (it's usually lunchtime at Yitz's) and the counter was crowded with experienced eaters, among whom I detected several professionals. ('Give me the roast beef sandwich on rye and don't forget the chicken fat.')

I had ordered impeccably. *Forshpeiz* had been gefilte fish and horseradish. Delicious. I had contemplated broiled liver steak with potato latkes and coleslaw but had settled for the chopped liver and turkey with a side-order of dill pickle. Perhaps tomorrow I would try the pastrami on rye and maybe the chicken matzo ball soup.

Judging from the décor, Yitz's dates back to the thirties. There are lots of old prints of New York and yellow photographs of the Yitzs at weddings and *Bar Mitzvahs*. A sign invites patrons to 'Say Shalom' to Mr Yitz,' a cheerful man in a red-ribboned boater who presides behind an old-fashioned school desk.

I was pondering the cherry strudel for nuchspeiz when there was a soft voice at my elbow. 'Pardon me, friend, I couldn't help but admire the expert and, if I may say, debonair way you handle the menu. I'm a stranger in town and I wonder if you could help me to order.'

I'm no good at small talk (nor big talk for that matter) so after agreeing a small consulting fee with this putative bore, I quickly returned to the personal column of the *New York Review of Books*. Recognition was coming late; but it was coming.

Going out I said, 'Shalom,' to Mr Yitz.

'Shalom,' Mr C. How was your lesson today?'

I couldn't think of a snappy Yiddish reply so I smiled, the way I do with my German mother-in-law.

Roger Collis

'Home, James and don't spare the nuances'
1983 Chief Executive; 1984 'If my boss calls...'

Heathrow airport on a raw winter morning. A sharp edge of anxiety breaking through the jet lag. James has the Daimler double-parked in front of Terminal Three. Now if *I* did that!

'Home is it, sir? I expect you'll want to freshen up. The meeting's not till half-past eleven.'

I sink gratefully into this black cocoon. Soft and warm. Unleashing a train of thought that any £300-an-hour analyst would relish selling back to me. Strange how the old libido stirs at the most incongruous times.

'Give Mel Geist time to arrive, I suppose.'

'Oh, Mr. Geist came in yesterday, sir. Quite a flurry of faxes. He had dinner with the chairman. Mr. Thomas was with them too, sir' I meet his eyes in the rearview mirror. Enough said. The Welshman's probably a major-general in the corporate KGB by now.

'I picked them up from Carrier's at 10.30, no, I tell a lie, eleven, and took them to the penthouse in Hill Street. They were talking about a dress rehearsal for this morning. Miss Angel brought documents over. A very late session it was, sir'

'What do you mean, Helen brought documents over?'

'Well, I understand Mrs Whitstable wasn't well or something. Oh, yes, Miss Angel gave me this letter for you, sir. Would you please give her a ring as soon as possible before the meeting?'

Premonitory notes from Helen. I wonder if she really knows what's going on. New agenda for the meeting. What's this? I'm down to make a presentation on my department. Three-year P&L, the lot! Management by surprise. Thanks for nothing, Mr. Chairman.

'James, give me some good news.'

'Depends what sort of good news you want, sir. We've drawn the first test in Australia. And apparently the Treasury has relented a bit on the taxing of dividends masquerading as up-stream loans.'

56

'Upstream loans!' Just as I'm about to shoot the rapids.

'Yes, sir. You know, sir, loans from an overseas company to a British parent. Means we're home and dry with those tricky inter-company transfers from Sweden. All that's left of the Treasury's 1981 proposals is a small part relating to tax havens. They've back-pedaled on everything else. What that means is that British companies with a stake of at least ten percent in a tax haven company will be liable to corporation tax on that proportion of its profits.'

'That doesn't sound very good news to me.'

'I know, sir. But Mr. Geist was saying to the chairman that we'd transfer our interest in the Panama entity to the States.'

Indeed! Why not transfer it to Brussels? Unless they're planning to eliminate Brussels. Take out the European management level altogether. That would fit with the rumor about decentralization. If the UK and Scandinavia became an operating profit centre reporting direct to New Jersey it would give the chairman a solid power-base. The game plan would be for him gradually to take over the other markets, like France, Italy and Benelux. So that when the pendulum swings back again and the corporation re-invents the wheel, the chairman would be in line for European vice-president. I shake out a Gauloise. I can only do it like Bogart when nobody is watching.

'No, I won't, thank you sir. Here, have one of these, sir. El Supremos. Mr. Geist gave me a box. Lovely smoke.'

'No thanks, James, I'm not a cigar person.'

I'm not a Mel Geist person either. Why this sudden largesse with the drivers? Trying to tap my stream-of-consciousness? Deliver a message? Message received. Okay, James, where's the hidden-eye camera?

'Word has it in the car pool, sir that you may be moving back to the States.' The statement hangs in the air like a question. You might call it subliminal insolence.

Tersely. 'Not just yet, James. I've got a busy department to run.'

But for how much longer? A department which is a cost centre. A high-cost centre. Genetic engineering costs big bucks. Literally. I'm billed in dollars to the UK company.

'The FT was saying this morning, sir that the pound's going to weaken against the dollar long-term.'

Of course, that's it. If we decentralize, the chairman's going to report in pounds. I could slide into the vortex.

'Gresham's Law, sir.'

'Gresham's Law.' Reading my thoughts.

'Bad money drives out good. Sir Thomas Gresham, sir. Said it all in 1566.'

I've never quite understood the paradox. But the chairman is going to want to save dollars and spend in pounds. And if I'm going to be integrated into the UK profit centre.

We are conspirators now.

'Your problem, sir, is how to stay here on the UK payroll.'

My problem is how to stay on the payroll. Period.

The swagman cometh

1983 Chief Executive; 1984 'If my boss calls...'

I confront a scowling morning. Nasty things in the mail and a diabolical hangover. And now this new voice breaching the switchboard.

'Mr. C? Oh good morning Mr. C. My name's Freedman. Mr. C, you don't know me but I would like to talk to you about doing some business in East Europe.'

A music-hall voice. Perhaps an actor enjoying a character role. Or, God forbid, my first wife's egregious lawyer trying a new disguise. But I detect an authentic mercantile ring. Soft and agreeable, yet seeming to uncoil for my delectation several yards of top quality angst.

As I reach for my polite forensic manner:

'Nice of you to call, Mr., er, Freedman, but I think you should know we already have an executive prospecting the East European markets. And in fact we are expecting our first order fairly soon.'

A steady hand on the *force de frappe*, a special answering device to confound the disingenuous. Just move this rheostat lever so, and the other party gets an earful of the *Prelude to Lohengrin*. Nothing like Wagner in the early morning to repel boarders.

'Oh I understand, Mr. C. Yes, I understand perfectly. But I think all the same we may be able to move ahead a bit quicker, you see. I've got some very well established business over there and I could offer you some interesting deals. I'm sure there's a lot of business we can do together. By the way, Mr. C, where's your stuff made?'

Still my annual report style: 'Well, we have a plant in Belgium and one over here. That's just Europe, of course, which is my responsibility.'

'Oh, I see. Very interesting. Yes. Well, look here Mr. C, I could get over there; there are plenty of planes, aren't there? Or should I send my son, Morris? No, I'd like to come myself. You'll pick me up at the airport? Oh, that's lovely. I'm sure we'll recognize each other. Yes. Well, goodbye Mr. C'

And the very next morning this small friendly man of sixty or so, umbrella at the trail-arms position, tipping his homburg back to smile. Pale watery eyes and an almost invisible ginger moustache. Specks of dandruff on his velvet collar give him a curiously vulnerable air. Reminding me of a little tailor I used to know.

'You've put on weight, Mr. C,' he would say lugubriously, 'about a stone.' And I half expect a speculative forefinger and thumb at my lapel.

But Freedman just takes my arm as we walk towards the car and says in a prophetic voice: 'There's a lot of money to be made, Mr. C. Yes, a lot of money. If you could let me have some of your stuff, about ten thousand cases? And of course, I want there to be something in it for you, Mr. C. Now I'm not talking telephone numbers, but would five thousand pounds in cash be okay?'

Over lunch I am introduced to the 'swag trade.' 'It's a bit like currency trading really. Only with well-known branded products. Buy them in one market at best wholesale prices and whip them out to another market in Europe or the States for a quick profit. Parallel imports, they're sometimes called. You profit, of course, from big brand advertising and differences in trade and retail prices in various countries.'

I think of the boardroom havoc caused by cut-price products from

England turning up in the New York wholesale trade. Or ricocheting off a spurious barter deal with Bulgaria.

'Take razor blades, Mr. C. Gillette... Wilkinson... I can give you an open order. And bicycles. You couldn't get me some bicycles could you? Ten-speed sports ones. We bought a lot from Poland but there's a two-year delivery now. I must say you can't complain about variety in this business. Yes. I mean... like I was in shaving cream last week. Are you married, Mr. C?'

Mr. Freedman spreads his hands... Uncle Reuben explaining the deal that got away. Euphoric memories of childhood breakfasts with poppy-seed bagels and cream cheese. 'It's all paperwork, Mr. C. You never touch the merchandise. You should see our phone bill. My son, Morris, spends all his time on the long distance. New York... everywhere.

'I want you to meet Morris. He's a chartered accountant, you know... in his own right. Got a new Jaguar. Yes, you must come and see us in London, Mr. C. Morris knows all the nice restaurants and places to go.'

Heady stuff for a slightly paranoid organization man. To become a swagman. Far from the world of investment plans and suave memoranda. Brazen trading, stripped bare of the fancy window dressing.

I know what you're thinking, Mr. C. Look, we'll give you all the paperwork you need. We've got some very impressive bills of lading and East European import documents. Or we can use our dummy company in Sarajevo. Then, when the stuff turns up in New York, you're covered. You just swear blind it was an okay deal.'

So fearful of my masters, yet savouring these proffered spoils. It's tempting to bite the corporate hand for a lovely millionaire's trip in Morris' Jaguar. Paid for with all these years of grey days.

This is the existential moment. As Freedman gently takes my arm he murmurs: 'Now you will give us a good price for your stuff, won't you, Mr. C?'

Standing up to the media

1980 World Medicine; 1983 Chief Executive; 1984 'If my boss calls...'

The young man in the strawberry pants petitioned the strings section of his imaginary orchestra for more restraint.

'Okay, Mr. Standing, now could you please try that smile again...? Nancy, I'm sorry, honey. This'll be the last time, then he's all yours... The thing we have to watch, Mr. Standing, is the left corner of your mouth turning up. There's nothing worse than a lop-sided smile when you're on camera. Okay? You've got it. Now, can you wrinkle your eyes a bit more? Perhaps it's a good moment to take off your glasses and look directly into the camera.

'What I want to see is deep corporate concern about the environment. You've got it, Mr. Standing. That's perfect. That's really sincere. Oh, my God... statesmanlike. Now, please remember, Mr. Standing, whenever you turn your head towards Mr. Bright or another guest, move it slowly, deliberately. No jerky movements on camera, okay? If you don't mind, I'll just go and check a couple of things with Mr. Bright.'

George Standing, chief executive officer of Honeydew Merryll, closed his eyes and succumbed gratefully to the make-up girl. He felt light-headed. No lunch and one too many, perhaps, in the hospitality suite. Over-refreshed, his wife would say. He wondered what they'd put in those martinis. He'd asked for Bombay gin. No discrimination these days.

There was that dull pain in his chest starting up again, and his stomach seemed to be forcing its way up into his throat. Nerves. He tightened his jaw. Ironic for a veteran infighter. High priest, judge, jury, executioner in God knows how many boardroom shoot-outs. Management by stiletto. Maybe his time would come...

Of course, this wasn't his first time on television. But you didn't get to be on the Johnny Bright show every day of the week. Good old Johnny. Son of a gun. They had both quarterbacked at Notre Dame. But there'd be no quarter given or asked for if the show ran true to form. Which it would do if recent ratings were any guide. TV talk shows were Everyman's Roman amphitheatre on prime time. Ladies and gentlemen, take up your nets and tridents for the next contest. Professional charmers versus professional villains. Not to mention professional personalities like his old friend Johnny Bright. Which is not to say that if things were to get really nasty with the Shatz woman, Johnny might not give him a helping hand. In the form of an appropriate one-liner.

He supposed there must be similarities between television and the management game. It's often how you behave, rather than what you accomplish, which gets you to the top. Titles do not confer competence. And style can be more memorable than substance in the ruthless dialectic of business.

Barbara Shatz certainly had style: a devastating amalgam of wit and rectitude. She was a ferret who could shred the fustian half-truths, baring the white bone of lies. But she could wield restraint as well as anger; the storm suddenly giving way to a deadly lenity. Barbara Shatz was the surrogate of every woman in America with militancy in her heart. And the furtive sweetheart of more than one man. No harridan she. Even George Standing would have to admit to the occasional pneumatic fantasy.

But tonight he was addled with angst. He thought of the distinguished panel and to whom he might look for support. Robin Weeks might support him, but Lord of the *Times* would only insist on fair play. He thought of the ketones spewing into the East River. Fifteen hundred tons a day. A necessary price to pay for sweet-smelling bath oils and colognes? He thought of his estranged conservationist son who had quit Harvard Business School in mid-semester to join a bizarre forestry protection group in California. He thought of the pressures on Honeydew's earnings per share. His forthcoming presentation to the Society of Security Analysts. And the controversial shareholders meeting in March.

The major shareholders paraded past him like ghosts. Frail but formidable blue-rinsed ladies arriving on that fateful day in their chauffeured Lincolns and Caddies. Sure, he could talk about the social audit. It gave them all a nice, warm feeling. Provided, of course, that when they got home and unwrapped the emotion and the social justice, the bottom line was alive and well.

The bottom line. The end of the rainbow, the crock of gold. George

Standing, 59 years old, had spent all his life in pursuit of the bottom line. That elusive quantum leap in the last year of the long-range plan. He'd spent nearly as much time worrying about it as about his management style and his golf swing. Of course, there had been sacrifices along the way. Two marriages and a third one shaking loose. His old friend Tim Matthews who had grown up with him at Honeydew… He opened his eyes to shut out the others.

The make-up girl had finished and look at him appraisingly. Was she admiring his famous leonine head? Would she succumb to management style? Where the hell was Strawberry Pants? Sweat prickled on his forehead and ran cold from his armpits down the inside of his shirt. Johnny might help with the timing of commercial breaks. But tonight he knew that he would die by his own hand. Of a malady not unrelated to abuse of the bottom line.

The selling of the business lunch
1974 Werbung/Publicite; 1984 'If my boss calls…'

Stanley Zilch, the celebrated soothsayer and raconteur, and I are lunching at Chez François. Over a nicely chilled bottle of vintage mineral water and the plat du jour (it is Stanley's treat), I am regaled with a long, convoluted anecdote about his latest indiscretion at Doberman & Pinscher. Stanley announces the denouement with a patrician chuckle. Then, he pats his pocket and with a sudden wry expression puts a hand to his forehead in a passable imitation of a world-weary gesture. This is usually the moment when he has forgotten his wallet in yesterday's suit.

I suppose I have a resigned expression. 'Relax, Stanley. I'll look after this.'

Stanley fixes me with a baleful eye (the other eye is busy with the waiter). 'That's rather uncalled for, old chap' (Legend has it that Stanley acquired the patrician accent at a bargain price back in the 'thirties from an out-of-work actor.) 'You might have more confidence in my hospitality. You wouldn't believe how much free advice and counsel, not to mention top-flight jokes and stories that I've given away over lunch. I mean, people seem to assume that just because they buy you a meal they're entitled to a couple of hours of free consulting. Predatory bastards.'

'Stanley, join the club. That sort of thing happens all the time. Guy invites you to lunch. Must talk urgently about a proposal. Big deal. So you break a previous appointment. You get all excited. Guy asks a lot of questions; he's very flattering. You spill the goodies. He's making notes all the time. Guys pays the cheque. "Great to meet you. We must keep in touch." The sincere handshake and that's it. No more talk about a proposal. He's got what he wants.'

'I've even had phony job interviews. Guy from Bent Elbow, Wisconsin, comes out to appoint a European general manager. You spend two hours explaining, as to a child, how to set up a tax shelter, how to structure profit centres, when or how to set up your own subsidiaries or work through distributors, and so on. And all the time he's nodding appreciatively. You're really doing well; you've already spent the first year's salary. And then, after lunch, the dollar signs vanish. "Well, it's been very interesting talking to you. You'll appreciate we haven't finally decided to make the appointment." It's strictly "Don't call us, we'll call you."

'And as for advertising agencies, I always buy them lunch these days; it gets to be cheaper. It's easier to control the menu and the numbers. And you avoid their commission on the lunch bill.'

'I couldn't agree more, old chap. Reminds me of my lawyer. I just can't afford to accept his lunch invitations any more. The chap has an unhappy predilection for the more exotic sea foods chez Wilton's — at my expense. I get a two-page invoice on the best onion-skin paper. "Two-dozen oysters plus time taken for eating them. Et cetera, et cetera." He probably charges me for having the damned invoice typed.'

'My sympathy, Stanley, but we've only got ourselves to blame. If we have the business acumen we're always boasting about, we should be able to find a way to market the business lunch. Stanley, I think I've got it! How about "Lunchtime with Stanley"? No, that sounds too much like a chat show. Hey, wait a minute… what's wrong with a chat show? I can see you in the studio, Stanley, at a glittering table surrounded by your guests. Camera panning on some choice repartee. Millions of prime-time viewers hanging on your every mouthful. "And now a word from our sponsor."

'But maybe we need a slightly lower profile. The concept needs class. I've got it, "Lunch of the Month Club," starring Stanley Zilch, for a £100 a plate. That would give people something to chew on. We could have a theme for each lunch, although I think the eclectic free-ranging style is your strong suit. Later on, we could sell franchises. "Good morning, Mr. Bloomgarden, I'm your Stanley Zilch lunchtime counselor."

'Of course, the ultimate would be private tête-a-tête lunches with Stanley in person for really top people. Can't you see yourself at the window table, Stanley? Actually earning money for having lunch with people?'

'I realize you're pulling my leg, old chap, but I think you may have hit upon something. It's a splendid idea. I might do something about it, if that's all right with you. It certainly sets the old entrepreneurial juices flowing.'

'You're most welcome, Stanley. Tell you what. As a kind of inaugural gesture, I'll waive my fee for the lunch we've just had.'

I guess, at bottom, I'm just a sentimental old marketing man.

How to choose an advertising agency

1973 Werbung/Publicite; 1983 'Business Matters,' BBC World Service; 1984 'If my boss calls...'; 1994 Resident Abroad

You are basking in a warm postprandial glow at the sixth agency presentation this week. It's certainly great to be the focus of attention from the agency people, who sit around in a carefully informal semicircle. The men are wearing their sincere suits and have tight anxious smiles. The showcase female flashes golden knees and gives you a cool predatory stare. Everyone looks like they've just come from Central Casting. You wave your cigar, making like a movie mogul, and accept just one more glass of the fine cognac. Swirling it around on your tongue, it has a mellow, expensive taste. Yes, it's been quite an ego trip, Mr. Prospective Client.

And yet down inside you there lurks a nagging inquietude. Nothing you can quite put your finger on, but you know it has to do with the awesome decision you have to make in the next twenty-four hours. Top management is leaning on you to get started with the new bath-oil campaign and you have no idea which agency to recommend.

You've been through your check-list six times and asked each agency about their television buying capability ('We're so glad you asked that question'), how many people they have in the research department ('Just tell us how many you want; we'll staff up to meet your needs') and how much time they'll devote to your business ('Our top management will give you their full attention; this will be our most important account').

You've seen case-histories of six new products which have naturally become market leaders. You've even seen the same campaign at two different agencies. The presentations have all been low key, carefully relaxed, the almost flip style so fashionable nowadays.

Each agency has put on quite a circus troupe for you. You remember the account executive who jumped through five successive hoops on Monday; the periwigged market research magician who conjured instant life-styles out of a hat on Wednesday; and most memorable of all, the bewitching bare-back rider in the white leather trouser suit who presented the creative this morning.

Of course the wiseacres told you to look carefully behind the façade; to wield your check-list like a totem; to get behind the plush carpeted areas and meet the real people who would work on your account; to forget the formal new business presentations and those great demonstration reels of prize-winning commercials.

And you've done your best. You've questioned and probed. The agency has been very understanding. They've nodded gravely at your favourite sermon on psychographics. They've laughed at all your jokes (They're very good at laughing at jokes.) They surely like you. Yes, it's been a great show. And yet swaying uncertainly on your pedestal, you suspect that your judgment may be about as reliable as the euphoria of that second martini before lunch.

The moral is: don't try to judge an agency by how professional they are (you won't find out anyway, until it's too late) but by how professional they appear to be. So forgo the anguish of trying to penetrate the façade and evaluate them by the quality of the façade. By the excellence of the lunch and the effulgence of the presentation. By the chemistry of the people you meet (you can't go far wrong with a white leather trouser suit). Use a different kind of check-list. Give the agency a Michelin test of crossed knives and forks. Remember that choosing an agency is a bit like an old-fashioned courtship. You can see how beautiful the girl is, whether she dances well and if she can cook. But you'll never find out how good she is in bed until after the wedding.

Naturally, the creative product is important. But just as the good creative person is primarily concerned with advertising that impresses the agency down the road, you should be concerned with advertising which impresses the Chairman (or perhaps more importantly, his wife). If it sells the product, it's an extra bonus.

This is why advertising awards are so important. Don't spurn them. Choose an agency which has a good track record at the major advertising festivals. There's nothing like a gallery of Hollywood awards and Lion d'Or's from Cannes on your office wall to keep your image bright. Then if you do have a bad run of ratings, you can ride out the storm with a fair amount of equanimity. Just lean back in your chair with an exasperated sigh and blame it all on the hapless sales department. After all, you point out, nobody has quite been able to quantify the effectiveness of advertising. Provided everyone loves the campaign, you're okay.

For one of the most important functions of an agency is to hold hands with your management, massage them regularly and give them subtle transfusions of confidence. After all, they need to feel loved, just like you – and to feel that they are part of show business.

So basking in the warm glow of the gourmet working lunch during the Chairman's visit to the agency of your choice, make sure the fine cognac is at his elbow to stifle any signs of post-presentation *triste*. And if there should be one of those curious silences when everyone stops talking at once, celebrate the moment. It will mean that an angel in a white leather trouser suit is passing overhead.

Roger Collis

But what have you done for us lately?

1974 Werbung/Publicite; 1984 Chief Executive; 1984 'If my boss calls...'

'Howard, come right in. I'm glad you stopped by. I know how busy you are but I do have a couple of things I'd like to go over with you.

'Let's sit over there, it's more comfortable. I'll just close the door. Helluva racket down that corridor. Like the art department's freaking out or something.

'Howard, just as soon as we're finished would you ask Marie to crank out another of her staff notes. I believe in creative licence but this is getting out of hand.

'No, I won't thanks, Howard, but you go right ahead. Karen's into a new cancer scare. That uncle of hers. Eighty-three. And of course, it just so happens he'd been a two-pack-a-day man all his life. Eighty-three! Jeezus. I reckon some of us will be lucky to make fifty in this game.

"Danger: Government health warning: The advertising business can seriously damage your health." How about that? We'll run it in the trade press as professional service advertising. But joking aside, I read somewhere that there are fifteen percent less people working in the industry than a year ago. Did you know that, Howard? Makes you wonder what happens to old agency men, doesn't it?

'By the way, have you had coffee? But you could use another. Mildred, would you bring an extra cup for Howard, please? Black with sugar, isn't it. Here, why don't you use this for an ashtray?

'Howard, I know you're not a numbers man, but as a stock optionee you should be aware how bad last year was for the agency. Well, I can tell you now that this year's going to be worse. Quite a bit worse. Yeah. Okay, billing's up slightly but profits are down. Sol tells me we'll be lucky to come in at three percent on gross billing. Before tax. That translates to a return on adjusted own capital of less than two point five.

'And even that's not in the bag. If that piece of British Airways that you're supposed to be handling shakes loose, we're really in trouble. I mean big trouble. And I can tell you, Howard, I'm not going to be fall guy when the you-know-what hits the fan at the shareholders' meeting. You've got to realize we're a public company now, Howard.

'Yes, I know you've been having problems with your account group. We all have problems. I'm not singling you out, Howard. I'll be talking to one or two of the other account directors fairly soon. No, what does concern me quite a bit is your approach to problems. Morale, motivation of your team. Not to mention client relations. People. That's what the agency game is all about, Howard.

'We should never have lost Sykes-Hughes, for example. Okay, I know he was having an affair with your wife. But look at the great work he's been doing since he moved to Doberman & Pinscher. And they've been using him to pitch for Seagram. But I don't want to get into that again. I know you've a number of real toughies. But remember, Howard, clients are very much how you handle them. Now Tom Guratsky at Diamond's taken to calling me. I think you'll agree you've got some fences to mend there. I shouldn't have to get into the account at all. That's your job, Howard.

'Now don't misunderstand me, Howard. I know you've put in a lot of hard work, and you've made some fine contributions in the past. But people are asking, what have you done for us lately? We've just got to trim the ship. Move to more variable costs. You know we've been using a lot of outside services. Particularly on the creative side. Remember we actually set Al Grayson up in business. He's making about twenty grand more as an independent TV producer than when he was full time with us.

'But what can we do for account people like yourself? I think you'll agree that account management just has to be in-house.

'You'll appreciate it hasn't been easy for us, Howard. I can tell you there's been quite a bit of heart-searching in the boardroom. And I know we'll miss you at the office party. Hell, twenty-five years is a long time. But I can see you've not been a happy man these last few months, Howard. And maybe that's been one of the problems. Perhaps you'd be happier somewhere else. For your own sake it may be best if we said goodbye. Of course, I shall be personally sorry to see you go. But this could turn out to be a blessing in disguise for you, Howard.

'I don't want you to think we're not grateful, Howard. You've got until this afternoon to clear your desk of personal effects, and we'll have your cheque ready by noon. We're going to pay you for the full month. I want you to feel completely free to drop in for a chat whenever you feel the need. And, uh, would you mind leaving the door open when you go out?

'Good luck, Howard. And thanks for stopping by.'

Introducing our very own cybernetic superstar
1984 Chief Executive; 1984 'If my boss calls…'

Roll of drums, cymbals, et cetera.

'Why, Mr. C, I didn't expect you so early this morning.'

'Morning, Helen. Yeah, I slept badly. I guess I'm still feeling the effects of that electrical fire in my right arm. So I had a lazy shower and a nice leisurely breakfast and knocked out a couple of dozen storyboards. I think I've solved the creative problem for the new Soulbad bath oil campaign. A meditation theme based on the mystical properties of the special Korean oil they use. A kind of massage-parlour-with-theological-overtones, if you see what I mean.'

'Gee, Mr. C. I'm sure the Mistral people will like that. No wonder they call you the Six Million Dollar Adman.'

'Oh, I don't know, Helen. But a funny thing happened to me on the way to the office. I was humming to myself in the car and must have left the tape-recorder switched on because, on playing it back, I found that I'd unconsciously composed the theme music for that 90-minute TV special we're doing on great ethnic sportsmen. Although I say it myself, it's not at all bad. Somewhat reminiscent of middle period Aaron Copeland…'

'Mr. C, I'm sorry to interrupt, but Mr. Guratsky's on the line. Red button.'

'Okay, I've got it… Tom, nice surprise. Good God. Sure, no problem. We can handle that. When do you need the final plan? Yesterday? That's okay if we make the presentation in the time capsule. I'll set a buffet lunch up in there now so it'll keep fresh. Tom, I'd better be going, we have to program the time warp.'Bye, Tom… Helen, would you book the time capsule for the day before yesterday.'

'Right away, Mr. C. Oh, I nearly forgot to tell you. You have five lunch appointments today. I guess you need to be there in person with Joe Stanley, you know how old-fashioned he is. That's at one o'clock in the Savoy Grill. Then, you should have time for a late lunch with Fassbinder of United Brands. Don't forget you have to dictate that new film script for him this morning. Then for your Media Circle speech, you'd best make a videotape and I'll have it biked over. You're hosting the Greenleaf lunch, so we'd better use the closed circuit television link. That leaves the Mackenzie Company working lunch at the Game Club. That's just across the park. I've got them to book a window table so you can participate live from here. It's a beautifully clear day. I've arranged to send Howard along to eat on your behalf. I think that's a gesture they'd appreciate. But I'll fix your martini drip so you'll catch the proper mood. You'd better tell me which arm.'

'Sounds great, Helen. Things are slackening off. It must be the long weekend coming up. Still, it might be a good idea to change my batteries and generally freshen up the voltages. I could use a few minutes in the bionic machine. Perhaps you could wheel it over, Helen. Then, let me see what I've got in my memory bank. Oh, yes. I must get across to the studio to shoot those dog food commercials. Then the agency presentation… What's this? Oh, yes. Check the printout of the new Mistral media schedule. I don't trust that damn computer. You remember the time I picked up an error in the gross ratings points comparisons in the TV and radio mix evaluation for Fassbinder? Well, I think that's about all I have this morning.'

'I have a couple more things for you, Mr. C. You promised to prepare a trade discount strategy for the Shoppers Drug Chain. They're sending a messenger along at eleven to pick it up. Then you have to translate the Mistral marketing plan into Japanese. That's due in Tokyo by Friday. Oh, and you have a sitting at ten for the life-size doll we're sending over to run the New York office. That nice young sculptress is coming. I think she's having trouble getting the exact way you hunch your shoulders when you make a decision.'

'Yes, it's important to get that right. There's so much more to decision-making than what you say. How are the electronics coming along?'

'Sol called yesterday. You should be able to control the doll subliminally. He's coming over on Friday to fix a new electrode in your arm... Just a moment, could you please take Mistral on the red button and United Brands on the blue? It's funny how our two biggest clients always call at the same time. Must be some kind of extrasensory competition... Why, Mr. C... Mr. C, you're not looking at all well...'

'Helen, would you get my engineer over here quickly. I think I've blown a fuse. I guess that old saying is right: an agency is only as good as the circuitry of the guy handling the account.'

Roll of drums, cymbals, blue smoke et cetera.

Madame Bellwether's establishment
1984 Chief Executive; 1984 'If my boss calls...'

With a great show of conspiratorial panache, Mainwaring stopped the taxi at the top of the rue Paul Valery and we crossed the street to walk the last two hundred yards. The house was tightly shuttered, a dark Balzacian fortress concealing God only knows what latter day *Comedie Humaine*. Mainwaring smirked and addressed a grille by the door. I felt a premonitory stirring of the bowels, and recalled with anguish a deeply traumatic occasion in Lisbon while engaged on a similar mission. Oh, well, I could always sit this one out with a drink, and wait for Mainwaring to indulge his flagellations or whatever his current predilection.

The door clicked open like a bank vault and we were ushered into a superb Second Empire salon by a simian party in a green baize apron who might have been a superannuated Mafia hit man. There was a tiny bar in one corner served by an ample blonde in black silk pyjamas. In another corner was a computer terminal built into a magnificent Louis XIII commode. Programmed no doubt for a zillion exciting permutations. We went over to the bar and ordered Chivas Regal and Perrier. We seemed to be the only guests.

Madame Bellwether entered on a cloud of Arpege. A tall woman in her fifties with a stirring military beauty. She greeted Mainwaring with an expensively groomed drawl. 'Such a nice surprise. It's been much too long. You know you missed our special marketing group sessions.' She made a moue. 'And your friend?' She offered me a vintage hand. 'I'll leave you for a few minutes. See if there's anything you fancy.' Madame handed us a slim leather folder and left on her cloud.

'Quite a woman,' I said as appreciatively as I could. 'But tell me, why was she talking about marketing? Some kind of special offer, I suppose, when business is slack?'

Mainwaring smiled. 'I'd better explain. You see, this is a very special house and Madame Bellwether is a very special kind of madame. I mean, would you believe she did the advanced management program at Harvard Business School? *Summa cum laude*, no less. Sorry if I brought you here under false pretences; but I thought it would be educative. Might give you some insight into the Welshman's behaviour; not to mention the Chairman.'

Mainwaring loves me to play straight man. 'I'm sorry, I don't understand.'

'Well, instead of catering for men's sexual proclivities, this is a house where managers at all levels can indulge their career fantasies by acting out corporate situations, real or imagined, with the specially qualified people that Madame Bellwether provides. Let's take a few examples to show what I mean.' Mainwaring opened the leather folder.

'Look, here's an interesting scenario. The boss and secretary. There are two basic variations. The man who fantasies about being dominated by his secretary or PA, and the other way round. Of course, there are all sorts of subtle variations one can program in to situations like this. They can pretend to be having an affair, for example. All the thrills of an office romance without the risk. Some of the girls who play secretary are highly trained psychologists. Imagine having a beautiful surrogate secretary sit on your knee and listen to how your wife doesn't understand you.

'Then, on top of that, you've got several scenarios where you can pretend to be boss. There are two variations of the chief executive scenario, for example: "It's lonely at the top," and "Total delegation." Some of the sets they have upstairs are very realistic. Like pilot training simulators in a way. All the paraphernalia of power. A lot of executives have fantasies about firing people.

'Madame tells me there are managers who come here two or three times a week just to fire people. It helps to get rid of their aggressions. In the office these are often the timid ones who are kicked around by their boss or their secretary.'

'I suppose it's really a kind of therapy,' I ventured.

'It can be,' Mainwaring said. 'And they do get some pretty kinky customers here, as you can imagine. Madame tells me she has one regular – a managing director of a big engineering group – who is obsessed with a desire to be humiliated in public by a beautiful woman vice president of human resources. Madame handles that one herself.'

'Yes, I can imagine,' I said.

'But most executives just want to play the big boss for an hour or so. Or perhaps hire or fire an advertising agency or outside consultant. Or play at marketing if they're in production and vice versa. There is quite an interesting scenario – I'm not sure that it's on tonight – where you can be a business school professor for a session of your choice. There's another where you can make an after-dinner speech at your old college. I've done that; it's not bad. Madame's scriptwriters provide the jokes and anecdotes. But look here, we should decide. Is there anything here that interests you? You're my guest tonight.'

'I don't know, really. Maybe scenario number five. "An evaluation interview with the chairman after a deserved promotion to executive vice president." I could do with some ego massage.'

'Excellent choice,' Mainwaring said. 'That's another that Madame handles herself.'

As I was being led upstairs by the Mafia hit man, I felt once again an ominous churning of the bowels.

In parenthesis

1977 Werbung/Publicite

Sunday afternoons around the fifteenth of the month will be sure to find me crouched over the typewriter pecking out the last elusive paragraph of this column. If you can fight your way through the Gauloise smoke you will see a lonely figure wearing an imaginary green eyeshade and chain-drinking Whittard's Earl Grey. Bereft of inspiration after a recklessly vinous lunch, I am throwing in my last hackneyed reserves to stretch an exiguous theme for a few more lines.

By six o'clock the situation is desperate. Madame is getting restless and reminds me we have a dinner date at 7.30. The post office in the Avenue de la Gare, in Lausanne, closes at eight for express letters, and I must get the thing in the mail tonight if I'm to make my deadline in Zurich tomorrow. So I hope you'll understand if the endings of these columns don't always match the promise of the leads.

This is my thirty-second column for *Werbung*. That's thirty-two beginnings and endings. Thirty-two take offs and landings. Someone said to me the other day, 'I just love your titles. Why bother with the rest of the piece?' I have some nice friends. But on the other hand, the title is often the idea, the starting point. An editor once said, 'You think in titles.' In a poem, the title often explodes the meaning. And if the final piece is defective, it may be because the theme needs either to be stretched, or cramped, into the Procrustian page format.

Perhaps the reason for this is the relevance of most of my themes to real business life. What starts out as light-hearted satire is often transmuted into bitter reality. Fantasy morphs into Realpolitik. Searching for material in everyday business life leads me to the chilling discovery that I live and work in a surreal world of pure satire.

They say that truth is stranger than fiction. I subscribe to that. And someday by way of proving it, I'm going to tape a marketing discussion – or maybe a session at our ad agency – and run the transcript unchanged in this column under a snappy title.

Roger Collis

We laugh at our own hypocrisies and doublespeak provided it is labeled 'satire.' Like the first time we hear our own recorded voices we do not recognize ourselves. Good satire should lean so closely to the subject it mocks that people have to do a double take. I once wrote some pieces for a German magazine which the editor insisted on flagging as *'werbesatire'* just to make sure that his earnest readers took themselves seriously, and not my column.

I also believe that the satirist should identify with his subject matter; have a spark of affection for his victims (who perhaps include himself). The best satire is mocking, but never savage. To satirize is to discover truth; particularly close to home. There but for the grace of God go I. Humor is a serious business; a maxim I abide by.

The problem is that satirists are always being overtaken by real events.

And there's no denying that business is a serious business; which makes it a great subject for satire; because business, or life in the organization, pervades, either directly or indirectly, almost every facet of our lives.

When Balzac wrote about the French bourgeoisie in the 19th century, he was writing about the interplay of human relations in a context relevant to his times. Today, he might write about corporate life – for life in the organization has a more intimate and potent influence upon the individual and the family than the nation state.

A fifty-year-old executive may be far more concerned about his new boss than a new president, or prime minister. A corporate reorganization may have the significance of a *coup d'etat*. We talk about freedom and democracy. But in practice, our freedom of choice is harshly circumscribed by our business relationships. Company politics is more the politics of everyday life than the politics we read about in newspapers.

So to satirize company politics and behavior is a serious business indeed. There are terrible sanctions for the executive who falls into displeasure with his masters. I was once nearly fired for mocking the industry in which I worked.

One reason I wasn't fired is that the pen is still mightier than the sword. Or maybe the pen has become the sword: A challenge to the grey organization men – which is what this column is all about.

And of course it's fun. I won't say that living with characters like Guratsky has made me a more effective executive. But it may have given me a better sense of balance, of perspective. Humor is a wonderful antidote to stress. And tuning the reflexes to funny situations can develop creativity. For creativity like humor is the harnessing of the absurd or irrelevant. What Koestler calls the 'bisociation of ideas.' That's one of Gurstasky's favorite quotations.

Incidentally, Guratsky is not my alter ego. Although I confess he does get near to being sometimes.

Physician sell thyself
1985 Werbung/Publicite

Sam Perkins groaning with frustration in a stalled taxi in Oxford Street. Six-thirty on a sticky afternoon in June. And now a thunderstorm bursting into the rush hour. Absolutely no joy sweating it out in this traffic. To miss his clinic. No coat, no umbrella; he wonders whether to make a wing-three-quarter dash through the rain to the Tube.

Blame it all on Diamond Laboratories. No, that's a bit unfair. He'd gone there of his own free will. And the first meeting of the Cardiology Club had been interesting even if he hadn't quite seen the point. It had certainly been nice to be included among the great and the good. Not often he gets a chance to rub shoulders with people like Simon Mangrove and Thurston Grant, his long-distance mentors. One learns. Always a chance to learn. And the lunch… Gorgeous smoked salmon with a fabulous Sancerre, and Chateau Margaux with the Cote de Boeuf en Croute. Must have cost Diamond a fortune. But after all they had to eat something. It was thoughtful though to take such pains.

His heart thumping now. He'd better watch his own blood pressure! Slow down. What was it last time? A hundred and thirty eight over ninety-two, with a pulse of eighty eight. And, of course, anybody with a diastolic of ninety-five and above should be treated. Start them off with a diuretic, a thiazide, and then add on a beta blocker or methyldopa. What was it that chap from Diamond called it? The 'Step Care Approach.' The theme of the meeting had been Post-Graduate Education. Yes, they'd started with that. Professor Wilkins had gone on forever about the pressing need for better knowledge of cardiology among general practitioners in the country. And then they'd been led off into discussing the protocol for this massive clinical trial with Extramet. It looked okay, double-blind, crossover study with 30,000 patients. But what was Diamond really trying to achieve? Were they really interested in the results of the trial? Or were they just using it as a new way of flogging Extramet? Bit of both, I suppose, if you want to be charitable.

He has to take them at face value. Diamond is into education in a big way it seems these days. It's all their reps really talk about. 'I've brought along our new mini-computer, doctor. Perhaps you'd like to ask some questions about the management of hypertension. Diamond wants you to feel free to use this new service.' And it's not as though Extramet is a new drug. Sam is still prescribing a lot of Extramet in spite of the lure of the beta blockers, and the side-effects, which have probably been exaggerated by the competition. He supposes most doctors must have had pretty well all their hypertensive patients on Extramet at some time or other. Of course, Diamond has a beta blocker of its own, but they seem to have been reticent about pushing it too hard. Some kind of ambivalence among the sales force one hears, and the lack of really solid clinical trials. It would have been interesting, for example, if they'd run a comparative trial with Salvatol. But they probably couldn't risk it reflecting badly on Extramet. And now they're going hammer and tongs against the beta blockers in bronchitis. Recently, they've been promoting Extramet as safe for pregnant patients with hypertension. No reduction of cardiovascular output, or risk of renal impairment. They've been running high-powered symposia up and down the country as well as abroad. Sam has been invited to a learned junket in Monte Carlo with wives. 'Hypertension in the Compromised Patient,' or some such. And now this massive clinical trial in an attempt to prove that Extramet can actually reduce left ventricular hypertrophy.

Surely, that's a worthwhile clinical exercise. At any rate, if Durston Grant thinks so, who is Sam to take issue? Sam fingers the soft kid briefcase with gold-embossed initials, compliments of Diamond Laboratories. What the hell! If Sam can get a publication out of this, it's all in a worthy cause. He has Jane to think about. And he badly needs a publication.

Back at the office, Ted Somerville pops an indigestion tablet and takes stock. A successful meeting. The idea of the Cardiology Club had gone down without a murmur, and they'd swallowed the protocol for the GP trial. If they got 9,000 doctors to participate, they'd be home and dry. Ted flicks on his calculator and punches out how many additional prescriptions for Extramet this will mean. Translate that to kilos and factory sales. A one-point-three increase in market share will translate to five percent above sales budget at the end of the year. And if he can keep promotional costs to seven percent of sales...

Of course, it depends what you mean by promotion. Promotion used to be an ugly word. It used to mean a million in journal advertising. A four-colour half-tone: 'Extramet, the first choice for hypertension,' with a little asterisk leading to the small print, 'in many patients.' And a reference to a tendentious clinical trial. Glossy brochures would cascade through doctors' letter-boxes, and Diamond reps would beard their prey in their morning surgeries with gizmos such as pens and desk sets marked with a bright yellow 'Extramet.'

But not any more. The new way to sell is to get the doctor to participate in the selling process. Get him to sell himself. As Diamond's president Sol Winkelreid puts it: 'Selling is education. Get the doctor to tell you what information he wants and give it to him – as a reward for prescribing our drugs. Diamond is in the business of providing good medicine at a good profit.'

Ted peruses his notes and asks his secretary to remind him to call Dr Samuel J. Perkins at the Royal Free Hospital. There's a pragmatic young physician with an eye to his career.

Roger Collis

Focus group victorious

1973 Werbung/Publicite; 1984 'If my boss calls…

'Hi, I'm Lucille Findlater and I'd like to introduce you to the Mishawaka Focus Group. You know, we're the folk who produce the ideas for the ads you see on TV. As you may have seen in the *South Bend Tribune*, we belong to the Michiana chapter of the National League of Focus Groups and have just been named winners for the second year running of the Concept Evaluation Cup. Yes, we're very proud, especially as we were competing against some strong groups from such famous test-market areas as Fort Wayne and Columbus, Ohio. That nice Mr. Guratsky from the Doberman & Pinscher agency sent us a congratulatory telegram and Mrs. Lipchitz baked us one of her special seed-cakes.

'There are twelve of us altogether if you count Estes and Ralph, who join us for the mixed discussions, and of course, our two teenagers, Anne and Debbie. Twelve is quite a coincidental number, I suppose. Mr. Guratsky says we must be the most balanced group in the country, demographically speaking that is. We'd make an ideal jury and in fact it's a wonder we haven't been called already. But perhaps they're saving us for something special. We've been working together for such a long time that we can always be relied on for a quick consensus.

'I've always said that the secret of our success is our teamwork. If at all possible we rehearse before a discussion. It's so much more spontaneous than reading from an agency script and you end up with such a convincing tape for the client. "Verisimilitude" is the word Mr. Guratsky uses. Anyways, one of the best, the most realistic tapes we ever made was the time Mildred (that's Mrs. Lou Harris) burst into tears during an open-ended discussion on grass-widowhood. I think she'd been rehearsing for years. We thought it was really a bit heavy and emotional, but Mr. Guratsky said, keep it in, and the client loved it. I think they were looking for a family membership concept for a country club.

'Of course, it's so much easier to run a good discussion if we know beforehand what sort of result the client wants. This is particularly true in the case of an agency that recommends a focus group discussion in order to buy time. For example: "Gentlemen, this area seems to be outside of present consumer experience so we advise doing a couple of focus groups just to kick the subject around a bit... What's important at this stage is to dig out some basic attitudinal information to give the creative boys and girls something to chew on... We can always quantify at a later stage." Or something like that.

'This is the sort of situation where good verbatims are important. A client loves a research report with lots of realistic verbatims, and creative people just eat them up. They're the life and soul of an effective discussion, I always say. There's usually a phrase or expression to suit everybody. With a couple of pages of well-chosen verbatims you can support pretty well any conclusion or recommendation you want. We've learned from experience always to keep a stock of verbatims in our word bank and before important discussions I get a fresh supply from my bridge club. Judy Galbraith (no relation) is our group intellectual and she can actually talk in verbatims; you can almost see the quotation marks. Judy has been quoted in several corporate marketing plans, and was once the reason for an agency account director being fired; but I think that was a typing error.

'People are always asking me how we manage to generate so many wonderful new concepts in the group. Well, I'd say that's one of the easiest things to do; it's the fun part, really. Training helps a lot, of course. I swim a good half mile a day in Judy's outdoor think-tank, and jogging is great too. It kind of gets everything swinging loose, if you know what I mean. We always read a page of the *Britannica* before going to bed, and call each other to discuss ideas. It drives our husbands mad. But we never stop creating. There was the time Mrs. Lipchitz was feeding us all chicken soup (we were very tired and depressed after a marathon discussion in Toledo and had bused back in the snow) when Mildred of all people came up with a brilliant idea for a miscellany gift page – "Just what I always wanted, a sterling silver bicycle chain" – that Doberman & Pinscher ran just before they lost the account.

'The toughest thing is when a client asks us to choose between alternative concepts. That's okay if we know in advance which one they prefer, in which case we simply rehearse a discussion which leads to the appropriate conclusion. "Consensus Management" is what Mr. Guratsky calls it. However, it isn't always clear what the client wants. So what we do is hedge our bets and split up into two or three teams, each one proposing a different concept. The client is then able to choose from a kind of smorgasbord. This can lead to a most entertaining discussion. Mr. Guratsky is talking about getting us our own talk show on one of the public service TV channels.

'Of course, being so successful we get many requests to lease our material, old tapes mostly, to clients whose budgets won't stretch to a live group discussion. But as a matter of principle we never release tapes before the original discussion has taken place. After all, we believe that if you're top of the league, you do have a responsibility to maintain high ethical standards.'

Management by accident
1984 Chief Executive; 1984 'If my boss calls...'

What I'd had in mind was a leisurely, introspective lunch at the hotel, a pre-emptive call to the Chairman while he was at lunch ('Of course, I'd forgotten you're an hour behind. No, just tell him I rang would you please, Mrs. Whitstable?'), a soothing something from the mini-bar, pack my papers and off to the airport.

After all these years my radar might have warned me. The Germans had practically eaten out of my hand; Mel Geist was in South America ransacking other people's reputations for a change, and I had a reconciliation dinner with the bitch-goddess Helen to look forward to in London. It was even a nice day; a thin winter sun burning off the early morning frost. Like an idiot I was actually humming to myself as I stepped outside. I should have been on red alert. After all, an optimist is simply a pessimist who is badly informed.

As it transpired, the thin winter sun hadn't had time to burn off a patch of black ice in the car park. This was skid row; the ultimate banana skin.

A professional stunt man couldn't have given a better performance. I did a kind of reverse somersault and landed heavily on my back in front of a group of secretaries who had just arrived from Central Casting. When I tried to move my leg, my foot flapped convincingly. A broken ankle, snapped right through. Somewhere in my mind the Welshman bellowed. 'Cut and print. Well done, squire!'

Slow dissolve to a hospital room in Frankfurt. Medium tracking shot of the protagonist, groggy with anaesthetic, reaching for the bedside phone. The Welshman on the line. 'Hallo, squire, I hope I didn't wake you. I'd forgotten you're an hour ahead of us. How did it happen exactly, squire? You just slipped? Well, that's what comes of skating on thin ice. What's that? No need to be offensive, squire. We were all very shocked to hear the news. Helen was in tears, if that's any comfort to you. And the Chairman said not to worry about anything for a couple of days. In fact, he asked me to keep an eye on your in-tray.'

Charming! Still, Helen could field any skeletons until the end of the week, until I was back on the road. Of course, with a plaster on my right leg, I wouldn't be able to drive, even an automatic. But I could use taxis and hop on planes. Perhaps the Chairman would lend me the company plane if he wasn't using it for Gleneagles. Or at least send James over to ferry me around. Maybe in a stretched Mercedes 600 with all mod cons, phones, computer, night nurse... After all, the German assignment was supposed to be top priority.

The chief surgeon was a distinguished looking *Wehrmacht* general with lugubrious news of the eastern front. He spread the X-rays out on the bed like campaign maps. His staff officers gathered around.

'A complicated situation, Herr C. You see here and here? Broken through on both sides. So we have inserted plates of surgical steel and screws to bring the bones exactly together. But it will be at least two weeks before you can leave the hospital, Herr C.'

Nothing to do but wallow in self-pity, fortified by intravenous transfusions of angst. Surgical steel, my God. Would I forever be a putative terrorist, setting off metal detectors at airport around the world? 'The giant slalom at Davos; my new racing bindings too stiff,' would be my line, accompanied by a tight, virile smile.

Most executives have to come to terms with diminished expectations some time in their careers; lower the sights of their ambition. Success to me right now meant getting to the bathroom and back without mishap.

And just how long could I rely on the Falklands Factor before a hero injured in the line of duty becomes a delinquent executive? Management by absence was the Chairman's prerogative.

The answer came at the end of the week, on the very day Sister Gertrude threw out the office flowers.

'Morning, squire, how's the German coming along; or more to the point, your German report? I think you should know, the Chairman's getting a bit restless…'

'Fahcrissake, Joe, I'm not exactly malingering.'

'Point taken, squire. But you must know we have to have a firm marketing recommendation, three-year financials, all the trimmings, by the middle of next week. If you can't make it, why don't you delegate to Karl? It could be a smart move; the Chairman's thinking of putting him in charge of a new mobile task force.' Karl had recently emerged as a mole in my department.

'Joe, I'm the first guy to delegate, you know that. But by the time I've got Karl over here and briefed him… I can wrap this up in a week once I get back on the road.'

'Your decision, squire. I was just trying to paint you the larger picture.' One thing about the Welshman; you could always see the brush marks.

The next day, I gathered up my lightweight executive crutches and limped bravely off into the sunset.

Airborne challenges for wide-bodied executives

2006 International Herald Tribune; CNN Traveller

Moments of truth seem to occur more often these days.

Boarding an Easyjet flight from Gatwick the other day (sharp elbows having got me pole position up front in the first row) I was mortified to find that the seat belt would not **quite** fasten.

Of course, one has to be sufficiently lean and fit to sit next to an emergency exit. Clever Easyjet, shortening the seat belts in these privileged rows. No point asking for a 'seat belt extender.' So I had to retreat to another row where I only **just** got the damn thing attached.

Coincidentally, perhaps, I have been assailed with weighty complaints from fellow travelers complaining about large passengers who 'invade their space' when they come to sit beside them.

Jane Ralls, a reader in Minneapolis, takes Northwest Airlines to task when on a flight to Detroit, 'this extremely large man lifted up the armrest that separated our seats, sat down and occupied at least one quarter of my seat space. People who cannot fit into one seat should be required to purchase two seats, rather than spilling over into someone else's space.

'It is my experience that armrests must be kept down, at least during take-off and landing. So how can this apply to large passengers who cannot physically fit in a seat unless the armrest is up? What are seat companion rights? How should one react? Can we demand a change of seat or an upgrade if no seats are available?'

Airlines require armrests to be kept down for reasons of safety and comfort during take-off and landing. So it follows therefore, that if an exceptionally wide passenger can't fit into a seat without raising the armrest, they should not be allowed to travel in that seat. They should either be required to buy a second seat, or upgrade to a more capacious class of cabin, if there is space, or else be offloaded on to a later flight.

Applying this logic (although when did you last see logic applied?) might have helped the husband of Joanna Bastin in Tournon d'Agenais, Lot et Garonne, France, who writes, 'On a flight from Atlanta to Frankfurt with

Lufthansa, my husband was in the middle seat, when an enormous woman sat down on one side of him and raised the armrest to squeeze into the seat; then, to his horror, a second equally large woman did the same thing on the other side. She complained to a cabin attendant who said there was nothing she could do because the flight was full.'

'I once found an oversize passenger on a flight occupying part of my seat space,' writes George Price in Washington, DC. 'I politely declined to occupy my seat, or take a later flight since the plane was full. As I recall, the airline got someone to take a later flight in exchange for some free travel. With obesity a growing problem and airlines jamming more seats into cabins, it is time for all passengers to send carriers a message by insisting on occupying the seats they've paid for.'

'British Airways advises anybody who has concerns about seat width to purchase more than one seat, but we do not have a weight limit for passengers,' says Jay Merritt, at BA in London. 'Our check-in agents and ground staff keep an eye open for passengers who may have a problem fitting into a seat. If a passenger cannot utilize a seat safely with armrests down for take off and landing, alternative arrangements have to be made. We can provide extensions to seat belts for those who can fit into a seat but cannot be safely secured by the normal seat belt; and special seat belts for anyone who has purchased two seats. Should issues arise on the aircraft, our cabin crew is trained to deal with problems using a common sense approach.'

American Airlines follows a similar policy; and Southwest Airlines, requires 'very large' passengers to purchase a second seat.

'We are sensitive to the needs of both larger passengers and those whose travel experience may be eroded through sharing seat space with them,' says Richard Hedges, director of corporate communications, Europe and Pacific, at American. 'Where there are instances of obese passengers whose bodies protrude extensively into an occupied adjacent seat, we may ask that they purchase a second seat at the same price or take a later flight. Passengers who find that their seating space is intruded upon by a fellow passenger, should raise the issue with one of our flight attendants, who will do everything possible to ensure the comfort and safety of both passengers.'

Understandably, some 'oversize' people feel that they are normal, and have a right to the space they need.

Leland Stuart in El Paso, Texas: 'I am 6 feet 7 inches and weigh 260 pounds with a 50-inch chest; I'm not fat, only "large." To say that I should have to purchase an extra seat seems unfair and discriminatory. I find it difficult to get in and out of a seat; the person in front of me cannot recline their seat as it hits my knees and the person in the next seat is cramped as I take some of their space. Airlines could accommodate large people by making six or eight seats in coach with a little extra room available only to them. There are certainly enough of us to keep the seats occupied.'

'I'm not particularly tall, but I am wide,' writes Edward A. O'Neal from Norfolk, Virginia. 'On long flights, my wife and I have bought three seats for the two of us; cheaper than business class and nearly as comfortable. We try to get a plane with three seats abreast in the middle – so both of us get an aisle seat with plenty of space between us. We just have to let the crew know so their head count will match up.'

Passenger bulk has never been much of an issue. But nemesis may be nigh for the laterally challenged traveler. Southwest Airlines requires 'large people' to purchase a second seat for 'safety and comfort.' Not an easy call if passengers book online and waddle straight to the gate.

Girth-stricken travelers might ultimately face simpler, more daunting 'baggage weight' rules if airlines were to adopt a 'total weight' system, whereby the passenger would be weighed along with his or her baggage. Add, say, 230 pounds for a wide bodied executive and 80 pounds of baggage and you've got an awful lot of avoirdupois.

It makes sense if you think that airlines have to compute the total weight of passengers, crew, baggage, meals and fuel in their cost-efficiency calculations.

Belinda Fogg in Tokyo is one of several readers who agree with this idea. 'The present system of weight limits for baggage unfairly discriminates against smaller people,' she writes. 'On a flight from Auckland to Tokyo, my baggage weighed in at 10 kilograms over the limit; but the carrier waived a $300 excess fee, probably because the plane was only half full. However, as I weigh only 53 kilograms, if you added 10 kilograms to my body weight I would still be lighter than many of my fellow passengers. Why don't airlines devise rules whereby they weigh people AND their bags together?'

Bruce Bogin in Paris suggests that airlines 'should make a total weight standard, for body weight with baggage, and charge for any excess? Say the standard is 275 pounds. Two passengers show up at check-in: A slip of lady weighing 100 pounds, with a couple of bags weighing 225 pounds – total weight, 325 pounds; and a man weighing 300 pounds, with small carry-on bag – total weight, 325 pounds. Both lady and man are 50 pounds over the limit and should pay an excess baggage charge.'

Let us not forget the plight of tall, thin passengers. M. Massimo in New York writes, 'I am 6ft 2ins tall with a back problem and cramped seats in economy give me a lot of pain. So is it possible to buy two or three economy seats as an alternative to an expensive business class fare?'

British Airways, Continental, Delta Air Lines, and Virgin Atlantic, say they accept such bookings. Sometimes extra wide passengers, or those carrying musical instruments or paintings, ask for extra seats.

Carol Fitzpatrick in Hartford, Connecticut, strikes a cautionary note: 'Make sure that the assigned equipment for all flights has armrests that are not fixed in the down position.' Many families with adjacent seating prearranged have found themselves split up because of such an occurrence.'

It is also wise to book directly with the airline and check on the aircraft type. You will have one ticket for all the seats you book. You can check on seating plans and get an advance assignment, online or with your travel agent. Seat pitch, width and angle of recline vary according to which carrier you choose, even with the same aircraft type.

Oh, yes, and try to make sure that your seats are pre-assigned – and together. I did hear of one wide-bodied traveler (this is a true story) who found to his chagrin that the two seats he had reserved for himself were on either side of the aisle!

Management by Absence
1990 Business Life

There was a time when I used to dread holidays. The very thought of taking off for a glorious fortnight (or heaven forbid, three weeks) to the sun-drenched Caribbean, the flesh-pots of the Cote d'Azur or one of those idyllic get-away-from-it-all islands in the Greek archipelago would be enough to send me into a catatonic tail-spin.

Ah, yes, I can hear you murmur; one of those born-again workaholics. Not so, I'm as intrinsically idle as the next man. And as a professional wheel-spinner, I've always been able to rationalize any amount of time spent away from the office.

No, I was a victim of what management theologians recognize as 'holiday stress,' a major factor in executive morbidity. Remove the day-to-day pressures and preoccupations of the office and a new kind of anxiety takes over. More insidious, more debilitating; a kind of free-flowing angst about your job and career that can make you a candidate for Paranoids Anonymous.

Holiday stress is endemic among business travelers and reaches an acute stage when the holiday is about to expire. This is known as the 're-entry syndrome.'

They say it takes the first week of a holiday to unwind, the second week to relax and the third week to worry about what you might find (or not find) when you get back to the office. Have they reviewed the budget figures without you? Can they do that? You bet they can!

Suddenly you see the dark significance of the chairman's parting words. Karl, your assistant, might be in the chairman's office right now mortgaging your department for the next three years. Maybe you are the chairman. But where was Mikhail Gorbachev during his management revolution? Unwinding at a Black Sea Resort with the BBC World Service of course.

You may fancy yourself as a latter-day Genghis Khan. But what are you going to do about the threat of a palace revolution if you're cruising on your mentor's yacht off the Turkish coast? To paraphrase Clausewitz: holidays are the continuation of politics by other means.

Roger Collis

So much for the aetiology of holiday stress; what can be done about it? A prescription of sorts was revealed to me in one of those rare Archimedean moments at the poolside of the Tel Aviv Hilton during a business trip last summer. I was exercising my management style with a toothsome bimbo at the bar, when I ran into my old friend Sammy Kalbfleisch. Shrugging off his entourage of American divorcees, he sat down to discuss the problem. Had I read Stanley Zilch's new book, *Zen and the Art of Holiday Management?*

It transpired that Zilch, director of Blue Skies Research Institute in Broken Springs, Colorado, had come up with a powerful management tool for salvaging the sanity of holiday exiles called Management by Absence. Since that fateful encounter, I've never looked back – except for an occasional glance over my shoulder when I go on holiday.

Sedulous practitioners of Management by Absence (MBAs) know how to stifle signs of incipient holiday stress by observing the following rules:

Make sure you are at the centre of the universe. Take the principal movers and shakers with you to limit the downside risk; send them on holiday themselves; or organize an incentive conference, say on a Caribbean cruise, during your absence. Or else hand them grueling assignments that will occupy them fruitlessly while you're away. One way to do this is to get your PA to release time bombs in the form of urgent memos every few days. Professional MBAs are adept at the 'planned crisis.' The idea is to create a diversion from any thought of insurrection by creating a problem that has to await your return for a miraculous resolution.

While you're away, keep in touch. This doesn't mean phoning the office every day, but using your laptop to send a stream of (pre-programmed) disquieting e-mails. 'Don't call us, we'll call you,' is an old cliché but a powerful one. Make ominous hints of a major reorganization when you get back to the office. Assign people spurious tasks to give credence to this eventuality.

Relax. After all, this is the objective. The best ideas are said to come in breaks between bursts of intellectual effort. Use the siesta to dredge the subconscious for new ideas.

Make sure you're missed. Nature abhors a vacuum. The planned chaos and confusion you have sown should make everyone clamour for your return.

This should always be unexpected – say the Friday before rather than the Monday morning.

With luck you may be hailed as a *deus ex machina*. In which case you might decide to take more holiday next year. It's a great way to run a business.

A crash-course in re-entry
1985 Chief Executive

It was one of those mornings when you make extra sure you don't step on the cracks in paving stones; the sky was an ambiguous gun-metal grey, darkening in the west, clearly waiting for a management decision to snow; I'd been tailed by a panda car for 15 miles along the M4, and my executive horoscope was less than propitious ('the new moon which has occurred in your birth sign seems to have raised doubts in your mind about the integrity and sincerity of someone close to you').

What's more, it was my first day back at the office after ten hermetic weeks at the Blue Skies Management Institute in the Swiss Alps, and for some disturbing reason, I hadn't been able to raise the bitch-goddess Helen at home over the weekend. Although I'd taken two of Dr Witherspoon's big reds, paranoia was still running high.

I arrived at 7.30 to check Helen's desk for time bombs before she got in; but you have to be very early to beat the Welshman, a close personal enemy, especially if he's on the scent of the walking wounded. I was riffling through the mail when he came loping across the reception area.

He leered. 'Morning, squire. You've been keeping such a low profile recently we'd forgotten how indispensable you are; and if you play your cards right we can keep it that way. Which is really why I wanted to catch you early. Helen has been helping Mel Geist, who borrowed your office while you were away. Mel won't be in today, but the Chairman suggested you use the conference room for an office, the one on the first floor, not the boardroom. Temporarily, of course.' He flexed his fingers like a concert pianist and played a few practice chords.

'Fahcrissake, Joe. I come back from an advanced management seminar and I don't seem to have a department any more. What's going on?'

'Good question, squire. I mean, you're general manager material now, aren't you? Field marshal's baton in the briefcase and all that. I suppose you'll be put on hold for the time being, so I suggest you check your automatic pilot. I wouldn't be surprised if the Chairman's got plans.'

Neither would I. Better check the bindings on my pewter parachute as well. The Chairman, of course, was still on his ego trip to the Far East. Meanwhile, I'd better go and chat up Mrs. Whitstable. I might have to sacrifice the box of hand-made Swiss chocolates I'd bought for Helen.

Reading my mind. 'Mrs Whitstable isn't in this morning, squire. I'd just settle for a quiet day in the conference room if I were you. Bone up on your case studies from academia. There's a phone in there somewhere. Look, don't blame me, squire, I'm only communicating.'

Of course, this was Diamond Laboratories' version of the 're-entry syndrome' we'd talked about at Blue Skies. As a professor said, 'One reason for sending mid-career executives back to business school is to prepare them for the transition from functional to general management. It's when companies fail to agree in advance on the purpose of these programs, what students are expected to achieve while they're away, and what they're going to do when they come back, that you find you have problems.'

Can't say I wasn't prepared for this. We'd had a two-day 'transition workshop' to prepare us and help us form our own re-entry strategies. The official line was to get executives to analyse how they had changed during the course and what effect this might have on their associates back in the office.

All very well. But this didn't take into account the strategies that companies adopt towards returning executives. Let them burn out in orbit? Undertake a major re-organisation while they're away so that they find their desks and telephones have been spirited away? I recalled the time when Diamond had eliminated the entire European management during the summer holidays. Regional managers in Brussels disappeared overnight, leaving country managers to report direct to Broken Springs. I feared that I had lost my marketing fiefdom to the egregious Geist. The real re-entry problem executives face is how to interpret their company's strategy (assuming it has one) in sending them on long management courses: for edification or elimination?

By 5.30 I had updated my resumé and worked out a half-plausible strategy.

I opened my little black book and turned to H for headhunters. I'd just got through to one in Geneva when a gaggle of cleaning ladies sailed into the conference room with vacuum cleaners. They came in noisily and emptied my ashtray with the unconscious percipience that cleaning ladies seem to have towards wealth and status, but forgot to close the door when they left.

There are few more eloquent barometers of executive health than that.

When the headhunter calls

1984 Chief Executive, 1984 'If my boss calls...'

The courtship ritual invariably starts with a discreet phone call.

'Are you free to talk? We're looking for a marketing vice president for a biotech group in Geneva.' (There follows a mouthwatering description of your dream job.) 'Do you know anybody who'd be suitable? You mean, you might be interested yourself? Why, that's terrific...'

With a budget meeting minutes away, you float into a Mittyesque trance. Your think-bubble fills with dollar signs and stock option forms, visions of a corner-office with a view of Mont Blanc and a lakeside house. Your ego is already basking in crisp Alpine sunshine. All of a sudden your present job has lost its savour. God, get me out of this hellhole!

Congratulations. You are being wooed by a headhunter. You've finally joined the movers and shakers. An *etat de grace* to be savoured, like one of Mel Geist's El Supremos, in the religious sanctuary of your office.

Unless, that is, you have the Welshman lolling in the visitor's chair, which somewhat takes the gilt (no pun intended) off the gingerbread. As I put the phone down, his think-bubble fills with asterisks and question marks.

'Not bad news I hope, squire,' he asks hopefully. (My side of the conversation has been confined to terse yes's and no's.)

'Just my broker,' I shrug unconvincingly. 'A margin call on some pork belly contracts.'

The Welshman leers. 'It's a mug's game, squire.' 'Come on, or we'll be late for the Chairman's budget meeting. Let's see if you have better luck with currency futures.' Everyone needs a daily dose of *Schadenfreude*.

For the next two weeks I ride a roller coaster of elation and despair as the affair develops. There are furtive meetings in restaurants and tacky hotels. It's not easy to find alibis. My boss is impressed by my zeal ('Bob, I have to get out in the field more often). The advertising agency is puzzled by my brief, otiose appearances at its strategically placed office in the West End. Suddenly, I need a dental appointment (the top management equivalent of the grandmother's funeral). The deception is worthy of John Le Carré as James ferries me to Harley Street. I wait on the doorstep for the Daimler to disappear, then nip around the corner and hail a taxi.

Helen is suspicious. ('That guy who won't give his name is on the line again') as I kick the door shut and grab the phone. And what's this envelope marked 'Strictly Personal' lying pointedly on top of my morning mail?

Any day, I expect to be caught in *flagrante delicto* in a Mayfair watering hole.

('Ahem, Tim, I don't think you've met my chairman, and, this is Joe Thomas, our production director.' *Maybe you could fix us all up with jobs!*)

For a week, I'm already in Geneva. Mental bridges are burning. So a couple of days without news from the headhunter threatens to send me into a catatonic tailspin. Dr Witherspoon checks my paranoia level and puts me on the big reds. Powerful stuff. Even the Welshman takes on a rose-tinted glow. How absurd of me to think that he's been monitoring changes in my comings and goings on his new computer software.

And God forbid that the headhunter should suspect that I'm becoming a candidate for terminal psychosis. The art of being headhunted is how subtly you intimate that you just might be prepared to make the big switch. Headhunters are like banks with loans; they'll never propose a job if they think you really need one. It's a game of bluff and counter-bluff. Try not to return too many of their calls. And never ever let them think that your resumé is ready for mass mailing.

The right approach is a nonchalant, 'Okay, I'll try to put a few words together for you over the weekend,' as you try your hand at 'career expansion.' This is a chance to show your creativity. As Peter Drucker was fond of saying, 'Don't talk to me about the death of the novel as long as we have resumés.'

Headhunters try to seduce you with expressions like 'high visibility' (perhaps he just means a view of Mont Blanc), 'a unique opportunity' and a 'pro-active control position.' But beware. Remember that headhunters work for their clients, not for you. They are very good at glossing over the negative sides of a job.

So ask some searching questions of your own. Test the headhunter's creativity. What happened to the previous guy? Was he promoted? Was he fired? Did he perform a lateral arabesque? Was he one of a long line of transient incumbents? Is this a new position? If so, why was it created? Why is the company recruiting from outside? Are you being set up as fall guy in a political manoeuvre or as the prelude to an imminent reorganization?

If you haven't yet been contacted by a headhunter, ask a close friend at another company to have his headhunter try to recruit you. Even better, call a headhunter to discuss a search assignment within your own company. (Perhaps a replacement for your boss.)

Another option is to become a headhunter yourself. All you need is a smooth telephone manner, a few contacts and half an ounce of chutzpah and you're in business.

The Welshman is camping in my office when the clinching call from Geneva comes through. I smile enigmatically. 'That was my broker. Good news on my career future contract.'

There's nothing as exciting as the euphoria of going into a budget meeting with a job offer in your pocket. It's the ultimate management tool.

My only problem is lunch with Helen afterwards.

Roger Collis

High flying aboard Management One
1985 Chief Executive

There's an earnest mood tonight aboard Management One. The reporters in the back of the plane are drinking warm *Veuve Cliquot* out of paper cups as they prepare to file their stories. Jacques Lecouteau is sharpening his management angle with an antique French infantry bayonet. Hans Weltschmerz is pecking morosely on his keyboard, while Judy Bagel is skillfully editing out a sense of drama that had crept into her early draft.

Up front in the Metternich Suite, Dr Mike Wunderkind is hard at work. He is drinking a glass of nicely chilled *Dom Perignon* and smoking an *El Producto* cigar, a gift from the Welshman, which is primed to explode at the half-way mark.

Wunderkind, without his cowboy boots, is shorter than his photographs allow. His great bald dome rises like a pink iceberg above a sea of raging white hair. Sideburns merge into a walrus moustache and granny glasses perch astride his long diplomatic nose. He is surrounded by bustling frock-coated aides, one of whom has just passed a call to the chairman at Diamond Laboratories. In a few moments we may know whether Diamond is at last prepared to sit down and discuss a joint venture with Zeitgeist International, the Swiss biotechnology group.

It was back in April that a consortium of merchant banks commissioned Wunderkind to handle these delicate negotiations. Half a million miles and 500 press conferences later he is being called upon to vindicate what the media has sardonically dubbed 'shuttle management.'

He has been tantalizingly close to success. Several frustrating weeks were spent discussing which brand of mineral water should be served at the conference table. Then there was the buffet lunch issue – exhaustingly examined in *Executive Gourmet* magazine, which ran a profile of the smorgasbord consultant who was called in to mediate. And then there was the 11th hour insistence by Howard Quagmire, Zeitgeist's chief executive, that he sit with his back to the window so the light would fall in the chairman's eyes. Wunderkind had come up with the brilliant compromise that they draw the curtains, only to meet with vigorous objections by Diamond to negotiating under artificial light.

And so it had gone on. Even more daunting has been the question of venue. The latest proposal is Paris, to which Zeitgeist has agreed provided a suitable hotel be found on the Left Bank. In plain PR language, there is a feeling of cautious optimism.

The stakes are high. Both Diamond and Zeitgeist are contenders in cutting-edge genetic engineering. It's still early days, but market analysts are hinting that a joint venture might lead to a breakthrough in selective executive breeding; a prospect neatly encapsulated by Judy Bagel in her recent headline: 'Blue Genes: Building the new breed of executive cowboy?'

'A lonely cowboy riding into the boardroom on a white charger,' is how Wunderkind described himself in a revealing interview with an Italian woman reporter. The overweening arrogance of this remark caused some consternation throughout the business world, not least because of the well-known shortage of executive stabling in many companies. But it had established Wunderkind as a cult figure. His diplomatic circumlocutions, such as 'Okay, baby just give me the punch-lines,' have formed the management style of a generation.

At Harvard, Wunderkind had gained a reputation as the only intellectual who transformed chess into a contact sport. After being expelled he became a Buckshee Scholar at Calcutta University, where he took a PhD (failed). Management diplomacy was the logical career choice. He now operates from an aircraft carrier somewhere in the South China Sea.

Management One has begun its descent to Le Bourget Airport when the call to the chairman comes through. Is Wunderkind on the brink of another diplomatic triumph? Or will his cigar explode in time? His aides gather round as he picks up the phone.

Roger Collis

Fighting inflation at the word factory
1971 Werbung/Publicite; 1984 'If my boss calls...'

I'm settling down after lunch when the careless girl at the switchboard puts Guratsky through.

'Good afternoon; sorry if I woke you.'

'No need to apologize, Tom, the phone was ringing anyway... Congratulations, by the way. How's it working out?'

(Doberman & Pinscher has won the account for a leading firm of word brokers, and our friend, Guratsky, has been named vice president, semantic services.)

'It's an exciting assignment. Right now I'm rationalizing our word production.'

'What does that mean exactly?'

'Well, our new Honeywell told us the other day that there's been a hundred and forty percent increase in the exchange of words over the past two years. Now that's even more than the unadjusted national inflation rate. It's clear we have to take action here at the Word Factory.'

'You shouldn't believe everything you read on a computer print-out, Tom. These younger generation computers are always out to kid you. Besides, they've no respect for the language.'

'I know you're prejudiced. Ever since that female Honeywell second-guessed you at that Harvard seminar. But even you should be concerned with the tremendous increase in the number of cheap, mass-produced words and ready-made epithets and phrases going into circulation. Of course, the government is largely to blame. At a time of raging inflation and high unemployment all they can do is to release more words – like printing semantic money. An utterly cynical, "let them eat words" attitude. It wouldn't be so bad if they were minting new expressions; but all they could do was to release the same old hackneyed ones; whole paragraphs, even speeches get recycled.

'Of course, industry is consuming many more words than before. For example, company reports need to be more verbose in order to compensate for declining profits. Marketing plans have become book length as their contents become more dubious. And in the advertising game, long body copy looks like it's here to stay.'

'Sounds pretty dismal, Tom. What's the prognosis?'

'Serious: radical measures need to be taken. It's clear the language is being ruthlessly diluted. If words are to keep their value, they must be used more sparingly; which means more thoughtfully. The problem is that word production cannot keep pace with world demand; there are so many more people using English today. We must arrest this profligate exploitation of a vital natural resource. Quite apart from word pollution, the nation cannot sustain the present rate of consumption.'

'Very eloquent, Tom; public spiritedness is a welcome new side to your character. I would have thought, though, that English is still a fairly stable language. After all, we still have a favorable balance of words.'

'Yeah, but that's not really the point. Sure, we export a lot of words. But on the other hand, the market has been flooded with Latin roots. Another thing. We've just done computerized "vocabulary prints" of a number of well-known people. Very revealing. For all their prolixity, some of these people are virtual cripples. Wordwise. Walking around with a puny vocabulary of a few hundred words – recycled, of course, thousands of times a day.'

'Well, what's the answer, Tom? Is Doberman & Pinscher going to run around snapping at the heels of wayward word spenders?'

'Very funny. We've developed a two-point program called "semantic rearmament." First, we're going to cut our total word production by fifty percent. Second, we plan to rehabilitate a lot of good, old words, and generally build better quality phrases for our customers. The keynote will be brevity. Texts will definitely be shorter this year.'

'I'm impressed, Tom. But assuming you succeed in reducing inflation, won't you be contributing to the unemployment problem? After all, you'll be throwing quite a few of your wordsmiths out of work.'

'On the contrary. We're actually hiring new wordsmiths. Don't forget – shorter texts take longer to write; we evaluate our writers by the number of words they leave out.'

Roger Collis

'I think I understand. What can I do for you?'

'Go back to sleep. I'll put our spring catalogue in the mail. We're having a special sale of cheap second-hand expressions that might interest you.'

The target group revisited

1971 Werbung/Publicite

It came to me in a rare Archimedean moment this summer at St. Tropez that the good old-fashioned 'target group' is not what it used to be. And that perhaps one cause (and effect) of the angst and anarchism in our midst today is that we are losing our sense of belonging. We find it increasingly hard to see ourselves as part of neatly packaged demographic packages each with our proper place on the 'socio-economic pyramid'. For today the lines of demarcation have become blurred. The poor consumer can no longer be quite sure to which target group he belongs. He doesn't instinctively know as in the past which products are meant to be advertised to him. Deep down in his consumer psyche he has become confused.

And as we know confusion can breed insecurity. And this state of affairs is the fault of the advertising industry and the insidious new fashion of 'lifestyle' advertising. In the old, simple, comfortable days before 'radical chic', creative boutiques, media 'middlemen' and such things were invented; when full service agencies still had a sense of identity, when media planners wore short haircuts and before every account executive came to look like Gunther Sachs, the 'target group' was a nice, easy thing to define.

Then the magic word was 'demographics'. 'Our prime target group for this campaign' the account executive would say, 'should be the AB demographic groups with some emphasis towards the CI's. If we are all in agreement we'll just run the cost per thousand comparisons through the computer and let the client have our final media recommendations in a few days.'

And the creative men would go back to their fibre-board cages und create advertising with an emotive appeal specially tailored for the office employee earning over 2500 a year, aged between 25 and 39 and living in a city with over 150 000 people. Or for the housewife of between 16 and 35 with two and a half children and who, goes to the cinema 2.3 times a month. It all used to be so simple.

But now the magic word is 'psychographics'. Target groups are defined by 'lifestyle' characteristics. Never mind whether a man is a taxi driver or a top manager. By some atavistic alchemy both can be made to share the yearnings of an exiled grand duke. And a new cologne or after-shave can evoke a sylvan nostalgia for the Romanov estates. Or again no occupation is too humble for a man to suffer (or aspire to suffer) from those minor ailments that are said to be necessary for an active, successful modern way of life. Nowadays the executive will say, 'Gentlemen, the research study shows that the psychographic profile of our typical user is not the man at the top, but the man who is struggling to get there. And, paradoxically, the man we want to reach wants to succeed as a means of expressing his latent hostility towards society.' Or something along those lines.

Yes, 'lifestyle' advertising is tearing at our social fabric. No wonder some consumers are becoming disturbed and neurotic. Some of the more enterprising consumers are building their own target groups. 'Trading up' is a common phenomenon. This is what the behavioural scientists call 'the aspiration or Walter Mitty syndrome.' Perhaps less common is 'trading down.' Sometimes called 'inverted snobbery' this is the millionaire who ostentatiously smokes cheap cigars or the English aristocrat with no money to pay the taxi. We see it too with the person who buys a Volkswagen not because it's a good dependable car but because he wants everyone to think that he really has a Mercedes 280 SE tucked away in the garage.

I saw it myself at St. Tropez. Part-time ascetics with expensively faded blue jeans. Able to muster the wherewithal to bum on this prohibitive shore withh fat portfolios hidden behind the shawls and beadds. the gold Dupont in the old denim shirt. An elegant flame licking up to anoint a daring joint. Vicarious identification with the 'alternative society.' I confess to be intrigued. It's time to cast off my old demographic habits. And so next year I plan to go back to St. Tropez in quest of a more exciting target group.

Roger Collis

Flower power in the executive suite
1972 Werbung/Publicite; 1984 'If my boss calls...'

The sun is rising across the bay from Sausalito as Mel Schlegel, president of Heavenly Happenings Herbal Tea Company, grabs the alarm and swings his feet onto the floor. He pulls on his jeans, flowered shirt and hand-tooled cowboy boots and ties back his shoulder-length blonde hair with a ribbon. His first important piece of business is ten minutes of meditation. Then he takes a steaming mug of hot tea out on the sun deck and watches a white bolster of fog slowly obliterate the Golden Gate Bridge. At half-past seven Schlegel climbs on his Yamaha and roars through the fog to his herb warehouse and tea-blending plant in down-town San Francisco.

You'll have gathered that Mel Schlegel is not exactly your Harvard Business School stereotype. Yet this 28-year-old entrepreneur is cutting quite a figure in the 'straight' business community with natural herbal teas and his concept of 'alternative' management. Wall Street scouts are sniffing at his heels.

Nobody punches time-clocks at Heavenly Happenings, and the hundred or so employees please themselves when they come and go, and meet in small teams to plan their work schedules. There is no hierarchy. The plant is near Fisherman's Wharf in the old Del Monte fruit-packing factory. After a communal 'organic' lunch in the canteen there's a volley-ball game in the antique warehouse. The women in long skirts and beads, and the men in faded jeans and unkempt Che moustaches. Afterwards, 'Schlemiel' Schlegel, as he is called with affectionate irreverence, presides over an open-ended spiritual question-and-answer period. The chief executive as guru. It's cool.

Schlegel discovered his genius for blending herbs when he was still at Berkeley. His salad dressings, containing as many as a hundred and fifty herbs, became legendary. It was during a trip to Mexico in his senior year with botanist friend, Harold Klein, that Schlegel discovered the felicitous combination of herbs that eventually became the famous Mexican Magic tea.

Mexican Magic (containing hibiscus flowers, rosehips, lemon grass, peppermint, orange peel, wild cherry bark and hawthorn berries) is a deep red brew which claims to have the spiritual uplift of 'a thousand angels flapping their wings.' It also has a one hundred and eighty percent gross profit. Mexican Magic has been described by enraptured fans as the 'ultimate organic drink.' (With fans like these who needs advertising?) It could one day replace Coca-Cola in the affections of the young and fashionably hip. Schlegel has dreams of Mexican Magic forging a 'universal bond of peace and friendship' among the growing army of aficionados.

Heavenly Happenings' catalogue can be described as 'sophisticated naïve.' It lists over two hundred different blends of herbal teas and organic tinctures like roasted dandelion root, Chinese star anise and passion flowers. The package designs are equally far-out. Cups of tea in quaint Victorian kitchens are struck by bolts of lightning. Flower-children walk hand in hand through orange groves. The packs carry quotations from Einstein and Timothy Leary. An organic coffee substitute named Morning Mocha has the most ambitious pack literature to date: a serial of Thucydides, *The Peloponnesian War*, which is planned to run for three generations. Inside the packs are Mao-like homilies about work, family and sex. All this is the work of the house advertising agency, Heavenly Expectations, which is staffed by a tribe of recycled scribes and artists from Madison Avenue lured from the arms of Mammon by the promise of spiritual fulfillment, propinquity to the Master, and all the iced tea they can drink. Strawberry fields forever.

While Harold Klein takes care of the mundane chores of running a profitable business, Mel Schlegel devotes his day to creating new herbal concoctions and devising new spiritual pathways for bringing the world closer to the warehouse at Fishermen's Wharf.

We are sitting in Schlegel's office-cum-laboratory. Cable cars are rattling by. A late afternoon sun, the colour of Mexican Magic, streams through a transom window. Schlegel ensconced in a water chair, his legs tucked under him in the lotus position. Inevitably, we are drinking tea. I am trying an insipid brew called Afternoon Mist. Schlegel expatiates on his plans for the future.

'We have two very important projects this year. First, we are perfecting a recipe for Iced Mexican Magic. This will be a ready-mixed drink which combines the tea with natural cranberry juice. Our problem is keeping it stable without adding any artificial preservatives. But it should be in the stores by mid-summer. Second is Morning Peace. This will be more than a new tea. It will be a program for bringing peace to executive suites all over the world. We want to share the alternative management concept we've developed here at Heavenly Happenings. You've seen some of the messages we print on our packages and on the tags attached to the tea bags. Well, we want to start a dialogue with executives around the world by using two sides of each Morning Peace pack as a kind of correspondence column. We'll also have a news-sheet inside the pack. We want to create a business community which is aware, which is tuned in to Heavenly Happenings. It's a heavy mission, man.'

I try to imagine the Morning Peace tea ceremony. Executives turning on with their brothers and sisters of the business world. It's cool.

Cold sweat in St Tropez

1977 Werbung/Publicite; 1983 Wall Street Journal; 1983 BBC World Service; 1984 Chief Executive; 1984 'If my boss calls…' 1993 The Times Magazine

I remember reading somewhere (or it might have been my subconscious playing tricks again) that holidays are not the happy, restorative institution that folklore and the tourist industry would like us to believe they are. In fact, holiday stress is being recognized as a major factor in executive morbidity. What I mean is: Remove the day-to-day pressures and preoccupations of the office and a new kind of anxiety takes over. More serious, more debilitating.

Of course, it may seem like paradise. No more tedious budget meetings; no more presentations to the board; no more secretaries to kick you around. A glorious fortnight away from the telephone.

That's just it. Better the devil you can see… Better a problem screaming down the phone than a problem screaming in your mind. On holiday, the normal three o'clock in the morning sweats can break out at any time of the day or night.

Imagine you're a prisoner on Tahiti Plage at St Tropez... or some other golden ghetto. There's a faint breeze coming in off the sea. Just brisk enough to stir the palm trees, set the beach boys to work tightening the parasols and waft the first pungent smells of the *plat du jour* across the serried rows of baking bodies. Monsieur Felix is starting on his rounds with a sheaf of menus. Fingers are snapping to order aperitifs. The beach is coming to life after a gloriously somnolent morning.

You've managed to empty your mind of practically everything except a teeming debate about whether you should chance a martini or move straight into the wine, when zap, a heavy thought threatens to engulf the fragile optimism of lunch. Suddenly you see the dark significance of the chairman's parting words. That's why Helen, your secretary, was evasive when you called the office yesterday. Have they reviewed the budget figures without you? No, they couldn't do that to you, surely. You bet they could!

It's the executive diaspora; the holiday exiles. Most mornings you can see them congregating at post office counters along the Cote d'Azur and those idyllic get-way-from-it-all islands in the Greek archipelago. That distinguished gentleman in the baseball hat and Hawaiian shirt is surely a vice president of something or other. He's been waiting in line at the telephone *guichet* for nearly half an hour trying to get through to his office in Bury St Edmunds. Sucking a nervous El Producto cigar and hefting a fistful of unfamiliar coins. '*Cabine quatre!*' Notice how authority soon loses its edge in the stale darkness.

Of course, he's got a terrible line. He clamps the phone to one ear and a cupped hand to the other. The roaring of a mighty ocean punctuated by electronic whirrings and burpings. Then the faint voice of his secretary.

'Helen, it's me. Yes, it's me. Can you hear me? Yes, I can hear you. I'm practically shouting. What's that? Operator, I'm trying to speak to my secretary. Yes, my secretary. This is Mr. Geist speaking. Thank you. Helen? We made it. Yes, we're all fine. Having a great time here. Yes, the weather's fine. Just perfect. Helen, listen, ah, the reason I'm calling. Ah, did the chairman say anything about that meeting he was going to set up? Yes, on the budget. Exactly.

'What do you mean he's had the meeting? He can't do that without my figures! What figures? What's that? Karl didn't give him any figures, did he? Karl's not authorized to give any figures outside the department, you know that. What's that? He fell out of a tree? He's upped them by three! Percent or tripled? Fahcrissake, he can't do that. Listen, he's no business doing that. I'd better speak to Karl; can you put me through? Sorry, I didn't get that. Karl's with the chairman! Helen, this is a terrible line. Operator? Is that the operator...?'

Out there, beyond Monsieur Felix's immaculately raked sand, stretch endless acres of job ads in the Sunday papers. Of course, there are the headhunters. But like bank managers, headhunters only offer you something when you don't need it. Right now, back at the office, they might be discussing you. 'I hear Tom's leaving Diamond.' 'Is that so? Does Tom know yet?'

Relaxation, they say, is the mother of anxiety. A Joe Thomas apothegm triggers an appalling stream of consciousness as you clamber aboard a martini. 'Even a paranoid can have enemies.'

An anarchic visitation

1966 The Guardian

She fell into my eyes one summer Sunday when the Swissair steward brought her up front of the Caravelle to sit by me at the window seat. Locks of flaxen hair framing a soft bronze smile. And carelessly gathered up on top of her head in a loose bun. She squeezed past me into her place smelling like an enchanted wood. An anarchic visitation. Spare a risqué thought for those ripe melons tipped no doubt with little gold stars. Naturally I looked nonchalant and relaxed but felt the need to slip my hand under my shirt to feel what the heart was doing. I could feel it pounding in my ears. On this bright afternoon in Copenhagen peopled by so many slender goddesses. And I was freshly tired from Chicago and slyly remembered the toss-up it had been at the last moment whether to break the journey at Copenhagen or

Mexico City. But visa problems and the Bergmanesque lure of Scandinavia spelled out the choice. I chuckled that old enemy Fate should have played so coolly into my hands.

'Fasten seat-belts, please!' And now bands of webbing tightly stretched. Our thighs almost touching, thanks to the happy geography of economy class. From the shield of my dark glasses I spied the blonde down on her long brown legs. And cherished her hirsute haberdashery. Only the night before in Rush Street, Chicago, I had feasted on girls who wore their thoughts right out front so you could serve yourself like hamburgers at an automat.

Now, how to make her unbutton a smile for me and not the steward hovering lasciviously with plastic trays. Wished I'd had time to visit my wordsmith about a new phrase. She gurgled like a child as we rose through grey banks of cloud to see the sun setting on top of a silky white sea. I wanted to take her hand longing for turbulence. But instead said, 'Mademoiselle, is this the first time you've traveled by Caravelle?' She almost smiled and said: 'No. I'm a student in Geneva and go home to Malmo three times a year.' I said how funny I live in Geneva too. And told her I was married and liked Bach. We talked some time and quaffed frothy beer and I ventured to admire her new blonde moustache. This time she laughed but soon came the cool dry handshake after the touchdown.

However, a few days later a miracle calling to my cluttered office and a golden brown voice floated among the thudding typewriters. Vouchsafing me a day or two in the country. Two get-away people driving into rural France through tunneled roads of tall poplars: erstwhile sentinels of la Grande Armée. Now sad golden branches of a premature autumn. We lunched near Macon in a discreet way on hefty steaks and draught Beaujolais. I was amazed where she tucked all those goodies in her svelte frame. And loved her mobile eyes as she mopped up the sauce with bread and thrust an intimate fork into my salad.

Please feel free to spear my lettuce while I gobble you up under the smooth silk. Oh, mademoiselle, you don't know me well, but on one of these chill autumn nights can't I creep into your narrow student's bed. In this arid autumn season of mine.

She said gently she did but not for me please and it was all a matter of chemistry. But she smiled as she said it and patted my sad knuckles.

That evening in the Casino at Annecy we danced until two and at the bar bumped into two people I knew. She understood at once and said I'll meet you in the car while I handed out several drinks as bribes. Later I found her asleep on the back seat like a lovely doll placed reverently there by a child.

Later that night I was tormented by the thought of her in the next room brushing her teeth and stretching like a tiger between lonely sheets. And in my own sleepless bed hopelessly islanded by a Siberia of raging linen.

A few days afterwards the telephone rang in my office space and I put the talking instrument to my grey face hoping someone would vouchsafe a few smiling words. She says can we meet for lunch, there's something I must tell you. I said sure I'll pick you up at twelve as I could use some sympathetic news.

And through the blood red goblet her wide green eyes almost misty as she said thank you again for a wonderful weekend. But you know it can never be. Even with all love's charity. Do call me again though sometime. But not too soon please. Turning away I was old. And almost wished I'd come back to Europe via Mexico City.

You'll find a friend at Discussion Partners
1985 Chief Executive

The idea came to me when I was browsing through the personal column of the *New York Review of Books*: 'East side Professor, youthful 50, open marriage, into white water canoeing, Indian artefacts, logical positivism seeks dominant woman, judo black belt preferred, for meaningful callisthenic relationship three afternoons a week. Discretion assured.'

Translate that into businessspeak: 'Chief executive, attractive management style, enjoys budget meetings, agency lunches, leveraged buyouts, seeks mature, upwardly nubile, female executive to share expense accounts and other good things in life, view collaborating on long-range plan. Sincere replies only please.'

From there it was only a short step to Discussion Partners. You'll find us tucked away in Charlotte Street. A bit seedy I admit. But we do have a refreshing view of the Telecom Tower on a clear day and I can offer you a decent cup of coffee and a sympathetic ear. If your needs are not too complicated we can probably fix you up right away.

You'd be surprised how many lonely, frustrated executives find their way here, from presidents to product managers. But don't forget the password. Security is a big problem. We have had quite a few plain-clothes headhunters snooping around.

We can handle pretty well any predilection. Here, let me show you. I'll punch in 'marketing' on the terminal and see what we get.

Quite a heavy demand this afternoon. Now, let me see… How would you fancy a six-foot three Swedish blonde, graduated *summa cum laude* from the University of Colorado in recreational sales, special interests include sports equipment and Wittgenstein? A bit heavy, perhaps, not to mention conspicuous in a hotel lobby. In fact I have a nice German sparring partner lined up for her: marketing director of a soft cheese firm in Stuttgart.

How about this one? 'Attractive Puerto Rican sales supervisor, petite, uncomplicated, presently finishing a product management course in London, anxious to discuss joint promotion with experienced, sympathetic executive who is socially aware and willing to share an interest in collecting Chinese restaurants.' That's not really your style either. You know, computer dating isn't nearly as simple as some people think. It's the factor analysis which dredges up all sorts of bizarre proclivities. Let's try later.

Meanwhile, let me tell you how we're organized. You know, of course, that we're officially listed as an escort service. In a way we are. But it's annoying to find ourselves between 'Let Chloe show you Paris by night' and 'Zizi welcomes old friends and new.' I'm trying to get our ads to appear under Business Opportunities. You may like to visit our site at www.bizpartners.com.

Imagine you're on a business trip to Paris. You've just checked in to your hotel after a sweaty flight from London. The French are being difficult as usual. They've left you alone tonight, part of the psychological softening up for tomorrow morning's meeting. All you want is a quiet meal and some soothing intellectual companionship. You can't bear the thought of room service or venturing alone into a rapacious city. You fling yourself on the bed in darkest despair.

Suddenly, a light bulb flashes above your head and you grab the phone to call Discussion Partners. An hour later, you are ensconced in a chic Left Bank eatery discussing the ramifications of your sales forecast with a zestful Parisienne.

The need to discuss is like a drug with some people. We have one human resources director on our books who has an overwhelming compulsion to interview job candidates at three o'clock in the morning. We sometimes have to pull people in off the streets and send them up to his hotel room.

We also have quite a demand for surrogate secretaries. It's the old story: an executive complaining to his wife that his secretary doesn't understand him. If an office romance is on the rocks we can often help by sending over a computer-matched temp.

Then there's our Samaritan service. You can phone in 24 hours a day and talk about company politics, marketing plans or whatever. If we can't find anyone to discuss your particular subject, we connect you to Sandra who leads you down the garden path and back again in a sexy non-committal voice. But most people don't really want to discuss: they just want someone to listen.

Close encounters of the management kind

1984 'If my boss calls…' 1984 Chief Executive

Mainwaring was so laid back he seemed to be ensconced in a superior incarnation. He had grown a beard and was wearing a white flying suit of strange shiny material. His Mayfair office looked like a set for Star Wars. Banks of computer terminals and huge reel-to-reel tape machines. One wall seemed to be a giant cinema screen. Tinted windows transmuted the wan winter sunshine into a weird green glow. I sat down in a water chair and unfolded the press release from Management Techtronics. Mainwaring filled his pipe with Acapulco Gold and gave a pregnant smile. I was glad to see his analyst had finally cured him of premature articulation. When he finally spoke, his voice was barely audible above the electronic hum.

'Essentially, what we've done is to combine several technologies, artificial intelligence, voice recognition and digitization, cognitive programs and the hologram, which, as you probably know, is a recorded three-dimensional image.'

'Something to do with lasers?'

'That's right. What you do is split a single laser into two beams and bounce one off the object you want to record and then onto an emulsified plate and the other straight onto the plate. If you then direct a laser beam - or in some cases ordinary light – at the processed plate you get a three-dimensional image projected as far as 20 yards away from the plate. This image is a hologram. Now if you do this with a multiple pulse laser you can get a moving hologram. Let me show you.'

Mainwaring tapped some keys on a console. Suddenly, we were sitting round a boardroom table with four executives who were locked into an animated discussion. The verisimilitude was daunting, except for the voices which were somewhat resonant. 'Too much bass,' Mainwaring whispered. He adjusted a dial. I overcame a compulsion to touch the pin-striped arm on my right. Instead, I flicked my Gauloise above the onyx ashtray on the table. The ash fell right through it straight to the floor. Our visitors (or were we the visitors?) were discussing some kind of marketing issue: how much media money to put behind a carbonated soft drink. What made the whole experience so uncanny was that they were totally oblivious of our presence. After ten minutes or so of this shameless eavesdropping, Mainwaring tapped the keys on the console and the visitors and their furniture vanished. My heart was thumping. Reality had lost all meaning.

'I'm impressed,' I admitted. 'That was absolutely unbelievable. But tell me, why did that guy on my right keep referring to today as Monday week?'

'You're very observant,' Mainwaring said patronizingly. 'What I just played you was a pre-recording of a hologram meeting which isn't due to take place until next week.'

'I'm afraid you've lost me.' The gratuitous fumes from Mainwaring's Acapulco Gold mixture were starting to get to me.

Mainwaring smiled indulgently. 'A new dimension to corporate planning. Who wants surprises at a board meeting? Wait till you see the software we've developed for advance decision-making. That will really blow your mind. By the way, did you notice anything strange about the way they spoke during the meeting?'

'Well yes, now you mention it. There did seem to be unnaturally long pauses between people speaking; there was no overlap or interruption. I mean, people actually waited until the other person had finished, whereas in normal meetings everyone speaks at once.'

'Exactly so,' Mainwaring said. 'That's what we call the "response time." You see each executive has his own tailor-made program which contains cognitive input from his career pattern as well as a range of personality psychographics which helps us pre-condition his responses.'

'So an executive is only as good as his software, his program?'

'In a way, yes. Career development these days does depend on the quality and scope of an executive's personal software. A good analogy is a famous comedian who would be utterly lost without his team of scriptwriters. The recruitment people don't bother with live interviews any more, it's done by long-distance hologram; the same as conferring and a lot of business travel.'

'Remarkable,' I murmured. 'But doesn't this make business entirely predictable.

'No more than it always has been,' Mainwaring said. 'It's still possible to have extemporaneous discussions. For example, the computer can be programmed to break in to coordinate or moderate a meeting on a random basis. "The free-wheeling factor' we call it at Management Techtronics.

'We've also developed a kind of joker which we call an "Action Prototype." This is either a simulated "virtual" executive or a famous executive from the past – say Alfred Sloan of General Motors – who can be plugged in to participate at a present-day meeting. A bit like Napoleon playing war games with Field Marshal Montgomery. Of course, every executive's personal program is adjusted from time to time. Rather like a golf handicap.

'What about computer pirates or hackers?' They could play havoc with decision-making.'

'I wondered when you were going to mention illegal access. We've got this 15-year-old schoolboy who lives in an electronic cottage in Wimbledon. If he were just to touch wires, so to speak between the Chairman and the Welshman... Might do you no end of good.'

'Mainwaring, that's the kind of state of the art I could use.'

Are top managers born under a lucky star?

1981 International Management

What do captains of industry have in common with famous generals and sports champions? According to Dr. Michel Gauquelin, the French psychologist, they all tend to be born under the influence of the planet Mars.

This extraordinary theory originated in 1949. This was the year that Gauquelin, then a student at the Sorbonne, set out to prove by statistical analysis that the so-called laws of astrology have no scientific foundation.

Gauquelin could find no evidence to support the idea that signs of the zodiac determine anything, or that horoscopes can be used to predict the future. But to his astonishment he did discover a statistically significant relationship between the positions of certain planets and the birth times of famous people.

In one of his early studies, Gauquelin found that 576 distinguished members of the French Academy of Medicine showed a peculiar tendency to have been born when either Mars or Saturn had just risen above the horizon or had reached its high point in the sky.

Another study of 2,088 sports stars showed that Mars was rising or at its zenith at the time 452 of these individuals were born. On a random basis the planet would have been in these positions only in the case of 358, or 17 percent of the births. The likelihood of such a divergence occurring by chance is one in five million, Gauquelin notes.

Over the last 30 years Gauquelin has gathered birth data on more than 20,000 famous people, including business leaders, actors, scientists, politicians and sports champions.

He believes that each profession has its own planetary influences. For example, while Mars is the planet for top businessmen, actors, politicians and journalists share a prominent Jupiter in their birth charts. Writers and musicians have a strong influence from the moon.

'Choosing success as a criterion,' Gauquelin says, 'allows us to examine the personalities in each profession who have shown most clearly those psychological qualities that are the hallmarks of their field.'

It is hardly surprising that Gauquelin has met criticism and even hostility from fellow academics. They have argued that he might have been biased in choosing birth data, incompetent in using statistics and mistaken in handling astronomical details. In an attempt to counter these objections, Gauquelin has regularly published his results along with the basic birth and planetary data of the many thousands of people he has studied. So far, he says, nobody has been able to fault his facts and his calculations.

Although Gauquelin has always been careful to point out that he is not an astrologer but 'a psychologist who just happens to be doing research in astrology,' he may, to paraphrase Moliere, have become 'an astrologer in spite of himself.'

I visited Gauquelin in his Paris apartment to discuss his methods and his ideas.

How do you calculate the positions of the planets at the time of birth?
This is fairly simple once you know the place, date and the time of birth. But it's important to have the exact time. In Europe, with the exception of England, most registers specify the time of the delivery. The same is true for the United States. But you'd be surprised how few people know their time of birth.

Once you have the birth data you can calculate the positions of the planets either by using astronomical tables or by one of the special computer programs which are now available.

In your work you refer to planets being in zones of high and low intensity. What do you mean by this?

We have found that the most powerful correlations between planetary positions and personality exist when a planet is either rising or at its high point in the sky. The other two significant positions are when a planet is setting or at its nadir. We call these four positions 'zones of high intensity'. Outside these positions are the 'zones of weak intensity' under which a person is unlikely to show much of the personality which we have found to be associated with that particular planet.

Does it follow that the position of the planets can determine a choice of profession?

No, I don't believe so. We have found that the correlations between the positions of the planets and birth times only hold true for high achievers. As you go down the pyramid the results are less significant. The greater the heights reached by an individual in his profession, the more likely he is to be born in 'planetary conformity' with his peers.

What we can say is that if you are born with a planet in a high zone of intensity you have a good chance of being successful; but not necessarily in any given profession. There are characteristic traits common to many professions. For example, successful businessmen reveal character traits like the ability to make rapid judgements, a high sense of realities, tenacity, combativeness and a certain need to drive themselves. This is a typical Mars personality. But you find the same traits among Olympic champions and military leaders.

In the final analysis, what is important is not the relationship between a planet and a particular profession, but with the character traits which are typical of that profession.

Success often depends as much on character as ability. A relative of mine wanted to become an actor. He was certainly very gifted, but he lacked what I call the Jupiter temperament. He was sensitive to criticism, he didn't know how to impose himself and he lacked ambition. But it can happen that a person who does well in a profession is not the characteristic type.

How do you collect and organize character traits?

We have assembled more than 50,000 traits from biographical references which we have analysed on a computer at the University of Paris. In the case of sports champions we compiled 6,000 character traits taken from 1,200 biographies such as the Dictionary of Sports. We established that, like the top business executive, the typical champion is energetic, dynamic, strong-willed, courageous, hard, tireless, lively and persistent. We found that Mars is very often rising or just at its culmination at the birth of people who have these traits. The odds against this happening by chance are ten million to one.

Can you give some examples of successful businessmen born under the planet Mars?

Marcel Dassault, the founder of the aircraft firm was born in Paris on January 22, 1892, at 8.30 a.m., a few moments after Mars had reached its high point in the sky. Then you have Gilbert Trigano, founder of the Club Mediterranee, who was born at St. Maurice, near Paris, on July 28, 1920, at 3 p.m. when Mars was also at its high point, The same is true for Livinus Gevaert, who founded Agfa-Gevaert, the photographic firm. So were many other successful businessmen.

What advice would you give on selecting personality types for management positions?

To keep it simple, let's imagine you are choosing from the five main planetary types. As I've indicated, your chief executive will probably be Mars. But he might also be Jupiter, which is a type of personality often found among successful politicians. Jupiter people tend to be ambitious and share many character traits with Mars. You might have a moon personality for your advertising or marketing person. Moon types are good communicators, which is why they are often writers and journalists and sometimes politicians. Your technician or financial person is probably a Saturn type, somebody who is precise and methodical. And then you might need a Venus type with a lot of courtesy and charm, possibly for some kind of public relations activity.

What is your own planetary type?

According to our research, I should be Saturn, the scientist, the investigator. But in fact I was born with Jupiter in the high point in the sky. I think this corresponds in my case with the fact that I'm something of an iconoclast, always trying to break new ground in unconventional fields. I'm always able to reply to my critics and have the last word. That is Jupiter.

How do you explain this relationship between time of birth and positions of the planets?

There are two possibilities. The first is the traditional view of astrology, that the planets directly influence the child at the moment of birth. This is hard to accept. After all, genetic characteristics have already been formed.

But there's another explanation. The planets act as a kind of 'trigger', with the baby selecting the moment to be born which coincides with certain planetary dispositions. But the planets don't change the child. Scientists know that the child controls the birth, or precipitates it, by releasing a minute amount of a certain hormone. And the planets may act as some kind of catalyst. The planets are simply a reflection of something that is already present in the child.

Two

Roger Collis

Executive Santa: an exclusive interview
1995 International Herald Tribune; 2006 Timesonline

'Ho! Ho! Ho! Yes, I have to admit that my organization is outdated, especially for a big mail-order business. And we do have a problem in maintaining contact with our customers. But I think you'll agree we still have a great deal of customer appeal! This is especially true among younger children coming into the market for the first time. Although we are losing business 'off the top' as it were as children reach the age of 10 or thereabouts. It's the old 80-20 rule – you make 80 percent of sales among 20 percent of the population.

'I don't want to appear cynical, but our old-fashioned image is something we actively cultivate. Heritage is all the rage these days. Management by Nostalgia (MBN) is what our consultants call it. Which is one good reason for keeping the Ho! Ho! Ho! (although we have updated the logo) along with my traditional dress and the reindeer. Mind you, I have had to give up the white ermine linings to satisfy the conservation folk. Nylon is so much more practical anyway. And we have had some flak from the animal rights lobby. No, I don't think reindeer pollute the upper atmosphere, do you? Well, not if they go before they leave. And anyway, the stuff is biodegradable, isn't it? Not like greenhouse gases. (Sorry about that! Ho! Ho! Ho!)

'You're right, of course, that sleighs are not the most efficient method of transport for the millennium. But the new 24-reindeer extended range sleigh which we brought into the fleet in time for this Christmas enables us to fly nonstop to Australia, traveling above the weather and commercial traffic. The trouble is we don't show up on radar screens, which makes it dangerous at low altitude with a full load. Nothing like as dangerous as dodging chimney pots in the old days mind you. I must say it's worth seeing the looks on airline passengers' faces as they flash past you on the way down.

'Distribution is still a problem. We're trying to improve it by bringing in toys by air freight direct from China and India to the regions. I'd say less than a third of toys are now made at our North Pole workshops. And we've extended our distribution points by appointing local Santas on a franchise arrangement. This has not only improved our cash flow but has broadened our equity base. This enables us to improve distribution in the under-privileged parts of the world. All part of the social audit as you can see from our Annual Report.

'I get sick and tired of critics who say that because we only work one day a year we aren't cost efficient. Well for one thing, it's three days if you count the time zones. And for another, we're kept pretty busy all year around. I mean talk about shop early for Christmas! We already have orders for next year. Then you have purchasing, manufacturing and management training. You won't believe we sent a dozen senior elves to Harvard Business School this year. (Harvard had trouble believing it as well.) We lost half of them to headhunters. So if you come across any little men with pointed heads in your business you've got Santa to thank.

'Of course we've been affected by the recession like everyone else. This has meant cost-cutting right across the board – except for the Board – on items like gift-wrapping, travel and entertainment expenses and company sleighs. We've also introduced a pay freeze, which can be pretty painful if you work at the North Pole.

'I'm expecting a vast improvement in customer relations when we finally come on stream with our computerized present system (CPS). At the moment, about half of all letters we receive go unanswered (much to parents' relief, I should say) and presents occasionally get mixed up. I remember a little girl in Ruislip got a Star Wars outfit while the little boy next door had to cope with a giant inflatable doll dressed in Tyrolean dirndl. It took one of our reps ages to sort out. Some kind of problem with the little boy's father.

'Boys will be boys! One of our worst problems came when a six-year-old hacked his way into our previous system and helped himself – and his mates – to hundreds of presents. He was only found out when he started running a 'cash and carry' business from his nursery school. I thought 'Ho! Ho! Ho! We can use talent like this.' So we got him to design our new inventory control software.

'People are always asking how we can possibly run a successful global business from the North Pole. I have to admit it used to be very difficult when we had to rely on postmen finding their way in the snow. Letters sometimes took months to get here. Children these days usually e-mail their requests to www.santa.com. Quite a few of our staff now telecommute from as far away as Africa and Latin America. And we have regular management meetings on our virtual reality conferencing system.

'Having an offshore headquarters has fiscal advantages as you'll appreciate. Ho! Ho! Ho! Holdings is incorporated in Lapland as a charity and pays no tax on repatriated earnings. The Santa Claus Foundation is domiciled under Swiss law as you're probably aware.

'A secret of our success has been an ability to constantly redefine our core business in contemporary terms. Should we continue in the business of distributing presents on a seasonal basis or start a package tour operation? These are some of our current concerns.

'Whether I exist or not is the great ongoing challenge. I can live with the credibility gap between my prime target children and their parents. The problem is that I'm finding it harder these days to believe in myself. But this is something all managers have to face.

'Still, I'm confident that I'll be around for quite a while yet. You may find my management style more durable than most people think.

'A Happy Christmas everyone. Ho! Ho! Ho!'

Small is beautiful
1985 Chief Executive

'Scale,' Guratsky said. 'The most important thing in business is getting your scale right.'

Guratsky was wearing his Sunday supplement smile; plastic, a trifle smug, a smile redolent of putative good living and possibly misplaced virtue. He was standing in front of the Arc de Triomphe, the sun shining dutifully on its refurbished façade. To his left was the Eiffel Tower and London Bridge, and over to his right the Empire State Building, the Taj Mahal and Chartres Cathedral. The backdrop to this architectural effulgence was the Bahnhofstrasse in Zurich on a busy Saturday afternoon. At his feet, a nuclear submarine of the latest 'Z' Class emerged from the sea like a sinister whale.

Guratsky was always master of the *non sequitur*, but this was a monumental performance. Facts must be stranger than fiction. Science fiction at that. I thought I could hear the roar of Niagara Falls just beyond the Paris *faubourgs* to the north of Guratsky's left shoulder.

'I thought it was all done with smoke and mirrors.' Humor the guy. My analyst says it's important to keep them talking.

'You're right. Illusion, in the form of models, is becoming more important than the real thing,' Guratsky replied. 'In some ways, models are more real than the real thing. A kind of transcendental reality.'

'Mmm.'

'Well, I would have thought these were eloquent enough.' A windmill sweep of his arms. 'But come down to the model factory and see for yourself.'

So the very next day we stopped by this green door in Wimbledon. A sign said: 'Model World: a member of the Doberman & Pinscher Group.' An unpropitious building; but inside a marvelous model world. There were Hawker Furies from the First World War flying sorties over the Hindenburg Line. Flower Class corvettes vintage 1942 shepherding a convoy on the Newfoundland run. St Paul's Cathedral majestic above a huge rural project for Fartingham Borough Council. We walk past serried rows of earnest young men and women making model barbed wire and dipping metal trees into glue and then dyed cork dust. The nubile Victoria serves us coffee in miniature mugs.

I learned about the intricacies of model-making; how you work with scale and white metal and how 50 different types of tree are made. And how it all started with architectural models and later diversified into stage sets and executive toys.

According to Guratsky, the detail is so good that model interiors (photographed through a kind of inverted periscope) are mixed with shots of real buildings and people to make a film of daunting verisimilitude.

'So who needs the real thing?' Guratsky said. 'Scale models can help management make better decisions by enabling them to understand complex projects in three dimensions. It's a case of seeing the future now. Models can even be an end in themselves. For example, why bother to go to the expense of actually building that new plant in Scotland when all the shareholders need to see is a photograph in a glossy annual report. Take this Greek factory. You see those model machines injecting creosote into the widgets? I tell you, these slides are going to save a busy executive a trip to Salonika.'

As we left the *atelier*, Guratsky was careful to double lock the door. 'You know, I expect the CIA is trying to break into this place,' he said.

'Now why would they want to do that?' I said, trying to humor him. 'I'm sure if they have a deep-down yearning for an HMS Dreadnought for the grown-up child, they can go to Harrods and swing it on expenses.'

'You can't be too careful in the model-making business. Did you see that large model on the left of the stairs? The one with the pipes and cooling towers and whatnot? That's a top-security nuclear power station. Tenth generation.

'Frankly, I'm more intrigued with the idea of model stage sets for television. Imagine being able to film a chat show or a sit com in the White House or Downing Street with a model set up in Shepherds Bush.'

'That's old hat. When we get to the car I'll show you a photograph of our new villa in Marbella. Hand-carved stone; Italian marble floors; heated pool. The real thing would have cost a fortune.'

I couldn't resist telling Guratsky what my analyst said about the difference between neurotics and psychotics. They both build castles in Spain. But psychotics live in them.

'I've heard that one,' Guratsky said. 'And the psychiatrist charges them both rent! But you must admit I'm getting better value for money.'

Executive star wars

1983 Chief Executive; 1984 'If my boss calls...'

I am with Mainwaring in his Mayfair office watching the computer screen. White-coated technicians are plotting zodiac charts on a huge electronic wall map.

Mainwaring's exegesis:

'The sun opposing the explosive Uranus on the 10th indicates that Diamond Laboratories' chief executive will experience a watershed in his relationship with his marketing director, while the full moon on the 12th will force him to cancel the New York trip he had planned for later this month.

'The fiery planet Mars is entering his opposition sign of Aquarius, indicating that this is a perfect time to exploit Diamond's fall in market share by more aggressive merchandising in Tyne-Tees.

'Saturn in Virgo turns to direct motion on the 23rd, suggesting a serious disagreement on financial issues. This could be a domestic row about a new washing machine, or the forthcoming budget discussions with the parent company; it should become clear when the sun has passed through Taurus on the 21st.

'The ruling planet Jupiter has re-entered the long distance travel angle of the CEO's personal chart and over the next several months the Sagittarius impulse for risk taking could have serious bottom-line implications for new product launches.'

Mainwaring rubs his hands in glee. 'Just what I was hoping. They are not going to wait for the next test market results before going national. Unwise. It could also mean that he's playing games with his new secretary.

'She is a Libra and with a full moon in Scorpio he may have reached the point of no return. But that's his problem. What happens now is that we feed this horoscope into an interactive program which will compute what should do on a rolling weekly basis.

'This will take account of market position and the planetary dispositions of all the key people, including the media and creative teams at the agency. The plan will be distributed in coded form to managers in the field on a strictly need-to-know basis.'

Mainwaring relights his pipe which has gone out in the excitement. 'I have to be a bit careful myself this week. I've got Virgo in my birth sign, which means I must avoid any kind of financial decision until Scorpio becomes dominant again. Fortunately, my assistant is a Gemini, so I can delegate to her for the time being.

'I believe we were the first company in Britain to use executive horoscopes in actual marketing operations. Of course, we'd been into management palm reading for several years. We'd found this quite useful. I had a weak career line corrected with plastic surgery a while ago.

'But it was Greenglass' statistical studies of horoscopes and character profiles that laid the foundations for the sophisticated planning that you're seeing here this morning.

'You may recall, back in the early 1970s Greenglass examined groups of successful people, top of their professions – sportsmen, actors, composers, political figures, business and military leaders – to see if he could categorize each group in terms of character traits. He then took each person's horoscope and found a remarkable correlation between career pattern and zodiac charts – after factoring in the actual position of the planets at the time of birth.

'Of course, we were fascinated by the findings and so we asked Greenglass to run a multi-centric analysis of 100,000 corporate executives and entrepreneurs broken down into key sub-groups – marketing, sales, financial, production, human resources and so on. The "Greenglass Effect" was found to apply in every case.

'What we did then was to recruit a team of astrologers and put them to work with our software people to develop a series of interactive programs, encompassing individual cognitive factors, for all aspects of management activity.

'I mean, you name it. Executive recruitment, marketing, financial and sales management, research and manufacturing, expense account management…

'We use weekly horoscopes – hourly if need be – to predict how competitors will react to changing conditions in the market. And the action we should take to counteract them. As you've just seen, we know more about the key executives at Diamond and what they should or shouldn't be doing than they know themselves.

'Incidentally, one very interesting aspect. We've found that the "Greenglass Effect" applies to companies as well as to individuals. It's perfectly possible to cast a corporate horoscope.

'It can be useful in deciding when to make a new share issue, arranging a propitious date for a meeting with the security analysts or shareholders' meetings – things like that. When people talk about an executive not fitting in with the culture of the company, that's when the individual and corporate horoscopes are out of sync. You have to take a slightly longer-term view to get anything definite out of this. But it does have useful applications in hiring and firing.'

We are interrupted by a personal message for Mainwaring. He studies it ruefully.

'Since your ruling planet is now passing by the mid-heaven part of your natal chart, you will be very much preoccupied with important career issues. The 20th would be a good day to update your resumé and make a mass-mailing; but do not answer any ads until after the full moon. Beware of Sagittarian headhunters.'

'Fascinating, I murmur. 'Tell me, what is Greenglass doing nowadays?'

'Oh, Greenglass still works for us as a consultant, although he is confined to a private mental clinic in Manchester.'

Eavesdropping on the Sunday Club
1985 Chief Executive

The scene is a conference room at Blue Skies Management Institute at a secret location in the Swiss Alps (in fact, the first management task for students is working out how to get there). With appetites stirring at this brisk altitude, seven men and a woman break off their discussion of a management case study and emerge for lunch. The conference room is sealed off with 'strictly private' notices. Outside two burly men in tweeds take turns to admire the view. It might be a routine classroom discussion at any business school, except for the elaborate security and the fact that today is Sunday.

The case too is unusual. Instead of being a disguised re-run of a historic problem for the edification of aspiring MBAs, it is a real life study being run in real time. And of pressing concern for the board of a major Belgian food company whose managing director and marketing director are among the group having lunch.

The men in the group are a Harvard professor, who is acting as moderator, four senior marketing executives from different packaged goods companies, and our old friend Guratsky. The woman is a behavioral psychologist from Bremen. They are exploring a unique experiment in management consulting.

The whole thing started a few months ago when Guratsky had the idea of bringing consulting into the business school. Or rather, bringing the business school into the real world.

Guratsky explains: 'It really stemmed from two observations. Firstly, that the case study has yet to be fully exploited. Sure, it's been brought to a high degree of sophistication as a purely teaching method. Students have a kind of simulated, or telescoped experience to draw on when they go out into the harsh corporate world. The cases they study are real enough, and sometimes rueful past protagonists come to tell them what really happened. But however imaginative the verisimilitude, the case study isn't the real thing. The real thing would be a case study developed around an actual problem which some company is anxious to solve.

'So we thought, how interesting if the case study teaching method were to be extended into a consulting mode. All you'd need to do would be to take real-life cases and replace the students by careful chosen experts.

'The second observation was that there's a vast reservoir of management talent throughout the world that might be more effectively exploited if full-time managers were to become part-time consultants. Not only would executives enjoy the intellectual stimulus of solving other people's problems, but they might be more insightful, certainly more hands-on, than your normal consultant.

'After that it was really quite simple. We formed an experimental group using top executives as "students" in discussing real-life case studies. We believed that such a group would work best under the auspices of a business school. An academic umbrella would help our "consultants" get permission from their management to spend their free time in this novel way. What's more, the business school faculty would be of great help in preparing the case material and moderating the discussion. We called the new group the Sunday Club. We never advertise and participants often conceal their names and origins. We run the club with the discretion of an intelligence agency.'

Today's meeting of the Sunday Club was planned three weeks ago. A phone call brought Stanley Zilch, the director of Blue Skies, to Geneva airport to meet the Belgian clients. The Belgians have been offered a license to manufacture and market a chocolate syrup. The syrup is a milk additive, competing directly with powdered chocolate products. Developed by a small company in Canada, it represents a real technical breakthrough in having no natural ingredients. Focus groups have shown that it has 'flavor parity' with the brand leader but is much more versatile in use. After six months in a Cleveland, Ohio, test-market, with minimal merchandizing, the syrup gained a 20 percent share at the expense of the two leading brands. A competitor would need an estimated nine months to develop and market a comparable product. The Belgians have a one-month option.

The 'consultants' are coming back from lunch. Millions of dollars of talent and experience devoted for one day to artificial chocolate syrup. By six o'clock this afternoon, the Belgians may feel they are in a position to make a go/no-go decision.

Roger Collis

Moonlighters anonymous

1984 'If my boss calls...'

Frankly, you won't believe the scene. I go up in this crystal cage suffused with pale blue light. It's like being inside a billion carat diamond. I step out into a penthouse office decorated in Deauville 1920s style. A blown-up advertisement of the new Panhard, chromium furniture and lots of black glass.

'Nice spread,' I say to Guratsky. 'So this is where you give the Charleston lessons.' Tom and I are old pals.

Guratsky, behind a desk of impressive vulgarity, sucks in his dewlaps. 'We subscribe to the furnishings library. They come and change the decor every six months. Would you believe Second Empire in a week's time?'

'I'd believe anything. I can just see you in satin knee-breeches. I have to admit though that moonlighting's bang up to date. Tell me about it.'

'It all started with a bunch of guys suffering from insomnia. We felt that if they couldn't sleep they might as well work. So we had the idea of starting night-time companies. We've developed an alternative noctural economy, banks, brokerage houses, advertising agencies ... We offer regular day time companies a complete night-time staff, from presidents right down to janitors. The night-time crew comes on board in the evening and take over the desks, telephones and files. Companies find they can literally double their productivity.'

'But surely there must be a conflict between day-time and night-time managements?'

'Sometimes. But that's not always a bad thing. Management by conflict, remember? And we've done quite a bit of research on the best times for decision making. The optimum time is three o'clock in the morning. So we usually suggest that the night president takes the key decisions. We act as coordinators. For example, we arrange breakfast meetings when the two management teams can meet. Breaksuppers we call them. We also run vocation clinics to help executives decide whether they are best suited for day-time or night-time operations. It's often a question of temperament.'

'I can understand that.' But don't you find executives become schizophrenic having to reconcile day-time and night-time careers?'

'Sometimes. What often happens is that an executive's night-time career develops faster than his day-time career. For example, you might be a vice-president during the night and only a product manager during the day. This can cause problems if the guy is working for the same company. The president can arrive in his office in the morning to find his decision of the previous day has been changed by his sales manager during the night.'

We are served coffee by a distinguished elderly man. A night-time banker perhaps. The glass telephone jangles.

'Hallo. Samantha! Yes, looking forward to seeing you. Byee.' Guratsky grins. 'That was Samantha Lane. She works in a typing pool during the day but runs her own night-time advertising agency. You'll have to excuse me. I have to prepare for a midnight lunch appointment.'

Contingency planning is never saying you're sorry
1976 Werbung/Publicite

The moment of truth: Mel Geist is in fulsome spiel.

'So you see for the last quarter of 1975 the lira was fairly stable at around forty. Then, of course, we had a sharp decline which resulted in the interruption of trading on January 5, when the cross-rate was thirty eight forty there has been a decline of twenty nine point eight percent against the Swiss franc. Yesterday's cross-rate was a little under twenty seven twenty. We can expect a slight recovery in the next few days, but this is technical due to an increase in spot and forward transactions. The prognosis is very grave. Particularly if the Italian government is forced to impose a new set of trade restrictions such as import deposit scheme; which is likely to be much tougher than the one we had last year.'

He pauses while two secretaries minister with coffee. There is a resounding silence. In some perverse way they are enjoying the drama. Mel fishes for a cigarette and continues.

'Now what are the implications for the Group? At the current cross-rate we have to have to face an unplanned loss of two point three two million Swiss francs for our Italian operations. As you are well aware, Italy accounts for twenty percent of Mistral's international turnover. And with the collapse last month of the UK distributor coupled with the decline of sterling the leverage on the whole group is huge. I'm particularly worried about the short-term cash flow implications. If we're going to be able to continue operations we shall have to make some drastic cuts here in Zurich. I'm sorry, gentlemen, I guess there was no way we could have foreseen this situation.'

Six pairs of suddenly preoccupied eyes are rehearsing un-neighborly incantations. Jaws are clamped in managerial concentration. Silence for several long seconds. Then Gottlieb offers a beleaguered smile. Normally they enjoy his schtik. The ursine spreading of hands…

'Don't all talk at once guys. Yeah, sure this calls for some, ah, radical measures. But there must be some way we can, ah, trim shall we say fixed overheads and at least maintain our marketing thrust. I mean, the fact is, ah, we have a good, well quite good, ah, lira business. Soulbad is holding a twenty-five percent share of the total bath addictive market, although we lost slightly to Neptune in the pharmacy sector. Of course, we can cut TV and go into radio and print. But the danger is if, ah, Neptune can afford to go on spending at their current rate, we could lose the, ah, market in twelve months. Remember, our current price increases are going to mean, ah, some reduction in unit sales.'

'You're right, Al, but if the political situation gets worse, we'll lose our business anyway. Wouldn't it be best to take as much profit from Italy now while we have the chance?'

'Cut our losses, you mean? It's probably too late, although we can try. But we're still going to have to let some people go. We can't afford to carry this kind of overhead. Otherwise, we'll be like some banana republic navy – all admirals and no battleships. We should have foreseen this situation; at least made some contingency plans.'

'Mel, I think that's a little unfair. You may remember in our long-range plan review meeting in September, we laid out strategies for decreasing our dependence on Italy and the UK. I'm thinking especially of the cross-licensing plan where we'd channel entrepreneurial funds into new product development in our key own-company markets. I believe we've been making some progress.'

The last sentence hangs in the air like a question.

'Yeah, but given that kind of vulnerability, shouldn't we have developed some kind of short-range plan to head off the situation we're now facing?'

Everyone is trying to recall reports which they never wrote.

'What you mean is we should have anticipated the probability of various "what if?" situations. Mel, you mentioned contingency planning. I guess what we should have done is to make a thorough evaluation of the product or geographical areas which exert the greatest actual or potential leverage on our business; and then developed alternative tactical plans which could be implemented quickly in response to possible crisis situations.'

'Marty, you've missed your vocation! You should be teaching at Harvard Business School. If I can translate for the others, what you're talking about is scenario writing. In other words imagining various catastrophes and having plans ready to use if one of them should happen. For example, we could have reacted much more quickly to the Italian situation by selling lire early and trimming TV commitments in other markets.'

Mel sums up. 'I guess there's only one scenario right now, gentlemen. We've got to decide where to make the cuts. I need three-quarters of a million by tomorrow.'

You can almost see the think bubbles, rising like ponderous Zeppelins; so vulnerable to paper airplanes, as six very personal scenarios are being written.

Roger Collis

The psychographic streamlined tangerine-flake computer baby

1972 Werbung/Publicite; 1986 Chief Executive

And now, folks, a brave new day in Consumerland. A wry rosy sun edging its way down the Bahnhofstrasse. Teeming citizens bustling to work. And in the research department at Doberman & Pinscher they are awaking this baby from twelve hours of restful cybernetic sleep. All the little circuits yawning. Open the windows to let in more electricity. Check the voltages on the bathroom scales. Fine. Tickle the memory disks. Nize baby et up all his programs.

But who is this hirsute executive joining us for breakfast? Why it's Tom Guratsky himself foraging for his client meeting at nine. Printouts for the Mistral media plan. TV and magazines, and radio and TV and magazines. Wow! And three alternative spending levels. Hey, what if they ask how we compare gross rating points with four color double page spreads? Mmm. We'll unleash Gottlieb who can do his thing on qualitative inter-media comparisons; importance of editorial and so on. Anyway, let's try this budget on for size in our prêt-a-porter boutique. Where the client is nearly always right. Depending, of course, on the size of his budget. Nize client et up all his presentation.

But for stream of consciousness buffs we'll move over to Studio Two where they are replaying the tapes of yesterday's focus group discussions. Digging out choice verbatims for the meeting: 'There's no point in acting out your frustrations in public.' 'I would consider myself a courtier rather than a baron.' 'Of course, the strength of the barons depends on the king.' 'Sure, the corporation is like a nation state.' 'Renaissance,' 'Politics, remember, is the art of the possible.' 'Politics is a fact of life.' 'Hell, so-called management science is just a continuation of the old-fashioned art of government.' 'Why should politics be a dirty word in business?' 'Being professional is getting things done unobtrusively.' 'Behind the scenes.' 'We're just applying historical methods to get to the top and stay there.' 'I'd feel happy with a fragrance that people associate with power.' 'Yeah, a power fragrance.' 'It would have to be really exclusive.' 'And instantly recognizable.' 'Prince Machiavelli is a great name.' 'Yeah, I could identify with that.' 'Prince Machiavelli? Wow, why not?'

'Of course, we need to quantify. But we've done some preliminary factor analysis among the thirty respondents who took part in the focus groups and found some remarkable life-style correlations among those who respond favorably to the Prince Machiavelli concept,' Guratsky's voice issues from a thicket of Fu Manchu moustaches. 'For example, they tend to prefer very dry vodka martinis on the rocks with five olives. They drive two point five cars and have been married three point five times. They have a mild obsession with candlelight and prefer meetings of no more than two people, including themselves. Humor rates only two point nine on the Chaplin scale. We still need to program their one-liners; but we haven't yet found any serious stand-ups in this group. Analysis of their career patterns shows a record of successful intrigues. Voice print and eye-camera analyses will be ready tomorrow. But I think we can say that the putative profile of the Prince Machiavelli user is beginning to emerge. Demographically, we have it, but we need to do some further psychographic studies.'

From an adipose prose a slender talent is starting to escape. Right on, Guratsky. And now the client is telling you about the Prince Machiavelli fragrance. The years of painstaking laboratory work extracting the essential oils from the sex glands of the Asian fox... the esoteric musky odour. Some regrettable badinage here; quickly hushed by news of the painstaking human trials, during which several promising young executives were sacrificed; a whiff of Prince Machiavelli across their bows. Splash a little on the jowls to scupper the opposition.

And the target group is developing nicely. Thanks to our baby who is humming productively in his air-conditioned room, after a light lunch of new demographic data; like the average number of castles in Spain; and how many of them are lived in the year round; and if there is a correlation between heavy coffee drinkers and the size of their briefcases. Guratsky's secret weapon is an analysis of all the books that each respondent remembers reading. Quite a meal. He says we are going to need a new computer programmer.

Programmer? Man, this baby needs a psychiatrist.

Recalling the good old days

1987 International Herald Tribune

As John Millar sees it, business travel was a much more civilized experience 50 years ago – especially flying.

Millar, a retired British aerospace manufacturer and former TWA captain (he flew DC-2s in 1935-6) is president of the World Solar Power Foundation. He now lives in Monte Carlo and has been an inveterate first-class traveler since 1936.

'Prewar one traveled by boat in the greatest luxury. The German line had the *Bremen* and the *Europa*, the French had the *Normandie* and the *France* and we had the *Aquitania*, the *Mauritanea* and later, the *Queen Mary*. There was none of this standing about in line for hours to show your passport and tickets. You went down by train to Southampton in great comfort. Then straight aboard the boat with your baggage delivered straight to your cabin.

At the other end, Immigration was on board, so that when the boat docked at pier 96 on the Hudson River, your baggage was put under your name on long tables. The customs officer marked them and a porter would take them to a taxi or car. There was none of this awful business of hanging about for hours. When one thinks of the beginning of trans-Atlantic and continental air travel in the U.S., it was a simple business too.'

And remarkably comfortable it seems. You checked in downtown at the airline ticket office and were taken out to the airport by limo. No waiting. You climbed aboard the plane and settled down in a reclining lounge chair. You were served a hot meal with real china, glass and linen. Then the crew would make up your bed – there were twin-size berths with separate dressing rooms for men and women – and you could sleep right through take-offs and landings until you arrived in the morning.

This is how it was on the Skysleeper service between New York and California which TWA inaugurated in June 1937 with the new DC-3 Sleeper Transport (American Airlines had started a similar service in September 1936). The overnight coast-to-coast flight took just over 11 hours, with stops at St. Louis, Kansas City and Albuquerque and from there into Burbank, California.

'It was all one class as I recall with 16 seats one on each side of the aisle and lots of legroom,' Millar says. 'They were very comfortable. Quality of travel in those days was probably due as much to the attitude of airlines and airport authorities as the in-flight amenities. You could do things that are unthinkable today.'

Even more luxurious were the Clipper flying boats that pioneered the Pacific and Atlantic routes. Pan Am started the first trans-Pacific service in 1935. And in 1939 it flew scheduled services between New York and Marseille via Lisbon. Then in 1945 came the Lockheed Constellation, which TWA flew half-way round the world (San Francisco-Los Angeles-Kansas City-Newfoundland-Lisbon-Paris-Bern-Rome). It had 16 berths and nine chaises-longues. This was followed in 1949 by the double-decked Boeing Stratocruiser, which had sleeping berths and a downstairs lounge. A very comfortable plane, according to Millar.

Millar says: 'I started an aerospace business in England in 1937 when I came back from flying with TWA and after the war I emigrated to America and built a factory at Newport, Rhode Island, on the local airfield. When I had to go to England, I'd make a reservation on BOAC and get an air taxi to fly me 200 miles down to New York. One time we arrived at Idlewild (now JFK) and couldn't get permission to land. I took the mike and said to the tower, "Look, my flight to England leaves in 10 minutes." The guy said, "Okay, you're number two to land. Your flight is at gate six." But when we taxied up, the Stratocruiser had left and was waiting to take off at the far end of the runway. I said to BOAC, "I'm terribly sorry, we've been circling half an hour." "That's all right, sir, we've sent a car for you. We'll fix it up with Immigration." So I went scooting off down the taxiway to the plane. They pushed my bags in one door, opened another door and pushed me into the bar. I climbed up the stairs into my seat.'

Slow dissolve to a recent experience with Pan Am when Millar took the direct Nice-New York flight. 'They said, we'll give you a free helicopter ride to 60th Street Skyport. Well we got to New York (a comfortable flight, no complaints; I had the front seat in first class, I hope you don't think it's a frightful conceit, but I always take my own silver tankards for champagne, it tastes so much better), then had to walk down endless corridors into a huge immigration hall which had 60-70 people in line before each booth. I had to wait an hour and a half – my fault I should have ordered a wheelchair. Then I had to get my luggage. I'd missed the helicopter and had to wait another hour for the next one. I got to the helicopter where a driver put the bags into a limo and without asking where I wanted go took me to 57th and Second Avenue. 'But I want to go to the Drake Hotel.' 'Sorry, sir we just leave you here. You can pick up a cab.' I said, 'It's my good luck it's not pouring with rain.' Next morning, Pan Am lost a bag of mine in Chicago. Do you think I have had any compensation? They haven't even acknowledged my letters.'

Millar says quality started to deteriorate in the late 1950s. 'I think we've gone about everything the wrong way. With hindsight it's easy to see why. If we'd seen the extent of the tourist traffic, we'd have said, let's have separate airports for first class and business passengers and keep them small. Instead they built bigger airports and bigger planes.

'I know you get a separate check-in. But, my God, what happened at the British Airways check-in at Heathrow? Half the girls never turned up for duty so there were huge lines stretching out into the street. It took me more than half an hour edging forward gradually.

'You've got this mass tourism thing. It's the same with hotels. In Atlanta the Sheraton gave me the wrong room. I said, I'm not taking this one. So I had to fight them. In the end I got the room I wanted and had reserved. But you see, one shouldn't have to go through all this hassle.

'In London I stay at Claridges, which is barely in the 20th century. But I love it. The food varies, it's not as good as the Connaught. But the bedrooms are wonderful; top quality sheets and marvelous bath towels that really dry you. The baths are big enough for two, at least in the old rooms. I have in my country house in southern France probably the only Claridges bath tub in Europe. I bought one and had it shipped out.'

Advertising a la carte

1985 Chief Executive

The stairwell was a Cape Horn of cooking smells which offered no respite to apfelstrudel lurking uneasily on top of the tafelspitz from Sacher's famous restaurant. Yes, you've already guessed; a windy day in Vienna. The mood was postprandial; dyspepsia engulfing the cautious optimism of lunch. I popped another Gelusil and groped for the lift.

Guratsky's office was on the top floor. A fly-blown blonde sat in front of an Art Deco sign which said: 'A la Carte Advertising Gesellschaft,' and in smaller letters, 'Thomas Guratsky & Associates.' I was wondering what Tom, that inveterate chameleon, had been reading lately when the man himself appeared in a white coat and neatly trimmed goatee. He had this genius for going native, sometimes in curious atavistic ways.

'Tom, you're looking great,' I lied. 'Not a day younger than when I last saw you. Tell me, what do you mean by the "A la Carte" bit? Does it mean you're no longer a full service agency or simply gone into the restaurant business?'

Guratsky narrowed his eyes, in the manner I remembered from tricky moments in client presentations. 'The innuendo, I'll ignore. I think you need a nice cup of coffee. Gudron, would you please... As a matter of fact we are having some problems with Frau Dr Oberholtz on the first floor. She's been doing a *cordon bleu* course in traditional Austrian cooking and does tend to be a little exuberant. On the other hand, she does our copy testing for us.'

It was my turn to narrow my eyes.

Guratsky smiled. 'It's obvious. When you're in the menu-writing business, you have to be sure that the dish sustains the promise of the advertising. Imagine we're creating a dish description for a client. "Tender prime cutlet of veal, cooked to a succulent turn, smothered in golden deep-fried onions and deliciously accompanied by a medley of exciting spring vegetables et cetera." That's pretty basic stuff. It always sounds better in French, of course; but we do sometimes get into real poetry.'

I smothered a grimace. This was enough to send the most relentless gourmet on to a crash diet. 'But Tom, if you're creating advertising copy, you surely don't have to go out and test the product as well?'

'Not exactly, but we have to make sure the product will live up to the claims we make for it. We don't want angry, disappointed diners on our hands who have been beguiled by the poetry, the eloquence, of the menu stuck outside. We specialize in-depth. We've separate menus for entrees, desserts and so on; and wines, of course. How about, "A very pretty girl in a short evening dress' to describe a Chateau bottled Bordeaux in a dubious year? Or, perhaps: "An unpretentious little wine with a heart of gold," for a New Zealand Chardonnay?'

'I'd prefer "A very pretty girl with a heart of gold." But seriously, Tom, you surely don't specialize in restaurant menus?'

'No, in fact we specialize quite widely, if you see what I mean. We have a team handling hotel brochures and another which does holiday advertising for travel agents. We're also in the media business, selling space on book matches, ball point pens, beer mats and the like. A good book match campaign can really move the stuff off the shelves. Right now, I'm negotiating to acquire an old established sky writing company.'

'Well, I've heard that the latest thing is a team of acrobatic parachutists forming a human slogan in the sky.'

'That's right,' Guratsky said, unfazed. 'Which reminds me; we're negotiating to take over a graffiti agency. Now that's something really specialized don't you think?'

'Graffiti!' I thought I could hear old Franz Josef turning in his grave; but it was only a tram rumbling along Grabergasse. 'But Tom, does that mean you have people going round all the public lavatories writing stuff like: "Zappo rules OK;" and "Kilroy washes whiter?"'

'Something of the sort,' Guratsky said. 'We've just done a media study which shows that lavatory wall advertising delivers a better cost-per-thousand than mainstream TV. People tend to enjoy the editorial content; and of course you have a captive audience. You can also buy demographics quite selectively.'

'Tom, the mind boggles. Even you still have the power to surprise me. Book matches, restaurant menus, sky writing, public lavatories.' I wondered whether Guratsky was still selling space on the side panels of his old hatchback.

There is a point, it seems, where advertising and graffiti merge.

King Fred's Tea Party

1967 The Guardian (inspired by a meeting with Crown Prince Leka of Albania, son of ex-King Zog)

He has a cool villa in a green suburb of Madrid. Twenty minutes from the cacophony of the Gran Via. At the end of a pale pink drive of dusty gravel. Among orange trees and the stately swish of water sprinklers under a big fat sun. We stopped in front of a tall, white gate and my friends told me to wait while they fixed the bona fides with old Gustave the royal bodyguard. I sat obscurely in the car while the right words were whispered through the fence. And then the proud entrance, casual as I could make it. Nervously adjusting my new persona grata.

Across spongy grass to the patio where there were wicker chairs and a round table of wrought iron thoughtfully laid out for drinks.

The king came down the steps tall in shirt sleeves. Fresh no doubt from his counting house and all the golden bars. Glad I'd remembered to wear my new purple tie. And I thought of bowing neatly from the waist but realized in time that this might be a mild lapse of taste.

The king's eyes spelled informality. I was struck at once by his long black hair and round tortoiseshell spectacles which looked engagingly out of place on his tired young face. And an American accent spread thinly over a dark brown Balkan sound. He might have been a king of Manhattan specially created by the public relations men. I thought of the sad immigrants stepping off the boat at Ellis Island. With a brisk Atlantic breeze to polish the homesick consonants.

But the king smiled into my reverie and said, 'Hi, friends, what's your poison?' I said, 'Thank you so much, please make mine a Scotch.' I stood with a fat crystal glass and cautiously helped myself to the tasty pastries. We talked a lot about water skis and the price of power boats. With Gustave all the time sternly omnipresent looking like it had never been the same since they sold the Hispano-Suiza.

This breathless afternoon soon fading, with the sun a giant chrysanthemum sulking behind the orange trees. And an impious wind coming to play with the sprinklers and speckle us all with water.

We said politely we really should go. But the king said no he wouldn't hear of such a thing and ushered us firmly into the drawing room.

We stepped from Spain into Austria-Hungary and a forest of dark furniture dangerously deployed. Something of a social mine-field. I nearly toppled a shako of the Imperial Hussars laid out no doubt for instant readiness. Sitting down for safety I could hear the whisper of satin and the sad bones of these old chairs. All the exiled ghosts imprisoned in this distant microcosm. There were wine-red drapes, small tables delicately inlaid, the ragged head of a deer and a schloss-sized chandelier.

I spied an oval portrait of great-aunt Sophie and a photograph which must have been the late king. He was splendid in sepia with uniform tunic bulging at the chest. And bristling Balkan moustaches. My king in magisterial pose raised his glass and gave his bare top lip an atavistic twist. How I envied those distinguished chromosomes. And thought of all my common ones palely lurking somewhere.

A Spanish maid in a black dress came with a tray of iced cakes and while the others were busy sinking polite teeth into the soft sponge, the king laid a conspiratorial hand on my arm saying he would like to show me around. Gustave, he assured me, was outside checking for anarchists. I thought of his slow silhouette stalking around the neat grounds. Perhaps with a Mauser rifle, vintage nineteen 'three, tucked under his arm and sadly couchant. Back in Bohemia there would have been crisp snow under his boots. The dogs smelling real blood as they stopped in their tracks. And the snuffling wildschwein careering between black Wagnerian pines.

This spring evening the king in his study. Great moon face solemn across the green baize. Around the room were displayed guns of all shapes and ages. Being a military man I could see that these shooting instruments were properly oiled and ready for any conceivable altercation. Neither was novelty forgotten. See this fountain pen. Just press the clip so and let go with a neat 22. Ideal for the ticklish tête-à-tête. I sat on an ammunition box and admired this swinging arsenal.

We smoked and drank champagne and when I rose to go the king said he hoped I'd come again. But before I went would I accept this parchment commissioning me in the Household Hussars. Naturally, I could serve on the General Staff. I knew a tailor in the Via Velazquez where I could buy epaulettes. Back in the drawing room to join my friends I clutched my proud document and thanked his majesty for a fascinating time. The king smiled. 'Hope to see you soon. And by the way all my friends call me Fred.'

Crunching away on the royal gravel I wondered what old Franz-Jozef would have said.

Designing a New Camel
1973 Werbung/Publicite; 1986 Chief Executive

'Okay, so we're agreed on the name?'

'Mel, I'm still not entirely convinced...'

'John, we have to compromise. Sure, the other name scored better in the research, but Legal insists that if we want to launch in September, we only have the one trademark checked out.'

'Yeah, well, we'll have to broaden the target group...'

'Frankly, I don't see why we should; what's in a name, fahcrissake?'

'Well, for one thing, Al, with the name we're now going with, we can't very well limit ourselves to a specific youth image. I mean, there's no way we can avoid diluting...'

'Sure, that means there'll be media implications. I'll have to get the agency to rework the media schedule. What I'm afraid of is sacrificing frequency by adding more titles. Sure, we'll have better reach but...'

'And if we have to trim spending... Dave Silver was making ominous noises in my office yesterday. John, how much...?'

'Look, I have a suggestion. Why don't we review the original concept? Then we can take a new look at the creative, media and spending levels in the light of our new investment guidelines. That should take care of Dave Silver. So, Dan, would you...?'

'Sure, Mel. Well, first of all, as you know, we'd originally thought of positioning this cigarette towards toward the nineteen to twenty-three-and-a-half year old motor-cycle enthusiast. Ah, no thanks, Al, I don't. No, you go ahead, I'll just open the window... Ah, where was I? Right. We hadn't worked out the exact male/female split but we were thinking in terms of 70/30. The name *Open Road* was intended to reflect a whole raft of social attitudes; a kind of anarchy, I guess. Not the dropping out kind, though; more of a creative radicalism.'

'The kind of person who reads *Rolling Stone* magazine.'

Right., you've got it – a fairly distinct target group, at least in psychographic terms. And economical to reach. But if we have to take a broader approach with a budget cut...'

'Look, Dave Silver wasn't explicit.'

'Dave Silver's never explicit'

'Maybe, but I think we'd better commit only 60 percent of what we'd planned. If we have to trim forecast sales by ten percent, we'll still be realistic with a broader target group.'

'Incidentally, has the agency got posters in the schedule? I think we should have a few posters, at least in the metro markets. They're very visible to top management.'

'They hadn't, but I can talk to them.'

'Look, fellers, if we could get back to the creative, I think that idea of my wife's might fit very well with the new name.'

'What was that, Mel?'

'The idea? It was showing a whole range of travel situations with a lot of different personalities. You know, Arnold Palmer coming down the steps of a plane...'

'Hey, you're not allowed to smoke coming down the steps of a plane.'

'Okay, I was just giving...'

'What about giving it a nostalgia image? Like the twenties. Something like *Voyage*. I think that's a tremendously evocative name. Romantic couple on the *Ile-de-France* enjoying a cigarette on the sun deck after dinner. Satin sea. Violins. Kind of a Scott Fitzgerald couple maybe.'

'Holy cow; I'm glad I'm not the one briefing the agency.'

'I would have thought that's fairly straightforward – if that's the way we want to go.'

'Listen, if we're going to make September, that'll mean checking out a new trademark.'

'Yeah, and can we reconcile smart set with Zen? I mean, the super-sophisticated traveler of the twenties with the hip motor-cyclist that was our original concept with *Open Road* remember?'

'But is that really...?'

'Anyway, that's the job of the agency. It's a matter of finding a psychographic common denominator. We're just developing guidelines here.'

'Mel, we haven't talked about sales promotion.'

'Right, John, I'd like you to have a go at that. But easy on the samples. Be selective. Remember, we haven't got cowboys in our target group.'

'But we'll need more money than Dave Silver'll give us.'

'You leave Dave Silver to me. Okay. Look, it's lunchtime and I've got to pick up my wife – she may have some more ideas. I'll get back to you all on the budget when I've talked to Dave. Meanwhile, Dan, if you could pull the new plan together on the basis of this morning's discussion, we'll be all set...'

Roger Collis

Whatever happened to the paperless office?
1985 Chief Executive

'In the old days it would take a week to crank out a five-page report that took the boss five minutes to read. Now it takes five minutes to print out a 50-page report that takes a week to read – or which nobody has time to read.'

This is how Stanley Zilch, our Brussels-based consultant in time management, describes the impact of the micro-processing revolution – a view shared with various shades of cynicism by corporate executives who have seen their offices transformed into putative global networks by telecommunications technology and computer power.

One thing corporate futurologists forgot on their way to the paperless office was the human factor (*pace* Graham Greene). They forgot that the sheer efficiency of computer communications systems would lead to more and more people getting more and more copies of more and more documents. In the past, managers tended to have too little information too late when they made decisions; now they suffer the even greater handicap of having more information than they can handle, and the automated office is cluttered with more paper than ever before.

It was a beguiling scenario. You start the day by logging into the corporate electronic mailbox from home with your Banana 3 laptop. You note incoming messages, tap out responses and print out anything that needs a hard copy while you were having breakfast. At your office workstation you can prepare and send out documents to other video display units anywhere in the world. Your telephone is a voice-mail system that allows natural voice messages to be stored and edited. You can hold teleconferences with far-flung colleagues, some of whom may be telecommuting from their electronic cottages (like the Welshman in Llandudno). If you need data from a file, you simply call up the electronic filing system on your screen.

But for most of us this is not the real world. Relatively few offices are fully integrated electronic networks. Most are at the half-way stage of 'stand-alone' applications: word processors, fax machines and personal computers, which may or may not be connected to the mainframe. Until we all have our own personal terminal or work-station, true electronic communications are not possible. There's still a lot of paper to shuffle around.

Of course, paper begets paper in a truly biblical sense. High-speed photocopy machines have a terrible fascination; making copies of everything is as compulsive as eating a bowl of salted peanuts. The photocopy area has replaced the water-cooler at Diamond Laboratories as the centre for office chitchat while people wait in line to make thousands of copies of their resumés.

Word processors are inveterate consumers of paper. This is not simply because of their prowess at high-speed printing, but because managers think it is so easy they send back draft after draft for correction. What efficient offices are doing is to use rough paper, like PR handouts or financial statements, for the first few dozen drafts of a report.

One danger of office automation is to assume that something becomes desirable just because it is technically feasible. Systems are naturally more important than the quality of what is communicated.

For example, back in the Stone Age, it might have taken the art department a week to make a dozen charts for a marketing presentation. So you had to be selective. What's more, your information on stock inventories was probably limited to ten percent of stores. This was more than sufficient for planning purposes. Everything was simple and precise. People would come away with a 20-page document that they could more or less understand.

Nowadays, you have the possibility of moving in on every store in the market and coming up with a zillion permutations, what happened to every brand by pack and flavor in every size on week days.

It's well known that paper proliferates, the higher up the organization one goes. Except for showcase examples of secretary-boss role reversals, most top managers are notoriously keyboard-shy.

'Senior management still wants lots of paper,' Zilch says, 'You might just persuade them to use this equipment, but when they start sending messages around, they worry about things like, how do I sign this? A laser pen isn't wholly convincing. They're also terrified that the Welshman might have got in and sent them a spurious message from the chairman.'

Roger Collis

Mind you, if you want to keep a secret from the chairman, just put a message in his electronic mailbox.

Nothing succeeds like success
1984 'If my boss calls …'

The film opens with the Boeing 747 bearing Patrick O'Malley, newly elected vice-president of Sunrise Holdings Incorporated, and 219 other passengers to New York, plunging across a turbulent sea of fractured cumulus. Bleak rows of business suits have usurped the colourful summer tourists. It is a black-and-white scene hardly relieved by the pale green olive in Patrick O'Malley's martini, his discreetly striped Union Club tie or the occasional stewardess's smile. The audience is invited to add suitable subtitles and think bubbles. Semi-classical music is courtesy of Pan American Airways.

Patrick O'Malley is a very experienced executive. So experienced that a team of graduate research students at the University of San Diego is tracking the statistical highlights of his career with a complex computer program. Cynics and admirers alike are fond of saying that Patrick O'Malley was born experienced as a result of some genetic alchemy wrought by his father, John Ryan O'Malley, the distinguished bootlegger and diplomat. Experience has certainly not stood in the way of his promotion.

The San Diego team has already published some mind-boggling figures. This is Patrick O'Malley's four hundred and fourth Atlantic round trip, not counting eighty polar crossings. This is probably why he remembers to keep his seatbelt lightly fastened throughout the flight and not to smoke in the toilets. In twenty years he has logged 3.2 million executive miles. He has attended 28,500 meetings and won or drawn nearly 5,000 of them. He has made 130 million phone calls, nearly 90 percent of them long distance, and received nearly a million miles of telexes. He has eaten 55,509 business lunches, consumed 65,000 bottles of wine and is now holding to his lips his twenty-eight thousandth martini. He has smoked a million cigars, personally fired 81 executives and closed 12 factories. Few executives at Sunrise can claim such a successful career.

And not to forget that Patrick O'Malley has his qualitative side. He is well educated: Harvard Business School and Brooks Brothers. He is good with table placings (up to six) and can find his way expertly round a menu. He knows his wines. How to choose a Muscadet, young, pale, like his new girl friend. 'Canton de Vallet? Excellent, waiter. We'll wait a few moments to let it cool some more.' 'Château Margauz, yes, a 1955 would be perfect. Let me see if I know the *domaine*. Ah, of course, that's old Bouchard père. Hand trodden these grapes.' In short, he knows a *premier crû* from an *assiette de crudités*. There's no finer school for the social refinements than the international business world.

Patrick O'Malley sips his martini and vouchsafes the pretty stewardess a self-satisfied smile. A top executive smile. He remembers the confidential facial expression seminar that the president sent him on. How to chair a meeting without actually saying a word. The teacher had been brilliant. A kind of oriental Louis de Funes. He practices another smile, crinkling the eyes and letting his lips twitch ambiguously. That one had earned him a few marks towards this promotion. He lights a cigar and makes a note for the San Diego boys. He thinks of working on his expense account, but surely he's earned the right to relax for once. In a while he will put on his earphones and allow himself to be lulled into a self-satisfied executive sleep.

He had been staying at the Ritz in Paris when the call from the president came. Lying in the bathtub, playing with his flotilla of First World War destroyers to be precise. Embarrassing. But better than being caught with his trousers down, so to speak. There had been that time in Milan when he'd had a two-hour conference call while trapped in the lavatory.

Success had started twenty long years ago when young product manager O'Malley had passed the asparagus test. He remembers to salute with another martini that fateful summer luncheon party in Wiesbaden all those years ago. He was being vetted for chief executive of one of Sunrise's smaller subsidiaries. It turned out to be Malta, but anyway … there on his plate was a mound of dripping asparagus. Inviting him to make the most momentous decision of his career: whether to cut the damned stuff or hold it precariously up to his mouth. He had never looked back.

He has risen steadily at Sunrise, heaping success upon success, eating and drinking his way around the world. He was one of the founding members of the Gastronauts, an executive dining club which meets every Wednesday in a different capital city. On the way up he has held practically every executive job in the company for a few months before moving on, carefully choosing his successors and predecessors so that he could ride on their success, which eventually became his own.

Our hero is asleep, snoring gently above the roar of the engines. The audience is invited to choose between *Singing in the Rain* and Vera Lynn's *We'll Meet Again.*

Ads with a ring in the tail

1984 Chief Executive

It was three o'clock in the morning in Madrid. Sound asleep after a bibulous business evening I was awakened by the jangling of the bedside phone. A slight pause as I struggled to remember where I was, followed by a faint transatlantic voice. 'Mister Cahlis, Mister Rahjah Cahlis?' I thought it said. A call from the chairman in Broken Springs?

But the chairman's lack of consideration for local time is invariably more subtle. He usually waits until I am firmly ensconced in the bathroom expiating the excesses of the night before. No, this was different, altogether more interesting. A nocturnal headhunter perhaps who had taken my resumé for bedside reading?

I croaked an expectant 'Hallo.' 'Mister Bern...' the voice said. The remaining syllables were smothered in electronic burps and whirrings. A pause, '...calling you from Los Angeles...' Another pause, longer this time, 'Hold the line, please...' A hurried conference at the other end, 'We'll call you back in two hours.'

Call me back in two hours! Los Angeles – the big L.A. Hollywood;

Sunset Boulevard; the Polo Club Lounge. Sammy Bernstein (pronounced Bernsteen) at the pool of the Beverly Hills Whatsit brandishing a huge Monte Cristo: 'You've found him in Madrid? Why, that's great. He's on the line now? Wait a minute, honey. Hold it, willya.' The starlet anointing him with suntan oil had reached a vulnerable spot. 'I better finish this casting session; why don't you tell him we'll call back in two hours.'

The dark three o'clock in the morning of the soul was transmuted into a rare euphoria. Your Walter Mitty lay in a delicious half sleep for the next two hours expending his author's prerogatives among a galaxy of starlets. It must be that screen play he had sent out. He was busy rehearsing the 747 seduction scene when the phone rang.

His days of fame were short-lived. It transpired that they were looking for a certain Robert Corless, a media executive in room three-thirty-five!

I was wondering if I could strike some kind of deal with this Corless man when I had a brilliant idea. The power of the telephone to conjure up fantasies and bring emotions to a shuddering climax should surely be better exploited. What about the phone call as a new advertising medium?

Of course, there's nothing new about telephone selling. We've all had to fight off encyclopedia and insurance salesmen. And there are specialized companies that have brought telephone sales to a fine art. No, I am thinking of actual telephone commercials.

For example, instead of the switchboard putting callers on to 'hold' with Vivaldi's Four Seasons, why not expose them to a few advertising spots? In fact commercials could pay the cost of expensive long-distance calls.

A five-minute local call, for instance, might have 15 seconds of advertising; while a call to the Far East or Asia might need several commercial breaks. No more phone bills

How would this work? Well, when traveling, instead of using your credit card or paying exorbitant hotel charges, you would simply use a free 'phone disc' which you would slot into the phone before dialing the number. The disc would contain sufficient commercials to pay for the call. Ultimately, phone companies might offer 'sponsored calls.' Imagine the following transatlantic conversation.

'Hallo, is that London two seven five seven four?' 'Speaking.' 'I have a call for you from Cleveland, Ohio, which is brought to you by the makers of Kennel-Burger dog food, the food that dogs just love to chew. Go ahead, please, your party is on the line…'

'Darling!' 'Darling!' What a lovely surprise; I didn't expect a call 'til Monday…'

'And now a brief word from your sponsor: Don't forget, Kennel-Burger contains 59 vitamins as well as hundreds of valuable minerals to keep your dog in tip-top condition.'

'Darling, could you say that again? There seems to be a lot of barking on the line…'

'And remember, dogs just love Kennel-Burger…' 'Hallo…'

Of course, we'll still get wrong numbers. The other night I was woken up by what seemed to be a long-distance Alka-Seltzer commercial. But I just slammed down the phone, took two tablets in a glass of water and went back to sleep.

When the Rue Bonaparte comes to Madison Avenue

March, 1981 International Management
'Ne dites pas a ma mere que je suis dans la publicite… Elle me croit pianiste dans un bordel.'

JACQUES SEGUELA

Ever since Madison Avenue became the fountainhead of advertising wisdom, 'copy strategy' has been the method used to create advertising campaigns. This approach assumes that a product has a tangible and exclusive consumer benefit that can be turned into a unique selling proposition (USP). But now from the rue Bonaparte, a quiet street located on Paris' Left Bank, comes a challenge to this time honoured approach. It is the 'star strategy;' the notion that by treating products like people, you can give them a 'star quality' that will boost sales.

The concept's prophet is Jacques Seguela, creative director and founding partner of Roux, Seguela, Cayzac and Goudard (RSC & G). Since its founding ten years ago RSC & G has enjoyed a meteoric growth to become France's second largest agency with gross revenues of $14.4 million in 1980. Instead of seeking a USP relating to a consumer benefit, the star strategy involves establishing a distinct and memorable "personality" for products such as washing powder or cigarettes. It does this by treating the product as if it were a person having a distinct character and style of behaviour. Having 'personalized' the product the advertising campaign aims to give it the charisma of a Hollywood movie star.

I visited Seguela in his office on the rue Bonaparte, to discuss the star strategy approach to advertising.

Copy strategy is a proven method of creative advertising. What makes you believe that your approach is better?

Copy strategy is a purely rational procedure which assumes a technical product advantage which can be translated into a consumer benefit or promise. For example: 'My washing powder washes whiter because it contains ingredient X.' Now there's nothing wrong with that kind of advertising provided there really is a product difference, a USP. But in the market place today most products are 'me-too's.' As soon as something really new is launched it's copied by everyone else within a few months. So originality must come from the advertising rather than from the product itself. That's why you can no longer think of the product as an object. We have gone beyond that to the notion of the product as a person.

But how can you compare a product with a person?

A person has three main features: a physique, a character and a style. Physique is obviously what a person looks like, whether he is tall or short, fat or thin. But physique is the least important feature. For example, Pierre Lazareff, the great editor of *France Soir* and the father of my professional life, was small, ugly and badly dressed. But in fact he was one of the most seductive and charming people I have ever known. That is character. Character is something profound in a person which stays with him throughout his life. Style is how the person appears before others, his special mannerisms. Style is the manifestation of character.

The physique of the product is the product itself. The bubbles of Coca

Cola, the formulation of Woolite detergent which makes it safe for delicate fabrics, the taste of Marlboro cigarettes. It's here that I part company with the copy strategy method. Instead of trying to find a consumer benefit based on the physique, I go on to give the product a character. This is the non-visible part of the product which turns it into a brand. And to unveil the character to the consumer, I find a style which will make it memorable. It is the imaginary universe created by the combination of character and style which is the real USP.

Character is the true capital of a product. It's something that should be thought about very carefully because it shouldn't be changed with every new campaign. Style is simply the executional device by which the character excites attention. It is the stage management of the brand. A product without style will not be noticed, without character it will not endure and without physique it will not sell. What makes a star is the fusion of all three. It's a kind of alchemy.

Are there any other reasons why you prefer this approach to the copy strategy or copy platform concept?
The time has come for a more intuitive approach to advertising by appealing to the consumer's imagination rather than his reason. Too much intellectualizing perverts imagination. Marketing people can destroy creativity by insisting on having rational ingredients in advertising. But advertising is an art, not a science. It has to do with the heart, not with the head. Creative advertising is there not to sell but to communicate. Once it has done that, once it has reached the consumer's sensibility, then it will sell. But the idea of selling should not dominate or even orientate the creative process.

The consumer society of today depends upon dreams. We Latins are dreamers and know how to bring imaginary product values to consumers. We are grateful to the Americans for having taught us advertising and marketing. But we believe that we can teach them something about communications.

Would you give me an example of the star strategy?
Well, take the case of Marlboro. As I've said, the physique is the taste of the American tobacco. The character is serenity. We need to relax and we find this

feature in the cigarette. The style of Marlboro is the cowboy. It's important not to confuse the character with the style. You may remember that when the Marlboro campaign first started, the Leo Burnett agency used much younger, more macho cowboys who had tattoos on their arms and pistols slung on their belts. This was a flop. It was only when the agency hit upon a more mature, more tranquil, middle-aged type of cowboy that the cigarette really began to take off and become a star.

But did Leo Burnett use the star strategy to produce their Marlboro advertising?

Not consciously, I think. Leo Burnett, who invented the cowboy theme, was a genius, one of the advertising greats. He was a creative man who understood instinctively how to give a product a character and a style. Many successful campaigns have used a kind of star strategy. But they lacked the label. What I've tried to do is come up with a structured way of working which will give us a better chance than others of producing great campaigns before they are launched rather than afterwards.

Can you give me some examples from your own agency?

I've mentioned Woolite. This is a detergent for expensive woollens and other delicate fabrics. We chose "seduction" as the character. We felt this was credible as Woolite is a premium-priced product. For something cheaper, more utilitarian we might have chosen a more functional character. The style we created was "Hollywood," evoking an almost cosmetic ambiance by using real stars like Romy Schneider, Jane Birkin, Sylvie Vartan and Marlene Jobert, who became the product heroines. The headline we used throughout the campaign was "I love Woolite." We tripled the market share in three years.

Another example is the Bon Marché department store. Back in 1977 when we first got the account, Bon Marché had a distinctly old-fashioned image. Research showed that the advertising had a fairly high recognition of around 50% to 60%, but an "unaided recall" of only 10%. Our brief was to generate some excitement for the store and, of course, improve the business. We had to do this with a budget of about one third that of the competition such as Au Printemps and Galéries Lafayette.

Roger Collis

We decided that the "physique" of the store was its prime location on the Left Bank, the *avant garde* section of Paris. So we created a character for the Bon Marché as the store which is the most up-to-date, the most "in" store in Paris. The style we used in the advertising to illustrate this was live models posing together with wax mannequins and a handwritten headline.

Three years later, the advertising had achieved an awareness of 65% and an unaided recall of 25% to 30%. In 1980, the Bon Marché registered the highest sales increase of any department store in Paris.

How do you set about developing a star strategy for a product?
We start off with a conventional briefing by the client who presents the technical features of the product along with any available research information and the sales and advertising history. At this point the agency starts getting the client to think and talk about the product as they would about a person. What sort of character would such a person have? Would he or she be passionate, aggressive, generous, stingy? What sort of clothes would this person wear and what type of car would he or she drive?

We transform the briefing into a psychological discussion and work closely with the client in defining the character of the product. We then check whether the character we have agreed is compatible with such things as price, distribution channels, the existing image of the product and its present and potential customers. Defining the character is the job of the marketing and creative people at the agency working together with the client. We believe it is vital for the client to participate in this process. He must feel comfortable with the character which is finally adopted.

This is quite different from the way the typical American agency works. What often happens is that the client will agree the copy strategy with account management at the agency briefing. Account managers will then brief the creative people. And the agency will work more or less alone until the campaign is ready to present to the client for approval. But we believe in having a constant interchange of ideas with the client throughout the development of the campaign. It's important for the creative people to be involved right from the start and participate in the definition of the product character. Their prime job is to create the style, which is the advertising itself.

You've said that the rational approach of marketing people can often destroy creativity. What are your views on market research?

I'm very sceptical about the value of market research in the creative process, although sometimes it can be helpful in stimulating the imagination. What really counts is experience and talent. The problem is that research only gives you an X-ray of the past. Opinion polls can be useful in tracking the evolution of consumer attitudes and behaviour. But I don't believe in pre-testing advertisements. Once a campaign is running it often has a force of communication which it doesn't have if you try to analyse the elements of it beforehand. No campaign which is really original, which is really creative, will survive a pre-test.

[When I met him in 1981, Seguela claimed to be a friend of Francois Mitterrand and to have invented the ubiquitous presidential election slogan: 'Mitterrand, La Force Tranquille.' According to Google, Seguela is alive and well in April, 2012 and reported to be a 'close friend' of Nicolas Sarkozy!]

The great consumer war
1973 Werbung/Publicite; 1984 Chief Executive

New York City, Tuesday: Heavily disguised in a business suit and a rented pair of magenta shades – a neatly folded hundred dollar bill tucked in my Gucci combat boots to simulate the distinguished limp, I saunter unchallenged through agency lines late tonight during a brief lull in the fighting when both agency and consumerist forces were collecting their wounded and preparing fresh propaganda material.

I am typing this dispatch on a battery-operated Telex in the sand-bagged reception area of an advertising agency somewhere between 35th and 52nd Street. Morale is high despite an acute shortage of olives which are being rationed to every second martini. Gin and vermouth, however, are in good supply. Stockpiles were established with commendable prescience and sense of priorities a few months ago. An armored ice-truck got through in the early hours yesterday.

A dog-tired agency staff officer in battle-scarred Brook's Bros. uniform, who had not slept for more than three hours, admitted that consumerist forces have strengthened a bridgehead on the East River side of Park Avenue and are now threatening Madison Avenue itself. Reinforcements of smoked salmon and olives have not yet arrived and it is feared that a relief column of junior executives from the First National Mammon Bank may have been ambushed and raped by a Women's Lib battalion deployed in force close to Greenwich Village.

Meanwhile, a great battle is raging for possession of the strategic Brooklyn Heights. More than 600 armored yellow taxis are engaged, recalling the North African struggles of 1942 in World War 2. From my window I can see the glow of burning supermarkets in Queens and the Bronx, set alight after looting by enraged housewives. In spite of liberal recourse to expense accounts, agency losses are said to be heavy, especially among more vulnerable account executives.

This particular agency has been under sporadic leaflet fire by detachments of the crack Ralph Nader Brigade. Although General Nader is reported to be in Washington preparing an important new campaign on the tensile defects of dog leashes (readers will recall his seminal book, Unsafe With any Hound), the troops are commanded by his loyal cadre of retired schoolchildren who are said to include several high school graduates. It is these intrepid surrogates who have been aiming sling-shots at this third-floor window with uncanny accuracy. Language on both sides has been regrettable.

It was, of course, the Nader Brigade who precipitated hostilities four days ago by the publication of the notorious Stomach Remedies Report. This carefully typed document alleges that a well-known brand of indigestion tablets is not 'hand made' as the advertising claims. It transpires that a 'limited edition' of a hundred million tablets, destined for the professional indigestion sufferer, were not in fact hand-crafted and numbered by Sicilian craftsman, but machine-made in Pittsburgh by non-union labor. The tablets which bear the embossed head of the company president have become collector's items, and with the banks closed in the present emergency, are now serving as a kind of legal tender. Some tablets have been defaced by members of the Consumers' Association.

The violent reaction towards the indigestion tablet fraud has spread to all types of branded products, even some of the more affectionately held species of peanut butter and 'authentic' mayonnaise. The militant Friends of Truth consumer group has predictably taken an 'extreme position,' branding all promotion for branded products 'a cynical attempt on the part of advertisers to force consumers to exercise free choice between competitive products in the supermarkets.'

So far, agency clients have been slow to replace the enormous amount of media commission and other financial materiel expended in the conflict, and it is clear that the agency general staff cannot sustain a long campaign. The fact that many creative folk from copy and art departments have been lost diminishes the prospects for an acceptable peace settlement. Indeed, some star copywriters have gone over to the other side, writing snide articles in the press under pseudonyms.

Even the most hopelessly sanguine 'new business' executives are reluctant to say when a ceasefire can be achieved.

However, I can reveal that 'a copy and art team' is working feverishly in a padded room next to me on what may prove to be the advertising idea of the century: the unbranded branded product.

The idea is diabolically simple. Branded products will not disappear, simply go underground. Product packs will be camouflaged in standard paratroop green and simply labeled 'tasty goulash' or 'super dishwasher detergent.' These will be trademarks masquerading as generic descriptions. This will enable both agencies and consumers to save face. An essential prerequisite, this correspondent believes, for a secure peace with honor in a brave new spirit of the times.

Roger Collis

The Italian connection

1973 Werbung/Publicite

We'd been chatting for a while about the economic crisis when the question of media costs came up. I told him we had rate increases of up to fifteen percent. And how tough it is now to get prime television time what with the stations shutting down early because of the fuel shortages. And, of course, with nice understanding clients breathing down your neck.

He clucked. 'Gee, that is bad; sounds a bit gloomy in London town. By the way I hope you manage to hang on to that bath oil account; Soulbad, isn't it? I read somewhere they've been talking to other agencies.' I detected a touch of Schadenfreude. The bastard's probably chasing it himself. Hard to be sure. He's a pretty cool customer on the telephone.

But he'd touched a nerve. It wouldn't be the first time I'd learned through the trade press that I'd lost a client.

'Yeah?' I replied. 'I wouldn't believe all you read in the papers if I were you Giancarlo. Anyway don't try and kid me it's all milk and honey down in sunny Milan. I hear the crisis is biting you even worse. Plus the usual chaos. Why, you're not even sure of the rates for this year. Not to mention the scramble for television air time.'

The soft, infuriating chuckle: 'That's true, my friend. But we Italians are infinitely resourceful.' He was aching to expound.

'Okay, Giancarlo. I'll be fall guy. What's the angle?'

'Well, you know how successful we've been with our Caroselli ?'

'Yes, I do,' I replied. Carosello is the prime-time TV programme where you buy what is effectively a two-and-a-half minute commercial. This can consist of only thirty-five seconds of product sell; the rest has to be 'entertainment.' The creative trick is to 'link' the 'entertainment' with the product. 'Don't you get incredible audience figures: twenty million or something like that?'

'That's exactly right. It's the top rated programme. And the secret is to use big name movie directors. You must remember that series we did with Gillo Pontecorvo.'

'Yes, I remember that. Real "Battle of Algiers" stuff; lots of grainy black and white photography. Great casting.'

'That's right. Well, we've just finished some electrical appliance spots with Giuliani Montaldo. His new film, "Giordano Bruno"; was released a few weeks ago. Tremendous hit. Even the fascist press had to admit that. It'll be coming your way soon. Anyway, Montaldo is going to start shooting a film on Dostoyevsky in a couple of months. The contract's signed with Carlo Ponti. They'll be on location in Leningrad. Incidentally you know that Antonioni is available for Carosello. Think what a splash that would make.'

'Fascinating, Giancarlo. I'm sure you'll be very happy in show business. I only hope your clients are going to understand when you can't buy them time on the programme. You told me that Carosello is booked up solid twelve months ahead. You'll be all dressed up with nowhere to go.'

'You are slow today, my friend. That's precisely the point. The idea is to get such fantastic publicity from making the commercials that we won't actually need to buy any television time at all. The whole of the media budget can go into public relations.'

'Giancarlo; sometimes I feel like I'm playing a sleepwalker in a Fellini movie.'

'Fellini? Look, I can get Fellini. About two million lire a day; nothing. But of course you have to fit in with his schedule and these guys use a lot of film. About eighteen metres for every metre used. But can't you just see it? Five columns across in the *Corriere della Sera*. "Fellini shoots new washing machine Carosello". Or "Fresh scandal on the Soulbad bath oil set". Then of course you'll get free television coverage – on the news programmes, my friend. We'll create a whole new cult of gossip columnists. Just to write about new commercials we're making. Why we could afford to fly Marlon Brando over for our soap powder campaign. Imagine. Crowds at the airport. "Er… Mr. Brando, could you tell our viewers about this new film you are making?" We'll have all the top stars and directors signed up. Top crews as well. Listen, I can get Pasquelino de Santis. He's Visconti's chief cameraman. We're going to clean up, friend. We'll be the biggest agency in Italy.'

'Congratulations, Giancarlo. Now that you've solved your crisis I'd better get back to mine.'

'Okay, I won't keep you. But we do have one problem. Actually it's the reason I called. Do you know anyone who wants to buy a good second-hand media department? Hardly used; only one owner. A snip.'

'Let me think about it, Giancarlo. We might be able to use some Latin guile. But I have one condition. I want you to book me for a series of lunches with Sophia Loren.'

Surviving le style français
1994 Resident Abroad

Anglo-Saxons tend to have a love-hate relationship with the French, which in my case – having lived in the country for the last (phew!) 15 years – translates to a rollercoaster of delight and despair. Catch me on a good day, and I'll regale you with the quality of life; catch me on a bad day and I'll hand you a diatribe on the Kafkaesque horrors of dealing with French officialdom (in France you have to contend with the bureaucracy of the French mind as well as the state) or a raw encounter with a French secretary.

Like the other day. I'd politely faxed this chap in Paris asking him to let me know when it would be convenient for me to phone him to do an interview. A secretary rang and said could I call at six o'clock? Fine. I called, was switched on to Vivaldi and passed round the houses, only to be told that Monsieur X was in conference. After some prompting on my part, I was asked (fairly politely) to call again at seven.

Similar treatment at seven except that the secretary finally said that Monsieur X had left the office. Had he left for the day? She neither knew nor cared. So I gave the woman a dose of vitriol at which she ventured to take my number. ‘Oh, that's in the provinces, isn't it?’ she said with ineffable disdain. ‘Yes, but we're not quite in North Africa,’ I said, hoping that she might be a *pied noir* – former colonials from Algeria, a pervasive mafia in France. Half an hour later, the chap rang me, with appropriate apologies. (The basic rule in dealing with the French is: *Il ne faut pas se laisser faire.* Don't let them run you over. Go in with a smile, but if you meet with a snarl, snarl back.)

This is when stereotypes emerge. If you have prejudices about a country you will surely find them confirmed immediately you arrive there.

The truth is that relations between the British and the French are mired in stereotypes and mutual incomprehension. 'Just consider 900 years of battle scars, rivalry and suspicion. The Brits say the French are dirty and dishonest, oversexed and ludicrously obsessed with their culture. The French say the Brits are cold, uncultivated, superficial and hypocritical,' says Polly Platt, an American sociologist based in Paris. 'One has always to bear in mind the completely different concepts of law – Anglo-Saxon case law and French code law – and education and the different thinking process which is linked to the different language. 'The basic thing is that the French are Cartesian, which means they want to map out a project completely – with all the interlocking elements – before they start on it,' Platt says. 'The Anglo-Saxons have a much more pragmatic and evolutionary approach, which is not necessarily spelled out. What this comes down to is that Anglo-Saxons will agree in principle and work out the details later, whereas the French do it the other way round.' 'Any foreigner who wants to understand the French cannot ignore Descartes,' says Aram Kevorkian, an Armenian-American international lawyer with a practice in Paris. 'The Cartesian method is a hodge-podge of *a priori* reasoning, formalism, deduction from unformed premises and verbal symmetry. The sign of a Cartesian is that he's always saying "*c'est logique*" and doesn't want to be bothered by ugly facts that would destroy his beautiful theory.'

In other words, truth (and ethics) is subjective: I've made up my mind, don't bother me with the facts. 'You get an unfriendly receptionist and then an uncommunicative secretary,' says the head of a corporate relocations bureau in Paris. 'The phone doesn't seem to work for the French. I find you have to go to cocktail parties and so on to get the chance to put your face in and meet these people. I forget who said: God invented the Parisians so that no foreigners would understand the French.'

One thing that's easy to understand is the importance of the business lunch to the French. Don't take it lightly. In my experience you always get a decent lunch, whatever the circumstances. There's always a great little bistro round the corner with the *patron* pretending to be angry with everyone and serving sublime food.

The French are almost Japanese in the sense that they have to get to know the person they are doing business with. They will want to know what you think about the refurbished Richelieu wing of the Louvre and the Delacroix exhibition. Remember that they want to be respected as cultural folk with a proud tradition. You may not be a gastronome yourself, but it is crucial to show a proper appreciation of food and drink. And the deal is not something to be talked about until near the end of the meal - between the pears and cheese, as they say; although a Frenchman who has been to Harvard or INSEAD business school at Fontainebleau certainly get to the point sooner. But a culinary faux pas can cut any deal stone dead. I heard a tale the other day worthy of a Bateman cartoon. An American - a former principal adviser on protocol at the US embassy no less - said, 'What delicious *paté*,' when served fresh *foie gras*. The French aren't going to do business with somebody like that. To show the depth of feeling about such things, consider the French businessman who was not simply appalled but 'humiliated' when his guest drank a great wine as though it were Coca-Cola.

Meanwhile, back at the office, don't be surprised if the chap keeps you waiting for a few minutes. And is busy with ten other things when you finally get in to see him; the French have a Latin notion of time. Nobody feels insulted when you arrive 20 minutes late – although it is nice if you phone.

Meetings themselves can drive Anglo-Saxons to distraction. The French style of working is often incomprehensible to us.

For example, in America or northern Europe, the point of having a meeting is to get decisions made or to allocate projects. The French meeting may not have a particular agenda. People simply talk and talk, with the idea of 'putting themselves in context' with other people; it's a form of jockeying for position, and networking; consequently, the French work very long hours. You often find French managers in the office at seven, eight in the evening. But they also work very hard and do get things done, although not always to deadlines, which don't always have the same awesome imperative as they do *chez nous*.

The French management style is much more authoritarian than in Britain or America, which is why it's hard to get decisions made.

The top man at most French companies has to sign personally and approve virtually everything from a newspaper subscription to a new fleet of cars. This derives from the Catholic tradition of authoritarian bureaucracy and centralism (*dirigisme*) – long before the Napoleonic Code. If a country priest in the South of France during the Monarchy wanted to repair the roof of his church, he first had to get approval from the Court in Versailles.

The effect has been to perpetuate a vertical hierarchy within the company (and society) in which there is little scope for true delegation of responsibility. And there is much less lateral exchange of information (in spite of the marathon meetings) than you find in Britain and America. Managers are less willing to take risks and will routinely kick things upstairs for a decision.

'There's a deep-seated formalism – which seems to be endemic in the Latin world – that nothing exists if it's not on paper,' Kevorkian says. 'Today I dealt with some bankers, and I signed my name to some documents. And they said, "Do you have your *tampon*, your stamp?" I mean the idea of seeing the guy and watching him sign doesn't count unless you add a rubber stamp.'

'Bureaucracy in France is much heavier than in Belgium - much more paperwork,' says Alain Smets, a director of Sabena who is currently on assignment in the South of France.

'My advice to foreigners is first to learn the language, otherwise it's hard to communicate, and second, adapt to the system, stick to the rules, don't try to change them.'

'You have to take into account the French class system, which is based on several things: what school you went to – ENA; Ecole Normale; HEC; Ecole Polytechnique; or one of the larger universities - intellectual classification is very important; then your profession, what is your title, what visiting card do you have – such as chef de cabinet, or diplomat?

It opens doors; then money – what is your financial status? – the ultimate being to have an *hotel particulier* in Paris and a place in Deauville or Cannes; then you come to the fourth category, artists, intellectuals, university professors - where it's not so much a question of money, but what you can give to Society.

'The French love this type.'

Whatever their reputation, the French can sometimes put on a class act. Especially in response to what you might call the disingenuous ingenuous approach.

I was on an assignment once with a photographer from New York. We entered the Negresco Hotel in Nice, the grandest of the Belle Epoque palaces on the Promenade des Anglais, in pursuit of a single room for him – he had not made a reservation. Nothing strange about that, you may say. Except that photographers can sometimes look very strange. And I was also looking strange, in my old black leather jacket, *espadrilles* without socks, and wind-swept hair.

But we were received with elaborate courtesy by the liveried doorman and desk clerk, and the *voiturier* smilingly agreed to keep an eye on my 2CV. And there was none of this, 'Ahem, how will you be settling your account, sir? May I take an imprint of your credit card?' Later, I congratulated the manager on the charm and discretion of his staff. He smiled. 'Ah, yes, you never know who you have in front of you these days.' I don't mind about the motivation as long as I get the benefit of the doubt!

One of the most compelling paradoxes is how pleasant and helpful local bureaucrats (sorry, *fonctionnaires*) can often be. (Especially if your going-in approach is, 'I'd appreciate your advice; can you please help me?') French civil servants do not just follow the rules from Paris; they have their pride as experts; they have their aspirations to social approval in their own community. And they can sometimes show you how to get around the rules.

A few years ago, I had a terrible shock when I got a vertiginous assessment from the tax people – I'd forgotten to fill in something or whatever. I rang in panic (you invariably have a name and a number to call on official forms.) The tax inspector said: 'Look, you really should have got in touch before. But I'll try and get it out of the computer.' She rang me back, asked me to come round at once, tore up the old form, and filled out another one in front of me.

That is what I call civic civilization.

French bureaucracy often allows you several *regimes* – or options –

whether for marriage (separation of assets) or for tax on revenue. I come under the felicitous category of 'writers and composers' – which is classified as 'non-commercial' revenue.

What you do is simply lump together all the money you've received during the year – whether from fees or reimbursed expenses, agree a sum (about 25 per cent off the top), and the rest is what you'll be taxed on. The thing is to be reasonably honest, and not let your lifestyle egregiously exceed your visible income. (Or should that be the other way round?)

'The French don't bother decent people; so you have to be decent and not cheat,' Kervorkian says. 'I trust the local tax inspector and the local postmaster – they are basically very decent people. The menace to the body politic doesn't come from them, it comes from the tremendous hold that the *enarques* have over the country. It's easier to bribe a minister or a mayor than your local *fonctionnaire*.'

There's also a lot of laissez faire.

Where else but France would you see a sign, 'Parking Tolerated'? Not that they won't tow you away if you push tolerance too far.

With all its rules and regulations, France is the only country I know where an unmarried couple can get an official *certificat de concubinage* from the local *mairie*. Notwithstanding that one or the other may have a legal spouse, the certificate enshrines certain legal rights. If you're into bigamy, come to France.

The loneliness of the long distance manager
1973 Werbung/Publicite; 1984 'If my boss calls...'

Air France flight 795 from Copenhagen to Paris is full; and it's been a long day. Martin Simon, European marketing director for the consumer products division of Mistral Laboratories, is wedged between a hirsute Swede and a disconcertingly attractive blonde. He balances a Scotch and Perrier on his open briefcase; and is in the familiar state of shifting mental gears between markets.

Roger Collis

Martin's thoughts right now are hovering somewhere between the pleasant meeting he has just left (after all Danish sales are on plan and the smoked eel was delicious) and the somewhat more combative session he expects to face tomorrow. The French company has a sales problem and is recommending that they trim their TV schedule to protect their operating profit. Martin is opposed to this; feeling that they are already spending close to minimum viable 'reach and frequency.' And to risk losing share of advertising at this stage of the market development might be disastrous for the brand.

Martin knows that from an overall European point of view he can easily compensate for a French profit shortfall by moving notional funds from the German market without hurting that business. (He suspects that the Germans have quite a bit more money 'sandbagged' in their budget.) But of course he has local sensibilities to contend with; there are few general managers willing to forgo a good end-of-year result for their country profit centres in the interests of the European area – especially to the consumer products division for which Martin is responsible. It is only too easy to cut 'discretionary' marketing expenses to the detriment of future sales and profits.

Of course, Martin is no stranger to this kind of scene. During more than fifteen years of multi-national marketing he has mastered some of the diplomatic arts; how to get results unobtrusively by letting others think that his ideas originated with them; he knows how to get inside the thought processes of the local people – much more demanding than simply speaking the language; an ability to project oneself into the wiles and wherefores and mores of the society. Culture shock is an endemic hazard for the international man.

Martin must also judge which battles are critical for him to win, and those which can be gracefully conceded to local *amour propre*. He has to know when and how to refer disputes to a higher court of appeal. In this case, he must judge whether the French really have a sound business case, or whether they are just 'being difficult,' interpreted as 'siege mentality,' or the 'not invented here' syndrome. He knows how crucial it is to be able to evaluate local recommendations in the light of other market priorities throughout Europe. Because, for Martin Simon, international marketing is not just marketing across frontiers; it means having an overview mentality – the ability to match resources with opportunities on a global scale. Local markets are competing all the time for funds, and for Martin's limited time. He needs to judge the priority and the quality of plans that are submitted to him – to reconcile each country's profit exigencies with those for the whole of Europe.

This is not easy. Mistral operates a 'matrix organization' in which Martin shares responsibility with the local general managers for his product division within their legal entities. Martin's divisional marketing managers only report to him on a 'functional' or a dotted-line basis; but to the country general managers on a line basis. Martin reports to the president, consumer products division; whereas each general manager reports to the president, international operations, both at the corporate Kremlin in Broken Springs, Colorado. It is a structure which exacerbates the inherent conflict between the European area and local management. 'Kinetic equilibrium,' is how Mistral's chairman described it. (The doctrine was later enshrined in a Harvard Business School case study: Chameleon Corporation.)

Martin believes it is better off trying to persuade than to legislate. The knack is to know whether a problem or issue requires a 'strategic' decision taken by himself or can be left to a 'routine' decision by his local people. The key to an effective relationship is personal credibility and trust. Martin's effectiveness derives in part from the dialectical tension between his role as a 'supervisor' and his role as 'consultant.' The reconciliation is particularly onerous in times of serious contention.

Striking the right balance will be the key to the French meeting. He will need to draw upon all his reserves of credibility.

The plane is on time at Paris Charles-de-Gaulle Airport, but the *autoroute* from Roissy is closed part of the way for one-lane traffic. It is half past eleven by the time Martin reaches his hotel – too late, perhaps, to call his wife in Brussels. He chats for a few minutes with Nicolas, the night porter; then takes a bottle of Perrier up to his room and goes through the French budgets once again. He knows that a conflict is inevitable.

Tomorrow morning he is on his own.

Roger Collis

Management lib

1971 Werbung/Publicite

Gloria Stern, forty-year-old mother of two, effulgent blonde, Harvard Business School graduate, owner of a mean backhand at tennis, semi-retired gourmet cook, and senior vice president marketing at Mistral Laboratories, is sitting alone in the main board room among the debris of the monthly planning meeting. It is five-thirty on a moist spring afternoon. Outside, she can hear her male colleagues gunning their cars in the parking lot. In a few minutes they will be heading for the fabled world of martini buckets and sympathetic bosoms.

Gloria shakes her long hair loose which gives her face a softer look. Little stress lines appear around her mouth as she tightens her jaw to apply lipstick. She is a beautiful woman whom time and the job have touched with an invisible shadow. She has a headache, her mouth is sour from too many cigarettes, and she feels her period coming on.

But the meeting had been good. They had approved her new medicated shampoo plans – in spite of a strong rearguard action from the pharmaceutical division. But it had been a close thing to get the budget allocation in face of so many other projects claiming priority. Gloria had had to summon all her reserves of restraint at times to disguise emotions which others would have pounced upon as being quintessentially female and therefore unbefitting a senior executive. And fortunately Dave Silver had been there.

Dave Silver is Gloria's division president and her mentor since she joined the group eight years ago. It is almost a father-daughter type of relationship. Dave has guided her through the two major hurdles that a management woman must face: the crucial transition into middle-management, and the quantum jump into the very top of the hierarchy.

In common with many successful women in business, Gloria was an only child and had enjoyed a strong and sustaining relationship with her father, which had lasted throughout her adolescence and college years. He had helped her to develop so-called masculine qualities and objectives without in any way abandoning her notion of herself as a female. Given her father's values, Gloria was given the support by both her parents to challenge the conventional limitations of the female role in business. In many respects, Dave Silver had taken over from her father.

Gloria had learned how to become a good team player. This was important to her in developing a male view of the organization and to share with men the ability to exploit personal relationships for long-term goals. Unlike many women, Gloria learned how to be flexible in-group situations, not to make a 'cause' of small issues and not to take criticism too personally.

The crux of women's problem in business is that while men are brought up to recognize that they will have to work all their lives, women typically hedge between a full scale career and the more conventional female role until they reach their middle to late thirties, when it is hard for them to make the major transition to middle-management. Consequently, women often tend to be more concerned with immediate job fulfillment than with long-term ambition. This can critically affect their attitudes towards people and their jobs in a way which reinforces their sexual stereotype among male executives, often potentiating their problems in the organization.

Ironically the stereotype derives mainly from childhood and adolescent conditioning, rather than any intrinsic differences in character between the sexes. As a result, women tend to become more task and skill oriented than men. They have a compulsion to prove themselves in the world of men by excelling in a speciality. This tends to make them good supervisors, but unable to delegate effectively at the middle-management level, in particular to male subordinates.

Gloria had been lucky. Her husband, Tom, understood the imperatives which her upbringing had instilled, and had helped her to make a definite career decision before she was thirty. They had married while Tom was still in medical school, and had the children early. Gloria was therefore better equipped than many women to make the crucial break-through into middle management.

It hadn't been easy. Gloria had decided that she could only move upwards through the organization if she proved herself more competent at her current job, at the job above her, and at the job below her, than any man available.

This took enormous amounts of energy and concentration, and threatened at times her life with Tom and the children. Along the way, she developed tactics for handling a range of potential embarrassments; from avoiding tears in public and unwelcome sexual overtures, to chairing recalcitrant peer-group meetings.

As she reached senior middle-management and became more secure, more sure of herself and her abilities, Gloria no longer felt a need to sublimate or make excuses for an essential part of her femininity. Not that she had led a double life in and out of the office. But she now felt more relaxed about herself as a woman and as an executive. She felt freer and more open in her work relationships instead of translating her perception of male styles into her behavior. Her transition into top management a year ago was accompanied by a sense of satisfaction and congruence; she had come to terms with the costs and rewards of building a career. And she had remained a woman, true to herself.

Gloria lights a last cigarette and thinks back over the meeting. It occurs to her that life would be easier if men were more liberated from their gender stereotypes with regard to female executives.

It's been a long way, baby. Gloria puffs on her cigarette and allows herself a few moments of silent, private emotion.

Three

Roger Collis

Jaime Sevilla's secret empire
1982 *Vision*

'Hymie? Hymie who?'

'Jaime Sevilla!'

The voice on the line is deep and muscular. 'What sign are you? I'm Sagittarius. Very Sagittarius!' Big chuckle.

I curse the switchboard for putting this lunatic through.

'Well, as a matter of fact I am Aquarius.'

A pause. 'Okay... Aquarians are good with Sagittarians. Look, I've just read your Gauquelin story in last month's issue of the magazine. And I think I've got something that'll interest you. Can you come over to Switzerland for the weekend? You can stay at my place. I'll arrange tickets and pick you up at Geneva Airport on Saturday morning.

What the hell; a weekend in Switzerland. And there might be a story.

Are top managers born under a lucky star? was a piece I'd written on Michel Gauquelin, the French psychologist, who claimed to have discovered through statistical analysis that each profession has its own planetary influences. For example, the planet Jupiter is prominent in the sky at the time of birth of top businessmen, actors, journalists and politicians.

My editor called it a 'flaky story'. But Sevilla was impressed. Sagittarius is ruled by Jupiter, the planet of expansion. This, surely, is the basis for the famous Sagittarian personality – optimistic, generous, strong love of change and excitement...

Sevilla is about thirty years younger than the voice on the phone. But with the bearing of a much older man. Heavy set. Big blue eyes in a big handsome face. Big smile. Big ego. Big *abrazo*. The supersalesman.

At 170 kph the loudest sound in a Rolls-Royce Corniche with the top down is Jaime Sevilla talking about money, his philosophy of life – and Sagittarius.

'Let me tell you... About ten years ago I began to notice coincidences. I began reading about Sagittarius and became interested to find out who is Sagittarian and who isn't. As soon as I find that somebody is Sagittarian

I find I like that person very very much. For example, Tommy Steele, Christopher Plummer, Walt Disney, Winston Churchill, Frank Sinatra, Sammy Davis Jr ...

'So I figured there had to be something. I looked at more and more characteristics, more and more phenomena. Nearly all my close friends are Sagittarians; and all my business associates. We all trust one another. I think that is wonderful.'

Fortunately, it appears that Aquarians are okay people as well. Along with Geminis, Aries and Libras.

'I was a dollar millionaire when I was 26. Speculating in foreign exchange. I made so much money I didn't know what to do with it. So I started a trading company – not so much to make money but to extend myself, learn about business, build a group of good people around me. As it happened I made more money.

'I hardly went to school, let alone university. But trading and running a company is better than Harvard and Cornell put together.

'What really pisses me off is when people ask me what I do for a living, especially Americans. What do I answer? "I produce results: that's my profession."

'Success for me is not making money but knowing how to spend it.

'I like my character. I've noticed that Sagittarians are basically very nice people, generous people. I want to do something nice, something good, like a modern Robin Hood. But take from everybody and give to everybody. Recycle some of that money.'

What exactly does Robin Hood have in mind? No less than a worldwide club for Sagittarians. A vast political and economic brotherhood!

Sevilla's lakeside retreat at St. Sulpice near Lausanne after a splendid lunch of *filets de perches*. Clutching a tall drink, I sink gratefully into a squishy armchair. The sun is shining. I am ready to suspend disbelief.

Sagittarius International will be a non-profit making association formed under Article 60 of the Swiss civil code. But soon it gives birth to trading and investment companies, shares being given to a special category of 'Charter Member' in return for a five-year debenture of $10,000.

'We're aiming for a million members throughout the world. Say everyone pays $100 a year; that's an income of $100 million. But nobody's going to touch that money. I want to create a helping hands club for Sagittarians.

'We'll have a computerized information service. Let's say a member in Madrid wants to find someone in Bogata to distribute his product. We'll put him in touch with a fellow Sagittarian. Or maybe someone's in trouble, in jail or something. The club will help him. That's the idealistic side.

'Then there's the commercial side. Members will get discounts on travel: air fares, hotels, restaurants... But our real aim will be to beat the retail system by bringing all kinds of consumer goods to members at factory prices. The club will do this by negotiating direct with manufacturers. One twelfth of all human beings are Sagittarians. Imagine what a force we can become.'

A deal with IBM to supply the computers; Sagittarius hotels; a Sagittarius airline. A Sagittarius island.

'We could have our own fucking country,' Sevilla shouts. 'Our own fucking country; Sagittarius passports, everything!' He starts reading from *The World Almanac & Book of Facts*. 'Listen to this: Kiribati, pronounced Kiribass, one of the old Gilbert & Ellice Islands, self rule since 1971... population 60,000, geographical area 264 square miles, slightly smaller than New York City, head of state Ieremia T Tabai, born, listen to this, born December 16, 1950. A fucking Sagittarian!'

Sagittarius Club will have a share capital of one million Swiss francs made up of 2,000 shares. This will be fully paid up by Sevilla in cash. He will then set about recruiting 980 charter members each of whom will buy one share at its nominal value of 500 Swiss francs. Collectively therefore, the charter members will own 49 percent of the club.

For each share that they buy, charter members will be required to subscribe a debenture of 20,000 Swiss francs. This will bear an annual interest of LIBOR plus one percent and will be paid back at the end of five years.

Sevilla lays a ruminative finger along his nose. 'What we'll do is create two commercial entities, a trading company and an investment company. Let's say they each have a share capital of $10 million. The club will own 51 percent of each and the remaining 49 percent will be distributed in the form of shares to the 960 charter members.'

I try to figure this out. 'You will own 51 percent of the club. But as it's a not for profit foundation, you won't be able to get any money out. Except expenses, I assume. So what's in it for you?'

'For me it's idealistic. I'll have the fun of running the thing. It'll be a sort of hobby forever, going around the world meeting Sagittarians, helping out where I can.

'I told you, I want to do something good, something nice, have unlimited amounts of money to give away. Working your arse off making money and keeping it in the bank. What for?

'When people are in distress they help each other a lot. A plane hijack for example. Twice on Concorde one of the engines blew out and we had to come back to the airport. Suddenly, everybody in the plane becomes very friendly. And then in normal times nobody gives a damn about anybody else. So I say, let's do something nice for a change. If we can have all the Sagittarians helping each other, that's a start isn't it? I don't need to make $100 million. I did many times… Well, once I did.' A grin. Remembrance of deals past?

How much is he worth?

'Nobody knows how much I've got. I remember what I have more or less, give or take a million. I use different names and account numbers at different banks around the world. And I don't keep all my papers in the same place.'

'Isn't there anybody who can put it all together?'

'No, it's too much fun this way. Every business knows just as much as it needs to know. The same goes for the people who work for me. I'm involved in lots of companies through nominees, through shares. Some of them I actually control, but they don't know about it.

'I'll probably take it all with me when I go. But as long as everybody around me is happy, why should they know?'

Indeed. The half dozen people I meet at Sevilla's office in London seem happy enough. But of course, it's early December, and being Sagittarians, they are all having birthday parties. Who's for spot of trading after a long liquid lunch?

At the end of the afternoon the acolytes are gathered in the discreetly plush offices off St James's Street. All eyes are on the high priest, massive at his desk. Black suit with a white silk scarf. Telephone tucked under his jowls. A drink in one hand, the other hand hovering over a calculator. Coiling cigar smoke and the hiss of air conditioning.

We're on the line to Sao Paulo. Something about a wolframite deal. I can't make out whether we're buying or selling. The transaction seems to be made more complicated by the price of tungsten ore at different stages of the refining process. Someone hands me a glass of ice-cold sherry. There is talk of the Brazilians having a hidden margin or something.

Lightning fingers on the calculator. A torrent of Portuguese. Sevilla puts the phone down. Has our side won?

'We're still making money; but not so much,' Sevilla says, with a rueful grin. The room relaxes.

That evening I'm sitting in the kitchen of Sevilla's penthouse flat off Berkeley Square. An impromptu supper of beluga caviar and bacon and eggs. A 1959 Chateau Margaux.

'I was born in Bilbao, but grew up in Zaragoza. We couldn't afford toys at home, so when I was about eight, I started a kind of business game with a file of clients, and coupons for money. Just dreaming. I'd buy and sell things; you name it, and cash it in at the bank. That's what I ended up doing in reality.'

He left home at 14 with 200 pesetas in his pocket. At Carinena, on the road to Madrid, he shoveled grapes in a winery; he worked on building sites; and slept rough under bridges and on the beach.

On the Costa Brava, Sevilla set up house with an English girl. They lived on the income from a travel guide that Jaime had put together, selling advertising to local shops and restaurants. The couple came to London early in 1968, and married so that Jaime could get a work permit. Armed with this and his Spanish, he landed a job with the Banco Espagnol e Londres.

'They were a pain in the arse. Not speaking English very well, nobody helped me. You'd think a small Spanish community in London would help one another. But there was so much jealousy. Obviously, being Sagittarius, I got crazy about this. I was making a lot of problems: if I don't like something

I'll say so!'

He found a better atmosphere at the Bank of Scotland where he spent his lunch hours downstairs in the foreign exchange trading room learning as much as he could.

'It wasn't my department but I was fascinated. I found I loved dealing – in money and in millions. You've got to be very very fast in your mind. Your head has to be very clean and very clear. Nowadays, you have the computers. But in those days you had to keep a position in your head.'

Sevilla's big break came in 1970 when another bank sent him out to Geneva to replace a currency trader for the holidays. He started to speculate on his own. He managed to borrow $100,000 which he parlayed into $1 million by 'selling forward against the Swiss franc.' He resigned from the bank in 1974 to work on his own. All he needed was a telephone, a calculator – and a bit of luck.

It's amazing what you can do with $1 million.

'If you have $1 million you can buy and sell $10 million. Let's say you sell $10 million forward against Swiss francs. That equals CHF32 million at 3.20 which was the rate in those days. The rate goes down to 3.10. You make CHF1 million profit. You still have $1 million in deposit. So when the dollar is coming off you can make a fortune.'

Sevilla traveled around the world, speculating, learning and enjoying his money. Four years and two marriages later, he started his first trading company by doing a deal with a Spanish bicycle manufacturer to export his products.

'How I made money was not by the trading margin that exists between buying somewhere and selling elsewhere, but through currency margins. You buy in pesetas in Spain at 180 days credit and you sell in the U.S. in dollars. If you buy your pesetas forward you get a number of points in your favor which alone justifies the purchase. Let's say today's value of the merchandise is three dollars. You go to the States and sell it for three dollars, the same price you paid for it in pesetas. You have the option of selling three dollars forward and getting 320 pesetas, or buying 300 pesetas and only having to pay 280 pesetas to the manufacturer.

'What I've done is apply my sophisticated financial knowledge to an unsophisticated business. In a country like Spain there are millions of dollars which nobody is making today. If I go to 20 or 30 manufacturers and say, "Let me take over your export markets. I will pay you 100 pesetas, I'll sell to your customer in France for 100 pesetas, and I'll make ten percent profit in between." They won't believe it; they'll think I'm crazy, or trying to screw them in some way. It takes time to convince them.

'The big money comes from the financial operations not the trading side. I tell you, I can buy at 100 and sell at 90 and still make a profit. That is an art.'

Sevilla believes in hiring people with natural talents rather than professionals.

'Most of my team has never done anything like this before. We have all sorts – an ex-airline manager, a professional comedian... We've all learned together, often finding the unorthodox, the creative solution. You either have natural talent or you don't. Professionals are brainwashed; they have lost their imagination.'

Sevilla is about to come full circle. He says he is negotiating to buy a 50 percent interest in a major U.S. firm of commodity traders specializing in gold, silver and 'strategic' metals. This is his first love; the business he knows best.

It is past midnight and we are still sitting in the kitchen. The Sony has been rolling for two hours, and I still don't know if I really have a story. This guy loves to talk. I'm getting tantalizing glimpses of his secret empire, but not many names I can use. I sense his ego wrestling with discretion.

We go down to the cellar for more Chateau Margaux and Sevilla yanks out a huge file. My God, what's this? A credit note from the Banque Populaire Suisse for CHF2.9 million dated March 10, 1980.

But that's nothing.

'You remember the silver collapse? I was behind one of the big contracts in Geneva. On February 22, 1980, I sold 75 contracts – five thousand ounces per contract – at $49 an ounce, the highest possible price. I bought at $18.47. Work it out. I sold in the morning; silver began to collapse in the afternoon. But if I'd sold all my contracts, I'd have made so much more money.'

Why did the market collapse so suddenly?

'For every ten members on the floor of the commodities exchange in New York, I would say nine were short and one was long on silver. If silver had kept climbing, most of them would have lost their shirts. That's why they put restrictions on the market. The same day silver started going down.

'I would describe it as the one before the last. Because it's going to happen again. The market is so artificial. Every ounce of silver you mine is costing between $16 and $17 an ounce. If the market price for silver is $8, you can't tell me that anyone's going to mine the stuff. Once the price of silver starts going up, there's no way it's going to come down. More gold is produced than silver. And look at the ratio between them – about 50 times. That's ridiculous.'

We're back to Sagittarius.

'Let's say we have a million members of the Sagittarius club, and everyone invests $1,000 to buy silver. That's one billion dollars. You only have to put up five percent on a margin call. So you can go to the commodities market and buy forward $20 billion worth of silver. Two and half billion ounces.

'You do it very carefully. When the delivery time comes, instead of selling back the silver certificates and taking your profit as everyone expects, you offer to pay the difference and demand physical silver. That's what Bunker Hunt did – he actually shipped the silver out in DC8s.

'The people controlling the market will have to go out and buy silver, go to the central banks. We'll break the system!'

A huge belly laugh. Sevilla falls about the kitchen laughing. 'I tell you, we'll screw the bastards.'

Sevilla doesn't explain how the Sagittarians are going to find the difference to pay for the physical silver, nor what the difference is. Nor the aftermath. But for one o'clock in the morning, it's a daunting thought.

'When gold reaches $320 an ounce, that's the time to buy silver.'

I'm sold.

Roger Collis

Do you sincerely want to lose money in commodity futures?

1984 International Herald Tribune

Should you be tempted to speculate in commodity futures, think again. You are likely to have as much luck – and more fun – trying to break the bank at Monte Carlo – unless you really know what you are doing. You can lose your shirt playing *chemin de fer*; but in commodities trading you can risk losing the shirt you do not even have!

According to Stanley Zilch, director of Blue Skies Futures Research in Broken Springs, Colorado, 95 percent of those who speculate in commodities lose money. Even successful traders may make most of their profits from five percent of their trades.

There are two broad classes of people dealing in commodities: speculators and hedgers. Hedgers are producers and consumers of commodities, banks and institutions, who want to protect a given price or position in a commodity. Hedging represents 50 to 60 percent of the total market. It is the speculators who take the major risk and provide the liquidity for the hedgers to operate.

Most traders never receive or deliver commodities, instead speculating on the rising and falling values of contracts for future delivery. For every trade there is a buyer and a seller. A buyer is somebody who thinks the market will go up; a seller is somebody who thinks the market will go down. For every trade somebody gains and somebody loses. It is a zero sum game.

Speculators normally trade on margin. What this means is that they pay a deposit to their broker of 5 to 10 percent of the initial value of the contract. When the market moves, it multiplies their profit or loss 10 or 20 times.

Imagine that you are trading a contract of gold at $44,000 with a margin of only $2,500. If the price of gold moves $25, you have either doubled your money or lost it. In the latter case you will get a margin call from your broker to cover your lost deposit. Normally, you can limit your loss to the amount of your margin by putting in a 'stop.' A stop is an order to your broker to get you out when the market hits your price or bounces through your price.

Punters will tell you to take your losses out quickly and let your profits ride. Advice that is sometimes hard to follow.

Says Zilch: 'If gold drops $100 overnight in Hong Kong as a result of some political news, and you are in New York with your contract of gold, the market in New York the next day is going to open $100 down. If your stop is in the middle, there is nothing you can do. You are stuck. A good broker can usually get you out. But you could be locked in a position and wiped out.

'It's the most anti-human character kind of game you can imagine. First, because in commodity trading the big money is made on the downside – selling short; which means selling something you don't have in the hope that you can buy it back at a cheaper price. Second, the only way you will probably make money is to accept the fact that you are wrong. Most people say, I am right, the market is wrong!'

Speculators can be categorised according to six basic types of trading style:

- **The Gambler:** a seat-of-the-pants operator with more money than sense. He has no strategy. He picks up bits and pieces of information and buys and sells without knowing what he is doing. For example, he has a friend who has just bought 50 contracts of gold. He wants to be one up on his friend, so he buys 100 contracts. If gold happens to go up, he does not know at what point to get out. The gambler will lose money consistently. After a while he will either be broke and quit trading, or he will get smart and develop a system.

- **The Wiseacre:** a gambler with a system. He has started over to win back the money he has lost. But he is going to make the same mistakes as the gambler because he is so clever that he tries to beat his system. For example, his charts tell him the golden moment to buy gold. Unfortunately, gold goes down instead of up. So he gets a sell signal on his chart. But instead of getting out with a small loss, he carries his long position and ends up with a large loss.

- **The Technician:** the technical trader is a professional. He follows a system based on strict mechanistic rules, like ratios, moving averages, relative strength indices and butterfly spreads. For example, with precious metals, he will buy or sell depending on the price ratios between gold, silver, platinum and palladium. Let's say the 'normal' ratio between gold and silver is 35 to one. If this moves to 40 to one, he would buy silver and sell gold forward and take his profit from both ends when the ratios move together again. He might also use moving averages to detect a trend that would signal a buy or sell decision. However, he is not infallible.

'Over the past few years, technical trading has done badly because we've been having down-trending markets that have bigger and faster reactions,' Zilch says. 'The volume diminishes considerably, the guys on the floor starve; they know where the stops are, and they come and grab you.'

- **The Cyclical Analyst:** a highly specialised technician who follows the past performance of trading patterns in a commodity over a particular period, which may be two weeks or 20 years. His buy or sell decisions are based on the assumption that exactly the same price levels reoccur in regular cycles. This does not necessarily happen!

- **The Fundamentalist:** a person who studies basic economic factors, such as gold production in South Africa and long-range weather forecasts that will affect crops. According to Zilch, he is likely to be right eight times out of ten. But his knowledge, for example, of an impending disaster for the cocoa harvest in the Ivory Coast, may not affect the market at the time he is trading. So he can end up taking a huge loss.

- **The Insider:** someone who has a fantastic tip from a friend who is close to one of the Russian oligarchs that Russia plans to buy two million tons of grain and sell 400 tons of gold to pay for it. So he buys grain and sells gold. Unfortunately, the Russians do a special deal with the U.S. Department of Agriculture and take the grain from stockpiles rather than the market. As a result, grain does not move, gold does not collapse, and the Insider takes a beating.

Zilch believes that the temperament and experience of traders determines their particular management style.

'In currency trading, for example, technical and fundamental styles can be very conflicting, and you don't know who is right in the end,' Zilch says.

Brokers are sometimes criticised as being more interested in the amount of commission they make on each trade than in giving sound trading advice to their customers. This is known as 'churning an account.' Good firms have compliance departments to control excessive trading. And in the United States, the Securities Exchange Commission is alert to this activity.

Another conflict that can arise, especially in London, is between the interests of hedger and speculator customers in the same firm. Zilch cites the case of a hedger who wanted to unload 3,000 contracts of cocoa. In order to avoid panic by throwing this amount of cocoa on the market, the firm sold it to another customer, a speculator, whose account he had carte blanche to trade. This ended in disaster for the speculator.

Another tale from London concerns a broker who doubled as a merchant, trading in physical commodities. A speculator had sold short 50 options on coffee. In the morning, he saw that coffee in New York was going through the roof. So he called the broker to buy 50 contracts when the market opened to hedge his options as he was short. Coffee opened in London at £3,000 a ton, the top of the market. It transpired that the broker had sold him physical coffee from his books because he had not stipulated that it should be traded from the floor!

The moral is, check out your broker. A good broker will also check out prospective customers.

'Brokers should want to know everything about a customer, even if he puts up $1 million; he'll want to know what is behind it,' Zilch says. 'The broker will then give a speculator a "trading limit," which is a mutual precaution. The rule is, don't speculate more than you can afford to lose in commodity futures. Try to assess the downside risk for every trade and if you are prepared to take it.'

Zilch stresses the importance of having a trading system. 'If you have a system and it gives you a profit, this will be about three times the size of a loss,' he says. 'I think that in the long run – up to 10 years – any system is going to be profitable, provided you stick to it.'

But to paraphrase John Maynard Keynes: In the long run, we are all wiped out.

Roger Collis

The entrepreneurial imperative
1982 International Herald Tribune

The great entrepreneurs of the 19th century forged the scientific revolution into the industrial revolution. They were the visionaries who turned dreams into profitable realities, who pioneered mass production, modern distribution and retailing, marketing and advertising, who built the great corporations which bear their names.

Yet many of these corporations would reject such people today. Big corporations are not always comfortable places for entrepreneurs. This is the age of scientific management. And in the complex hierarchies that managers have constructed, reward systems tend to favor bureaucrats and conformists and to reject risk-takers, creative mavericks and entrepreneurs. The entrepreneur is seen as a threat, a deviant who rocks the corporate boat.

That is why many such individuals have quit or have been forced out of large corporations to start up their own small firms. The entrepreneur is mainly thought of in terms of small business. Yet what is needed today is more entrepreneurs in big business.

Corporate executives and bankers talk comfortably - and patronizingly - about encouraging small firms. About the need to be entrepreneurial. And in the United States and Europe, there are a large number of agencies set up to finance and nurture new small firms. These small business movements are helping entrepreneurs to identify and fund their new ventures. Small firms are widely recognized as a rich source of jobs and innovation.

But large corporations should start by creating a climate for entrepreneurship and risk-taking within their own organizations. It is rather like a father telling his son to show lots of initiative and go off and do his own thing without setting an example himself.

In his book 'Management and Machiavelli,' Antony Jay described the entrepreneur as being made up of two antithetical archetypes: the 'Yogi' and the 'Commissar.' The yogi is the contemplative, creative, man; the commissar is the man of action. Put them together in one person and you have the entrepreneur.

Jay pointed out that the one organizational factor that most inhibits the evolution of the, entrepreneur today is the cleft between design, production and sales.

The entrepreneur often works through capability rather than conscious knowledge; he is the angel who dares to tread.

The manager cherishes his rules and guidelines, whereas, according to Ronnie Lessem, who teaches entrepreneurial management at London's City University Business School, the archetypal entrepreneur 'gets kicks out starting from chaos, which gives him his freedom to maneuver, and out of chaos creates his own sense of order.' Corporations are scared of taking risks.

This is because many are undercapitalized and the tax structure often discourages risk-taking. So they tend to be more interested in short-term payoffs rather than long-term investments. Companies that have a strong market position around the world are spending more and more of their capital resources to protect this position. This means that less money is available for new, innovative development.

With layer upon layer of management, decision-making power in many big corporations has turned into decision-blocking power, wielded by serried rows, of time-serving, middle-management bureaucrats. A terrible paralysis pervades the organization. It is the entrepreneur who creates the business; it is the manager who maintains the systems to keep it going. E.F. Schumacher recognized the need for both imagination and control. In his seminal best-selling book, 'Small is Beautiful' he wrote: 'Without order, planning, predictability, control, instructions to the underlings, obedience and discipline – without these nothing fruitful can happen because everything disintegrates.

'And yet without the magnanimity of disorder, the happy abandon, the entrepreneur venturing into the unknown and incalculable, without: the risk and the gamble – without this, life is a mockery and a disgrace.'

But inevitably bureaucracy corrupts.

There comes a time in the life of a business when the entrepreneurial spirit is stifled rather than enhanced by systems and controls. The corporation loses its sense of mission, its entrepreneurial zeal and becomes preoccupied with running the machine for its own sake than as a means to an end.

What are the symptoms? Departments proliferate. There are more research staff but fewer people actually doing research. Overheads grow faster than turnover. The company may be making more money from currency transactions than from trading. There are fewer new products and more reports that nobody reads. Customer service falls off. Products no longer reflect the changing needs of the market.

Most management pundits agree that the key to rekindling the entrepreneurial spirit in a company is to decentralize into smaller, more autonomous business units. But size in itself is neither good nor bad: James Hayes, chairman of American Management Associations, said, 'Size of companies has a tendency to fit size of managers. And size is relative to function.' Peter Drucker, the doyen of management thinkers, said, 'One doesn't start with organization, one ends with it.

Form follows function and function follows people.'

Mr. Drucker, believes in starting with people at the top. 'You've got to build a top management team having diverse points of view,' he said. Managers of old companies all tend to look and think alike. Like carbon copies, they are weak. There's a lot to be said for the old habit of recruiting top management from the outside – but bringing them in at the second level, just below the chief executive. Any further down the line, by the time they reach the top they've already been brainwashed. Senility sets in very fast.'

Jacques Horovitz, professor of business administration at IMEDE business school in Lausanne, said, 'Entrepreneurship is part of the company culture. And that is set by signals from the chief executive. It's important that he sets a climate for risk-taking and allows mistakes to be made.'

Mr. Drucker has a three-point prescription for reforming the organization. 'First, think through your business, define your mission; think it through and again. But keep it simple. In hard times one can't manage complexity. Second, abandon. Sit down with the research people and evaluate what they're doing. Take a hard look at staff services, at old products. Where are they in the life cycle? One can't measure until one has defined and understood. Don't keep the past alive, but zero-plan. An innovative company is one that always abandons on an organized basis. And third, make sure you focus on opportunities. Put them on page one of the agenda. And don't mix promising new projects with established operations or they will die.'

One way to encourage entrepreneurship within a company is to give the managers the chance to succeed, or fail, in building a new project or idea into a profitable business. Mr. Hayes said, 'You've got to force people on the way up into innovative roles where they can fall flat on their faces. They have the safety net of their old jobs if they fail. And they often will. One of the characteristics of the archetypal entrepreneur is that he fails first time. That's difficult for managerial types to accept.'

But the 'sink or swim' approach will work only if the reward system in a company positively encourages innovation and risk-taking. Brian Allison, chairman and chief executive of the London-based Business Intelligence Services, said, 'It's essential to give key executives, those with the ability to make things happen, not only a profit share in their own unit but an equity share in the whole business. It's almost magical to watch the change in a person once he becomes a shareholder and is actually treated as such.'

Mr. Drucker advocates a two tiered compensation scheme, part entrepreneurial, based on performance and innovation, part hierarchical, based on conventional rewards of seniority and function. Most scientific compensation plans, he said, penalize the innovative manager.

Mr. Lessem talked of a new breed of corporate entrepreneur or 'intrapreneur' to use the new buzz word, which he calls an 'enabler.'

This is someone who is able to recognize, develop and orchestrate entrepreneurs within the company. 'In a sense he combines the skills of a management trainer and business broker,' he said.

'He is able to bring people and markets together, so that by developing other businesses, he creates his own.'

What are business schools doing to develop entrepreneurial managers? Not enough, according to Mr. Lessem. He deplored what he called the 'cognitive imperialism' of many business schools.

'Conventional management training is primarily concerned with organization and planning,' he said. "Entrepreneurial management is to do with vision, imagination, enthusiasm and self-assertion You have to emphasize capability rather than just knowledge.' Jean-Pierre Jeannet, also a professor of business administration at IMEDE, said, 'Entrepreneurship is more a matter of mental attitude than skills, it is part of personality. It's non-cognitive, a general ability to suspend yourself in a risk situation.

To develop this attitude, you've got to take people outside the organization and to re-energize them.' Mr. Jeannet believes that the lack of entrepreneurial spirit among managers stems from the changing values of society.

The white-hot urge to build has disappeared. 'This is due to pressure from society; the temperature has dropped,' he said.

Confessions of a headhunter
1971 Werbung/Publicite

Headhunting is said to be the most profitable branch of management consulting. It is certainly the most controversial. Executive recruiters, as they prefer to be called, normally charge client companies twenty-five percent of the yearly salary of the individual hired. Overheads are low, except for the telephone which the client pays for anyway. The headhunter often strikes fear and hatred into the hearts of company presidents (unless of course they are looking for a job) who resent seeing their best executives pirated away to a competitive firm. On the other hand, rising young executives monitor their status by the number of times a month that the headhunter calls. Headhunters operate in a shadow world of disguised telephone calls (Er.... are you free to talk?), envelopes marked 'strictly personal and confidential' and furtive meetings in airports and motels. So furtive in fact are these encounters that some executives have found themselves recruited by mistake into the CIA or even back into their own companies.

Olaf Olafsson is the consummate headhunter. From his ice-palace headquarters (no pun intended) in Reykjavik his telephone calls are feared or cherished, as the case may be, in executive offices throughout the world.

Apart from his telephone, Olafsson owns a German sheep dog and a private gunboat. He has not been seen in public for the last twenty years. The last published photographs show a heavily built blonde man with orange-framed tortoiseshells and a Delphic smile. We asked our special correspondent, Guratsky, to conduct a telephone interview with Olafsson and lay bare what many people have called 'the black art of executive recruiting'.

GURATSKY: 'Good morning, Mr. Olafsson.'

OLAFSSON: 'Good morning. I hope you can hear me.'

GURATSKY: 'Perfectly. You have a reputation for always keeping an excellent line. Mr. Olafsson, you have not appeared in public for over twenty years. Have you appeared in private during this time?'

OLAFSSON: 'That's a difficult question. It's a matter of definition. Let me say that I invariably communicate with my family and close associates by closed circuit television.'

GURATSKY: 'I admire your discretion. But tell me, how did you first get into ... er executive search?'

OLAFSSON: 'Well, I majored in corporate politics and tribal studies at Harvard Business School. And then I really learned the tricks of the trade at the CIA and ITT. It was when I saw all the fired advertising men and retired army majors claiming to be experts in human relations that I thought I could do better. So I acquired my own telephone.'

GURATSKY: 'Mr. Olafsson, how do you plan an executive search?'

OLAFSSON: 'First you make a list of what we will call "target areas". A good man can often be found in unexpected places. Like a call to the men's room. That's what makes a creative recruiter. He can smell them out. The real secret is research and contacts. We have, of course, extensive files. And then we have a corps – a secret fraternity, if you will – of Olafsson men in companies all over the world. We actually build the careers of our men, headhunting them from one job to another until they reach the top. Then it's too late. They are beholden to us. Sometimes we'll keep a man inactive for years in a company until he can be of use. "Moles", they call them in espionage.'

GURATSKY: 'Interesting. But isn't it rather unethical. I mean, headhunting a man you've just placed with a client?'

OLAFSSON: 'Well, we do undertake not to raid a client company until two years after the assignment. Otherwise we'd soon run out of clients. Obviously if we were searching in the automotive industry and we could not touch Ford or General Motors our value as a recruiter would be pretty limited. We do make an exception to the two year rule when the executive who calls us in to do the search is really only looking for a job himself. It's a subtle way of saying, "I'm available".'

GURATSKY: 'What do you feel about the "cult of youth". Has the executive lifestyle changed over the years, in your opinion?'

OLAFSSON: 'I believe the "youth cult" was part of the economic upsurge of the sixties. Our average candidate is between thirty-five and forty-five. I'm forty-eight now and have always tended to work with people of about my own age. The problem of youth is recognising how to deal with people. There's also an ambivalence I think between the newer business graduates and the older professionals. The trouble with many MBA's is they are not trained to make money but to run a business. There's too much preoccupation these days with running the machine for its own sake. Companies are just there to exist. Many of them are past the profit motive altogether. At least the entrepreneurial drive.'

GURATSKY: 'You talked a few moments ago about the need for creativity in recruiting. Could you expand on that?'

OLAFSSON: 'Yeah. What I meant was the search has to be creative, not the executives. Normally when a client calls us in they have tried to find the man themselves. After all, eighty percent of top management appointments are internal. We tend to get the tough jobs. That's why we have to rely upon safe, middle-of-the-road men. We can't take a chance on the too imaginative candidate. I guess that's a kind of "natural selection" for all the grey corporate men around. Incidentally, I'd be happy to see your resumé anytime, Mr. Guratsky.

After ten days and twelve thousand dollars, what have you got to say for yourself?

1989 International Herald Tribune; 1992 Business Life

'I have one ground rule for my language students: Never worry about remembering anything and never try to remember from one moment to the next. Responsibility for learning is with the teacher, never with the student.'

So says Michel Thomas, founding guru of Michel Thomas Language Centers in New York, Washington DC, and Beverly Hills, California.

'There is no note-taking and homework is not allowed - not even mental homework. Relaxation is the key ... to eliminate the tension and anxiety associated with learning languages. One gets confidence from the experience that it works. And that confidence is achieved very quickly.'

Confidence is something that Thomas has in abundance - an essential part of his method, one suspects. He claims to distil years of language training in a few days. With sure-fire results. He guarantees success ('I'm talking about proficiency - fluency is something else') after just 10 to 12 days of full-time study. This means being able to speak, read and write almost any Western language (Japanese, Russian and Arabic may take a few days longer!) 'We offer results, we're not selling blocks of lessons,' Thomas says. 'You can take as long as you like to cover them.' And if you do need a refresher you can come back for free any time.

Sceptical? Yes, I was until I began talking to some of Thomas' students. He has a fanatical following. The proof of the pudding is in the speaking.

'I was as sceptical as anyone until after the first hour with Michel,' says Joan Sherman, a business consultant who lives in Monaco. 'I've made nine round-the-world trips since January - time is the most precious thing. I went through the first part of the course in four, I must say, gruelling days. I could read French fairly well, but I had a need to communicate. His technique is unique in that he manages to zero in on those things that inhibit you – on the blocks – and figure them into his method. If I knew how he did this technically, I'd be in competition with him.

'He makes it so simple. The key to retention is understanding. Michel kept reminding me not to memorise. Which is hard to do. But once I let go of that I found that weeks... months later things were popping out of my mouth that I was not actually memorising. I was going to say almost hypnotic, subliminal. That's exactly what it is. When I read French I actually hear Michel speaking. He has this quiet, soft voice. I mean you have to have such tremendous respect for the man...'

None of this comes cheap. A 10-day course is $4,200 ($2,700 per person for two) with a regular teacher and $12,000 if you opt for Thomas himself. There is a two-and-a-half-day crash course for a mere $1,250. And a bargain basement two-day course aimed at giving a functional use of French, German or Spanish for travel purposes for $380 per person based on a minimum group of four.

But the gift of tongues seems to be priceless for the galaxy of showbiz and corporate luminaries who have graduated with Thomas - Michel, as everyone calls him - and rave about the method.

Thomas has plastered the walls of his New York offices with fulsomely inscribed photos from Raquel Welch, Natalie Wood, Barbra Streisand and Bob Dylan. Thomas claims that Woody Allen learned as much French from him in 10 days as Yves Montand did in English.

'Grace Kelly was my student before and after she became Princess of Monaco,' Thomas says. Corporate clients include CocaCola, Chase Manhattan Bank and AT&T 'We gave Spanish to American managers at Westinghouse in Madrid with English for Spanish managers. We gave a German course in Zurich for an American stockbroker firm. And the University of Pittsburgh at Johnstown gave our course for three consecutive four day weekends last May in German, French and Spanish. On Monday, we have Robert Halmy, a film producer, who knows no French and has a great need of it for a business trip to France. By Wednesday, say Thursday, he will be speaking the language. You can talk to him in French if you'd like to.'

Too late for my deadline. But Yue Sai Kan, a Chinese-American TV producer in New York, who returned my call early that week, says, 'Fabulous. Michel is a brilliant teacher. I speak quite a few languages, including

Cantonese and Mandarin, but I had never studied French before. I came out after ten days with enough of it to move around in Paris. He has a way of helping you to remember things based on what you already know in your conscious and unconscious minds.

'He's like a Zen master, you never feel pressurised. And he makes you feel very smart. I don't think anyone else teaches that way.'

Thomas, a courtly, soft-spoken man in his mid-sixties (he won't reveal his age) is reticent about his background. He says he grew up in Lyon and Bordeaux and studied at the Sorbonne. He was an authentic hero of the French Resistance during the second world war and then worked for American counterintelligence in Germany. In 1982 he was decorated by the Academie Française for 'services to languages and education.' After the war, he moved to the United States, starting his first language school in California in 1947. His English is reminiscent of Central Europe, like a psychiatrist from Central Casting.

So what is his mother tongue? French, he insists. 'I speak 11 languages, so maybe my accent is little bit of everything.'

'Michel's past has never been completely understood,' says a former student and close friend. Thomas claims it took him '25 and a half years' to perfect his tapes, which play a key role in the teaching method. The course consists of the two five-day phases. During Phase One the student is pretty much left alone in a comfortable room with a cassette player; although a teacher is present for review sessions. When you listen to the tapes it's a bit like eavesdropping on two people (often celebrities) along with Thomas. (On the Spanish tape, for example, you can hear Herb Alpert and his wife.)

Says Thomas, 'Having two students on the cassette is a teaching device, a learning situation for three. The most important thing for you to do is relax. And whenever I ask a question, for you to hit the pause button and respond out loud, release it and you'll get the response from one of the two students. Then I will repeat it and spell out the words. It's essential to learn how to spell mentally. You'll experience a constant sense of learning which is mentally stimulating, exciting and self-rewarding. There's no fatigue; you don't want to stop, break for lunch you are so excited.' The aim is for you to be able to converse comfortably 'and at every level, in all tenses, and read newspapers and books.'

Phase Two, conducted exclusively in the language, is tailored to individual needs. 'We have specialists who do role playing, not only to break the language barriers but cultural barriers,' Thomas says.

'I told them I wanted to talk about business, the Middle Ages and Crusades, and the French role in Algeria and Indo-China,' says Nicholas Gardiner, head of a New York-based executive search firm, Gardiner Stone.

Did they deliver? 'Not in every case, but the instructors were really very good. It was a little like throwing away crutches. After the first 30 to 40 hours I never spoke English again which was quite terrific. But I do not think it's as passive as Michel says it is; if you're highly motivated and have a tremendous need to learn it's superb. I took 12 to 14 weeks to finish, not 10 days. I think that's nosense. There is no quick fix. I feel Michel is a master teacher but I don't feel he has totally institutionalised his system – he tends to over – promote the organisation.'

Maybe part of this motivation comes from paying all that money. 'What Michel pushes is the idea you must speak the language, which was very effective for me,' says Donald Beldock, chairman of Fundamental Properties Inc. in New York, who took courses in French and Italian with Michel Thomas. 'I was a product of the best American schools, but in French I'd lost what fluency I'd had. I studied for several months with Michel and got over my inhibitions. He deals with those anxieties that seem to prevent most Americans speaking another language. I manage business effectively in French. In Italian I can carry on a social conversation with some ease.'

What seems to impress students most is the tapes – which, incidentally, are never released from the premises. 'I'd say he has created an algorithm which gets you into a language probably in the way you learn it as a child,' says Warren Keagan, a professor of business at Pace University in New York. 'I created my own schedule over a 12-day period of 50, 60 hours – I was getting ready for a trip to France. I'd learned a lot of mistakes at school and couldn't speak a word. Afterwards I was interviewed by a woman professor at Colombia on Wall *Street Journal Report*, a TV programme, and did just fine. It is for real. I checked him out. It worked for me, but I did work very hard.'

'After years and years of French in U.S. universities – including Alliance Française – I could read quite well but couldn't speak worth a damn. But after two solid weeks with Michel, I was in Stockholm covering a meeting and was perfectly able to talk to delegates in French,' says Janis Kelly, a medical journalist in New York, who was mid-way through a crash course in Hebrew when I spoke to her.

'The method is so simple and logical; it organises your brain; you can reach for words and find them.' But does she have a problem not being allowed to take notes?

'Not at all, because part of Michel's genius (he's a real systems person) is the built-in redundancy. The tapes are like a fugue, the same themes keep recurring, with slightly different variations. So that by the time you've been through the whole thing you've hit all the major areas of grammar 20 or 30 times.'

I've had a go with the German tape. I wasn't relaxed and kept forgetting to hit the pause button. But I found I was talking along with the two students and after an hour some useful sentences had stuck in my mind. But my German wife is more moderate with her praise. 'Correct, but he doesn't always use the best, the most elegant expression,' she says. Something to do with cognates.

Never mind. Give me another half an hour and I should be able to hold down a conversation with my mother-in-law about the weather. *Au revoir. Auf Wiedersehen...*

Roger Collis

Bailing out the banks with frequent flier miles
2008 International Herald Tribune

Back in my corporate days, the rule was that for every 'problem' identified in the marketing plan one had to find a commensurate 'opportunity', however spurious, in subsequent 'brain-storming' sessions.

I was having a quiet brain-storm of my own the other day, wondering if the present turmoil in the banking system might be an opportunity to transfer my overdraft to a safer haven, when I happened upon a cartoon in The New Yorker, which had a man pleading with the mugger who had snatched his wallet, 'Use the platinum card – I need the miles!'

Exactly! There is nothing like black humor for unleashing productive ideas.

If frequent flier miles are as good as gold, how would it be if miles were actually to replace money as convertible currency? Mileage millionaires would then replace derivatives traders and hedge-fund managers as the new 'Masters of the Universe.'

Frequent flier programs are said to be the most successful marketing idea of all time. Since American Airlines launched AAdvantage a quarter of a century ago, more than 124 million travelers count miles with one or more of 140 airline programs, many of which have scores of airline and non-airline partners, hotels, car rental firms and credit card providers. Some FFPs have as many as 200 partners. Nobody needs to fly to earn miles. Many airlines make money from FFPs by selling miles to program partners. United Airlines and American Airlines are said to generate more money in this way than by selling airline seats.

That's quite a universe.

No sooner had my think bubble filled up with asterisks and exclamation marks when a call comes in from my old friend Stanley Zilch, the fecund chairman of Blue Skies Travel Research Institute, a think tank in Broken Springs, Colorado.

Great minds think alike!

Stanley reminds me that with 14 trillion unredeemed miles sloshing around the system there is more liquidity mileage, so to speak, than in today's beleaguered monetary systems. And with each mile worth an estimated 2 U.S. cents, that adds up to $280 billion.'

'Surely that's not enough to bail out the banks. And what about the airlines? If an airline goes bust, surely the miles become worthless.

'Not at all! The idea is to package up what you might call "sub-prime" miles, and any other dodgy loyalty award schemes, into structured indebtedness vehicles, and mileage derivatives. Nobody knows what they contain; but so long as people believe they have a value...'

'Didn't Warren Buffett describe derivatives as 'financial weapons of mass destruction?'

Zilch is unfazed. 'You can search for WMDs but everyone knows by now that they don't exist!'

'But surely some miles are more equal than others, because FFPs have different rules, such as award levels or the category of fare that earns miles and "elite" membership privileges. How would you be able to exchange miles that have different values?'

'This happens now: The three main airline alliances, Star Alliance; One World and Sky Team, allow travelers to earn and redeem miles on their partner carriers – that's a total of 32 major airlines. Frequent travelers often have several accounts. Thus by pooling their mileage in a single carrier, they are able to achieve elite status more rapidly and become mileage millionaires. Elite members would be kept loyal by awarding them "stock options" in miles. This might help solve the present problem of too many miles chasing too few aircraft seats.'

'Yes, but how do you encourage airlines to start lending to one another again?'

'Airline Alliances will act as banks, underwriting the issue of miles, collateralized debt obligation bonds, and credit default swaps. The new Central Mileage Fund will act as lender of last resort, pumping as many miles as necessary into the system.'

Zilch stresses the importance of confidence. 'These miles exist only because people believe that they do. It's like the cartoon character who only drops through the air when he realizes he has walked off the cliff, he says. 'In the long run, any system will be profitable as long as you believe in it.'

A brief history of the future: Flying villages and space spas

1999 International Herald Tribune

Airborne between Paris and Hong Kong on a Global Airlines Boeing 2000ER, John and Jane Harbinger are lingering over lunch in the gourmet restaurant on the top deck (not much point in fast food on a 16-hour flight) figuring how they're going to spend the rest of the afternoon. Jane decides on a soothing séance in the beauty parlor: John will make a few calls from the business center and polish his presentation. They'll meet for drinks at six in the suite before dinner. 'Would sushi hit the spot? I'll book a table downstairs.' John asks a passing 'skycop' for directions. 'Head down the main corridor towards the tail and take the elevator down to the bottom deck.'

Planes such as this three-deck 1,000-seat Goliath – which entered service in 2015 – are derived from the 600-seat super jumbos promised (or threatened) by Airbus and Boeing in 1999. They are flying villages, allowing infinite scope for social congress, with half a dozen restaurant concessions – from classical French to McDonalds' – casinos, shops, cyber-cafes with Internet access, and health clubs. About the only things missing are a pool and an outside jogging track. But you never know!

There is no such thing these days as first, business or economy class. The price you pay depends on your choice of seating, cuisine and entertainment along with the kind of service you want on the ground. Accommodation ranges from standard cattle class and ergonomic sleeper seats with more personal space to air-conditioned cabins with beds, bathroom and butler service, that convert to a daytime lounge. For an extra charge, the airline will deliver a container to your home or office, transport you through the airport and load you onto the plane. Some tycoons have converted their offices into flight containers, re-creating the private railroad cars of a century ago – the ultimate in seamless travel.

Many people travel 'a la carte.' You book a seat or cabin and pay extra for meals and in-flight facilities and lounges, limos and other trimmings on the ground. Traveling cattle class is no longer much of an ordeal. You only have to stay in your seat for take-off and landing; the rest of the time you can move around freely. Skycops patrol the crowded aisles ready to deal with unruly or abusive passengers who can threaten not only the well being of other passengers but the safety of the aircraft. After all, on a long-haul flight you can be in the air for up to 18 hours – almost long enough to get married, start a family and get divorced, although not necessarily in that order. Some enterprising agents are using reservations computers to help people choose in-flight companions. They punch in your high-altitude likes and dislikes and match you up with a suitable seatmate.

Global Airlines is one of three mega-carriers that together share 80 percent of the world air travel market – the culmination of the giant airline alliances and code-sharing deals that carved up the skies in the late 1990s. These compete with consortia of regional airlines in Europe, the Middle East, Africa and Asia Pacific, along with half a dozen long-haul carriers mainly serving the business market.

Code sharing, whereby two or more airlines operate the same flight, and 'block seat' arrangements, whereby one airline sells seats on another airline's flights, became commonplace by 2000. The abundance of space on the super-jumbos allowed several airlines to share the same plane with their own fares, flight attendants, in-flight cuisine and service.

This led to the concept of the 'virtual' airline. You don't need to own aircraft and infrastructure when you can 'brand' your own cabin in a super-jumbo. Travel agents can buy blocks of seats (and hotel rooms) and market them under their own brands to corporate customers.

Since 1999, super-jumbos – along with advanced technology for better control of the airways with new satellite navigation systems and new airports and terminals – have diminished the specter of gridlock in the skies by quadrupling air traffic capacity since 1999. But the challenge was daunting.

Roger Collis

Since 1999, air traffic has been growing at around 10 percent a year.

Thus the number of passengers has doubled every seven years, reaching a staggering 20 billion in 2020. Where are all these people going? And, more to the point, why do they all seem to be going with me?

The growth of tourism in China has been phenomenal. The Chinese government set the ball rolling when it cut the working week to five days, giving the nation's workers an extra half-day off a week.

This was even better news for the travel trade, because – assuming a workforce of 750 million from a total population of 1.2 billion – it meant an extra 15 billion days' leisure time coming on stream. And with more disposable income and the liberalization of passports, the Chinese have become international travelers.

According to the World Tourism Organization, China now generates more out-bound tourism than any country in the world apart from Japan, Germany and the United States. China has also become the world's top tourist destination with 137 million visitors in 2020.

The world's top 30 airports will handle more than 16 billion passengers this year. The traditional mega-hubs such as Chicago O'Hare, Los Angeles International, Atlanta, London Heathrow, Hong Kong's Chek Lap Kok and Singapore's Changi are bursting at the seams, each handling around 200 million passengers a year. But an airport building boom, especially in Asia, has added capacity. China has built more than 50 new airports since 1999.

Meanwhile, the creation of 'wayports,' or new hubs, in remote parts of Norway and Siberia has siphoned off a large amount of connecting traffic. More than 30 percent of the people milling around Heathrow, for example, were simply trying to get somewhere else.

Supersonic travel has become space age with Orbitol, a 50-passenger space plane that travels in low earth orbit enabling it to fly from London to Sydney in 45 minutes. Unlike the old space shuttles, Orbitol takes off and lands under its own power. After accelerating through Mach 5 to 80, 000 feet, the plane leaves the atmosphere, continues to accelerate and becomes a satellite itself after reaching 250,000 feet – around four times the cruising altitude of Concorde – with an orbital velocity of Mach 25 to 30.

More down to earth, high-speed maglev (magnetically levitated) trains traveling at 300 miles per hour have replaced air travel on journeys of up to 500 miles, releasing slots at major airports, most of which have train stations, for long-haul traffic.

Regional airlines serve 'thinner routes,' enabling business travelers to avoid mega-hubs. Thus 'regional long-haul' services allow travelers to fly point-to-point between cities such as Manchester and Osaka, Seattle and Perth, Stuttgart and San Francisco.

Mega-hubs, with a larger daily population than many major cities, are no longer a means to an end but an end in itself, destinations in their own right. They form a worldwide network of alternative cities – what you might call the terrestrial equivalent of space stations – with their own business communities and civic amenities, hotels and conference centers. Who needs to go downtown when you are already there? Many people don't travel to cities any more, just to airports.

John Harbinger, on-line to his office in Broken Springs, Colorado, asks himself a routine question: whether he really needed to make this trip.

Technology enables (and requires) him to be totally wired at all times. The No. 1 rule for business travelers is wherever you are, always to be on the phone to somewhere else. So why travel? John rationalizes that this is a working vacation – a chance to bring Jane along. He's looking forward to a round of golf with his Chinese associates. And he and Jane plan to take off for a five-day airship cruise among the Hong Kong islands.

Modern airships are safe, comfortable, and environmentally friendly, as they sail and hover less than 100 feet above the ground. An airship cruise is a spectacular way to see many wonders of the world, such as the Amazon and what's left of the rain forests in Brazil and Peru, chateaux of the Loire, fly along the Nile to see the pyramids, explore Venice or make an air safari in Kenya.

'Virtual conferencing,' has done away with the need for many business trips. A 100-inch (256 centimeter) illuminated high-resolution screen with 'wrap-around' sound makes everyone seem life-like and gives the illusion that you're in the same room. This means that you can participate normally in the discussion; using the same body language.

Travel was in danger of becoming an end in itself. I am therefore I travel: I travel therefore I am. Travel is about human interaction, hands-on experience. Getting the best return on your 'interaction expense' is a trade-off between cost in terms of time, money and hassle and the opportunity of staying doing something more productive somewhere else.

Of course, there's sometimes a need to be somewhere in person – the eye contact, the real, compared to the cybernetic, handshake, the impromptu meeting and, of course, the social dimension can be pure gold. It is not something you can quantify; it's intuitive, gut feeling. Who goes to a conference to listen to the speakers? You can pick up a transcript or receive it live in your office. It's real-time networking that counts.

In the words of Alfred Lord Tennyson's Homeric hero, Ulysses, back in 1842:

> I am a part of all that I have met;
> Yet all experience is an arch where thro'
> Gleams that untravelled world, whose margin fades
> For ever and for ever when I move.

But business travel is less poetic and a good deal less sentimental. Which is why John Harbinger makes fewer trips these days. This excursion with Jane is a fairly rare experience in real-time reality. Like most other road warriors, John embraces the new 'travel avoidance' technology, such as virtual conferencing and virtual meetings in real or 'displaced' time, with chiliastic zeal.

The technology is rooted in voice recognition software developed back in the late 90s that enabled you to call a computer from anywhere in the world, check your e-mail your voice-mail and faxes, either by computer or through the telephone. You could convert them from voice to text, or vice versa, and re-direct them by any medium.

Recent advances in artificial intelligence make it possible to hold an open-ended discussion through a computer. The machine not only understands the meaning of what you say but replies to you in a normal voice – which might be the digitalized voice of a real person.

John Harbinger, along with his colleagues, has had his voice 'digitalized' and stored on-line. Early computer-generated voices sounded robotic because words were mechanically strung together into sentences, thereby losing the rhythm of the dialogue; whereas digitalized voices are produced by recording entire sentences, then shoehorning in numbers and letters of the alphabet.

Voices are recorded in three ways. If you say the number nine, for instance, at the beginning of a word, it sounds different from if you say it in the middle or the end. The same applies to words and phrases.

It's hard to detect a digitalized voice in displaced time from a real voice in real time. Meetings can thus be conducted in real or displaced time. You program your responses, to say, a budget meeting, in advance and your digitalized voice conducts a dialogue on your behalf. Cognitive programs are being designed whereby John can participate vicariously at several meetings while he is away. It beats the old way of having answering machines talk to one another, or batting e-mails back and forth, communication lost in fruitless volleys of non sequiturs.

Back in their suite, the Harbingers are mentally packing their bags for an 'out of this world' space vacation. They have been armchair astronauts for years and are looking forward to five days in a Disney Space Resort 300 miles above Earth. They will take off from Cape Canaveral, Florida, in a NASA space shuttle adapted to carry 40 tourists, experiencing weightless for about 15 minutes.

The resort accommodates 300 people in cruise-ship luxury. It takes an hour and a half to make a complete orbit of the Earth, spinning like a roulette wheel at about one revolution a minute, thus developing artificial gravity.

You stay in an outer ring, where you experience about half of normal gravity – just about half your normal weight – so you can use bathroom facilities and such at practically normal conditions. A central column section has zero gravity. This is the entertainment and recreation center, which guests can visit for an hour or so at a time. There are windows in the central column to view the Earth.

There are lots of entertainment possibilities at zero gravity, including a gym with padded walls. Astronauts have found that blood that is normally drawn down to your legs is released and drifts upwards. You become thinner, your chest expands by two to three inches, your face fills out and wrinkles disappear.

While Jane muses about a second honeymoon in space, John is thinking about the final frontier in space travel – to experience Einstein's paradox of relativity, that if you travel faster than the speed of light, you are younger when you get back than when you left.

Daunting implications for the international manager.

Too many discounts confuse business travelers
1992 *International Herald Tribune*

With all the promotions and deals around, how about a loyalty program which keeps executives busy in their offices instead of reward them for traveling?

In today's buyers' market for business travel, many corporations are spending more management time on finding travel bargains than doing business when they get there, according to Stanley Zilch, chairman of Blue Skies Travel Research Institute in Broken Springs, Colorado. And business strategy often stems from travel opportunities. Stanley and I are intimate enemies from my corporate days. So when this landed on my desk, I called to ask what he meant.

'It all stems from the cutback in travel during the recession. Airlines worldwide lost $4 billion in 1991. And when you think that business travelers account for a third of seats but more than two-thirds of revenue, that's an awful lot of leverage. Hotels too. Occupancy levels in the States fell to 62 percent, less than break-even. That is a lot of leverage. What's happening is that companies are putting all that leverage to work by smarter purchasing of travel services."

"So there are some great bargains. What else is new?"

"Stay with me. The problem is just that there's such a blizzard of great deals from so many sources – airlines, hotels, travel agents, club membership and card companies, not to mention all the frequent-flier and frequent-stayer programs – that travel planning can be even more of a nightmare than the trip itself."

"You're saying frequent travel can mean frequent confusion."

"Absolutely.

Even straightforward trips – such as Paris to Los Angeles – can involve heavy management decisions.

Do you fly Air France to earn the last 5,000 miles that you need for a free round-trip ticket between North America and Europe on United Airlines' Mileage Plus program? Or American Airlines via Dallas to top up your Aadvantage miles for a free Caribbean cruise?

Pay with American Express at the Hilton and get double points in the hotel program. Or get the corporate rate somewhere else.

Then you might want to fly KLM through Amsterdam for a free stopover package. And if you want to rent a car you have as many options as possible moves in a game of chess: fly/drive and fly/stay/drive packages; discounted rack rates; non-discounted pre-booked rates. And so it goes.

"This is why travel management has become an end in itself, rather than a means to an end. Instead of asking: Is all my travel really necessary? People are traveling more often just in order to save money. I am therefore I travel: I travel therefore I am."

"I think I see what you mean. But how does all this affect how and where business is done?""Simple. Every piece of research we've done confirms that people travel more to places that are easy to get to and where they can get the best deals. The hassle factor is important. People are looking for user-friendly airports and convenient schedules. Remember the number one rule for business travel is never to do business in the office you are visiting, but constantly be on the phone to somewhere else. It's one way to beat jet lag – or pass on your jet lag to somebody else. And keep people in the subsidiaries on their toes. We call it Management by Absence. So from the business point of view, it doesn't really matter where you travel, if the price is right."

"This is why it makes sense for my English friends to meet me in New York. It's cheaper for them than flying from London to Nice."

"You got it. That's another thing about bargain travel – companies often find it is more cost-effective to keep around 50 percent of executives on the road rather than at their desks. There is widespread recognition that foreign travel, especially to conferences, has made a major contribution toward full executive employment. I mean there are tens of thousands of executives flying around, and attending conferences, who might otherwise be standing in line at employment agencies and executive soup kitchens.

"As more companies change from centralized, functional types of organizations into decentralized, divisional ones made up of profit centers, or business units, they are shedding up to 30 percent of their staff. In fact, up to 50 percent of personnel can be casualties in a major reorganization.

"Instead of firing these people, however, many companies find it more cost-effective to send them out on the road or the conference circuit. It's a question of balancing travel costs against the expense of golden handshakes.

"What's more, companies are finding that they can cut overhead costs by allocating one office to several executives. There are special computer programs for this. We find inventory control software is useful in working out the probability of any one manager needing the office on a given day."

"But to come back to the mechanics of travel: what can we do to keep track of discounts through a maze of airline and hotel tie-ins, corporate rates and bonus offers?"

"You're talking about our new super CRS, which should come on stream in the summer."

"A computer reservations system?"

"No, we call it a consumer research system. We enter your personal profile, likes and dislikes, what discounts you already have, whether you are primarily interested in saving money, or comfort and convenience.

We search through the jungle of options for the best deal for you.

"You should join our frequent-flier program called The Program of

Programs. It's based on membership in all of the 40-odd airline and hotel frequent-flier and frequent-stayer programs. The big payoff at one million expense-account miles is two weeks in the office. Along with a full no-trip guarantee."

"That's quite an award!"

"Yeah, it comes down to 'contingent liability.' Airlines and hotels lose less money by paying frequent travelers to stay at home."

A million dollars is still a lot of lamb chops
1984 'If my boss calls …'

Who was that apparition I saw you with on the Bahnhofstrasse in Zurich the other day? That was no apparition that was Guratsky played by a Damon Runyon character from Central Casting. George Raft suit, black silk shirt and white tie, two-tone shoes. He had a new toothbrush moustache (or it might have been second-hand) and his usual air of quiet desperation. Perhaps the cops had towed away his 1932 Packard roadster. Or more likely Doberman & Pinscher was about to lose the vintage cheese account he was handling.

'Hallo, Tom,' I said. 'I recognized your dorsal fin from across the road. How's business?'

Guratsky gave me a manic leer which I politely handed back to him. 'I always have a problem with this sharkskin suit. Business is okay. We got an important new client last week.'

He told me about it over coffee in Baumgartners. 'You've surely heard of Fleischkopf & Rumpelmayer, the international commodity brokers?' He offered me a soya bean future from a small wash-leather bag.

'Yes, of course, my dentist is always talking about them.' Dear old Dr. Feinstein. Who else could give you the spot price of gold right off the top of his head and then go on to quote you for a miniature replica of the Forth Bridge in precious metals. 'Aren't they tied up with the First National

Mammon Bank, or the Dentists' Benevolent Association?'

'That's right; they're a wholly-owned subsidiary. They've given us an assignment to promote lamb chops as a reserve currency.'

'That'll give the international banking community something to chew on,' I said. 'I can just imagine you organising the world's first Lamb Chop Symposium at the Dolder Grand. All the political fat-cats and central bankers. You might get someone like Paul Bocuse to make the key-note speech. I wonder what wine he'd choose. With a nice *côtelette d'agneau à la Provençale* you wouldn't go far wrong with a Pauillac or a Saint Julien …'

'You can be as facetious as you like' Guratsky admonished. 'But you'll see. One day lamb chops will take their place alongside gold and Special Drawing Rights.'

'Excuse my ignorance, Tom, but isn't today's monetary system complicated enough without getting into lamb chops?'

Guratsky removed his moustache and stroked it thoughtfully.'Look, I don't want to get too technical, but it's a question of international liquidity. You see, the growth in liquidity needed to   finance the expansion of world trade has been limited by the physical output of gold and the supply of dollars and sterling. Of course, Euro-dollars and Special Drawing Rights have added to the supply in recent years. But many bankers are now pressing for a new currency similar to that which Keynes first proposed at the Bretton Woods conference in 1944. He argued for a unit of international currency, the "bancor" he called it, that would not be subject to the technical progress of the gold industry in a few politically sensitive areas of the world like South Africa and the Soviet Union.

'We believe at Doberman & Pinscher that the lamb chop can fulfil Keynes' dream of an additional reserve currency. Of course, it will be convertible against gold, sterling and the dollar.'

'That's all very well, Tom. But you haven't answered my question. Why choose lamb chops? Wouldn't it be better to have something less perishable? Like copper wire or worn out typewriter ribbons?'

'Of course not. Because like gold and silver the things you mention have very little intrinsic value. Whereas lamb chops have. You can eat them.

Underdeveloped countries like Zambia and the United Kingdom will be able to grow their own currency reserves and live off them. Literally.

'And think of a nuclear war,' Guratsky continued with the same crucifying logic. 'You could emerge from the shelter into a devastated city and starve to death with a pocket full of gold coins. That's why people will keep their money in the refrigerator instead of under the mattress.'

'Or instead of in their teeth,' I added, thinking of Dr. Feinstein.

'Exactly,' Guratsky said. 'And another reason for investing in lamb chops is that they're an excellent hedge against inflation.'

'How's that?'

'Look at the lamb chop exchange rate against the dollar over the past year or so. You're getting less bites for your buck. Or putting it another way, more dollars for your chops than a year ago.'

No point arguing. 'Okay, what's going to happen to the banks?' I said.

Guratsky produced two butcher's aprons with Pierre Cardin labels. 'Come and see for yourself. The First National Mammon is converting its strong room into a huge freezer with individual ice-boxes for private depositors.'

To paraphrase Damon Runyon: 'I am walking down the Bahnhofstrasse feeling like a million dollars. And a million dollars is an awful lot of lamb chops.'

The middle-management menopause
1971 Werbung/Publicite

John Harbinger knows he won't get the job. The interview wasn't bad at all. He had quite impressed the staff guys with his technical knowledge – the trade structure in the main European markets, the TV scene in Germany, and so on. Hell, twenty years experience doesn't hide itself under a bushel. And he had got on well with the chief executive too; they had been together at a business school seminar. He had felt very comfortable in his new Cardin suit, his graying hair nicely styled, fashionable steel-rim glasses. These young lions, just give him a chance, he'll eat them up. No match for this young forty-six year old.

But that's what they'd kept coming back to. His age. Wagging their heads in a kind of reluctant doubt. Not that he's too old to hack it as vice president. And there is his fine track record… But could he please tell them what he has achieved recently?

Let's face it; he has been slowing down a bit. It used to be four or five markets in as many days. Positively itching to get into things. Now he prefers the Hilton to the milk plane.   And he has to admit that fifteen years with Mistral has worn away some of his creative edge. When was the last product launch he had sponsored? He's stronger now on experience than ideas. Same brands, same markets. It has been a long time since he felt the spirit of adventure in preparing say, a new business presentation. He reckons his reflexes are still pretty good. But what *has* he achieved recently? Has he been coasting? Yes, he's afraid that the younger candidate will get the job.

In his final interview with Mistral all those years ago, they had asked him a question which they had neglected to ask this morning. 'Where do you see yourself in ten years time?' As a young product manager, he had looked his questioner heroically in the eye. 'I want to be the president of this company.'

Today, after that fateful interview, John Harbinger admits for the first time to his secret self that he will never be a president. Maybe not even a vice president –though they seem to be ten a penny these days. Like the middle-aged majors he had known in the army who had known they would never make that quantum promotion to colonel and beyond.   They were bright enough, they had the experience, but somehow, almost imperceptibly, their career trajectories had flattened out, like spent artillery shells at the end of their range.

Coming to terms with the ineluctable can be harder than the moment of truth itself. To have the sights of ambition suddenly lowered, to accept diminished expectations.

Paradoxically, John Harbinger feels a curious sense of relief. He has been saved from the fear of success, the terrible obligation to go one notch higher on the ladder. The true Peter Principle is not so much being promoted to the level of one's incompetence, but to a level of anxiety that can defeat ability to perform an exacting higher-level job. Perhaps John Harbinger's subconscious anticipation of this anxiety, this, what you might call, hierarchical stress, may have contributed to his recent lack-lustre performance; with the danger that this might feed upon itself to cause nervous depression – a personal as well as a career crisis.

Executives often reach an 'anxiety threshold' when they move into a new job in which functional or trade skills are less important. For example, a sales manager promoted to product manager; a copywriter who becomes an account executive; or a vice president finance who is elected to managing director.

Unfortunately, the reward system in most company hierarchies tends to favor the generalist; the position of 'general manager' is more highly esteemed than that of the functional specialist. Of course, there can be exceptions – the esteemed research scientist (although too often it's the patronizing, 'Oh, come in doc!'), or the media specialist – but all too often there is relentless pressure upon the individual to have 'top management' aspirations.

Perhaps one solution is the 'horizontal' hierarchy where the top functional people – finance, production, marketing – are on the same 'level' as the managing director, the arch-generalist, the spider in the web, who co-ordinates all activities. (Although, one can argue that the MD has a specialist role. But that's another story.) The functional jobs are then seen to be of equal importance and prestige. They can even be more important, as in the case of an advertising agency where the creative director makes the running and the managing director handles the admin.

But perhaps the only practical solution for John Harbinger is try to recapture his old fulfillment with his role of marketing director at Mistral. Recognizing and accepting diminished career expectations is half the battle. He now has a sound base for exploring new ways in which he can develop, broaden perhaps, his present job. He can relate to his peers and his subordinates with less apprehension, perhaps directing some of that old competitive energy into finding and training young marketing whiz-kids.

Coming to terms with the 'Management Menopause' means recognizing that 'success' is how you define it and can be achieved at all levels in an organization. The pyramid gets smaller near the top. Middle-managers need to find fulfillment with their reduced expectations if they are to keep their sanity and self-respect.

A Friendly Voice on the Road

1998 International Herald Tribune

Road warriors of the millennium are slaves to progress. In-flight phones and faxes, laptop computers that pack the punch of desk-top PCs, e-mail, voice-mail and the new generation of digital mobiles enable (and compel) you to catch up with office work and keep in touch with anyone anywhere in the world at any time; and, more ominously, for anyone to keep in touch with you. There's no excuse these days for not being totally wired at all times.

Stunning advances in speech-recognition technology now allow travelers to dictate documents, such as faxes and e-mail into a laptop computer at twice the speed of the average professional typist and to have e-mail and fax messages read back to them. All you need is a microphone/speaker and some inexpensive software. Should you find yourself without your laptop, or a friendly neighborhood PC, you can do much the same thing from any touch-tone phone. You just call a personal 800 number from anywhere in the world to have e-mail, faxes, or travel information, such as airline schedules, read to you with voice or touch-tone key commands. You can respond to, say, a fax, with an e-mail or voice-mail message, or edit and redistribute faxes and voice messages as e-mail

Talking to a computer, either direct or on the phone, is the ultimate user-friendly interface with your personal cybernetic secretary. No need to type or click with a mouse, just speak to your PC to open files, send e-mail, format text or surf the net. Premiere Technologies Inc. in Atlanta offers a product called Orchestrate that allows you to receive and redirect messages between one medium and another through a laptop via the Internet or by telephone. You sign up for an e-mail address – your own home page – with a 10-digit access number and 4-digit PIN on the Orchestrate Web site at www.orchestrate.net plus an 800 number that you can call from anywhere in the world to do much the same thing via voice prompts. Steve Walden, vice president for Internet strategy at Premiere Technologies, says: 'Your personal 800 number virtually makes the telephone and the computer interchangeable, so as long as you have access to the Internet, you can go to your personal Web page and check your voice-mail, your e-mail and faxes either through the screen or by voice through the telephone.

'But let's say I just have a phone – I'm changing planes in London. You dial your personal 800 number and a voice says, "Good afternoon, Roger. Would you like to hear your messages?" It will play your voice-mail, read your e-mail or faxes and then it will give you options, through a series of voice-prompts, to which you respond by hitting numbers on the telephone key-pad, such as, Do you want to forward this? Do you want to respond to this? The voice will take you down a decision-tree: You have six e-mails, two voice messages, 12 faxes, which would you like to listen to? You can decide what messages you want to listen to, store for later or delete. You can also direct a fax or e-mail to a fax machine near you if you want it on paper. And on the Internet version, you can attach a voice message to an e-mail. You can go quickly through a list of 25 e-mail headings and decide what you do or don't want to hear.

'There are two levels of voices: A pre-recorded voice with the 25 to 30 prompts that are needed to take you through the menu; and a digitized voice that recognizes texts and translates them into speech. The next stage will be actual voice recognition where you won't need to give a password.'

David Dingley, a travel and transportation specialist at IBM in London, says: 'You have to make a distinction between a machine understanding your dictation and turning your words into text, and a machine understanding the meaning of everything you say and replying to you – an open-ended conversation. That is a huge challenge and I'm not aware of anyone having got near that yet. What we do have is software that will understand and act on relatively simple commands in what you might call a bounded context, such as travel or emergency medicine.'

PureVoice, offered by Qualcomm Inc. in San Diego, a company that develops wireless communications systems and Internet messaging products, provides enhanced voice quality on the Web.

'PureVoice produces a very clear reproduction of your voice in a digital format with high compression, which means a smaller file and fast transmission,' says Arnold Gum, product manager for PureVoice. 'That format is something that you could e-mail, use in a program over the Internet. PureVoice enables you to add voice attachments to your e-mail. A lot of people like to hear a message in a natural voice; it's more personal, and it allows you to communicate more information faster than a typed text. People say: We love sending e-mail, but we don't type. So you add a PureVoice message to your e-mail message.'

'The next step toward voice recognition is, will this thing understand what your words mean and interpret a relatively complex command?' Dingley said.

'We recently gave a demonstration of a flight inquiry system to IATA. "Show me flights from London to New York," we said, in the way a normal person would phrase it. And the system read back the flight times. We had all sorts of people asking it about flights any way they chose, and it was giving the right answers most of the time. You could certainly do that over the phone.

The next layer up, if you like, would be slightly more complex spoken commands and turning them in effect into a transaction against some system behind it.

You've got to take the spoken word and parse it into something simple and structured so that the system understands it in the same way as human operators.

'There are other devices that you can talk to and they'll do things for you. For example, if you ring up our lab in Hawthorne, you can say, "Connect me to Sally," and it does.

It's like the flight inquiries thing, a bounded context. Another approach is when I speak to this thing, can it identify me as Dave Dingley with enough accuracy for it to be a secure device? In other words, whenever I speak to it, whether I've got a cold or a hangover, it will know it's me. There are rumors that some military establishments are capable of doing that. But we're talking serious computer power.

'One use for voice recognition is in customer service. Right now we're running an exercise with a major airline. Imagine a situation at check-in with agents walking around without a keyboard and the need to interact with the computer and the customer at the same time. They could be wearing one of these tiny microphones, so that when they say, "Good morning Mr. Dingley," to the customer, they would get a voice whispering back in their ear from the computer, which had looked up Dingley, saying something like, "Dingley, flight 123, difficult customer, look after him."'

How to count words and influence people
1979 Werbung/Publicite

Jean-Michel Bourdier was uncompromising. 'Motivation? You can forget about motivation, consumer needs, inhibitions and all that. Motivation has nothing to do with the day-to-day practice of communications. In order to communicate you have to be understood. And understanding depends on speaking the same language. So what we do is to analyse and compare the two languages; that of the advertising message and that used by the consumer in talking about the product. This tells us a lot about the message, whether it has been received and in fact whether there is a message at all.'

This is the stuff that revolutions are made of. Bourdier took a long pull from his Gauloise and seemed to blow gun smoke through his nostrils. Give this young iconoclast some more rope.'And how do you do that?' I asked.'The first thing we do is quite simply to count the words which are used, when talking about or describing a product. The words are classified according to occurrence and frequency. Of course we've developed a computer programme to do this. We end up with a hierarchical index of words which are listed from the most frequent to the less frequent. This is expressed in the form of a curve. Zipf's curve we call it in lexicology. We then select the key words which may represent only 20-25% of the dialogue or the text. Usually we analyse as well the language around competitive products.'

'Just a minute, Jean-Michel. All this sounds a little mechanistic. What about meaning? Surely meanings of words are to a great extent personal, individual. How can you reveal this with a computer?'

'That's not the computer's job. The computer is there to count words and analyse their contexts. It can handle massive amounts of material at high speeds. I agree that meanings are crucial. But it's the context which gives a word its real, its practical meaning.'

'Jean-Michel, you've said that you ignore motivations, consumer attitudes and so on. But what people say, the words they use, whatever the meanings of the words, doesn't necessarily correspond with what people do. How is language different from motivation in telling you whether or not people will buy or not buy a product?'

'The answer is we're not looking for a cause and effect relation but correlations with sales, consumer fidelity and other measurable forms of behaviour. We can say after doing hundreds of language studies that for products which have a high sales performance there are many words in common between the advertising message and the language used by the consumer. Of course it isn't enough just to use the same words. To build an effective communication or message you have to use them in the same sense as the recipient, the consumer.'

'Okay, I think I understand. But what does that give you exactly?'

'It gives us those words and themes which must be used or avoided in promoting a product at any given time to a defined target group. In effect a detailed language recommendation or brief. Advertising has two functions; first to be noticed, second to be understood. The first is the artistic, the creative side. Understanding is the business of lexicological analysis. Or course the two should form a synthesis. The advertiser often thinks of research and the creative as two separate domains. They're not. Research and creative become a continuum. Creation, feedback and control, trial, it's a constant dialogue.'

'Isn't there a risk that creative advertising developed from linguistics will lack fantasy, imagination?'

'Fantasy is always possible. Sure, we have developed fairly rigid structures of communication and rules and guidelines for developing the advertising. But this doesn't in any way prevent the final expression of the message being varied and exciting. Look at the Bach concertos. Highly formal mathematical structure but my goodness... You have to appreciate that in the last fifteen years the human sciences and particularly psycholinguistics and semiology have made an enormous contribution to the art of communication.'

'I can see how your methods can work for existing products, repositioning and so on. But what about new product launches where there's usually no consumer dialogue for you to analyse?'

'In that case we analyse the language, the semantic universe, of competitive products. You can often identify and develop new concepts, trends, advertising approaches, from the marginal meanings of words. We do this by looking at the 25% less frequent words in the discourse rather than the 25% most frequent.'

'Jean-Michel, there's something still bothering me. If you develop a message by analysing existing language how do you expect to change a consumer's behaviour by playing his own words back to him?'

Bourdier smiled and lit his millionth cigarette. 'Common words are necessary for the communications mechanism to function. Once you have that you can add "doses" of new information into the circuit to progressively change behaviour. But you have to be careful not to overload the circuit. Here, what I'll do is analyse the tape of our discussion and tell you whether you've understood what I've been saying!'

Roger Collis

Games product managers play
1984 'If my boss calls …'

Scene one: New York. Five minutes to five Friday afternoon this bleak December. Thirty-five floors up from the swirling fog at Doberman and Pinscher Advertising. A stealthy exodus of top management heading for the sanctuary of commuter trains and martini clinics. Bill Haysmith, account director on Soulbad Bath Oil, is making preliminary desk-clearing moves. He drops a voucher copy of Penthouse into his briefcase. The phone rings. It is long distance from Jerry Greenwald, product managed on Soulbad at Mistral Laboratories. Bill's think-bubble fills with asterisks and exclamation marks.

'Hi, Jerry. Nice surprise. What can I do for you?'

'Bill, I'm sorry to grab you this late on a Friday, believe me. But I'm in one helluva bind here. You know Charlie just got back from his Far East trip. Okay. Well, I had lunch with him today and he's talking about a whole new concept for Soulbad. An idea Marcia had when they were in Bangkok. A kind of meditation theme. You know, Buddhist monks anointing themselves and that kind of thing. "Take a soul trip with Soulbad." I reckon Charlie's pretty serious. He was wearing one of those copper bracelets and took a rain check on the third martini.

'Bill, we've got to come up with something pretty fast. Charlie's out of the office again on Wednesday for three weeks. Can you guys let me have something for Tuesday morning? I've set up a meeting for ten o'clock sharp. You could get the late United flight through Cleveland. I'll book you in the Holiday Inn.'

'That's a fascinating concept, Jerry. But with respect I do think we should wait a week or so. After all, it isn't as though the product's not moving. As you know, the agency's view is there's a lot more mileage in the soft-skin positioning. Jerry, I honestly believe we should wait till the September/October Nielsen comes in. We should be getting the top-line figures …'

'Look, fella. I appreciate your position, I really do. But you'd better understand mine. Okay? This thing could have serious political implications for both of us, unless we move really fast with Charlie's new idea. And by the way, he asked me for the marketing plan. Which incidentally I'm still waiting for from you.'

'Jerry, you'll have the plan in a few days. You know we had to re-do the media tables a couple of times because of the budget changes. But Jerry, on this new concept, I just don't see how I can produce a whole new campaign by Tuesday morning. This week's shot. That leaves one working day. If you could give us another week …'

'Fahcrissake, Bill, I don't wane come the heavy-handed client. And I don't want to go over your head, believe me. But I want a new campaign by Tuesday. Period. Now, I don't expect finished stuff. Coupla storyboards and a few rough magazine executions. But I leave that to you. I'm confident you can do a fine job, Bill.'

'Okay, Jerry. We'll put something together. I can maybe catch one or two of the creative guys over the weekend and kick some ideas around before Monday.'

'Bill, that sounds great. I really appreciate your attitude, believe me. I'll make sure you get full marks with Charlie and your own people. So we'll see you bright and early Tuesday. Give my love to Jane. And have a nice weekend.'

Scene two: Mistral Laboratories. Eleven-thirty Tuesday morning. Bill Haysmith has been cooling his heels for nearly two hours in the general office area. Word has it that Jerry Greenwald is tied up in a meeting with Charlie, who is leaving at noon for New York. Bill has drunk six cups of coffee and read *Business Week*, *Fortune* and *Advertising* Age from cover to cover. He wears a complex expression of frustration, anger and deep visceral anxiety. Suddenly Greenwald appears with arms outstretched and a wry apologetic smile. Like a neglectful host at a crowded cocktail party. The Muzak is playing a soft Gregorian chant.

'Bill, I do apologise. Keeping you waiting all this time. I guess you've had coffee. Bill, I know you'll understand, but we've had to make a couple of changes this morning. Charlie's off to New York unexpectedly. And so we can't have our meeting. I'm sorry Bill, believe me.'

'That's okay, Jerry. I understand. These things happen. Look, let me show you what I brought. The guys worked right through the weekend. I think we've got quite an interesting campaign.'

'Ugh… Huh. Why, that's great, Bill. I can see you're fired up. But the fact is we're not going to need a back-up campaign after all. We got the top-line Nielsen in this morning. Soulbad is up 30 percent on a year ago. And share of the market is up nine. Charlie said to tell you he's very pleased with the soft-skin concept. I explained your position. But Charlie doesn't want to see any new creative material right now Why don't you just leave the stuff with me and I'll go through it when I have time.'

'But Jerry. That's not quite …'

'Bill, I'm sorry. Believe me. But I guess that's showbiz. Come on, cheer up. It's twelve o'clock. I'll let you buy me lunch at Katz's.'

Anything for the weekend?

1993 Business Life; 1995 The European

Combining business with pleasure always reminds me of that felicitous French custom near the end of a meal of asking for a little cheese to finish off the wine. Followed, of course, by more wine to finish off the cheese… First back to the office is a sissy.

Not that you have to look very far these days for an excuse to build a holiday on the back of a business trip – or vice-versa. Airlines, tour operators and hotels are all hard at work undermining the Puritan Work Ethic with a smorgasbord of weekend offers for the 'business extender,' ranging from half-price rooms (with 'welcome' fruit baskets, flowers, champagne and a 'personal thank-you' from the assistant house manager) to elaborately packaged mini-holidays (with 'gourmet' dinners, excursions, tickets to a show, tennis and golf), insidiously favouring double-occupancy where two can often stay for the price of one.

Take your pick from the galaxy of 'theme;' 'special interest' and 'activity' weekends being purveyed by the travel trade.

There's something to suit most tastes and proclivities, I imagine: from parachuting and medieval management to falconry and competition Ludo. Even stuff I can hardly imagine; like murder weekends and adventure games for those who missed National Service. (You can take the chairman on either, it seems.)

One of the wackiest weekend breaks I've come across is a 'final fling' for divorcing couples, proposed by a hotel in Essex. A choice of double or single accommodation is offered with the idea that the couple can 'reminisce over the good days of their relationship'. There are flowers, 'gourmet dining' and wines included. Two copies of a photograph of the couple are provided on departure. A two-for-the-price-of-one tariff is charged over the three nights, but full-rate is charged if the couple decide to stay married after all. If you enjoy a macabre touch 'A local solicitor will be invited to join the couple for their final dinner together.'

The same hotel is offering 48 hour 'Breakfast Heritage' breaks during which you can sample more than 50 breakfast dishes. You start on Friday evening with a Saxon breakfast of cold pork and ale, followed by a medieval one with frumenty (a form of porridge), boiled beef or mutton, herring and beer and a Tudor version with bread, cheese and bacon. Saturday is spent sampling a 20-course, 12-hour Victorian breakfast, interspersed with croquet, archery, tennis ('I say who's for breakfast') and golf putting. Sunday brunch – accompanied by a jazz trio – includes eggs Benedict, fillet steak and pink champagne. Excellent training for power breakfasts in the City.

How you rationalise all this – as the pause that refreshes, or as a buffer for rest and recreation, the working break, to get your act together for vital meetings, especially in a new time zone, or as a blow in the cause of saving money – is up to you. Or down to your management style. In fact, it wouldn't be a bad idea for companies to restrict all business travel to weekends; could save a fortune. Take that idea a step further and we might see a new weekend working week emerge – from Thursday to Tuesday. Companies could double their productivity and halve unemployment by having weekend and weekday crews, from chairmen to office boys, sharing desks, telephones and files: the value of weekend decisions versus weekday decisions and sundry schizo-socio-economic devil-maycare desiderata – the ultimate in Management by Conflict.

Clearly, the top priority for most business travelers is to get there and back as quickly and comfortably as possible. But the professional extender will typically stop over somewhere, take off the middle weekend, or add two days to either end of a ten-day trip for rest and recreation.

Successful business extension needs both a strategic and tactical approach. Look after long-haul trips and the side-trips will look after themselves. You could describe the ideal extension as a kind of planned surprise getaway – the paradox is that thoughtful preparation can lead to impromptu discoveries.

First, plan your long-haul itinerary for opportunist stopovers. If you are flying business or economy you may be able to earn a free airline package, say, in Madrid or Copenhagen, as a reward for flying through those hubs. Or combine a money-saving point-to-point fare on the way back with multiple stops on the way out. Always point out how much you are saving the company. ('In that case, Tom, you may as well take your partner with you.') Piggyback as far as you can on expenses and then take off with a local air pass or series of cheap excursion tickets.

Extending within Europe can involve some tricky management decisions. Let's say it is Friday in Vienna and your next appointment is 9am on Monday in Paris. So do you fly home to Zurich tonight, or stay in Vienna? You would have a chance to unwind, see something of the city for a change, or work on your expense account should you have a creative urge. Or you could fly to Paris and spend the weekend there, maybe bring your loved one (or prospective loved one) over for a surprise treat.

Whatever you decide, there is always the risk of becoming a victim of your flexibility. Back at headquarters in Broken Springs, Colorado, they are plotting to dislocate your schedule. A weekend's golf – or, heaven forbid, a carefully wrought assignation – goes down the tube with a request you be in Munich on Monday morning. In these days of instant communications, it's hard to go seriously missing.

Professional extenders never permit business to interfere with pleasure.

The secret is pre-emptive planning. You make sure that whatever pre-trip (or mid-trip) crisis occurs, you are not included.

One way is to plan your own crisis: 'Charles, I'll have to miss the emergency budget meeting: it's absolutely crucial I meet Karl in Frankfurt on Friday. We can always talk on the phone.'

Two crises are better than one. So sandwich your golf break or tryst between two 'inviolable' business meetings. Should you need to go off the air for opportunistic reasons, invoke an urgent 'field trip' ('Charles, Sven wants me to help check out the crayfish stocks in the north of Sweden.' Or, 'Charles, you know this is the first time anybody has actually talked to our customers on the French Riviera.')

An almost sure-fire way to prevent an extension being scuppered at the last minute is to make complex non-refundable bookings.

An Irish-based friend has developed this stratagem into an art form. Whenever he flies to Paris on business, he saves his company money by going to the Cote d'Azur for the weekend.

I've never quite understood the legerdemain, but down here we all enjoy his extension – and expense account.

Taxis: how to avoid being taken for a ride
1997 International Herald Tribune; Highlife

Hugh Thomas, the British historian and author of "The Spanish Civil War," once said that fascist parties are composed primarily of waiters and taxi drivers: "the middle classes at their worst." I think this may be going a bit too far. Let us just say they are both sedulous practitioners of the old admonition never to give a sucker an even break. There is something about driving a taxi that seems to bring out the worst. Perhaps it's because many are self-employed, streetwise entrepreneurs, working long hours with scant thanks from clients. Whether out of anger, frustration or innate cupidity, they have often acquired a mastery of asset-stripping that would leave a corporate raider gasping with admiration. Some, like those in New York, have developed rudeness to an art form, although taxi drivers in France (especially in Paris) have little to learn in this respect.

So I was cheered to learn that the Paris taxi drivers' association offers a 13-week charm course to its members to teach good manners, map reading and a selection of English phrases along with a smoothing out of body language. No more jabbing of the thumb behind them as a rude way of saying, "Get in!" Although we shall still be able to witness the ineffable resignation of the Gallic shrug.

This may sound perverse, but I have a residual affection for those romantic times when many Paris taxi drivers were exiled White Russian Grand Dukes. That was a period of elaborate politeness. I was once driven in from Le Bourget (No, I hadn't just arrived from Croydon with Imperial Airways - I'm not quite as old as that) to my hotel by an octogenarian descendant of Czar Nicholas. (Or maybe it was the Czar, I can't remember. They all seemed to be called Nicholas.) Mind you, he ripped me off, in the nicest way by taking me to an expensive Russian restaurant he just happened to know on the Left Bank. (I had to go to the bank next morning.)

More recently, there's been a new wave of exiles from the Supreme Soviet. It makes a change to be driven around the Place de la Concorde by men in square-cut suits and wearing trilbies. For Nicholas read Mikhail and Boris. Dialectical materialism managed to reconcile a generous tip. Along with a new line in back-seat repartee: "Have you read Marx?" "No, but I've seen the movies." "Je suis Marxiste - tendance Groucho".

Even the locals complain. A taxi from Nice Airport to Cannes or Monaco costs about the same as a helicopter (around 300 francs, or about $60); more in rush hour. A 10-minute ride to the center of Nice will set you back at least 150 francs. And that's on the meter! So it goes in the south of France. I heard the other day - from a usually unreliable source - that Jacques Medecin, the disgraced former mayor of Nice (last reported selling T-shirts in Uruguay), gave local taxi drivers the freedom to charge pretty well what they wanted in return for ferrying Medecin's supporters to polling booths. So it goes in the South of France.

But at least you have more chance of getting an English-speaking driver than in New York where the 10 percent of American-born taxi drivers are typically Puerto Ricans. In an effort to encourage more English speakers, the city authorities have plans to cut taxi-driver training to seven hours for "native New Yorkers" and double it to 80 hours for immigrant drivers. Question: What's the shortest measure of time? Answer: From when the lights go green to when a New York taxi driver honks behind you.

In central Manhattan it's a question of, "Shall we walk, or do we have time for a taxi?" Except when it rains and you can't find a cab anyway. Or, speeding uptown at night you might identify with Woody Allen in his movie "Manhattan": "God, you're so beautiful I can hardly keep my eyes on the meter."

But there's no such thing as a free lunch. Remember that most taxi drivers are self-employed entrepreneurs working long hours stuck in traffic with little thanks from customers, and frustrated that they're not running the country. If you are being taken for a ride, my advice is to close your eyes and think of market forces.

This is not hard to do in New York, where many taxi drivers have acquired a mastery of personalised asset-stripping that will leave the most rapacious Wall Street raiders gasping with admiration. (Question: What is the shortest measure of time? Answer: From when the lights go green to when a New York taxi driver honks behind you.) In central Manhattan it's often a matter of, "Shall we walk, or do we have time for a taxi?" Unless, of course, it's raining, when all self-respecting taxis disappear.

A Dublin taxi driver helped me give up smoking. I offered him a cigarette as we drove into town from the airport. "No, I won't, thanks all the same," he said. "The doctor told me that if I didn't stop smoking I could expect to live another six months." He caught my eye in the rear view mirror with the look I imagine a priest might throw you in anticipation of a more comprehensive confession. "So I thought, if I'm going to give up smoking I might as well give up drinking as well." "How do you feel?" "I feel grand. The only thing about it is that if you don't smoke and you don't drink, you have an awful lot of time on your hands."

My analyst couldn't do as well with £100 on the meter.

One of my most daunting experiences was arriving in Tokyo jet-lagged out of my mind and thinking I'd got a kamikaze driver at the airport when the cab shot out of the rank *onto the wrong side of the road*. I never dreamed the Japanese drive on the left like the British. The next day I was launched into an uncomprehending city with a taxi driver whose only recognisable word of English was Hilton, who had been briefed by the hotel porter and who was clearly losing his way. My advice is to take not only the address written out in Japanese but a survival kit of "deaf and dumb" cards bearing contingent expressions such as, "Take me to your leader," and, "I am British, take me to the nearest gin and tonic".

So I must say it's nice to be home, even though London taxi drivers are not quite as cuddly as the guide books like us to believe. But at least they know their way around (except for one genial mini-cab driver recently, who seemed to be following a street map of Karachi on the way out of London to Hatfield. My uncle Reg took to driving a taxi when he retired from the police. I didn't much care for his prowess at the wheel, but he knew London like the back of his hand.

Mind you, I always try to strike up a conversation with taxi drivers. First to establish credibility ("Do you think it's best at this time of night to take the Lincoln or the Holland tunnel?") and catch up on the news.

Usually they are ferociously well-informed on everything from sport ("Which brand of cigarettes will win the Monaco Grand Prix?") or affairs of state ("Is John Major trying to grow a moustache?").

Perhaps they should be running the country.

The people factor

1993 Business Life

'We consider our people to be our most important asset,' are familiar words in many a chairman's annual report. Words (if not sentiments) which ring a trifle hollow these days on both sides of the Atlantic as some of the bluest of blue chip companies shed thousands of staff in a desperate attempt to stem a fatal haemorrhage of cash and profits, like BP, British Aerospace, even IBM – 'Big Blue' itself. General Motors, the world's largest industrial corporation, with a turnover of around $120 billion, lost $17 billion on its North American car operations over the three years to the end of 1992. That's more than half the GNP of Ireland. This will mean closing 21 plants with a loss of 74,000 jobs from a total workforce of 360,000 over the next two years. Pundits say GM is impossible to save in its present form and may be sliding towards bankruptcy.

Blame it all on the recession, the economy. But hell, these companies are the economy ... no company is an island unto itself. Blame it on the Japanese.

Yes, yes, the Japanese. Japan Inc! They flood our marketplace with better products at better prices. How do they manage that? Not by the tired clichés: singing the company song at six in the morning; lifetime employment; quality circles; consensus decision making and bottom-up communications. But by better management. The bottom line is the end not the means. Market forces rule okay. What we can learn from the Japanese is interdependence; between people in the company and between the company itself and the community – reconciling social and corporate needs. And if corporate success is to be durable, it has to be based on the satisfaction, not only of shareholders, but of all the other stakeholders in a business – customers, suppliers and the community as well as employees. Arguably, it is unbridled, purblind pursuit of earnings per share, with high dividends to shareholders in the short term, especially in Britain, which has led to a neglect of critical long-term future. Short-term financial opportunism focuses attention on wrong criteria and often encourages managers to asset strip or close rather than to develop a business.

Japanese management focuses on the long-term prosperity (in the spiritual as well as material sense) of those in the firm and the community. Companies do not live by the bottom line alone. Interdependence – a team spirit rather then the competitive, often disruptive individualism we encourage in the West: the 'them and us' between managers and employees and between corporations and the community (akin to the adversarial tradition of Anglo-Saxon law – whereby justice does not necessarily evoke the truth). This means much more than lip service in the western sense to things like the 'social audit' (how green are our profits – or losses!). 'Get rid of the 14th floor,' Ross Perot said about the plush executive offices at the top of General Motors' Detroit head office. He wanted GM's managers to learn their business by working alongside the folk who actually make cars – which is what the top managers of Japanese car firms do. Dare I call it corporate socialist democracy? Yes, I dare! Contrast this with the finely-tuned pecking order of directorial perks at my last corporate job. How very *infra dig* to make coffee for my secretary, lunch in the canteen with my guys, answer my own phone, et cetera. Talk about management practice. It was small wonder they asked me to practise somewhere else.

On my first visit to Tokyo I asked a Mitsubishi executive how many people his company employed. About 400,000 he replied. Then quickly added, 'But we have over a million in the family.' He showed me a gold lapel badge: '25 years with the company," he puffs out his chest like a schoolboy. And he brought a printed card from his pocket: 'Our company philosophy.' It's easy to be snide. But there's something worthy, something daunting in truly believing. This is not just my meal ticket but my life. It stands the greed creed on its head.

A characteristic of organisational structure in companies today is that managers are given more responsibility than authority. The onus is upon them to come to terms with themselves in an ambiguous, more demanding role. What is vital today is the qualitative people side of management. The Japanese have taught us the crucial importance of the softer, human and visionary skills compared with the hard-nosed cognitive skills of our Western business culture. Which is why Japanese companies are often more successful at coping with a fast-moving, unpredictable business environment in which the only thing you can plan for is change.

Takeo Fujisawa, co-founder of Honda Motor Company, said that 'Japanese and American management is 95 per cent the same and differs in all important respects.' This is one of many maxims and paradoxes from a pathfinding book, *The Art of Japanese Management*, by two American academics, Richard Tanner and Anthony Athos, published in 1982. The authors illuminate the five per cent in a way which must make Western managers think very hard about all their duties and opportunities and we must endeavour to change who we are, as well as what we do, the authors urge.

I'd lost my paperback copy when it was 'borrowed' by a Swiss friend. So I was delighted to lay my hands recently on a hardback edition which contains a stimulating new (1986) introduction by Sir Peter Parker, the present chairman of Mitsubishi Electric UK – a Japanese speaker, Confucian scholar and a vocal admirer of Japan and her culture.

'The message is unmistakable. The Japanese win in so many markets in the world ...Why? Because of the skills of Japanese management,' Parker says. 'If we want to understand the success of Japan, and believe me, we all do, it's difficult, I believe, without studying some Confucianism ...This is basically optimistic, whereas Christianity is pessimistic. We need our Commandments, we need our Heaven and Hell, but in Confucianism there's a much more civic sense of the key virtues of a life – a sense of group loyalty, which is above all. Japanese management always builds on the unity of social and commercial purpose while Western management has not seen that as part of its job specification. That limited vision is the difference between us, West and East.'

The difference comes to light in a comparison of two archetypal companies: the giant Matsushita Electric Company, still presided over by the 86-year-old Konosuke Matsushita, and ITT under the less than benign auspices of notorious Harold Geneen. It was an uneven contest resulting in a 'spiritual knock-out for Geneen.' Whereas Matsushita 'has become a great corporation that makes more than money – an organisational system that meets the demands of its executives and employees, and it is "programmed" to adapt as may be necessary to changes that may come.' ITT fell apart after Geneen retired in 1979. Geneen made profits but at great human cost. He 'had not built a great corporation ...that achieves multiple goals ...the firm may not always have served the values of society at large, and could not withstand his departure ...To concede victory to Matsushita is to celebrate excellent management.'

The authors show that the striking differences between Matsushita and ITT were not in the so-called 'hard S's' – strategy, structure, and systems – but in the four 'soft S's' – style, staff, skills, and 'super-ordinate goals', the human values beyond profit to which we can dedicate our productive lives. We are talking about team spirit compared with the disruptive individualism that is encouraged in our business schools. There are fascinating chapters on Zen and the Art of Management and Bridging the Differences. As Sir Peter Parker writes: 'This book is a sophisticated revolutionary handbook for management.'

The revolution may emerge from the new political Zeitgeist in the Western world. At the heart of President Bill Clinton's economics is a preoccupation with asserting public goals in private markets. If his friend, guru and close adviser Harvard professor Robert Reich has any influence, he is aiming at the reorganisation of the entire framework in which companies operate – much more direct investment in human skills, and the infrastructure and environment - a new wave of interventionism (you might want to call it interdependence) which reflects Japanese (and German) models.

'The challenge of the Japanese art of management,' Sir Peter Parker says. 'It defines afresh just what the full-scale definition of entrepreneurial management adds up to... Increasingly and inescapably, the future manager – especially the international manager – will have to attempt the reconciliation of social and commercial worlds.'

The bottom line is that excellence in management as shown by the Japanese involves a holistic vision: an amalgam of science and art – of pragmatism and human values.

The Art of Japanese Management is published by Sidgwick & Jackson at £12.95. *For Starters, the Business of Life* by Sir Peter Parker has just been published in paperback by Pan at £6.99.

How to be a professional expatriate
1982 Rio Tinto Gazette

About 100 years ago, when I was running the European markets for a big American drug company, I was promoted, or exiled (I've never quite figured out which) to head office in Broken Springs, Indiana, from my regional headquarters in Geneva, Switzerland.

Of course, my job was the same; the company was simply undergoing a periodic swing of the pendulum from a decentralised to a centralised type of organisation. I exchanged my panoramic view of Lake Geneva for conditions more compatible with the puritan work ethic; an inside office with an inspiring view of the typing pool.

I accepted the challenge by keeping both my flat and office in Switzerland, getting the company to buy furniture for my pad in Broken Springs for the same cost as they would have incurred shipping my own stuff out, and making trips back to Europe so often and for so long that by the time the corporation had reinvented the wheel and decentralised, I was back in Geneva more or less unscathed – from a career point of view, that is. After all, as an outwardly – if not upwardly – mobile 'third country national,' I knew what to expect.

I received a change-of-address card the other day from an executive I had recruited in Toronto for a job in Madrid and then in Geneva. He had moved on to Manila with another company, then Caracas, Melbourne and Bern. He said he was off to Minneapolis this time, 'this is our 10th move in 17 years.' Neville, I'll call him, has made a career out of relocation, not simply moving up in the hierarchy but getting rich on a raft of allowances, from cost of living and offshore tax arrangements to education and home leave (home to Switzerland where I brought him, no less).

What these tales illustrate is that relocation is what you make of it: some survive, others thrive; it's a question of attitude – on the part of the person and the company. The needs of both must be congruent; get it right and you have a happy executive pursuing a successful career within the company; get it wrong and you have unhappiness, recrimination and expense. Most successful executives in multinational companies have learned to be professional expatriates. And the most successful multinational companies have learned that overseas postings can be a means of motivating and training executives with top management potential.

Relocation can provide an executive with the stimulus of job changes within the same company and work experience he or she might otherwise seek with another firm. The problem many mid-career executives face is how to make the transition from a functional role in marketing, finance or production to general management. A general manager may need to develop his international skills or further develop a specific functional skill. Relocation may be the answer in both cases, either to run a small subsidiary or to be finance director in a large one. This is a way for a company to nurture its executives and make sure they're still around when opportunities occur.

Easier said than done. US studies show that as many as one in five people sent to work abroad never finish their assignment – typically three years with major MNCs. A tremendous waste of human and financial resources, when you think that an overseas job shuffle can cost a company as much as $400,000.

It is often the family which is the cause of the problem. The executive has the excitement of a new job, familiar company procedures and a secretary to shield him from most local bureaucracy; his wife, however, has to face the full brunt of culture shock, and alien values in the minutiae of everyday living. She may find herself bored, frustrated, ill-at-ease and resentful – especially if she has had to give up a job of her own back home. And then, just when she most needs him, her husband takes off on the familiar round of business trips to the country they have just left. This often stretches a marriage or relationship to breaking point.

Then there may be a question of what to do about children's education – do you send them to a local school, an international school or a boarding school in the UK? This depends on how old they are, the quality of local schooling and how long you expect to stay. In my experience, children are good to have around; they pick up a new language with humiliating ease (my four year old daughter is teaching me German via her mother and corrects my French). They are also great ambassadors and are a sure-fire means of making new friends among the natives.

Living conditions vary so much from one country to another that it's almost impossible to give anything but general advice for adapting to a new life. The US government gives bonus payments to its employees posted abroad. They range from zero for countries considered most desirable (most European countries, Rio de Janeiro, Mexico City and Singapore), up to 25 per cent for countries such as Bolivia, Kuwait, Nigeria and some parts of Thailand, where significant hardship is likely to be experienced. Countries such as Jordan, Poland, Bahrain and the Philippines rate 15 per cent, and Egypt, Syria, the USSR, Pakistan, Peru, Jeddah and Riyadh in Saudi Arabia and Shanghai and Peking in China rate a 20 per cent hardship bonus.

Even countries which share Western values, such as Germany, France, Italy, Spain, the US and Australia can be a cultural and social minefield for the unwary; business etiquette such as relations with subordinates and ways of negotiating are fraught with danger. Wise companies take pains to select the right person for the job and brief both executives and their families, often on a residential course, before unleashing them on a subsidiary abroad. The professional expatriate is able to tread the fine line between adapting to the new environment and becoming too integrated. One doesn't want to live in a golden ghetto – cocooned in a sterile and inbred world of fellow expatriates, who have nothing in common except their language.

On the other hand, one needs to avoid fitting in so well that you're considered indispensable to an overseas subsidiary. You don't want to be like Lord Cockfield, who, some would say, had to leave the EC Commission for being a too enthusiastic advocate of the European ideal, or the Evelyn Waugh character: "The chap's gone native ... taken to wearing a belt instead of braces and ready-made shoes." Not the best augury for a promotion to head office, or even a lateral arabesque to a subsidiary in Zambia.

It has been said – and I'm the last to deny it -that successful executives have a talent for choosing predecessors and successors - the idea being that if you have three years in a job, you have one year to blame the previous guy, the second to reap the rewards and the last year to cook the books for the next guy (who, if he's astute, repeats the cycle). This is known as Management by Blame. I know people who have been thus promoted from disaster to disaster and ultimate triumph as chief executive and then to another company. But that's another story. Professional expatriates look out for the next posting almost as soon as they arrive by making sure they train and anoint their successor. Call it Management by Replacement.

I often wake up at three o'clock in the morning here in the South of France wondering what job I might have now if I'd had the sense to complete my stint in Broken Springs.

Kami's future: 'Only change is predictable'
1983 Chief Executive

Dr Michael Kami is one of the world's leading strategic planners. Formerly corporate director for long-range planning at IBM, and vice president, planning, for Xerox during the super-growth eras of both companies; he is now one of the most soughtafter advisers to corporations around the world.

Kami's own organisation, Corporate Planning, based in Florida, publishes the *Kami Strategic Assumptions*, an international quarterly newsletter for top management that focuses on socio-economic analysis, forecasting and management planning.

To his clients, who pay $5000 to hear a group lecture or $4500 for a day of individual counselling, Kami preaches a vision of the future where only change is predictable.

Kami says he grosses $1m a year for only working one day in four. This he finds adequate to finance his 200 or so days of what he calls 'unstructured time.'

What does he do with it? 'I study. Management, economy, social change. New *mores* of the American consumer. New shifts in pluralism. All very important. Above all, I have time to think. A normal executive doesn't have time to think.'

Kami believes that the biggest problem for business in managing the future is the inability of chief executives to adapt to change.

'The tragedy of modern management is either top management that does not want to move or top management wanting to move but middle management that drags its feet,' he says. 'In fact, middle management has become almost obsolete. You need good workers and top management, the rest can be done by computers.'

Kami says that his strategic planning system is more a philosophy of thinking. The key to it is getting the priorities right, deciding what is important and then concentrating on just that.

'The rest will fall into place. Someone in the organisation is going to do it. And if they don't, maybe it doesn't need to be done.

'If you have an obsolete product, focus on getting the product right. If you also focus on marketing, personnel and manufacturing, what good is it if the product is bad? If you could delegate the ten most unimportant tasks down the line, you'll end up with 20 people having 100 of the least important things to do. Maybe you should get rid of those people.

'Top management only spends 10 per cent of its time on important matters.'

I talked to Kami during his recent visit to Europe. This is what he told me.

RC: You ask us to plan ahead in an era of unpredictability, to 'expect the unexpected'. But isn't this a contradiction in terms?

MK: It sounds like a contradiction but actually if nothing would happen you wouldn't need to plan. The more unpredictable the conditions, the more you have to plan. You just have to plan on being flexible, on adapting very fast to changing conditions and be able to change in one second, on a dime as we call it, the policies of a company.

RC: What's the difference between "strategic planning" and the long range planning we've been doing for years?

MK: This is mostly semantics. People talk about short-range planning, about long-range planning, strategic, tactical, operational planning and so on. I say all that is bunk. You have to plan forward by an integrated planning process that takes care of the short and the long-range at the same time.

Roger Collis

RC: *How far ahead is it possible to plan?*

MK: The question is not how far ahead you can plan, but how far ahead you should plan. You should plan ahead for the length of time you take between making the decision on Monday morning and accomplishing that decision.

If it's a research programme, it may take seven years, so you plan seven years ahead. If it's a marketing programme that takes you six months to accomplish, you plan six months ahead. Don't plan ahead on the basis of some strange, theoretical five-year plan, because that doesn't make sense.

RC: *How do you build flexibility, adaptability, into your strategic planning?*

MK: The most important thing is to plan for the company. Survival of the company comes first: Let's say you have 1200 workers, It's better to let 300 go than lose the whole company. A great deal of flexibility is involved in being able to sub-contract, to change rules, to change production, to change your manufacturing, marketing, service organisation faster than ever before. That means, if you are able to change in a given time period, then divide that time period in two, and you have a faster, more flexible organisation.

RC: *There must be some areas you can plan for and some areas you can't plan for.*

MK: There are areas of international instability, of currency fluctuation, of governmental rules and so on, that you cannot really plan on. You can only set two assumptions; if it happens what will we do? If it doesn't happen what will we do? We should have an ability in the company, by looking at what is happening, to move in one or the other direction. This is the 'suppose if' type of planning.

RC: *You mean a kind of contingency planning?*

MK: Contingency is a bad word. It means you do some alternatives in case. Alternative planning means that if something is here (a) you do (a), if it's (b) you do (b). Sometimes (b) is better than (a).

RC: *Take the case of unpredictable currency fluctuations and raw material prices. How can a company come to terms with this through strategic planning?*

MK: Companies that are heavily dependent on a supply of raw material, whether it's silver or platinum, or oil, must be prepared in the future for three types of alternative planning: one, staying with the present raw materials if the price increase isn't too severe, two, being prepared for higher prices and checking out substitutes, and three, and most important, eliminating the need for a raw material.

You have the case of electronic cameras developed by the Japanese which eliminated the need for silver. So you have to choose the right road at the proper time – standard raw material, substitute of the raw material or elimination of the raw material. All that requires more thinking, a cleverer organisation, more segmentation of research and development, marketing and so on. These seem like buzz words, but they are very important for a company strategy.

RC: *Some pundits talk about the long-term business and economic cycle that lasts for 50 or 60 years. They say we are presently in a 'down wave': And that different strategies are required for an 'up wave': What are your views on this?*

MK: I do not believe in a wave which has a fixed cycle. This is because we have a geometric progression, an exponential progression, of technological change. If you say that the waves will be here, but they will be reduced in time and increased in amplitude, I would say, yes, that's a good theory. So, forget the "fixed time" pundits, this is as good as the ground hog day or whether the shadow is here or not, or counting lemons on a tree.

RC: Small firms tend to be innovative and a breeding ground for the new technology Is there any basic difference in applying your strategic planning system to small as opposed to large companies?

MK: The interesting paradox is that now all big companies would like to have entrepreneurs - what I call 'intrapreneurs', because a true entrepreneur would not stay in a large company. The key is to create many small companies within a large company. This can be done through a horizontal organisation, multi-profit centres and so on. We *do* want this innovative spirit. Small companies have a lot of future; they can move fast, they can take risks. So, very interestingly, the small companies should not try to be like the big companies. But big companies should try to get organised as if they were a series of small companies.

RC: To what extent is risk a part of strategic planning?

MK: Risk is an integral part of strategic planning. There is a basic policy that must be understood in the years to come: doing business is going to involve bigger risks than ever before because of change and unpredictability. In times of stress most companies want to reduce risk: But, by doing this, they increase risk. It's a good idea to subdivide your risks among a number of profit centres.

RC: *Doesn't a company have a problem finding and rewarding entrepreneurial managers?*

MK: Absolutely. The key need for a company, the only need for a company, is to have talent. And to have talent you have to attract talent. The problem is that large companies lose talent rather than attract it. How do you attract talent? You need to create a culture, an environment, rewards, that attract in unusual, undisciplined, innovative, non-organisation men. You ask them, "What do you want?" If I have a talented person, I give him what he wants, because he makes the difference. The rest of the people, the other 95 per cent, are average. Average people are expendable. Therefore, don't worry how the talented people dress, or how they behave.

RC: *A prime characteristic of the traditional entrepreneur is his intuition. To what extent is creativity and intuition a part of your planning process?*

MK: I have a formula; fifty per cent intuition, fifty per cent data and facts. If you are a hundred per cent intuition, you're flying by the seat of your pants. This person is very dangerous. If you're a hundred per cent data and facts person, you'll have paralysis through analysis and never make a decision. Fifty fifty. I don't want an entrepreneur, I don't want a bureaucrat. I want a combination. I call him a strategist.

RC: *Some companies have done well in the recession, some have failed. Can you give me some reasons why this has happened?*

MK: Some companies have a tremendous knack for adaptation - IBM for example. Traditionally, it only sold through its own salesmen, but when it saw there was a market for the personal computer, it completely changed its marketing strategy and started selling through department stores, agents and mail order. This is a tremendous adaptation to need. Other companies can see the need, feel the need and will never change a policy, because that is a tradition.

RC: *To what do you attribute the success of Japanese companies?*

MK: The Japanese are not as traditional as folklore seems to say. They are ad hoc, they adapt to the environment in a very pragmatic way. When other countries put up tariff barriers against them, they change their tactics, come into the country, set up a factory, and are able to out-produce the local people with the local labour. How do they do that? The Japanese have a dedication to quality and performance. They work through the entire level of management all the way to the worker on the floor.

RC: *Who in a company should be involved with strategic planning?*

MK: Certainly not a planner. I don't like planners. Planners should be planning coordinators; planning educators. The only people in a company who should plan, strategically or operationally, are the line managers, people who really have the responsibility for the profit and loss. So the first planner in a company is the chief executive officer. Staff is fine, but staff is only a tool of line management, not vice versa.

RC: *So keep strategic planning to the entrepreneurial cutting edge of the operation?*

MK: The top edge of the corporation, because at the top you have to determine which segments you want to enter, where you want to go. Once you determine that direction, then within that direction let's have entrepreneurial entry. You cannot be entrepreneurial on everything. You'll be so superficially spread that you won't have what we call 'critical mass' of entry. We have to be very segmented, but in each segment there must be a critical mass of action.

RC: *What do you see as the broad priorities and issues in the next two to three years?*

MK: There is a major change in the industrial complex of the world that has nothing to do with the recession. The so-called 'smokestack' industries, the heavy industries, will not be able to be profitable in industrial countries like Europe, United States, Canada. These heavy industries will be heavily mechanised and operated with cheap labour in Taiwan, South Korea, and Indonesia. We have to accept the continuing decay of the heavy industries, and rationalise. On the other hand, there is a plus to every minus. The plus is that the heavy industry making mass-produced commodities, will be replaced by high technology, fast moving, customisation. The service, knowledge, communications industry is really growing at 30 to 40 per cent per annum So we're in a major change from one type of economy to another.

Paws for thought
2005 International Herald Tribune

It's hard to separate fact and fiction these days. A letter from Joan Draper in Ramat Gan, Israel tells of her dog Turtle creating mayhem in transit at Paris Charles-de-Gaulle Airport, when he escaped from his unlocked cage, might have been a scene from Keystone Cops.

To lock or not to lock the cage of a traveling pet is a crucial concern for civil aviation.

But the arcane domain of frequent flier programs becomes even more surreal with news that Virgin Atlantic has launched a 'Flying Paws' reward program for traveling cats, dogs, and ferrets. (Rabbits, hamsters, crustaceans and ornamental tropical fish are left to make their own arrangements (www.defra.go.uk)

On their first flight Virgin Atlantic gives jet-setting pets a 'welcome onboard pet pack.' Dogs are given a 'Virgin doggy t-shirt and sparkling dog tag.' Cats are given a toy mouse called 'Red' and a Virgin collar tag; and ferrets receive 'a cool limited edition flying jacket and collar tag.'

Pets that travel on the European Union's Passport for Pets scheme are given a passport 'which not only gives them a record of all their flights, but allows them to collect "paw prints" which they will be able to redeem for gifts.' After 10, 15 and 20 flights pets can claim rewards from 'blow-dries and pedicures to Prado, Burberry, and Gucci pet clothing, to a personal "Pawtrait" from famous artist Cindy Lass, renowned for her paintings of celebrities [sic] furry companions around the world.' One paw print is awarded per flight; five paw prints brings a galaxy of goodies, such as handmade Virgin bowls plus a non-slip mouse mat so they can 'dine in style' or choose to donate their rewards 'worth £50' to their favorite animal charity or sanctuary.' 'If they're feeling especially loving toward their human friend, they can show their true feelings by donating 1,000 bonus air miles to his or her "Flying Club" account.'

How do I deal with readers' letters asking how to convert pet miles into people miles?

Question: 'My ferret Joshua has accumulated 100,000 pet miles in the Virgin Atlantic program. Can I redeem these for an upgrade to business class on my next flight to Orlando?'

Answer: 'Joshua and you should have reciprocal rights on flights taken separately or together. But check the exchange rate between pet miles and people miles. Joshua could be entitled to elite status with access to the cargo hold lounge. But do make sure that Joshua, or heaven forbid, the animal rights folk do not get to know what you are planning.'

Airlines have different requirements about carrying pets on board. Virgin Atlantic, in common with most carriers, does not allow pets to travel in the cabin with their owners. But they are individually collected at check-in and travel in a separate part of the hold from the baggage, with controlled temperature, and fed water, according to Marianne Jenson, a Virgin spokeswoman in London. Air France, one of the few dog-friendly airlines, allows dogs up to 5 kilograms to sit in the cabin; United Airlines allows 'small dogs or cats' to travel in a cage under the seat; guide dogs are confined to the hold. British Airways requires all pets to be checked in as 'excess baggage;' except for guide dogs which are allowed a seat of their own. Pets should not be sedated and given a light meal before traveling.

Take care to check quarantine and vaccination rules and make sure you have the documents you need. You'll find useful tips at www.hotdogsholidays.com.

China Southern Airlines joins our ongoing debate on the crucial issue of traveling with pets, with a charmingly succinct release in the apocryphal ('There's a French widow in every bedroom') guide book tradition.

'Pets are not allowed on board the aircraft, except for dogs for the seeing impaired.' This is because 'once a dog or a cat becomes agitated... it may run about the cabin and is very likely to bite off its restraining leash, or hamper flight attendants in their duty.'

Or 'the pet could carry bacteria or parasites and since the cabin is a sealed and constant temperature environment which is favorable to the multiply [sic] and infection of the bacteria, it could affect the health of passengers and aircrew.' What is more, 'some pets, such as mice, could easily throw passengers into a panic; and pets of any species can leave their droppings randomly in the cabin.' China Southern provides exemplary specifications on the size and the ventilation of pets' traveling boxes, 'which must be firm enough to prevent the pet from opening it from the inside, and able to hold the pet's droppings during the flight and ground handling,' along with the need for quarantine certificates.

'If you consign your pet to China Southern, it will enjoy a first class cargo service; it will not only be looked after before the boarding but also be supervised during the entire trip,' we are assured by Li Kun, chief operating officer at China Southern Airlines.

I am pondering the possible fate of my ferret Joshua on a hypothetical flight to Guangzou, when another release from China Southern, this time with a Chicago dateline, hits my mailbox.

It transpires that 470 'Canadian breeding pigs' were flown to Shenzen; 'accompanied on board with their own "welcoming ceremony" of a three-step disinfection.' After the 14-hour flight to China 'the foreign travelers were greeted in the Middle Kingdom with fire hoses and showered disinfectant.' Quarantine clerks 'inspected all swine documents' to see that there were 'no illegal aliens.' The 'porkers were humanely treated and had three in-flight meals during their journey.' That we should be so lucky! On the other hand – 'they did not get to see an in-flight movie, nor earn Sky Pearl Club frequent flier miles.'

So pigs *do* fly! Have a nice year.

Despite draconian measures to restrict hand baggage since the airline bomb scare last month, that still forbid one to bring liquids, whether bottled water or hand lotion, into the cabin on some flights, it is pretty much business as usual when it comes to traveling with pets; an issue of crucial concern to a growing number of readers.

While pets and their containers may now be required to pass through an X-ray machine, in addition to a metal detector, Air France (one of the world's most pet-friendly carriers) still allows cats and dogs of up to 5 kilograms to travel under your seat in the cabin; larger animals are consigned to the hold. British Airways still allows guide dogs to sit next to their owner free of charge; while Virgin Atlantic will welcome dogs, cats and ferrets (in the hold) and award them 'pet miles.' KLM hosts pets at an 'animal hotel' at Amsterdam's Schiphol Airport, where they are fed, walked and watered, and their cages cleaned before re-boarding. Humans should be so lucky! Itineraries and choice of airline can depend upon whether you can take a pooch or feline with you on board. So I was hardly surprised to learn from the American Pet Product Manufacturers Association, Norwalk, Connecticut, that 'pet travel soared 33 percent last year to a record 80 million and a full 14 percent, or 29 million, Americans travel with their pets.

'People love their pets, and love being with their pets, and that means hitting the road with them,' says Leslie Downey, director of communications at TravelersAdvantage.com.

'The surgingtrend in pet travel has put more bark in luxury vacations, and airlines and resorts are listening.'

I can hardly wait to take my ferret Joshua on his first flight with Virgin Atlantic, when he can claim his 'cool limited edition flying jacket and collar tag.'

Meanwhile, I am wrestling with a rising tide of anguished letters from peripatetic pet owners seeking the right airline, and the best route to fly with their pet – vaccination documents and quarantine rules, and arcane rules on certain breeds banned from cargo holds.

The latest pet conundrum arrives from Hans Carl, a reader, recently resident in Montreal-du-Gers, France, who asks how he can bring his 'hand-fed female green-gold yellow head Amazon' parrot over from Massachusetts.

'We have searched for information from American and French veterinary authorities, but have nowhere been able to get firm advice on what is needed,'

Carl says, 'Can she travel in the cabin (a cat cage does fine)? If not, is the hold safe for a bird?'

Alas, I can find no way for him to bring the bird – short of getting her to talk her way through security and on to a flight, or fit her with a homing device to fly the Atlantic. British Airways, Air France and Virgin Atlantic say they do not fly birds either in the cabin, or in the normal baggage hold, although nobody could explain exactly why (aside from a frivolous suggestion that a parrot might cause a noise disturbance in the cabin, especially if it were to bark commands in a strange tongue).

Warwick Smith, a spokesman at the Department for Environment, Food and Rural Affairs, in Britain (Defra.gov.uk), explained that there is a 'temporary ban on importing live birds' into any European Union country until December 2006, because of the risk of spreading avian 'flu, although there are exceptions in the case of 'endangered species.'

Yours revealingly

1994 Business Life

'The heavy blue notepaper crackled as the man signed his name… a dashing autograph, bigger by far than any of the text. It began well, rushing forward boldly before halting suddenly enough to split the supply of ink. Then it retreated to strangle itself in loops. The surname began gently, but then that too became a complex of arcades so that the whole name was all but deleted by well-considered decorative scrolls. The signature was a diagram of the man.'

No, this is not a graphologist's portrayal of my own unfair hand. It is author Len Deighton describing actor Marshall Stone in the opening paragraph of his novel, *Close Up*. I'm afraid you have to read the book for the exegesis.

I would have been more interested in some graphological revelations about Bernard Samson, the protagonist in the Deighton spy trilogies. Presumably,

Samson would have written in invisible ink. Although an office-coffee stain would no doubt have left him vulnerable to a Rorschach test. His handwriting may bear the angular traces of his childhood in Berlin. I would expect to see independence (wide spacing between words and lines); intuition (no initial hooks; long *t* bars to the right of the stem, and breaks between letters within the words) and humour (*i* dots as dash or arrow formation), in contrast to John le Carré's spook George Smiley – exacting and efficient – who would have a tight and angular hand.

Whether or not handwriting actually reveals character is far less important than our willingness to believe that it does. Graphology is like extra-sensory perception, astrology, and palm-reading in that most people hope that there is something in it, somehow, somewhere, and preferably for us.

I must say I've dabbled in them all at some time or other. I used to spend hours trying to analyse the handwriting of various girl friends (with conspicuous lack of success); I once thought of asking a famous clairvoyant to intercede with a headhunter on my behalf; I had a half-fledged entrepreneurial notion of marketing executive horoscopes; and after a palm-reading session I thought of having plastic surgery to correct a weak career line, followed by a laser job to ensure the fortunes of my love life.

Handwriting, though, is not easily managed. I have always suspected that my deteriorating scrawl has been trying to tell me something I would prefer not to know.

Time was when I wrote with great speed, if not gusto, and putative aplomb. Nowadays, I can barely read my own notes. I am amazed that the bank still recognizes my signature from that of 30 years ago. There is less confidence now in the mushroom sort of *R* and the way it trails off at the end. And I have taken to underlining it which apparently shows a craving for recognition. Thank heavens for the anonymity of the computer, except I hear they can now analyze your key-strokes. And they've brought out a screen which you write on with an electronic pen. Welcome to the science of computer graphology.

Graphologists (who like to think of themselves more as forensic psychologists than handwriting experts) claim extraordinary powers of percipience and prescience. The science goes back a long way. Nero is said not to have trusted a courtier 'because his handwriting shows him treacherous.' Not a subject for fiddling.

Apparently, the CIA used graphologists to suss out spies during the Cold War – although Cyrillic script can be tricky I'm told. *The Economist* reported that at least five percent of U.S. businesses use graphologists to pick staff. And quoted an American graphologist as saying that Germany had, in 1980, almost as many graphologists as dental surgeons. Something for graphologists to get their teeth into.

Graphologists sometimes try to gain credibility by pointing out the obvious traits of famous people – retrospective analysis, or hindsight. This is fairly easy with the monsters of history: the 'vicious and jagged strokes of Himmler;' 'muddy pressure of Joseph Stalin, which gives a clue to his innate brutality' (I know lots of people with 'muddy' writing); 'compare the evolving signatures of Napoleon: in his prime – tenacity of purpose; forcefulness and power with a ferocious underscore – and after his defeat – more reflection, with unhappiness in the downward slant.'

On the other side of the page as it were, it's easy to discern the 'lyrical spirituality' in the handwriting of St. Francis of Assisi, and in Beethoven, 'the genius for counterpoint,' which is shown in single down-strokes; while in the analysis of a famous tycoon, 'single down-strokes with no lower loops means a balanced judgment.'

It seems easy to spot the obvious traits in handwriting, such as ambition, drive and energy in soaring lines; temper and tenacity in strong pressure and 'finals with hooks;' sensitivity in wide loops; vanity or vulgarity in ostentatious and embroidered capitals; or how introverted or extroverted a person is by the size of their writing. But I find it hard to believe that a strong letter *I* necessarily denotes selfishness; that a capital *S* written like a dollar sign has anything to do with financial ability, or that an *S* like a musical clef means an interest or ability in music.

Graphologists go further than this. They claim to spot the typical features of talent and aptitude for any vocation or profession you care to mention. For instance, the handwriting of a successful business executive shows 'constructive ability' in his or her printed capitals, along with 'strong will, sense of direction, and a capacity for organized, judicial planning' shown by heavy, even pressure and large writing. An advertising man will have larger writing 'which shows a desire to do things on the grand scale; small letters may not always be uniform, showing difficulty in concentrating because so many ideas often flash into his mind at the same time.' You think you're a salesman? Think again if you don't have 'a down-stroke in the *t* bars indicating aggressiveness', and if the writing does not flow to the right 'showing you want to be of service to other people, while trying to impose your will upon them at the same time.' A creative salesman has all this and much, much more, such as a tendency to make breaks in words, which show he is 'intuitive, inspirational.' You want to be a doctor? Eat your heart out if your handwriting is not entirely illegible. (Sorry, I made that up.)

If graphologists can read character from a person's handwriting, it should follow that my changing your handwriting you can change your character, or at least redress a few bad habits. Step into better handwriting and build a better career.

I hardly had time to applaud my prescience (shown by the breaks between letters in my handwriting) when somebody told me about the Greenglass Graphology Clinic in the heart of Tunbridge Wells. It transpired that Professor Barrie Greenglass – a fugitive from orthodox graphology – had developed a therapy to revive graphology analysis victims. What he does is 'reconstruct' errant handwriting through what he calls 'designer traits.' Take your choice from Machiavelli and Clausewitz to Sigmund Freud and Harry Houdini.

New careers for old. 'Yes, Mr. C, there are faint signs of culture in your separate, small printed letters though I suspect you're just doing that in a hopeless attempt at legibility. Your *t* bars are catastrophic, flying away in all directions. Have you considered a career in French polishing?

'What can we do about it? Well, I suggest you firm up the *t* bars to show purpose and self-control and later, later, make them fly off a bit at the end to show a modicum of ambition. Then I want to see high *i* dots: this shows imagination and ability to plan ahead, sharp vision... and then your capital *I* as a simple down-stroke – no hooks please! – this shows essential analytical purpose. And you must start using Greek formations of *d* and *e* and the *g* made like a figure 8, to show a cultured background and an ability to adapt. People making this kind of *g* have intellectual flexibility, and are able to manage, no matter what they see ahead. Remember, no lower loop shows good judgment.

'You want I should go on?' Greenglass went on. 'Yes, well, you want to start connecting up letters, perhaps sometimes words. This will show power, mental energy, and executive ability. And finally, I must insist, no initial hooks. You've got to show yourself a quick thinker, with a copious flow of ideas...'

Bizspeakmanship

1994 'Roger and Out,' Business Life

In the old days, the adage was 'It's not so much what you know but who you know.' These days, it's also a question of 'how well you know how to say it.' In bizspeak, that is. In other words, if you want to be a 'mover and shaker' with a 'pro-active control position,' you'd better acquire 'intrapreneurial' skills (entrepreneurial skills inside the company). Of course, it depends how 'buttoned down' (how formal or bureaucratic) the company is. Get it wrong and you may find yourself making a 'lateral arabesque' or worse, becoming a candidate for 'outplacement.' So make sure you have a 'golden parachute.' You may also need to consult a neologist or attend a seminar in advanced semantics at Harvard Business School.

Talking of seminars, I had a deeply disturbing semantic experience during a lecture on 'artificial intelligence' when the only expression I recognized as belonging to the English language was the term 'Chinese walls.' It came up so many times that I decided to risk a 'high profile' intervention by raising my hand and asking what it meant.

There was a brief Batemanesque moment, after which it transpired that a

Chinese wall is a means of prohibiting the exchange of sensitive information between two or more departments or systems, such as the underwriting and brokerage areas of a financial institution.

Imagine my surprise when people came up to me at the coffee break and said 'We're so glad somebody asked that question. We didn't know exactly what Chinese walls are either!'

'China hands' will recall 'Chinese Wallpaper' (junk bonds of the 1960s – don't ask me what junk bonds are); the 'Chinese water-torture tactic' (a takeover ploy where a predator gradually buys more and more shares in the market) and 'Chinese fire drill' (mass confusion within management).

Bizspeak has been with us for a long time. In the army – pioneers of management science – I underwent a course at OCTU (Officer Cadet Training Unit), having successfully passed WOSBE (War Office Selection Board) interviews. Everyone spoke (or shouted) in acronyms – we had a class on 'army abbreviations.' I'm sure you're dying to know that CIGS means 'Chief of the Imperial Staff,' not a packet of Rothmans.

Nowadays, everyone speaks bizspeak. An American I met on a plane was worried because his credit card had 'maxed out.' I suggested that he should acquire a 'revolver' (credit which when repaid can come round and be borrowed again). This, I pointed out, is different from a 'bullet,' a loan on which the principal is payable entirely at maturity and the interest is payable periodically. The guy wasn't amused. But that's life at the sharp end.

All of which leads me to think that when the CHIPS (Clearing House Interbank Clearing System) are down, jargon has two main functions: short-cut communications between initiates, and to repel (no pun intended) outsiders. At its best, it reveals meanings; at its worse, it obscures them. Obscure, imprecise, language reveals opaque thinking (we think in words, but should never let words do our thinking). At its worse, bizspeak is muddy and pompous: at its best, it can be concise, colorful and nicely ironic; enhancing or 'exploding' the meaning rather than obscuring it. What's sure is that bizspeak is washing over us in an ever-swelling tide. Language is made up of current usage whether we like it or not. So we may as well come to terms with it and have some fun as well.

Roger Collis

The first step to bizspeakmanship is to buy a copy of Biz Speak by Rachel S Epstein and Nina Liebman, published last year by Franklin Watts in the U.S. The authors have assembled and defined 2,000 words and expressions alphabeti cally in dictionary style; emphasis ing the 'new and humorous'. They cover 15 fields: Accounting, Banking, Computers, Economics, Finance, Human Resources, International Business, Management, Marketing, Media/ Publishing, Non- Profit, Operations, Real Estate and Retail. At the back of the book is an index of all terms according to category. And entries are cross- referenced, which can set you off on an endless adventure trail.

Some of the most colorful terms come from the world of high finance (along with low ethics) and asset-stripping (ripple dissolve to 2008). For example, 'greenmail,' paying off a raider by re-purchasing shares at a higher-than-market-price (for which you have to pay 'feemail' – what lawyers charge for greenmail cases). 'Landmail' is similar to greenmail, except the raider is bought off with land. Both might start with a 'bootstrap offer,' a takeover ploy in which a raider first uses a small shareholding as collateral to raise his stake, which might be followed by a 'bear hug,' in which the 'wooden tops' (directors) are offered a deal they cannot refuse.

A classic defence to a hostile takeover is a 'poison pill' (not to be confused with a 'suicide pill'). A 'white knight' may come charging to the rescue, failing which a 'white squire' defence (getting a friendly investor to buy a large block of shares) may save a victim from takeover. A new ploy is the use of 'shark repellents,' devices such as selling the 'crown jewels' (the most desirable parts of a company), which are sometimes offered to the white knight). Some companies employ consultants ('shark watchers') to identify the buyers of large blocks of its shares.

However, none of these are 'golden rules.' This means, 'he who has the gold
However, none of these are 'golden rules.' This means, 'he who has the gold
makes the rules, which probably means he is a 'heavy hitter' – a powerful person with a lot of money or brains.

Management provides semantic gold in the form of 'golden hellos,' 'golden handcuffs,' 'golden circles,' 'golden eggs,' 'gold plating,' 'golden handshakes,' and 'golden parachutes.' Along the way, you may be wooed by a 'body snatcher,' or perhaps a 'body shop' – headhunters who throw lots of bodies at clients in the hope that one is sure to stick. For how long will depend on the 'commitment window' – the length of time a professional manager is willing to give to one company – not to be confused with a 'launch window', a marketing term which means the opening through which a product is unleashed on the world, or a 'time window', as in, 'I only have a window of three hours a day with New York.'

If you find yourself to be 'down-sized' humiliating at the worst of times – or 'involuntarily defenestrated' (sorry, I just made that up) you may be in line for one of the 'golden goodies' (gee-gees?). And so it goes.

Then, of course, we have the versatile 'management by...' epithets. Epstein and Liebman list four: the once fashionable MBO ("Management by Objectives"); "Management by Exception" (MBE); "Management by Intimidation" (MBI) and "Management by Wandering Around" (MBWA), a form of "hands-on" management.

My own contributions to management bedlam and strife (MBS) include Management by Rumour (MBR); Management by Surprise (MBS); Management by Absence (MBA); Management by Blame (MBB); Management by Consensus (MBC) and Management by Replacement (MBR). All of which may involve 'Mickey Mouse' (big effort with few results), and it may be advisable to KISS (Keep it Simple Stupid); preferable to KITA (Kick in the Arse), a practice which, according to social scientist Frederick Herzberg leads to 'movement without motivation.' In the course of which, you may be awarded with an OBE (Overtaken by Events). At any rate, MBJ (Management by Jargon) seems to be here to stay.

'Consumer motivation' is, of course, what marketing people worry about. One of the first steps in creating advertising is to define your 'target group.' This used to be a simple matter of 'demographics' (Our prime target group should be the ABC1s, with some emphasis towards the C2s'). Now we talk about 'psychographics' and 'lifestyle' advertising. This will take account of 'aspirational undercurrents' (hidden dreams) and may be combined with 'wet-dream' demographics' (the discovery of 'very exciting' customer groups).

We all know about yuppies (young urban professionals), but I wonder if you've heard of 'yumpies' (young upwardly mobile professionals); 'ruppies' (rich urban professionals – yuppies who have made it); 'dinkies' (dual income no kids yuppies); 'guppies' (ecologically minded yuppies); 'coruppies' (yuppies of dubious ethical standards); 'doppies' (divorced older people); and 'woopies' (well-off older people).

Sooner or later, some 17-year old genius is going to combine product with target group and name a breakfast cereal after one of these acronyms. What you might call 'yupscale positioning.'

A worthwhile book from this side of the Atlantic is Longman/Guardian's New Words, a dictionary of politics, business social issues and leisure. It gives the etymology of each entry as well as examples to show how a word or expression has been used in the media. Existing words have taken on new meanings ('hacker'), new compounds have been assembled ('lap-top', 'off-the-wall') and completely new words have evolved ('greenmail', 'mega merger').

The book complements that of Epstein and Liebman in surprising ways. I found examples of how prefixes, like 'mega' (mega-loan, mega-worry, mega-bid, mega-sulk, mega-buck ...), and suffixes, like 'friendly' (user-friendly, customer- friendly, audience-friendly ...) are crucial building-blocks in bizspeak.

There's even a reference to 'yuppie-gate', a scandal involving five young financiers (The Yuppie Five) accused last year of stealing secret information and of insider dealing.

But my favorite is the '-gate' series from William Safire, the columnist and pop-lexicographer of The New York Times, who wrote the other day about the White House aide who padded his expenses in a 'Double-Billingsgate'.

'How to' books on management style have become a major growth industry. Kenneth H. Blanchard and Spencer Johnson, authors of The One-Minute Manager, and Thomas J Peters and Robert H Waterman Jr., who wrote the bestseller, In Search of Excellence, are laughing all the way to the bank (see, Laughing all the Way to the Bank, by Arnold Fishmouth). Fans are no doubt looking forward to sequels: Sons of Excellence and Sons of Excellence Ride Again, The 30-Second Manager; Playing for Time; Bogus Management; and How to look like somebody - without being anybody at all.

Other seminal titles include Twenty Ways to Improve Your Presentation Power; The Art of Getting Fired, or Beyond the Peter Principle, The Invisible Hierarchy, and Zen and the Art of Holiday Management; Japan on Two Faux Pas a Day by Stanley Zilch, and Clausewitz's classic Holidays: the Extension of Politics by Other Means,

It's certainly been nice interfacing with you. And I hope this has been consumer-friendly. My message is, don't wait for bizspeak to zap you. Next time someone off-loads a lot of semantic kludge that you don't understand, the chances are that he doesn't either. So zap him back with a blizzard of acronyms. You'll find plenty in the books I've mentioned (real or imagined). Or else do some zero-base wordsmithing of your own.

At the end of the day, this is the bottom line.

It's not what you say... It's how you say it
2002 The Survivor's Guide to Business Travel

Ralph Waldo Emerson's counsel 150 years ago that 'No man should travel until he has learned the language of the country he visits' is reflected in the boom in language learning for business travelers. The key to success, we are told, is to do business in the other person's language.

But unless you can really cope in that language, it's usually best to save it for social chat. A little learning is a dangerous thing (although a few gracious phrases in, say, Chinese, Arabic and Russian, are always appreciated.) English, of course, is now accepted as a *lingua franca* for business travelers in most parts of the world. But forcing people to speak it when they're not completely fluent can lead to serious misunderstanding.

There was the case of a former German chancellor who was presented to the Queen during a visit to London. He had brushed up his English for the occasion. But when he was introduced to her he said, 'Who are you?' instead of, 'How are you?' She replied, 'I am the Queen of England.' That's supposed to be a true story.

A good compromise is for both parties to speak their own language, which may bring a dialectical if not an entirely cultural, meeting of minds. Although it may be worth remembering the old German adage that you should sell in the other language and buy in your own. A variation, perhaps, of the maxim 'Dress British, think Yiddish.'

For most people this means speaking through interpreters. But the ability to work well with one is a technique, a skill in itself. You have to make sure that your message is received in a cultural as well as a linguistic sense.

You have to be very careful about using humor on formal occasions. If you make an after-dinner speech in the UK, you're heavily criticized if you don't make a joke; in France you'll be criticized if you do. They'll say, he's a clown, he's a lightweight. The British self-mocking humor is not understood.

It can be quite disconcerting with simultaneous interpretation. You make a witty remark and those people listening in English laugh; then the French and Italians laugh; then there's a pause because the Dutch and Germans are waiting for the verb at the end of the sentence before they get it. Meanwhile, you're saying, 'yes, but to be serious I must make an important point.' At which point the Germans and Dutch burst out laughing.

The Japanese seem to have found a face-saving solution to this contingency. The story goes of the Japanese interpreter who said: 'The British gentleman has now started telling a joke. When he stops speaking, please laugh and clap loudly – or I'll be in trouble.'

Another solution when faced with strange English from a non-native speaker is to tune in to the French translation – or tune in to space music on your iPod.

Alas, this is not always possible in face-to-face meetings. Everything depends on the skill of the interpreter. Confusion generated by faulty translation is less hilarious. Experts recommend that both parties in a negotiation bring their own people to interpret for important discussions. It's convenient, but dangerous, to rely on the home side's interpreter, who may unconsciously represent the interest of his or her employer.

Keep sentences short and simple but avoid oversimplifying – which may give an impression that you're condescending – and pause frequently. Avoid vague and imprecise expressions; use visual aids when you can; and look at the person with whom you're dealing – not the interpreter; look for signs of confusion; keep eye contact when culturally appropriate (in the Far East it's sometimes interpreted as aggressive or challenging behavior – only the occasional glance into another person's face is considered polite).

When it comes to the Far East, it's not so much 'read my lips' as 'read my mind.' The silences between utterances are just as meaningful as what is spoken. The Japanese method of listening comprises a repertoire of smiles, nods, and polite noises. The idea is to keep you talking, usually misinterpreted by Westerners as agreement.

If the Japanese have a reputation for inscrutability, it is because they have developed ambiguity of expression to an art form. They have delicate ways of voicing personal opinions. The British may have invented circumlocution (not to mention elocution) but the Japanese have made it an art form. It's not that they're hypocritical. But they manifest quintessential politeness, which can mean they say 'yes' when they really mean 'no.'

The Japanese are concerned with saving face and have developed a set of rules to prevent things going wrong. So try to avoid saying no or asking questions when the answer might be no. If you do hear a no in Japan, it is likely to be expressed as a sucking of breath through the teeth. The closest anyone will get to articulating the word no is, 'It is very difficult,' or 'We will need to give this further study.' The real message is likely to be, 'Let's forget the whole business.'

Closer to home, there are defective cognates between languages like English and French. The *entente cordiale* was in jeopardy when the French head office of its recently acquired subsidiary in Britain faxed: 'We demand your latest profit figures…' *Demander* in French means to ask, not to demand.

Much more important than language, the psychologists, say, is your 'non-verbal behavior,' your awareness of different 'business modes' and 'nonverbal behavior' or body language. This must take into account different notions of politeness, manners and social rituals. Actions speak louder than words. Saying the wrong things – eye contact, hand gestures, touching, bowing, using first names, how to eat and drink can be a minefield for the unwary.

Roger Collis

The snappily-dressed young Chinese in Hong Kong with the portable phone may seem to talk the same business language, but if you unintentionally offend him, you may lose his trust – and his business.

You first need to know whether you are dealing with people from so-called 'low context' cultures (North America, Britain, Sweden, Switzerland, Germany), who spell things out verbally, or 'high context' cultures (France, Japan, Spain, Greece, Saudi Arabia, China and Korea) who communicate more by nuance and implication and are less dependent on the spoken word.

For example, the Swiss and the Germans like to lay their cards on the table. Talking to a Frenchman or a Spaniard, what is unsaid is often most important. Low context folk need to attune their listening skills; high context folk should try to be more explicit. 'Your context or mine?' is the dialectical ideal.

Every executive looking for a short cut to the top pays attention to essential subjects, such as strategic wardrobe management; office politics and etiquette; resumé expansion (as management guru Peter Drucker was fond of saying, 'Don't talk to me about the death of the novel as long as we have resumés') and how to make buzzwords work for you.

In the real world the only thing that counts is performance, recent performance; anything that happened before the close of the last quarter is ancient history.

But while cutting costs, increasing market share and reducing employee turnover are good measures of performance, they are not enough. When a company evaluates executive performance, perception is reality.

You have to project the right image at all times if you want to rise above second-rate jobs like vice president.

Let's take 'moving and shaking.'

First impressions are important. The handshake is your first line of offense (no pun intended) when meeting clients or colleagues. There are many types of handshakes used in business and it's important to master as many of them as possible.

Here's a guide to expand your repertoire and your ability to 'read' the handshakes you receive.

The straight shake: Hands meet fully extended and clasp with moderate strength for no more than three seconds. This classic shake developed after long hours of practice is the international standard for business executives everywhere. Use this shake accompanied by at least five seconds of eye contact and a sincere, slightly wry, smile, when you want to break the ice at board meetings or job interviews.

The sincere shake: This is a variant of the 'straight shake' except that you use your left hand to cup your opponent's elbow or pat him on the back. You may or may not want to extend it into a hug.

The two-for-shake: This hearty variant of the 'sincere shake' is the favorite of enthusiastic types everywhere, such as salesmen and real estate agents.

The trick here is to reinforce the 'straight shake' with a blind side attack with the left hand; also used by drunken acquaintances at conventions, especially if they're trying to weasel a job or contract out of you.

The shake down: This is the hall mark of jovial athletes, or self-made millionaires who regard every encounter as an opportunity for hand-to-hand combat. It is similar to the 'straight shake' except for the intensity of application and the more extended duration.

To perform this shake, first work out for several months with a wrist exerciser. Give your opponent a solid six count before you deliver the release.

The golden handshake: This one is particularly effective when dealing with foreign governments, local politicians, or journalists posing as Middle Eastern oil sheiks. It is also known as the '**sheik down shake.**'

The soul shake: This is basically the old 'peace and love' shake of the hippie era; helpful when you want to show contemporaries that you haven't lost that phony maverick anti-establishment spirit. It's mostly used between men, especially old friends, or former colleagues, who often greet each other somewhat ironically.

You raise your right hand (or left hand, if you are a southpaw, or want to nonplus your opponent) while keeping a close eye on the other guy's approach. If his arm is more tipped upward, you should quickly adjust and move in thumb first. The shake may or may not be followed by the sliding of the hands and an additional grasp of the fingertips and a pop on the release.

Women executives should avoid this shake as it can send the wrong signals. Each of these variant techniques has its place. If you find yourself in unfamiliar surroundings, or in any doubt whatsoever, opt for the low risk strategy and deliver the 'straight shake'.

The handshake is probably the most common form of greeting in the world (except in Japan). But even this simple gesture is fraught with complications. The British handshake is firm but used sparingly; in Italy and France – where handshaking is something of a national pastime (the French are said to spend 30 minutes a day shaking and re-shaking hands) –a gentler, kinder grip may stand you in good stead.

In Germany and Denmark, you nod your head when you shake hands as a gesture of respect. Somebody who does not know this may interpret it as aggression (which it may well be). People in Mediterranean countries sometimes tilt the head back when they shake hands. Northerners may interpret this for arrogance (which it may well be). Anglo-Saxons learn to look people in the eye. This is sometimes interpreted as aggressive or challenging behavior, especially by Orientals, for whom only an occasional glance into the other person's face is considered polite.

Unless you really know what you're doing, close bodily greetings are best avoided.

Kissing has many pitfalls – unless you are fortunate enough to have been coached by a French general. You need to know which cheek to start with. The British start with the right cheek. In Belgium and Switzerland you start with the left cheek; left, right, left. The French generally kiss twice; left, right. In some Middle East countries they kiss three or even four times – men kiss men, women kiss women. (In Saudi Arabia, greetings are particularly elaborate: after shaking hands a Saudi is likely to kiss you on both cheeks then take your hand in his as a gesture of kinship.)

Should you ever summon the nerve to kiss a lady's hand (a French aristocrat says it takes three generations to learn how to do it properly), your lips must never actually make contact. In Spain, men who are close friends often give a bear hug, or *abrazo*. The story goes that a British businessman so shocked the Americans he was with when he greeted a Spaniard with a hug, that he almost lost the contract he was negotiating. Look out now for the Slavonic bear hug.

Women executives are constantly confronted with male counterparts who are unsure whether to kiss, shake, or use an alternative technique, such as a smile and an awkward bow.

If you don't want to be kissed, put out your hand when your opponent is at least five feet away and offer them the 'straight shake;' if he or she ignores your signals and tries to kiss anyway, stop them cold with a bone-crushing 'shake down.'

One area where handshakes, kissing and (heaven forbid) bear hugs have not become established is Japan where such bodily contact is considered impolite. On the other hand, the Japanese custom of bowing can be daunting to a Western businessperson. (Let your hand slide down towards your knees, back and neck stiff with eyes averted.) The act has crucial social implications, depending on title. It is essential for Japanese to know the ranking order within any group because rank is applied to all circumstances – whether business or social.

The way other cultures like to put people at their ease can be confusing. The American use of first names as an instant form of friendship does not go down well in countries like Germany, even England. (Germans like to be addressed by their last name with full academic titles, like Professor Dr. Schmidt, rather than Willy or Ilse. In Austria, you have to contend with Dr. Dr. Schmidt. In Italy, address anybody over 40 wearing a suit as *Dottore*.)

The British and Americans share at least one thing: they like to break the ice with a joke, which means sometimes being thought flippant. We in turn may think the Japanese are amused if they giggle: but they may sometimes do this when they are perplexed. In Japan, Korea and China, laughter is often a sign of embarrassment. In the Philippines it can mean, 'Take note! I'm about to say something important!' And Thais laugh at tragic news to cheer you up. (Something we are all getting used to now!)

The classic Anglo-Saxon 'time is money' approach to negotiations is unlikely to go down well in Asian societies, which are based on personal relationships and building reciprocal trust before agreeing to clinch a deal.

Roger Collis

The cold call often brings the cold response.

The Japanese in particular set great store by long term relationships and human value. They need to know the sort of person they are dealing with. An evening's karaoke or a day's golf isn't enough. One must submit to an exhausting spiritual inquisition. 'What are your first impressions of Japan?' Four pairs of liquid black eyes are hanging on my reply. I venture something about the felicitous co-existence of tradition and the modern industrial state. 'What impresses me,' I hear myself say, 'is that traditional values seem to be an integral part of the business and social fabric. And that tradition is more than ever relevant in these protean times...'

I seem to have passed the test. My host smiles. 'It is important for the Japanese to explore the heart of the person he does business with.' And refills my cup from his own *sake* flask, a gesture of friendship.

Consequently, the Japanese take much longer than business people in the West to make a decision. They are more committed to group consensus. But once everyone is on board, implementation can be swift. The getting-to-know-you process often takes weeks or months instead of hours and days. Reaching an agreement takes five times longer than it does in the west. But it's usually time well invested.

If you're late for a meeting or dinner in the Philippines nobody cares. But elsewhere in Asia it's a fatal faux pas. But don't be surprised at constant interruptions during meetings in India, Africa and the Middle East, especially with ministry officials. People rarely instruct the secretary to hold calls or tell unscheduled visitors to wait. This would be inexcusably rude to legions of friends and relatives who are likely to drop by unannounced at any time.

Meetings themselves can drive Anglo-Saxons to distraction. The French style of working is often incomprehensible to us. For example, in America or northern Europe, the point of having a meeting is to get decisions made or to allocate projects. The French meeting (which can go on for three or four hours, even longer than the business lunch) may not have a particular agenda. People simply talk and talk, with the idea of putting themselves in context – as the sociologists say – with other people. It's a form of jockeying for position and networking. Consequently, the French work long hours. You often find French managers in the office at seven in the evening. They manage to get things done, although not always to deadlines, which don't have the same awesome imperative as they do *chez nous*.

People set great store by details of etiquette. Gestures need not be extravagant or deliberate to be considered offensive. For example, in the Middle East, never give or receive anything with the left hand (which was traditionally used for cleaning up after bodily functions) or sit showing the sole of your shoes. And it's often considered impolite to refuse refreshments.

Even a classic Anglo-Saxon OK sign – a thumb-finger circle – can get you into trouble. In Brazil, Russia and Greece it is considered vulgar, even obscene. In Japan it signifies money and in France zero or worthless. In Finland, folded arms are a sign of arrogance, while in Fiji, the gesture shows disrespect. In Java, placing your hands on hips means you are looking for a fight. So place your hands on the table out of trouble.

Except at an English dinner party, of course, when they should be placed on your knees, when you're not actually eating. (In France, place them by the side of your plate.) And in Japan remember not to speak when you're eating (not to be confused with speaking with your mouth full). And, of course, Americans have this curious habit of cutting a piece of something, putting the knife down then switching the fork to their right hand. No wonder they invented fast food.

People do business with those whom they feel comfortable. It comes down to sincerity and spontaneous good manners.

If you're not sure how to behave in someone else's culture, then at least be polite in your own. Unless, of course, you are into power behavior.

But that's another story.

Roger Collis

Some survive, others thrive

1993 Resident Abroad

Some years ago, when I was running the European markets for a big American drug company, I was promoted (or exiled – I've never quite figured out which) to the corporate Kremlin in Broken Springs, Colorado, from regional headquarters in Lausanne.

Of course, my job was the same (only harder to carry out); the company was simply undergoing a periodic swing of the pendulum from a decentralized to a centralized organization. I exchanged my panoramic view of Lac Leman for conditions more compatible with the Protestant work ethic: an inside office with an inspiring view of the water cooler.

I accepted the challenge by keeping my office and apartment (plus company car) in Switzerland, persuading the company to let me buy furniture for my new place in Broken Springs for the same cost as they would have incurred shipping my stuff out, and making my trips back to Europe so frequent that by the time the company had reinvented the wheel and decentralized once again, I was back in Lausanne more or less unscathed – from a career point of view, that is. After all, as an outwardly – if not upwardly – mobile 'third country national,' I knew what to expect.

I received a change of address card the other day from an executive, Gerald, whom I had recruited in Toronto for a sales job in Madrid and subsequently in Lausanne. He had moved on to Manila with a soft drinks company, then to Caracas, Melbourne and Bern. He said he was off to Minneapolis this time: 'this is our tenth move in 17 years.' Gerald has made a career out of relocation, not simply moving up in the hierarchy but getting rich on a raft of allowances, from cost of living and offshore tax arrangements to children's education and frequent home leaves.

What these tales illustrate is that relocation is what you make of it. Some survive, others thrive; it's a question of attitude – on the part of both the individual (and his or her family) and the company. The needs of both must be congruent. Get it right and you have a happy executive pursuing a successful career within the company; get it wrong and you have all-round unhappiness, recrimination and expense.

Most successful executives in multinational companies have learned how to be professional expatriates. And the most successful multinationals have learned that overseas postings can be a means of motivating and executives with top management potential.

Relocation can provide an executive with the stimulus of job changes within the same company, and with work experience he or she might otherwise have sought elsewhere. The problem that many mid-career executives face is how to make the transition from a 'functional' role in marketing, finance or manufacturing to general management. A general manager may need to develop international skills or further develop a specific functional skill. Relocation may be answer in both cases, perhaps to run a small subsidiary company or to be finance director in a larger one. This is a way for companies to nurture their executives and make sure they're still around when opportunities occur.

Easier said than done. Studies have shown that as many as one in five people sent to work abroad never finish their assignment – typically three years with a major multinational. A tremendous waste of human and financial resources, when you think that an overseas job shuffle can cost a company half a million dollars or more.

How then can an executive cope? The professional expatriate is able to tread the fine line between adapting to the new environment and becoming too integrated. One doesn't want to live in a golden ghetto – cocooned in a sterile and inbred world of fellow expatriates, who may have nothing in common but a language of sorts.

On the other had, you should avoid adapting so well that you're considered to be indispensable to an overseas subsidiary, or to have 'gone native.' Not the best augury for a promotion back at the Kremlin, or even to make a lateral arabesque to a subsidiary in Zambia.

It has been said, and I'm the last to deny it, that successful executives have a talent for choosing predecessors and successors – the idea being that if you have three years in a job, you have one year to blame the previous guy, the second to reap the rewards and the last year to cook the books for the next guy (who, if he's astute, will repeat the cycle). This is known as Management by Blame.

Professional expatriates always look out for the next posting almost as soon as they arrive by making sure they train and anoint their successor. Call it Management by Replacement.

Even now I often wonder what job I might have now if I'd completed my stint in Broken Springs.

It's been a hard day's week
1972 Werbung/Publicite; 1984 'If my boss calls...'

Monday: Make it to the office before eight to check my secretary's desk before she arrives. My office seems smaller somehow. Someone must have moved the bookcase away from the wall. But strange. Slight churning of the bowels as I glance through the mail and phone messages. I just can't take any unpleasant surprises after a trip or the weekend. May need a few minutes to compose myself. The bitch-goddess, Helen, has an almost triumphant way of announcing bad tidings. I'll never forget that time I caught all that grief on the meditation claims for Soulbad. One of my more quixotic forays into truth in advertising.

I'd just come back from Europe and walked into the office like the proverbial lamb to the slaughter. Helen greeting me with that mocking half-smile. Those dangerous green eyes. 'Have you found yourself another job?' Oh, my God. But nothing devastating. Mendelsohn, that dissembling shrink from Personnel, called five times on Friday. Must be about the management palm reading program. Yes, I could use some plastic surgery on my career line. I'll wander over to the other building and see what he wants. What's this? Lunch with John tomorrow. Wow, a three martini lunch before the budget meeting.

Catch the men's room before the morning crowd. My favorite stall by the door. You can tell guys' have got magazines smuggled under their jackets. Could spend the whole day in here if they had telephones.

Like that hotel in Milan. Taking a conference call from Fort Paradise while sitting on the john. There are still a few ways left to express one's anarchism.

Put in some time on the Soulbad marketing plan which is a fairly painless way to kill the morning. My friend, Manny Selzer, drops by at noon and treats me to a 'Bunch 'O Lunch' at Shakey's. Manny says George is planning a big purge. Obviously to assert his authority after taking over from Bob who was kicked upstairs. The *tricoteuses* in the typing pool are flashing their needles. Manny is relaxed because it seems Walter likes the wild life series that Manny bought from BBC Television.

I chew so many antacid tablets during the afternoon that I feel sick and go home early.

Tuesday: There's definitely something wrong with my office. The ceiling seems lower and the outside wall has moved inwards. I'm so nervous this morning that I barricade myself in the men's room with *Advertising Age*.

Lunch with John at Prichett's which is filled as always with Mistral brass. A weak joke about whether we qualify for the 'Business Man's' steak. John is suspiciously genial. Even praises my revised sales forecast and twists my arm for a third martini. Ironic how a bucket of martini seldom offends the puritan work ethic while a glass of wine at lunchtime will get raised eyebrows. Like the time Miguel came up from Colombia. A wino image after half a bottle of Californian Chianti.

An uncomfortable budget meeting but nobody gets hurt. John oozes proletarian camaraderie. I have to admire his 'I'm a people person' routine.

Wednesday: Meeting in New York with Midas & Walsh. John cancelled out at the last moment and asked me to handle. That way he can second guess me if George doesn't like the new Soulbad concepts. Siw Anja Walsh the creative director, sat in for half an hour, scissoring her gorgeous knees. Can never be quite sure if she's flirting with me, or not. Have to be very careful what I say as she has a direct line with Walter.

Thursday: John is tied up all day in a meeting with George. I am very nervous. There's no doubt my office is smaller than it used to be. If I were Groucho Marx I'd call Personnel and ask them to send round a larger office.

Friday: George dismisses the old palace guard. Manny Selzer tells it best: 'Late in the morning sixteen pink slips appear without comment on sixteen desks. Then, following a forty-five minute lunch break for the recipients of the pink slips they all move over to the Holiday Inn where the egregious Mendelsohn explains quite convincingly why none of them is indispensable to George's corporate renaissance. Following this each of the discomfited is granted a fifteen minute interview with the Commander-in-Chief. The interviews are conducted in alphabetical order since none of the unhorsed has any rank left. Then, George holds a kind of prayer meeting for the bereaved secretaries. Nancy Hamburger is so disgusted that she walks out. "I'm too old for this kind of playacting."

Manny says it's all so incredible that if I were to write about it in one of my crazy articles nobody would believe me.

Back in my office I find a flushed and impatient Helen. 'I've been looking for you all afternoon. George wants to see you in his office before you go home.' She pulls back a curtain of blonde hair and gives me a long, appraising look. Maybe she is thinking this is the end of a beautiful love-hate relationship.

As Kurt Vonnegut would say, 'So it goes.'

Are you sure you want to save time?

1984 'If my boss calls…'

One lean Monday morning, with a nagging hangover, a deadline looming and not an idea in sight, I was scratching around among the papers and business magazines for something to plagiarize, when I came across this intriguing item: 'Take time to manage your time.'

As a professional wheel-spinner I've always been able to rationalize the amount of time I spend away from the job. Idleness is in the mind. It's one thing to spend the day lying on the beach when you're supposed to be working. But it's quite okay if it's 'freeing the mind' as a prelude to a frenzy of productive activity.

Procrastination can take many forms. Mundane is re-arranging your workspace, grinding coffee or discovering you need to make one more call for that last-minute piece of information. Neurotic is saying, 'I can't possibly work without another check-list. Creative is exploring the siesta as a means of dredging the subconscious on those days when the juices steadfastly refuse to flow.

So here, I thought, might be some heartwarming advice on the subtle art of how to be involved with work rather than actually working. And how to reconcile this with the rigours of the Puritan work ethic.

But no. What I found was a report on a time-management seminar imported from where else but the U.S. The seminar, destined for top managers, was being held in time-honored fashion at a luxurious château on the outskirts of Paris.

Apparently, the aim of the seminar is to disabuse managers of the cherished notion that because one lacks time one is important. And it teaches that time must be managed just like any other commodity and that it should work for you as a management tool.

The seminar starts with each participant submitting to a kind of activity test. This is very revealing. Most managers it seems show an almost pathological tendency to rush around doing things as though they are bulls chasing after a red rag.

Participants are then asked questions such as: 'What would you do if you had only six months to live?' (Light the blue touch-paper and retire immediately.) 'What would you most like to achieve in the next five years?' (Why, a golden handshake of course.)

The idea is that by answering such questions the participants are able to establish a series of objectives for their lives, their careers and their jobs. This enables them to recognize the various contradictions that often exist between these objectives.

The final part of the seminar is to establish an action plan. This is supposed to match the objectives with the means available for achieving them. Participants are shown various ways of managing their time, such as using a miniature recorder for trapping fugitive ideas and establishing a priority rating for various activities.

All this was stewing in my mind when my old friend Guratsky called. It transpired that he'd just returned from the seminar.

He said he'd found it fascinating. It was only when he got back to the office that the problems started. 'Budgeting your time is okay as far as long-term objectives are concerned,' he said. 'It's the daily routine that makes life difficult. Telephone calls, meetings, delegation, the flow of paper in the office … checking out how every minute the day is spent.'

I said I didn't understand. Didn't this help him to save time?

'That's precisely the problem,' Guratsky said. 'I saved so much time that I found I could get all my work done in less than half an hour a day. Now I'm a candidate for redundancy!'

Perhaps what we really need is a seminar on how to spin out time rather than how to save it.

'I miss you too!'

1991 International Herald Tribune; 1994 Resident Abroad

As every executive knows, rule number one when traveling on business is never to do business in the country you are visiting, but always contrive to be on the phone to somewhere else. You need to call the office incessantly to make sure you're still at the centre of the universe, and to keep other third-country nationals on their toes. The expert leaves a trail of unrequited requests to call back ('Ah, he's just left for the airport. You may be able to catch him in Sidi Barrani.')

Rule number two is always to ring home at least once a day. There are two main reasons: first, to check that your loved one misses you; second, to reassure your loved one that you are having a ghastly time struggling to bring home the bacon against all odds. But this is harder to pull off as the executive lifestyle becomes more transparent. ('I expect you're having a cosy dinner with that PR woman.' 'Sweetheart, this is my job!')

And there's competition between working couples. ('Darling, I had to go and be nice to Fingelstein, he knows my boss.' 'Helen, is that the television I can hear?' 'What do you mean, I wasn't in? We'd just gone out for a pizza. You're not the only one...!') Hypocrisy rules OK.

I spend a lot of time chatting up all sorts of people I shall (fortunately) never meet. So I was intrigued at the chance of a natter (on the phone, naturally) with Dr Guy Fielding, a psychologist, on a subject close to my heart: how to build healthy 'tele-relationship.' It seems that people who master this 'find a better understanding of each other by the intimacy and focus of having to rely exclusively on the phone.'

'If your relationship is central to you,' Fielding says, 'it will provide a number of needs, like intimacy, comfort, nurturing or challenge.' You can put a relationship "on hold" for one or two days – but if you don't work at it, it will die; it has to be fed and watered. For some people their relationship will be threatened by telephoning when they are upset; for others, that may be the way in which they keep the relationship no only going, but actually progressing.'

This is all down to the exceedingly intimate nature of the phone. You acquire more information in listening to what people are saying and how they're saying it than you do from watching for visual clues. Intimacy is honesty. This means it is easier to tell if someone's lying to you on the phone than face-to-face. But if you really mean what you say, you're going to sound more convincing.

'In a sense, the telephone is as confessional as a psychoanalyst's couch, because it allows you to talk to somebody without distractions. You are focused entirely on them,' Fielding says. 'People often find it easier to deal with intimate or difficult topics. One of the things that the telephone does for you is to choose the right moment of contact, and to treat each moment as a peak experience. You then get samples of the person at their best, rather than as they are in general relationships at home.

'A lot of people we talked to think that separations have brought them benefits. There are several ways in which that is important. First, the fact that we have to set priorities, which means choosing to telephone them, rather than someone else; that's an explicit affirmation of the importance of the relationship.

'Second, people did more talking on the phone than they would have done face-to-face, because when the call came it was very focused, and it meant that they did not allow themselves to do something else at the same time or be interrupted.

'The third thing was that the phone forced them actually to listen to what the other was saying: their tone of voice and whether they were sounding upset and the particular words they were using.

'Then the final thing is that when people are apart and talk on the phone, they actually have to make some things explicit which face-to face they can let go by. That they miss each other, for example, which may never be said otherwise. What the phone does is allow people to get things sorted out and to build up, if you will, a set of explicit, shared understandings, which they may never have talked about together at home.'

People who are successful with a 'tele-relationship' say they don't expect to 'move the earth' with expressions of affection: it's the act of calling that is important, talking about things that would perhaps not in themselves justify a phone call.

Women seem to be happier about it than men, both on the road and at home. This is because they are more conscious of the basic need to communicate – and less concerned about what is actually said.

An international opera singer told us: 'We don't go in for these grand declarations of love; we're too old for that. But it's very important for us to make it clear how we feel about each other,' Fielding says. 'There is this delicate balance between not being overly dramatic and yet being prepared to express things on the telephone that reassure the other person.'

Couples can help prevent resentment from the partner stuck at home by sharing the responsibility for keeping in touch, rather than putting the onus on the one who travels. 'By calling from home, the non-traveling partner can show valuable support for the relationship,' Fielding says. "Companies can play an important role here by meeting the cost of calls, and overcoming the practical difficulties of contacting a partner on the move.'

Have expenses, will travel
1987 International Herald Tribune

You may not have heard the story of the salesman who is summoned by his boss to explain an egregious item in his expense account. 'Now see here, Joe. I know you've had a tough month chasing the Fingelstein order up in Niagara Falls. But $2,000 for an overcoat! You know there's no way I can approve that. You'd better go away and re-work these expenses.'

The next day, Joe's boss is apoplectic. 'Joe, these expenses of yours come to exactly the same amount as before. How come; what about that overcoat?'

Joe is unchastened. 'Ah, yes, Mel, I know it's the same total. But you find the overcoat!'

Had Joe's company given him a fixed daily allowance for meals and entertainment expenses, he could perhaps have bought the overcoat with a fairly clear conscience by skipping a few lunches or dinners – or getting himself invited. Or, by making a pre-emptive call to his boss. 'Mel, I've landed the Fingelstein order. And he has invited me up to his place in Yellowknife for the weekend… Mel, listen; it's cold up there; I'm going to have to buy an overcoat.'

'Have expenses, will travel' is a wistful mantra of the past to the present generation of road warriors as they struggle with tougher rules, and a heightened scrutiny of their travel expenses.

Back in my corporate days, we faced a dialectical dilemma between the creative exploitation of the rules and grand larceny, rather like the legal difference between 'tax avoidance' and 'tax evasion' – between being smart and being dishonest.

The moral: Travel expenses – however outrageous – should be transparent, or seemingly so. The best place to hide something is out in the open; you can get away with (almost) anything if you can show that you are (1) saving the company money with astute travel planning and (2) getting results beyond the call of duty. Make the most of your moral mileage – not to be confused with frequent flier mileage. And always ostentatiously deduct personal expenses. There is no point in being virtuous unless you are seen to be virtuous.

Traditionally, 'Travel Management' in most organizations is mainly about accounting control of 'travel and entertainment' – who gets to travel first, or business class, stay in certain categories of hotel, how many signatures are needed to sign off on expenses. Nobody bothers much about whether a trip is necessary as long as the company gets the best value for money and the correct procedures are followed. Look after the expenses and the trip will look after itself.

The converse of travel management is Management by Expenses: the creative exploitation of the rules that are enshrined in the corporate travel policy.

Expense account *aficionados* swear by corporate plastic. A corporate credit card helps no end with personal cash-flow. But it can lead to hassles with the bean counters when you're trying to sort out who owes whom at the end of the month. This is fairly clear cut when you're 'extending' a business trip from say, Hong Kong, to a long weekend in a Thai resort with your loved one by getting the travel agency to 'pro rata' the difference to your account. Trying to get a hotel cashier to let you pay for personal items on the bill with cash or your own plastic can be a nightmare. Checking out is bad enough at the best of times.

In my corporate days, I preferred to use my own plastic in felicitous conjunction with a cash advance (better you owing them than them owing you) and then ostentatiously deducting personal expenses, like personal phone calls, drinks in the disco, or the cost of a friend joining me for breakfast.

Make the most of full-fare business tickets by exploiting two-for-one promotions or free or half-price companion fares. Some airlines offer a free 24-hour stopover package as an incentive to fly through their home hub. Or combine a money-saving point-to-point fare on the way out with a fare that allows stopovers on the way back. And, of course, traveling full fare allows you to earn more expense-account miles to buy yourself upgrades or free tickets.

'Planning business trips can be more daunting than doing business when you arrive – assuming you still know what you're supposed to do there – says Stanley Zilch, director of Blue Skies Research Institute in Broken Springs, Colorado. 'We've developed a kind of "yield management" system for the expense-account traveler called Expenses Monitor which flips the whole expenses reporting system upside down.

'Let's say your boss wants you to visit customers in Hong Kong, Bangkok and Tokyo. But you could also visit customers in Sydney, Chicago and New York. And yes, it would be nice to spend a weekend in Bermuda. Expenses Monitor allows you to "model" these factors, along with how you can maximize your earning of frequent flier miles, and come up with an optimum travel solution – such as a first-class round-the-world ticket.

'You might even get your boss to believe that it's his idea.'

Then you could say you have arrived – expenses-wise.

Can absence make the heart grow fonder?
2008 International Herald Tribune

It seems obvious really: When you are traveling you always call home. But apparently, having the 'space' to think about loved ones when away on business, can actually enhance relationships, promote domestic harmony, allowing couples to reflect on what brought them together in the first place.

This is the conclusion of an online survey of 740 business travelers based in the UK conducted by Crowne Plaza Hotels & Resorts. Three quarters of travelers said 'I love you' more often when away from home; and 40 percent admitted to sending text messages to their partner during business meetings. Distance is an important factor, with 60 percent of travelers saying that the farther away they are from their loved ones, the more likely they are to call them.

Over half the respondents said they would 'check in' with their loved ones at least once a day, with two thirds waiting until the evening to call from their hotel room so that they could catch up properly – and privately. And over 55 percent said that when away, they learn more about their partner's day through phone conversations than they would normally; that catching up on the phone allows them to move away from the mundane and instead have a more meaningful and focused conversation. People may even have more direct contact when apart than at home, where, on a typical evening, a third prefer to unwind in front of the TV than talk to their partner, with over a quarter admitting that eating dinner may be the only time spent together in the same room all evening.

'Psychologically, two things are going on here' says Susan Quilliam, a relationship psychologist in Cambridge, 'the first is when we are with our partners, we can get habituated, take them for granted. Distance helps you look at things in a new light you suddenly start to appreciate them more, miss them more because you don't have the touch-down time – for men in particular, for whom physical contact – I'm not talking sex here – is important.

'The second is that for business travelers, the experience of being away can be quite an alienating one; you're in a foreign town, an anonymous hotel, the challenge of meeting new clients, so the need to go back to your roots, and contact with the people you love is much greater.'

The survey shows that women are more likely than men to be better focused on the job, more dedicated, less emotionally tied and far less easily distracted when they are away; with men calling home more often than women, especially on longer trips and the farther they go: 28 percent of men call home once, twice or three times a day compared to only 25 percent of women; 17 percent of women are likely to call their partner only once every other day. Three quarters of men, but only 68 percent of women said they sent text messages to their partner during an important business meeting and with men more likely than women to send something romantic.

'Gender differences are not overwhelming,' Quilliam says. 'But there are contradictions. While there's a slight tendency for women to be more focused when they're away from home, they also feel guiltier than men about traveling on business.'

I can understand that one can become more homesick, and have a greater need for reassurance, the longer one is away. But why should distance alone make such a difference to a tendency to call more often?

'This is because subconsciously you know it's going to be more difficult to get back, in the sense you couldn't get back,' Quilliam says.

'So the farther you are away, the more likely you are to check in to see that everything is all right, and to make strong statements of love.

If there's a huge distance it makes contact more important and probably more emotional; we all need more bonding contact, even in long-term relationships. Men are more emotional in many ways; they will have fewer intimate friends. Women will have a big network; and men are far more likely to be dependent on one significant other.'

I suppose saying, 'I love you,' is really saying, 'do you love me?' 'That would be a lovely way of putting it,' Quilliam says.

'It's almost entirely down to your need for reassurance; because you are the one who's out of the information loop; at home they are stable, secure; they don't have this alienation thing.' The late Canadian media guru Marshall McLuhan said that radio is a 'hot' medium, whereas television is a 'cool' medium. Like radio, the telephone is an intimate medium, making one focus entirely on the voice, the spoken word. One can acquire more information in listening to what people are saying and how they're saying it, than searching for visual clues; especially true with loved ones. There is a sense in which the phone is as confessional as the psychoanalyst's couch; which is why it might be easier to deal with intimate or difficult subjects. Phone conversations force people to actually listen to what the other is saying, their tone of voice, whether they are sounding upset, and the particular words they use.

Some relationships may survive in spite of or because of frequent or prolonged absence.

So what is the secret to a healthy long-distance partnership?

'Do exactly as the survey describes,' Quilliam says. 'Keep in regular contact in private time; and also take the opportunity of being separated to remember what's good, the things that at the beginning of the relationship just overwhelmed you; regain that sense of appreciation, not as something you resent. And see separation as an opportunity, not a problem.'

Much appreciated

1994 Business Life; 1995 Resident Abroad

How to express appreciation is an art which few executives appreciate and which even fewer have mastered. Knowing how to motivate people by praising (or thanking) them for the right things in the right way is a crucial management skill. Get it right and you may improve productivity beyond the dreams of your masters. You may even – as once happened to me – boost morale beyond the dreams of your people.

About a hundred years ago, when I was a corporate executive in Switzerland, our travel agent offered me (as managing director) a round-trip ticket on an inaugural flight to Hong Kong.

Nowadays, I'd snap it up for myself. But having just come back from a course on Behavioral Decisions in Organizations, I decided to organize a sweepstake for the ticket among the staff. The chap who won it was our very deserving, very staid, Swiss book-keeper – I'll call him Willy – who returned with a gorgeous Thai girl whom he'd met in Bangkok on the way back. ('How did you meet her?' we asked in wonder and admiration.'I met her in a shop,' Willy averred.)

My secretary Marion had been known to straighten my tie before an important meeting, but Willy's Thai lady did things that would set a self-respecting feminist's teeth on edge – like stirring his tea, or tying an errant shoelace! I'm not sure whether Willy's acquisition did much for company morale. But it shows that a little appreciation can go a long way.

One lesson I learned from my roller-coaster career is to reward someone both as an individual and as a member of the team. But praise should be relevant as well as sincere (in many respects, expressing appreciation is like choosing a present; it's the thought that counts): spontaneity, surprise, an element of the unexpected can be important too.

Here's an assortment of views from sundry suits of my acquaintance:

'Genuine consideration is the best form of appreciation and in this busy life it's the most difficult thing to do, consistently to make time to care about people. If you do that, you are sensitive to the person and sufficiently alert to praise them for the right things, to avoid an automatic response. People see through expressions of gratitude which aren't related to something that they ought to feel good about.'

'Appreciation, like criticism, should be fair, properly meted out without a barbed edge. It's wrong to over-compensate someone for only a marginal added-value to what they had to do anyway, but important to recognize when extra effort has been made.'

'Single out the exceptional things that are done; don't go overboard in congratulating people for what they're paid for – you can devalue the currency very easily.'

'Too often we give praise for things that people feel they shouldn't be praised for and ignore the things that they feel they should have been praised for. A lot of managers say: "I get a great performance review every year but for the wrong reasons; they are giving me credit for something that I have no ego invested in."'

'If the general objective is met, there's a lot of praise for that, but then the people involved all have individual motivations for having met it. How often has anyone had the opportunity really to sit down for an hour or so and talk about themselves with someone really listening? The boss is too busy satisfying his boss or doing what really needs to be done. Just to listen and respond is a great form of appreciation.'

'Today you're going to be faced with a mounting wall of cynicism in management groups, no matter how much they're appreciated,' says one soothsayer. "'They're just telling me this now before they let me go." There's insecurity in any executive job today. Cynically, if we want to get rid of people, then by all means let's not appreciate them, then they'll go away.'

I lost a lot of battles when I was a corporate suit. But I always tried to build a team of individuals and motivate them by helping them recognize and develop their own skills so that, come what may, they could take both their skills and recognition somewhere else. One of the best ways to express appreciation is to level with people, so that they can say, 'I did well, even if they don't want me any more.'

I look upon management as achieving results through other people: by picking the right people and providing them with an environment in which they can be most effective – both for the organization and for themselves. And this is what appreciation is all about.

Golfing holidays may handicap your career

1987 International Herald Tribune

How you behave on the golf course can reflect how you behave in business. Your management style is on the line each time you tee off. Who said vacations were just for fun?

These are the findings of a survey of 100 American executives carried out by Hyatt Hotels Corporation early this year. Respondents were senior managers (vice presidents or above) earning more than $100,000 who had played at least six rounds of golf over the past twelve months. The sample was split 78 percent men and 22 percent women, matching the actual percentage of female golfers in the United States. The mean age in the study was 51. Nearly a quarter of the 30 million golfers in the country are top management executives.

Predictably, almost all executives say that 'playing golf with a business associate is a good way to establish a closer relationship,' and over a third say 'some of my biggest deals are made on the golf course.' But while nearly all say 'playing golf is a good way to relieve stress,' half have thrown or broken a club after making a bad shot; 12 percent say 'golf is more important to me than sex' (slightly more women than men); more than a third of those (55 percent) who admit cheating at golf have also cheated in business at least once; and 47 percent say that 'the way somebody plays golf is very similar to how he or she conducts business.'

'If I want to get to know someone, start to do business with them, I play golf with them,' says Darryl Hartley-Leonard, president of Hyatt Hotels Corporation in Chicago. 'They have let you into the inner sanctum of their life. I really believe that more deals are being done on the golf course than any other place in America. I think it is because, on the whole, you can make a pretty good assessment of someone when you spend about four hours on the golf course with them.

'The obvious thing is whether that person cheats — because golf is a game where it's completely down to your own integrity as to how you score. Someone might overplay what there handicap is. They might say, my handicap is 12, you play with them and they shoot 78. You know that that person's major interest is winning, not telling the truth. It's so indicative of that person. When you know somebody like that you just won't want to do business with them. Or the person goes into the trees looking for a lost ball and you just happen to notice later on the green that it is a different ball. Or they can nudge the ball or kick it away a bit. The other side is when someone does a chip shot, accidentally hits the ball twice, which you didn't hear happen, then calls that extra shot on themselves. You say, I like this guy. Then there are people who throw clubs, who lose their temper and scream at the caddie. I have seen outrageous behavior on the golf course from people who are seemingly honorable, decent, family types.

'You can tell someone's management style on the golf course. What if this person is too slick, too glib, cheats, abuses the caddie, or the environment? Is the individual a caring person with people around him? Is he a tenacious person? Do I trust this person?

'Sales people are very interesting to watch. They will often throw a game if they assess that the person they're playing with needs to win. What does it say about somebody who needs to win all the time?

'Say you're thinking of hiring somebody. You'll see a person who maybe starts out with two or three bad holes and they will give up. "I've blown this round." Not trying to fight back. Well, you can imagine what kind of aggression they are going to use to fix things that go wrong in business.'

As in all self-respecting surveys, there are several types of demographic and psychographic profiles to choose from:

Power Players – the most likely to link playing golf with doing business. They are most likely to believe that golf is a good way to develop business contacts. These are the most fanatical golfers – 91 percent will play golf in terrible weather, and 77 percent agree that 'I am happiest when I'm on a golf course.' They spend the most money on golf equipment and are the most likely to gamble and show their temper on the golf course. They have a higher income than the rest of the sample.

Non-Competitors – mainly view golf as relaxing and fun (55 percent of the women researched are in this category.) They are most likely to be women, play less often than the other groups, less likely to associate golf with business and less likely to gamble. They score lowest as risk-takers in business.

Gunslingers – most likely to cheat and the largest group (75 percent) who say that 'gambling makes the game more enjoyable.' They are the most frequent golfers (89 percent played at least 21 times in the past year) and are likely to use oversized clubs with balls that don't hook or slice. Nearly 90 percent are young (48) married males, who have been playing golf for over 20 years.

Escapists – most enjoy playing golf on vacation (80 percent) and are also competitive golfers; 64 percent say 'I always play to beat the others in my foursome,' while preferring to play with people who play better than them. They are the group most likely to take lessons from a pro (66 percent). While they seem confident in their financial future, they are the one group that is most likely to say 'I basically do not like my job' (12 percent). This group is slightly older (53) and has played golf longer (25 years) than the others.

'What surprised me about the study is that people agreed with it, but had not realized that that's what they had been doing.' 'People said, 'Yes, I know that, but I never concentrated on it.' Also, I didn't realize how many people cheated, in a game that sets itself up as a paragon of virtue, where cheating is the most abominable thing,' Hartley-Leonard says.

'More women are saying, "I've got to get in this game in order to do business." But men don't like playing golf with women, because women approach the game totally differently; although women don't mind playing with men. Women follow the rules much more stringently. And, like a lot of things in life, are far more disciplined. With women, golf is not a big case of win or lose it's seen much more as a leisure activity, to relax. Men have got far more ego on it, far more insecurity.'

Golf and skiing seem to spearhead the growing trend towards activity vacations.

'I would no longer build a resort without a golf course,' Hartley-Leonard says. 'People don't want to go to the beach and just lie there in the sun all day. They are looking for new experiences.

'We're also looking at shorter and more frequent vacations. In the course of this year, I'll probably take seven three- to four-day trips either to ski or play golf.'

Honey, did you pack the divorce papers?

2008 International Herald Tribune

'Ah, if only we could get away,' is a frequent lament from office slaves this side of summer. But while it may seem grim minding the fort while everybody around you is away, going on vacation is a minefield for the unwary.

This is why some people opt for a 'staycation,' or what the travel trade calls a 'home-based vacation,' instead – not necessarily staying at home, but staying over for a night or two at local hotels, or resorts; splurging on fine dining: simply an extravagant extension of normal life.

Of course, it may seem like paradise; getting away from it all to that beach hotel on the Cote d'Azur, or an idyllic island in the Greek archipelago, with your loved one for a glorious week or two.

And that's the rub. Vacations are an ideal time for couples to rediscover themselves – and each other. But unaccustomed periods of 'unstructured' time; the break from routine, can play havoc with relationships. If you are used to having time apart, being together all day, every day, for several days, can send the best relationship into an acrimonious tail-spin.

I have known relationships to survive, not so much in spite of, but because of the regular absence of one partner on business trips. Absence really can make the heart grow fonder. Hence the adage, 'I married him for better or for worse; but not for lunch.'

Couples on vacation are often forced into proximity and interdependence for which they may not have a script.

When away from routine, there should be a new division of privileges and responsibilities, and a rediscovering of each individual's role.

According to Jackie Walker, a relationship coach based in Edinburgh, early September and mid January – the periods just after a vacation – are peak times for couples to seek relationship counseling, or initiate divorce proceedings.

'Vacations are stress times for relationships,' Walker says. 'People go back to work after end-of year and summer holidays and say, "I can't go on living like this any more; I'm not going through another year."

They suddenly realize they have little in common with their partner; and the time they spend together is either spent proving who is right, or blaming each other rather than enjoying their relationship and supporting and encouraging one another.

'In daily life, couples can be so busy with work and social commitments that they spend little time together,' Walker adds. 'But sometimes all day, every day, for a couple of weeks is too much. If you are used to having time apart in your daily lives, allow for this when you are on holiday. Accept that he might want to try scuba diving and she might want to visit historic sites, and you can limit resentment and conflict, and have great stories to share over dinner that night.'

Vacations are a good time for taking stock; and reflecting upon our lives.

'But if you've been burying your head in the sand about relationship problems, long, hot, leisurely days can allow time to admit that something is very wrong,' Walker says. 'Many couples take a holiday in the hope of reviving a foundering relationship, but it's the late summer that I get a high level of inquiries for counseling – the divorce lawyers are busy at that time too.'

Paradoxically, relationships often founder when a couple returns from vacation, perhaps after having a wonderful time. A return to the reality of daily life convinces them that they will happy only if they leave their partner.

'That affects a lot of people,' Walker says. 'They may be right; but sometimes it can be helpful to recognize the things you need to change about your life so as to feel happier all year round.'

Walker says there are three parts to a relationship. 'There is him, there is her, and there's the relationship. And very often the third part is forgotten; people work on the assumption of "I'm doing this," and "I'm doing that," and forget about the "we' part. The general run of what goes wrong in relationships is because people have forgotten how to look out for one another; to recognize that they are serving one another. I believe it is important for couples to support and empower the other person; and so often what happens is that people start blaming, shaming and knocking, rather than working together.'

If you are still thinking of taking a late vacation this year, here are some tips for 'divorce-proofing' your relationship:

– Decide what you both want out of a holiday and agree in advance on joint or separate activities. Give each other space.

– Agree who takes responsibility for what: booking flights, hotel and car rental.

– Agree on a budget and who's paying for what.

– Try something different; if you always do beach holidays, try a rural retreat, somewhere quite to go and walk, and talk, or an activity holiday with friends.

– Go on holiday without your partner and come home to a revitalized relationship.

– A lot of the pleasure is in the expectation; but be realistic; expect the unexpected, and for things to go wrong.

Roger Collis

Sleepwalking sets off alarms

2008 International Herald Tribune

Few things are more disconcerting on a trip than to wake up in a hotel room, and for a few bewildering seconds wondering where I am, which hotel, which city, why am I there? Even which day it is, never mind the time.

But a release from British budget hotel chain Travelodge, reporting that sleepwalking among guests increased seven-fold in the past year, mostly involving naked men, has set me worrying about a more alarming kind of amnesia: What am I getting up to while I'm asleep!

According to Travelodge, which runs 310 hotels in Britain, more than 400 night-time wanderers appeared at reception in the past year asking such questions as 'Where is the bathroom?' 'Do you have a newspaper?' or 'Can I check out, I'm late for work?'

One naked male sleepwalker even managed to get himself locked out of the hotel and later arrested. On other occasions hotel staff was able to direct somnambulists safely back to their rooms.

The top five sleepwalking activities are: opening the curtains; watching TV; getting dressed; eating and drinking; and going for a walk.

Studies have found that sleepwalking can be brought on by such factors as, stress; alcohol; cheese; eating too late; too much caffeine.

Chris Idzikowski, a sleep expert at Edinburgh Sleep Centre says, 'The Travelodge figures are a surprise. Sleepwalking is a serious disorder that can develop for a variety of reasons. It can be triggered by a stressful lifestyle, sleep deprivation, alcohol abuse, or not breathing properly during the night. Sleepwalking is most likely within an hour or two of going to bed and slipping into a deep sleep.'

'Part of the brain switches into auto pilot, and can manage well-learned movements, Idzikowski adds, such as walking, bending or sitting, even detailed activity such as talking, texting, eating and drinking, opening and closing doors, even driving a car. Sleepwalkers will awake quite unable to recall any of their actions. Other forms of sleepwalking may involve acting out dreams.'

Leigh McCarron, director of sleep at Travelodge says, 'My job is make sure guests get the best nights sleep possible; by making sure we purchase the right duvets, with good linen, and comfortable beds. But we are seeing more cases of sleepwalking so we have issued our staff guidelines so they know how to help sleepwalkers when they meet them.'

Idzikowski's recipe for a good night's sleep is to allow at least an hour 'of non-work-related activity,' to empty the mind, to wind down, however late it is, along with silence, darkness and comfort. 'We have shown that light from a laptop or Blackberry is concentrated enough to signal the brain to stop secreting melatonin, the natural hormone that produces sleep.'

'After a business meeting, go to your hotel room, sort out the results, what you're going to do, put that aside,' Idzikowski says. 'A hot bath can be relaxing, especially for women; there is no point in going to bed and not sleeping. Caffeine: a general rule is to avoid it for six to seven hours before you turn in. I am pro-alcohol; a nightcap is not a bad idea, but low doses basically. Above 80 milligrams it is catalyzed down, the brain reacts to lack of it, you get a rebound effect, and three to four hours later you wake up again.'

Idzikowski recommends sleeping in darkness and being progressively woken by an alarm clock with a light that slowly increases in intensity, simulating a sunrise; although you might draw the line at seashore, nature or city sounds.

Thinking outside the box
2008 International Herald Tribune

We have all been there: Stuck in a windowless meeting room, fighting to keep awake, surreptitiously checking our e-mails, letting the imagination roam behind half-closed eyes, lips tightly pursed against judiciously steepled hands, while rocking slightly forwards and back, thinking about lunch, or plans for the evening, or making mental lists.

So I was intrigued to read the other day that two in five bored business travelers spend meetings daydreaming about holidays; one third fall asleep during 'especially dreary meetings,' with 35 percent often 'catching themselves on the brink of dropping off;' while 83 percent treat meetings 'like a long telephone call with a relative – only paying attention for the first half, when they can expect to hear 'all the bits worth knowing.'

These are the 'shocking' conclusions of a poll of 1,207 British business travelers by Crowne Plaza Hotels & Resorts.

Tactics for staying awake include doodling (59 percent) and 'fiddling' (52 percent); and 'playing with a pen when the mind wanders off the topic' (33 percent). More than half the respondents said that 'looking out of window is their biggest distraction;' 73 percent admitted 'they'll pay no attention if a person conducting the meeting has a monotonous voice.'

Crowne Plaza promises an end to boring meetings with the 'Think Box' designed by Roger von Oech, a California-based 'creativity consultant,' known for his book, 'A Whack on the Side of the Head.'

The Think Box (of brushed aluminum about 18 inches by 14 inches by 8 inches) is the latest gimmick in Crowne Plaza's 'Think Tank' campaign to stimulate business guests with tools and tips from 'innovators and visionary thinkers.' Boxes will be distributed in hotels across Europe and Middle East.

Think Boxes contain three items designed to overcome three key hurdles that Von Oech claims beset meetings. They are: Loss of focus; lack of creativity; and achieving meeting goals.

– The Inspire Boards use brain teasers to help get people focused at the start of meetings and stimulate creative energy activity.

– The Ball of Whacks, a rhombic triacontahedron puzzle made up of 30 detachable magnetic blocks, is a 'tactile tool to release nervous energy, prevent distraction and to reinvigorate creativity during a meeting.'

'The Ball can be taken apart and manipulated into a lot of different shapes,' von Oech says. 'Using your hands and eyes together stimulates the brain.' (Squeezing the Ball in your hand and showering your neighbors with magnetic shards is certainly a great way to break the ice!)

– The Think Cards contain 32 of von Oech's strategies for creative thinking and to get a new perspective on an issue. One card says, 'Avoid arrogance;'

others say, 'Laugh at it;' 'Drop an assumption;' 'Slay a sacred cow.' 'Picking cards at random can get you off thinking in other directions,' von Oech says. What you might call, thinking outside the box.

'Meeting planners typically look at the technical needs for the meeting, such as space, catering and audiovisual needs,' von Oech says. 'But not enough attention has been given to how you energize the thinking of people in the meeting, and to spark their creativity.'

The Think Box might be great for brainstorming; but I can think of meetings where using it would be unthinkable. Surely it depends on the type of meeting?

'Absolutely not,' Von Oech says. 'There are three or four different types of meeting; some where you're just disseminating information; others where you trying to come to a consensus; making a decision; then some where you're trying to come up with ideas – to the extreme of a brainstorming session. Some of the products can be used for a stepping-off point, or as an ice-breaker. People are more engaged, participatory, rather than being lectured at, or power-pointed to death.'

Well, yes. But after a short meeting with myself I've decided to go on thinking without the box.

Space Tourism Ready for Liftoff?
1997 *International Herald Tribune*

Don't pack your bags yet. But serious people in the aerospace and travel industry are taking the idea of space tourism seriously. Pundits predict that the first space tourists could be in orbit by 2005. Tourists would travel by 'space plane' to 'space hotels' 200 to 300 miles (320 to 480 kilometers) above Earth. NASA's Space Shuttle is capable of flying 60 to 70 passengers on each flight. In fact this was envisaged by Rockwell engineers in the design of the Shuttle 25 years ago.

There seems to be plenty of interest from armchair astronauts. More than

40 percent of Americans yearn for an 'out of this world' vacation, according to the 1997 Yesawich, Pepperdine & Brown/Yankelovitch Partners National Leisure Travel Monitor, based on in-depth interviews with 1,500 U.S. households.

Forty-two percent of those surveyed say they are interested in a space cruise that would offer amenities similar to an ocean-going cruise ship while 34 percent specifically say they would be interested in a two-week vacation aboard the Space Shuttle and be willing to spend (on average) $10,800 for the trip. Aviation Week & Space Technology magazine recently reported similar surveys in Japan, Canada, Germany and the United States that found "an enormous unsatisfied desire among the general public to travel in space."

'Space travel is about 10 to 15 years away if NASA and the private sector develop the necessary research and technology," says George Diller, NASA spokesman at the Kennedy Space Center at Cape Canaveral, Florida. "I think you'll see commercial initiatives, but it'll be pricey. Ten thousand dollars won't get you to the launch pad. You'd probably be looking at something closer to $50,000 for a trip lasting an hour, allowing the passenger to experience weightlessness for about 15 minutes."

For space flights alone, Bob Citron, a former aerospace executive and director of the Foundation for the Future in Bellevue, Washington (an organization dedicated to scholarly research on life during the next millennium), speculates that $3 billion to $5 billion would be needed to buy 24 to 45 space tourist vehicles, four or five launch sites and staffing for 1,000 to 2,000 flights a year with ticket prices of up to $50,000. 'A Space Shuttle vacation is certainly real in terms of consumer interest,' says Dennis Marzella, senior vice president at Yesawich, Pepperdine & Brown. 'The technology is there, but it needs to be adapted to accommodate tourists – comfortable seats and big windows.'

Patrick Collins of the University of Tokyo and the Japanese Rocket Society, speaking at the International Symposium on Space Tourism in Bremen, Germany, last March, estimates the development of a reusable, vertical takeoff and landing rocket for passengers would cost $10 billion and take six to seven years. "We need a lot of windows and we need bars, and the Japanese need a karaoke bar," Collins says. "A gym with padded walls for zero-gravity sports would be a really fun place.'

The space plane designs may draw on the experience of "Hotol," a pilot project of British Aerospace and Rolls-Royce a decade ago.

Hotol was to have been a 50-to-60-passenger plane that would take off from conventional airports.

After accelerating through Mach 5 to 80,000 feet, the plane would leave the atmosphere, continue to accelerate and become a satellite itself after reaching 250,000 feet – about four times the cruising altitude of Concorde – and an orbital velocity of Mach 25 to 30.

Maximum flying time, ground to ground, to anywhere in the world would be about 70 minutes. Unlike the Space Shuttle, such a space plane would need no external fuel tanks and would re-enter the atmosphere and land under its own power. A space plane would be ideal for picking up and delivering tourists to a space resort en route.

Space Islands Project has an intriguing scenario for a space resort hotel based on a '20-year-old Rockwell idea' for joining up a dozen or so of the Space Shuttle's empty external fuel tanks into a wheel-shaped space station. Each external tank measuring 28 feet in diameter and 154 feet long (a tad shorter than a 747 fuselage and walls four times thicker than those of the Mir space station) would be divided into three decks. The space station could accommodate 300 people in 'cruise-ship conditions.'

'The external tanks would be joined up end to end in the form of a ring with two more tanks joined up passing through the center like an axle through a wheel, like the orbiting Hilton in the 1969 movie, "2001: A Space Odyssey,"' says Gene Meyers, director of Space Islands Project, 'a loosely knit group of engineers, educators and architects,' in West Covina, California. 'The station would take about an hour and a half to make a complete orbit of the Earth, but the ring itself would be spinning like a roulette wheel at about one revolution a minute thus developing artificial gravity. People would live in the outer ring where they would experience about half of normal gravity – they'd just be half their normal weight – so they could use bathroom facilities and suchlike at pretty well normal conditions. The central column section would be zero gravity. This could be the entertainment and recreation center, which guests could visit for an hour or so at a time. You'd have windows in the central column to view the Earth.

'There are lots of entertainment possibilities at zero gravity. Astronauts have found that blood that is normally drawn down to your legs is sort of released and drifts upwards. Astronauts' legs become thinner, their chests expand by two to three inches, their faces fill out and wrinkles disappear. Shots of men in their forties before launch and an hour after launch look like father and son. Shannon Lucid, a 53-year-old American astronaut in the Russian space station last year, said she looked 20 years younger in space.'

Meyers and his group are looking to corporate sponsorship to meet the $10 billion to $15 billion cost of building the first space station. "You'd need about 16 of these external tanks. If we can get companies like Coca-Cola and General Motors to sponsor them for $500 million each, you'd cover big chunks of your costs for the first station; the second station would cost roughly half as much, and the third and fourth stations would be about 10 to 15 percent less.

'Space Islands Project is privately funded right now. We've budgeted $20 million for this first push to bring in some of the larger sponsors. The payback for them will be enormous. Coca-Cola, for example, spends $8 billion a year on marketing. So we've suggested that if they were to pay the cost of a shuttle launch – $400 million to $500 million – they could have the external tank painted white with their logo splashed all over it. This would give them two to three years of broad international exposure. We're talking to Carnival Cruises, Hilton Hotels, Universal Studios, Radisson Hotels and Disney to support the project.'

Jet lag: The time to stay on your own time

1993 International Herald Tribune

One of the hardest management decisions I ever made was not to self-destruct on vintage Champagne and a premature lunch when I flew Concorde from London to New York for a job interview. I compromised with a glass or three of Moët et Chandon and a cup of coffee. I finally lunched with my inquisitors at around 5:30 P.M. my time and flew back economy (this was before business class) at 7 P.M., which was midnight for me. I landed in London at 8 A.M. (3 A.M. in New York) in quite good shape. I unwittingly beat jet lag by staying on my home time. (I got the job by the way; but they sent me back on a 747.) Jet lag, of course, is what happens when the biological clock gets out of step with the chronological clock of a new time zone. Your body is geared for sleep at a time you are expected to be awake, and vice versa. Most people say they get more jet lag flying east than west. They find it easier to cope with a longer day than a shorter night. The reason is that the circadian rhythm has a natural tendency to run at a sleep-wake cycle of 25.2 hours. So if you fly west you're gaining on yourself all the time and the clock has to run a bit faster whereas coming the other way it has to run slower, which it seems is hard for it to do. Westward flights produce premature awakenings plus sleepiness in the evening. Eastward flights result in difficulties staying asleep and morning sleepiness. Light is the main trigger, or synchronizer, of the clock, although social cues, like mealtimes also affect circadian rhythm. Most people adjust at the rate of one time zone per day. This means you would need a week to properly adjust to a flight from, say, Europe to the Far East.

Ask a dozen frequent travelers how to cope with jet lag and you're likely to get a dozen different answers – from elaborate diets, in-flight aerobics, and aromatherapy to seeking nirvana through meditation (or medication).

Conventional wisdom says you should adjust as fast as you can to local time by resetting your watch and thinking in the destination time the moment you get on the plane. Expose yourself to bright light – especially sunlight – depending which direction you are traveling. From London, for example, traveling to Tokyo, try to get out in the sunlight later in the day when you arrive: Going west to Los Angeles try to get a good dose of sunlight as soon as you arrive.

The idea is that light suppresses melatonin – a sleep-inducing hormone, secreted in the late evening, and thought to be the master synchronizer of circadian rhythm.

However, a recent study by SAS of jet lag among air-crew members suggests that the best strategy for trips of up to 48 hours is not to adjust but stay on your home time. British Airways is offering similar advice to passengers in its new 'well-being in the air' program of diet and exercise.

'We haven't got the full results of the study yet, but it's perfectly clear that if you are not staying longer than 48 hours and have to work when you come back, it is important to stay with your home rhythm and try to eat in the right way with light meals,' says Dr. Christer von Hedenberg, medical director of SAS in Stockholm. He tells crew members to wear sunglasses at times when it's dark at home, get artificial light to simulate sunlight when it's supposed to be daytime there and not to sleep when they shouldnt. 'Going west, i.e. from Stockholm to Los Angeles, we feel people should go to bed as soon as possible and get what we call anchor sleep for, say, five hours. You can still go out for late dinner.

It's important to get plenty of sleep before you leave home. And napping can help.

'But you have to compromise between what is going on where you're going and at home: you'll find there's an overlap of some four hours. If you're going for longer than 48 hours, adjust as soon as possible to local time. It's definitely a strategic decision that you have to stick to.'

Dr. Jim Dunlop at British Airways in London says: 'I don't think it's quite as dramatic. It just seems easier in a 48-hour trip to attempt to stay on your home time, but in 72 hours probably you wouldn't manage it. The thoughts we had with the 48-hour touch were that if you can somehow keep more or less to your own sleep pattern, even if you're going to bed very late – like 1 o'clock in the morning-or waking up very early – like 6 in the morning – depending which direction you've traveled, you'll probably get away with it for 48 hours. You wouldn't need to try to shift your circadian rhythm – and if you did you'd get totally confused because you'd just have started to move it, and then you'd come back home and have to move it back again.'

The real problem comes when traveling to the Far East with a 7-to 9-hour time shift.

Says one old Asian hand (I'll call him Gerald): 'I've tried leaving Europe in the morning and getting to Hong Kong first thing in their morning; and I've tried leaving Europe in the evening and arriving Hong Kong at 3 or 4 the next afternoon – by far the best. There is nothing worse than arriving at 7 in the morning, when you've been up all night and you're confronted with a full day ahead of you. You can't even check into your hotel for another five or six hours. Whereas if you arrive at about 3 in the afternoon local time, then you can either have a quick nap or even better hold off until 9 P. M. local time and then go to bed.'

Gerald subscribes to trying to stay on your home schedule. 'Your day starts later and finishes later – so plan your business meetings for the afternoon and evening. The worst part is not so much the time change, but how much sleep can you really get on that long, 12-to-14-hour eastward flight. Beyond that, even if you try to adjust immediately to the local time it catches up with you about the third day.

'Therefore, in a perfect world, if I am flying out east for more than 48 hours, I would fly on Wednesday so that on the third day when this loss of sleep hits you, you are on a weekend to recover without losing any business.'

So next time you face a midnight lunch appointment, make sure you get a proper day's sleep.

Four

Roger Collis

Remembering the days of the Concorde
2000 International Herald Tribune

I have flown Concorde three times to New York, although I never made the round-trip. With the one-way fare costing around $5,000 (for which you can make 10 round-trips in economy), the people picking up the tab rightly felt that the "time is of the essence" rationale for getting me over on the Concorde didn't apply to getting me back on my own time. I got to arrive in New York an hour before I left London (the 10:30 a.m. flight arrived at 9:25 a.m.), but I never had the experience of beating jet lag by taking the 1:45 p.m. Concorde from JFK and arriving at Heathrow at 10:25 p.m. for a normal bedtime. I had missed the era of trans-Atlantic liners (the QE2 is too tacky to count). The nearest I got was breakfast in the first-class dining room on the Queen Mary when she was in Southampton, an invitation my colonel had secured when we were playing at soldiers in the area.

And alas, I never rode the 20th Century from New York to Chicago back in the mid-1960s, when I was going that way. Seize the moment is the moral.

The Concorde was such a moment. One of the hardest management decisions I ever made was not to self-destruct on vintage champagne and premature lunch when I flew the Concorde from London to New York the first time for a job interview. I compromised with a glass or three of Moet et Chandon and a cup of coffee. Which was just as well, because the guy sitting next to me drinking mineral water turned out to be one of the people interviewing me (this is a true story!) We introduced ourselves when we were picked up by the same limo. I finally lunched with my inquisitors at around 5 p.m. my time and flew back economy (this was before business class), arriving at 8 in the morning jet-lagged out of my mind. But I got the job.

Some wag writing in a travel magazine the other day enthused about Concorde being the 'ultimate in fast food.' I suppose at Mach 2.2 and at 15,000m, he had a point. But at $45 a minute from London to New York that compares with the more egregious tourist traps on the Cote d'Azur – except you do get transportation thrown in – along with those never quite requited poetic menus endorsed by designer chefs who have gone into public relations full-time. I might have gone for the poached salmon and a touch of Puligny-Montrachet 1986. But how much Puligny-Montrachet can you drink in three and a half hours? Quite a lot, actually.

I remember the Concorde for the exquisite discomfort of sitting in a 100-seat cigar tube.

You have about the same legroom as cattle class, but you feel no pain. After all, you're getting there in half the time. How good you feel about it may depend on how much you value your time – as distinct from how much you think your time is worth. But social cues have a lot to do with the legerdemain of supersonic travel. Arriving in New York at 9:25 a.m. instead of 1:25 p.m. (in the case of a 747 leaving at the same time as the Concorde, 10:30 a.m.) gives you four hours' extra time – to have a meeting, do lunch and make the 1:45 p.m. Concorde back to London if you must.

And the people you might meet. The Concorde is divided into two identical cabins. The less noisy rear cabin was, for some reason, considered less chic than the front of the plane, the place to sit if you aspire to rubbing shoulders with the high and mighty.

Frequent fliers had their favorite reserved seats and were greeted by name. "Morning Duchess, morning Mr. Connery, morning Ms. Pfeiffer." Travel often enough and the gold dust may come off on your shoulders, the pundits said. But it never happened to me. Maybe I should have saved a magazine article many years ago that revealed seat numbers of Concorde regulars and put my management style on the line. It would be just my luck to be stuck next to the wrong kind of celebrity – a banker perhaps rather than a publishing mogul.

However nonchalantly you play it, there has to be an authentic thrill when you step on board the Concorde. At 60,000 feet (18,300 meters), far above the clouds and weather, the sky is deep purple. And the slight jolt you feel when you break the sound barrier at Mach 1 (675 miles per hour), then watch the needle on the bulkhead dial reach Mach 2, is exhilarating. My second flight on the Concorde, in 1985, was what you might call eventful.

The idea was to write a story on how to travel from Nice (via Paris) to New York, do lunch in Manhattan and be back in Nice the same day.

Roger Collis

We left Charles de Gaulle in Paris on time at 11 a.m. An hour and a half later, halfway through the gourmet lunch, there was a brusque call from the flight deck for everybody to return to their seats and fasten belts. . The cabin crew cleared the tables and we lost speed and altitude. This was a moment of high-quality stress.

Then the captain announced that we had 'lost a hydraulic system.' There was no danger, but we would have to limp back to Paris at subsonic speed and change to the Concorde that Air France kept in reserve. This destroyed my story, of course, and I later wasted hours at JFK before getting a 747 back home in the evening. But I sympathized with a fellow traveler, on a less frivolous mission than mine, who missed a crucial meeting with banks that morning in Manhattan.

The last Concorde trip I made, an afternoon flight from London to New York about 10 years ago, was less eventful. Quite good wine, I remember, but the food was dire and there was nobody to talk to. People were tapping away at their laptops or huddled together in conspiratorial tête-à-têtes. The girth-stricken steward, almost as wide as the aisle, had little time for me.

Clearly, I was not a fully paid up member of the club.

What's more, the person I was supposed to meet in Manhattan didn't show up. So I spent most of the time I had saved flying the Concorde switching TV channels in the hotel room.

The Hotel room of the future

2004 International Herald Tribune

Welcome to the hotel room of the future: an ergonomic, open living area 'that guests can tailor to their individual needs.' Mod-cons include 'fiber optically lit carpet swaying to star lights twinkling on the ceiling above the bed,' the rooms will offer a feast of sensual delights, including textured glass walls 'that can be transformed with adjustable colored lighting' and 'a personal beverage station will be filled with the guest's favorite drinks.' Guests will be able to create their own 'wall of art,' from images of tropical beaches and famous monuments. Music selections can be personalized and air currents can be programmed to breeze setting.

This is the future, or, rather, it is Holiday Inn's vision of a model room for the needs of the traveler in 2054.

'The key is flexibility, allowing them to control their environment through technology, allowing them to create a true home from home,' said Stephen Powell, Holiday Inn's senior vice president for sales and marketing for Europe, the Middle East and Africa.

It will be, in the words of the 20th century's most influential architectural thinker, Le Corbusier, quite literally 'a machine for living in.'

For example, the personal exercise area would include virtual links with fitness instructors to a virtual marathon through a city of your choice. Press your feet down on the workout mat for a calorie count, body weight and blood pressure reading. Mirrors in the shower area can analyze your 'facial image' and give examples of, say, how your hair could look. You could nurture your nostrils from the "atomizer selection" with smells like newly cut grass or baking bread.

The bed can become a seating area with light or heavy support to suit your comfort, and the multi-function table area provides a practical working surface with keyboard functions and a touch screen that transforms into to a dressing table and mirror.

The hotel room has come a long way since the 1960s, when I started traveling on business. Driving down from Michigan to Indiana, I would look for the Holiday Inn sign as a guarantee of a comfortable bed for the night. Rooms were exactly the same at each property: a bed, a small tub and towels; you knew the coffee-shop menu by heart. The only gizmos were a black-and-white TV and a 'massage boy' – insert a quarter and the mattress would vibrate for a few minutes. You did your own "virtual" experience.

Since those simpler days, travelers' expectations have kept pace with their requirements. Everybody expects a comfortable bed, power shower, color TV with umpteen channels and Internet access. Business travelers want more recognition, more control; the hotel bedroom has become a command center, not so much a home away from home as an office from home.

For the futuristic room, Holiday Inn recruited British interior designer, Laurence Llewelyn-Bowen, to create computer graphics, and Martin Corbett, professor of psychology at Warwick University in Coventry, England, to predict what hotel guests might want in 50 years' time. 'We've looked at cultural trends. People want a home from home, a sense of comfort and reassurance,' Corbett says. 'They want to have mastery over the technology they're using, to be in control, the power to create their own experience and their own environment – not just access to the Internet, but the climate of a room, the sound of a room; and involving the senses.'

What happens to the old-fashioned notion of hospitality?

'This kind of technology saves us time learning about your needs,' Powell says, 'We've focused on room design, but it should include service through connectivity. For example, you can communicate with the guest better. When you want the room cleaned, rather than ringing room service, we'll have a processing system through loyalty cards with chips. We'll meet expectations because they will have been anticipated.'

Video Conference: a global view

1998 International Herald Tribune

If you have ever felt that stepping off a long-haul flight into a business meeting is a form of virtual reality (Couldn't we have done this on the phone?), here comes Rosenbluth International – the second-largest travel management company in the world – with virtual reality in the form of 'virtual conferencing,' a new product developed by TeleSuite Corporation, which it is offering to corporate clients as an alternative to business travel.

TeleSuite claims to achieve what ordinary video conferencing 'has always promised but never delivered.' Participants appear life-sized and you have the illusion that they're in the same room – which means that you can behave naturally and don't have to change the way you normally communicate. You use the same body language. What's more, you don't need a Space Invaders helmet. 'Ultimately, we're in the business of connecting people,' says Danamichelle O'Brien, vice president and chief travel scientists at Rosenbluth International in Philadelphia. 'Virtual travel is the next logical step for our business. And TeleSuite allows us to connect our clients from point A to point B in a shorter amount of time.

As we've seen in all business practices from overnight delivery to e-mail, this era is about time compression – allowing people to do more – faster.

'"Don't leave home" is not typical advice from a travel company,' O'Brien says, 'but if it makes sense for our client, we recommend it. Virtual conferencing, video conferencing or PC-based conferencing will not replace travel. There will always be a need to be somewhere in person. Just as the fax machine and the postal service coexist, so can virtual travel and actual travel. What we're creating with TeleSuite is virtual airlines. It may allow people to make three trips instead of five, or travel the same amount and just speed up their business cycles.'

Scott Allen, vice president of corporate communications at TeleSuite in Dayton, Ohio, says: 'We set out with IBM Global Services and NEC Technologies to design a new video conferencing system that didn't have a roll-about monitor with a camera sitting on top.

Normally, you can only have your head life-size on a monitor screen, and if you see someone moving around, the image is very jerky.

'We wanted people to feel that they were in the same room, like sitting across the desk, not just because they are life-sized and make eye contact with you, and the voice is coming from their direction, but because they're standing on the same carpet in your office, with the same wall covering, the same decor,' Allen said.

'We have built what you may call a virtual environment – a tele-presence whereby you are projecting yourself into someone else's virtual reality.'

Picture this. Take a conference room with a circular or oval table. Then chop the room in half right through the table and put a 100-inch high-resolution screen down the middle and pull the room apart – 100 or 1,000 miles – and connect the two halves with a very high bandwidth cable. When the screen illuminates, you see the other half of your table completed as a mirror-image drawn on the screen with participants from the other site sitting around the table with you as in a normal conference room.

You make a call to TeleSuite saying you want to use the system at such and such a time. TeleSuite makes the bookings with the various locations involved.

Half an hour before the conference the locations are automatically connected, the lights come on, the screen is illuminated, and you just walk into the room and engage the other participants face-to-face, just as you would in a meeting room down the hall.

'We are right now facilitating a nine-city meeting for IBM to train people to use a new software program,' Allen says. 'Of course, it would be chaotic if 29 locations tried to communicate one with the other,' he says. 'But we have done up to six meetings that are fully interactive – it's just that participants need to be self-disciplined and not all speak at the same time.

And, of course, you have to make the picture smaller.

But you can have the illusion of being in the room with up to three sites. You can have a voice-activated system whereby whatever location is talking, they are the ones on full screen. Some people like that; others like windows on a split screen.'

The TeleSuite conference room comes in a modular design that can be erected as a room within a room at corporate locations. TeleSuite has 17 public locations in the United States available for hourly reservations at Hilton hotels, including the Waldorf-Astoria in New York, the Capital Hilton in Washington, and the Atlanta Hilton and Towers.

A recent link with the Grand Hyatt Hong Kong allows you to conduct a one-hour video conference with up to 10 participants from each side for 120,000 yen ($886) – less than an undiscounted round-trip economy fare between the two cities. The hourly charge from the Grand Hyatt Hong Kong is 75,000 yen. It costs around 87,000 yen to link up with Britain or France. Kate Burchill, a Hyatt spokeswoman in London, says that video conferencing is mainly used for monthly strategy sessions and troubleshooting, client presentations, training sessions and interviews of job candidates.

Video conferencing is probably less about saving money on travel and more about global teamwork. It enables people to attend meetings who might not normally attend if they had to travel – for example, senior managers or specialists.

Does the Meeting Deliver the Message?

1998 International Herald Tribune

You have spent a chunk of your budget bringing the troops to Hawaii or some other sun-blessed archipelago, for this high-powered meeting to celebrate your new software product. And all has gone smoothly: the travel, the meeting logistics, the multimedia presentations, the gala dinner and the fireworks. Yes, it has been a great event; everyone seems fired up; congratulations to the meeting organizer.

But are the troops properly prepared to go out and sell? Has the medium delivered the message?

The answer, as Sam Goldwyn might have said, is a definite maybe. For here comes Meeting Planners International, a charitable foundation based in Dallas, Texas, with a study, 'Making Meetings Work: An Analysis of Corporate Meetings,' published last month, which examined key success factors in sales meetings, management meetings and education-training meetings. It concludes that there is 'often a large gap between how senior managers and attendees view the success of a conference or meeting' and between expectation and fulfillment. While 85 percent of senior managers think that their meetings are successful and 'are pleased with facilities and arrangements,' they have concerns 'about what happens with the attendees after the meeting.'

'The focus is on what meeting planners should be doing to help management achieve its goals,' said Nikki Walker, a spokeswoman for MPI in Brussels.

'Traditionally, senior management has taken control of the contents of meetings themselves and left meeting planners just to handle the logistics and making sure the equipment works. What we're saying is that they should sometime take the advice of professional planners on the content as well, to make meetings more motivational, more effective – avoiding some of the classic mistakes, like having sessions that drag on too long, where the message is lost, and making sure that the corporate goal is actually being achieved.'

MPI plans to develop a system that rates 'proven success factors' to enable corporate meeting planners to develop their own 'gap analysis' of their company's sales, management or education meetings.

'The idea of a successful meeting must be expanded beyond "satisfaction" to the "achievement of corporate goals,"' the study says.

'Meeting content needs to be addressed in a strategic fashion, not just an operational one, so you need to be asking your boss or client, "Why are we having this meeting?

What tools will measure its success?"' said Vanessa Cotton, managing director of The Event Organization in London.

'The message is, let's plan the meeting and what we want to achieve and then we'll think about venues and hotels, hot food on plates and the color of badges.

'A lot of meeting organizers think on a micro level – getting small things right.

That's important; but getting the big things right means understanding the strategy and reinforcing that throughout the event, and how delegates will evaluate the event – whether it's value for time and money.'

'There's a definite feeling in organizations these days that time equals money and it's essential to get an efficient return on peoples' time invested,' Walker said. 'Making sure that speakers are delivering the message: That comes out over and over again in the MPI survey. The traditional five-day company conference has been cut to two and a half days. Europeans stick to European destinations to limit time out of the office and traveling time. A one-day meeting at an airport hotel in Frankfurt or Paris saves commuting time downtown.'

Meetings and conferences have become more purposeful and less glitzy. Meeting planners talk about getting the right balance between 'motivational values' and strategic and tactical 'imperatives.' A good conference, or meeting, is a catalyst, a means to an end rather than an end in itself. Objectives should be clearly defined along with a clear idea of how you measure success.

Manuela Ranzanici, meeting planner at Hewlett Packard in Geneva, said: "People these days are very, very busy – they don't want to spend half a day or a whole day getting there. There's a tendency to start or finish a meeting over a weekend, taking advantage of APEX fares and weekend hotel rates – instead of arriving on a Monday and getting back to the office on a Thursday, It's starting on a Sunday and back in the office Tuesday afternoon or Wednesday morning latest. Or start on a Friday and go back on Sunday.'

What is coming up now, Ranzanici says, is a trend for people who travel a lot to bring their partners – even kids – along to a conference, depending on the program, although they might have to pick up the tab.

'It's contradictory, in a sense,' Ranzanici said. 'But it's all to do with "new values – work-life balance."'

Choosing the venue is sometimes the hardest part of organizing a meeting. If you have people from more than one country, you might want to meet on neutral ground, such as a beach in Jamaica, or the new conference center in Hong Kong.

'Whenever the economy takes a lurch, companies adopt a leaner, meaner persona – steering away from, say, the French Riviera, which is excellent for meetings, but may give out the wrong message,' Cotton said.

"So they meet in The Hague, Berlin or Birmingham. But places like Rimini, just slightly out of season, are incredibly cheap.

Then you need to think of communications – bringing people in, either as a group or individuals.'

If there's a recession, Cotton said, the meeting industry will be affected as it was the last the last time around. 'What companies have learned in the past is to keep talking, not only to their staff but to their customers.'

Executives on Vacation: not all play
1991 International Herald Tribune

Executives in the United States do not take vacations just for fun these days. Time off is spent working hard to cope with stress, prevent burnout, increase productivity and improve relationships back at the office. People are seeking new and exciting places to go and more activities. And vacations are shorter and more frequent as you go up the corporate ladder.

These are the findings of a survey of 500 American executives carried out by Hyatt Hotels Corporation in May and June this year.

Respondents ranged from managers/directors to presidents/company owners with average incomes of $113,000.

The study included telephone and in-person interviews of executives on vacation at resorts. The sample was equally divided between men and women.

Average age was 47, with 58 percent age 45 or older.

Predictably, executives admit they 'play more, eat and drink more, become more athletic and sexually freer' when on vacation. This accompanies a change of personality, which makes them 'more devilish' (55 percent), and 'more of a risk taker' (53 percent). Nearly half take work along.

A 'spouse or significant other' is the preferred vacation companion among both married and unmarried executives.

Executives look upon vacations as a 'psychological investment' and in spite of increased pressure to perform with the recession, 78 percent believe vacations are 'absolutely essential to prevent executive burnout.'

Women are more likely than men to view vacations as a 'vital part of their lives.'

They are far less bound to the Puritan work ethic, and are probably more ready to give themselves permission to take the time off.' Women seem to suffer more than men from pre-vacation stress, and work longer hours before they get away.

Respondents average four vacations a year, with 53 percent saying they've become shorter the higher they rise in the corporation. Sixty-two percent say they should take more vacations in the future. Wherever they go, a majority (70 percent) say the office knows where they are at all times. Company owners, presidents and CEOs are most likely to be 'constantly calling the office' (30 percent).

As in all surveys, there are several types of demographic and psychographic categories to choose from:

Power Players – who make the smoothest transition from work to play and back again.

On vacation, they take work with them, stay in touch with the office, and believe that this enhances their ability to relax.

Calm, cool and confident at work, they stay like that way on vacation.

And unlike most other executives, they don't become more athletic or outgoing while away. Since they mix work and play so successfully, they do not notice a significant improvement in their job performance when they return to the office. (About 21 percent.)

Stress Fighters – use vacations as missions to relieve stress. While away, they aggressively pursue athletics and are obsessively health-conscious. They prefer vacations that conform to their lifestyles and do not take the time to meet new people or discover new places.

They believe vacations have a positive effect on job performance. (21 percent.)

Fugitives – in spite of their high level of achievement, are unhappy at work, worried about financial security and see vacations as the great escape. And yet they can't stop worrying about their jobs, the money they're spending, and the homes, pets and the children left behind. They tend not to take all their vacation time. (25 percent.)

Fun Worshipers – who see vacations as a healthy balance to a happy work life. Out to enjoy the break from the office, they leave worries behind, like to party, and become more outgoing and athletic and tend to say vacations enhance marriages. They return to the office reinvigorated, and consequently see an improvement in job performances. (13 percent.)

Schedulers – who believe the longer and more you plan a vacation the better it will be.

They see planning as one of the most rewarding aspects of vacations and schedule most daily activities ahead of time.

Schedulers believe vacations reinvigorate them, but do not have much effect on job performance. (19 percent.)

'What surprised me is that I am not unique in feeling much more comfortable being active in business on vacation. I find you can relax much better by doing that,' says Darryl Hartley-Leonard, president of Hyatt Hotels Corporation.

'For years my wife would say, "Look, you'll never be able to relax if you don't stop calling."

'Yet finally, even in our family, she realized, look, give him that half hour a day that he's in touch with his office and he will be able to relax for the rest of the time.

'People misinterpret the need to be in touch with work as a kind of insecurity. I maintain that because work is part of my personal environment I have no desire to escape from it. The study really makes you look at yourself differently.'

Having decided that vacations are a good thing, what kinds of vacations are executives looking for?

'Our research shows that people are looking for new experiences. They want to climb a mountain, go on a hike, camp out, ride those river rapids for a day, go scuba diving,' Hartley-Leonard says.

'They may like the idea of sitting on a beach for a couple of hours but I think the group we were talking to find that when there's too much leisure, too much sitting doing nothing, the mind starts to wander back to the work place.

I can sit there reading a book and after four or five pages I'm not reading any more.

But if somebody puts me on a rock face, I'm not going to worry about occupancy in Des Moines.

The more activities, the more rest, the more regeneration you're getting.'

The recession has had the effect of encouraging the trend to shorter trips. 'We have far more weekend business than ever before,' Hartley-Leonard says. 'But the long-term vacation, the 10-day trip to Hawaii, has really been hurt. Right now it's a buyer's market: it's a bloody war out there.'

'Mobile homes' on the high seas
2002 International Herald Tribune

You could call it the ultimate mobile home – a $270 million luxury 'floating condominium' that will have called at 120 ports in 40 countries by the time it drops anchor at Honolulu on New Year's Day.

This is not a cruise ship, according to Nikki Upshaw, vice president of sales for ResidenSea, its operating company. "This is the first ocean-going luxury resort," Upshaw said. 'We are selling a lifestyle.'

Built in Norway for the billionaire ship owner Knut Kloster Jr., who came up with the slogan 'travel the world without leaving your home,' The World has 110 apartments costing from $2.2 million to $8 million.

Rentals range from about $45,000 for 30 days to $514,000 for 300 days. The 12 story ship has so far attracted 80 buyers. About 40 percent of The World's resident population is Americans, 20 percent Britons and 30 percent from other European countries. Most are 55 to 60, Upshaw says, and self-made entrepreneurs. They need to be. Owners have to pay 5 percent of their purchase price every year in service charges.

The World may be large as ships go, but it's only about a 10-minute stroll from prow to stern. You can break your walk with a visit to the pool, the library, the casino, the tennis court, the art gallery, shops or the golf range. When at anchor, golfers can drive biodegradable balls, which dissolve after four days in the sea, at a green on a floating island trailing behind the ship.

A visit to the deli on the 'village' deck yielded few of the staples required by new homeowners. On display were Champagne, caviar, foie gras, smoked salmon, fresh pasta and pastries.

Other shopping temptations range from jewelry to original art. The ship has a theater, four gourmet restaurants, footpaths with real grass from the Spanish coast and a fully equipped hospital. The World sailed up the Thames to Greenwich in southeast London this month on its inaugural voyage, which began in Oslo and stopped in Hamburg. Then it headed for Lisbon and a relentless global itinerary. Many of The World's ports of call have been planned so that the visit coincides with 'major world events,' such as the British Open at Gleneagles, Scotland, and the Cannes film festival.

Jeremy Scott, managing director of CruiseFare, a travel agency in London, says, 'Do I think it is going to work as a cruise product? Probably not, because a cruise ship is all-inclusive of entertainment, meals,' and The World is not, 'and there's no companionship on board. It's a floating resort, the ultimate time-share. You don't have to worry about swapping it to be where you want to be. It's a means of transferring from one resort to another. Buy an apartment and it moves for you.'

If The World seems too high a price to pay for a global home, you might want to wait for the Freedom Ship (www.freedomship.com), a 'floating city' nearly a mile long (four times the length of the QE2) and 25 stories high. This latter-day Ark will have 17,000 'residential units,' ranging in price from $150,000 to nearly $10 million for the penthouse, plus 3,000 'commercial units.' The ship will 'circle the world once every two years,' and can house as many as 115,000 people to 'live, work, vacation or visit.'

The vessel will house a hospital, schools, shops, banks, hotels, restaurants, entertainment facilities, offices, warehouses, 'light manufacturing and assembly enterprises' and a trade center for companies 'to showcase their products in a different country every two or three days.' There are 200 acres (about 80 hectares) of open space with 'parkland, grass, trees, waterfalls' on the outside decks, and a wide range of recreational and athletic facilities.

Norman Nixon, chief executive of Freedom Ship International Inc. in Palm Harbor, Florida, says: 'We're an engineering and construction company and have been working on this project for nine years. We're raising the money, around $11 billion, and hope to get started with construction by the end of the year; then it will be 38 months before it's operational. So we're talking about three and a half years. Freedom Ship is basically a flat-bottom sea platform with a conventional high-rise built on top.'

The ship is as large as it is because that is the minimum size required to make the community economically self-sustaining and an attractive place to live, according to Nixon. The greatest interest, he says, has been shown by trading companies that want to do business in a different country every week or run a dot-com business out of the ship. And there are a lot of people who want to get a job on the ship – teachers and nurses want to buy units. An airport on the ship's top deck will serve private and small commercial aircraft carrying up to about 40 passengers. 'The Freedom Ship has not been conceived a tax haven,' Nixon said. 'While the community itself will levy no taxes, citizens of countries such as the United States will not realize any income-tax savings by residing or running businesses on board since we are taxed on worldwide income – and receive no tax deductions if we reside on a ship.'

In search of the 'boutique experience'
2012 OAG

How often do travelers find the clichés of the glossy ads, and the PR hype, redeemed by that elusive amalgam of true friendliness, service, recognition, and efficiency that I call 'hospitality,' whether in hotels, airlines or cruise ships?

It is hard to find that authentic welcome, a true home from home, to coin another cliché; it is palpable but at the same time elusive; it is hard to define, except in industry clichés, but seasoned travelers recognize it at once – typically in the first ten minutes of stepping into a hotel, or boarding a jet.

Travelers cherish recognition, whether they are traveling for business or pleasure, or both. Hotels that treat every guest as 'mystery shoppers' can reap dividends in goodwill and future business. But 'recognition' means different things to different people. It can mean simply being greeted by name by the staff; having the deputy front manager steam across the foyer to welcome you; flowers, fruit, or maybe a nice chilled bottle of your favorite vintage in the room.

Legend has it that Fats Waller, when asked for a definition of jazz, replied: 'Lady if you have to ask, I can't tell you.' (It is a nice analogy when you think that jazz engages both the brain and the feet.) The immortal Billie Holiday said, 'Blues is a mixed up thing; you have to feel it.'

I call it the 'boutique experience' – the gut feeling that the smiles are real, not the plastic smiles, switched off nanoseconds after they turn their heads – real smiles are smiles that linger; the feeling that you are a 'guest,' not a 'customer.'

It comes down to training and example which has to come down from the top through the organization. It has to be dyed deep in the culture and in the reward system of a company; and permeate through to every employee whether in direct or indirect contact with guests.

'People are our most precious asset' is a corporate mantra that has a hollow ring in many organizations, whether it applies to staff or customers.

'Boutique' is an overused word describing any small environment with 'luxury' facilities. But small is not necessarily beautiful; although there does seem to be an optimum size – and a staff/guest ratio of typically one to three. It is the 'software' – the soft-skills of the people who provide the service – that can make or break the experience.

Bea Tollman is founder-president of the Red Carnation Hotel Collection of fourteen boutique hotels in outstanding locations – five in London, two in Dorset, Guernsey, Geneva, Palm Beach, and three in South Africa. She inspires awe and affection among the staff.

'The boutique experience for me is that people feel they are walking into a home where the welcome is warm, genuine and where they are recognized for who they are. Every guest should be made to feel special; that is what we really aim to do. And we do this through training and leadership example – how you genuinely feel about people. But to make a real boutique hotel you should have less than a hundred odd rooms; I think that's the optimum number really.'

Guy Young, president of Uniworld, a self-styled 'Boutique River Cruise Collection,' based in Los Angeles, says. 'What makes us unique as a river cruise operator is that the décor on our ships has a different look and feel... plush, intimate and warm; we're not a cookie-cutter company. We average about 130 guests, with one staff member for every three guests. So they get to know the guests personally, and greet them by name when they come back on board after an excursion; it's like a big family on board, and our staff work very hard to express that sincere, caring attitude. And there's a lot of interaction between the guests.'

The Virgin Limited Edition of boutique properties includes the Necker Island resort in the British Virgin Islands, along with the Necker Belle, a 100-foot catamaran; Kasbah Tamadot in Morocco; a private game lodge in Ulusaba, South Africa; the Roof Gardens and the Babylon restaurant in London; and The Lodge in Verbier, Switzerland.

The Lodge, a large chalet style hotel, consists of two big communal floors and nine en suite guest rooms; and 14 staff.

Hannah Allen, general manager of The Lodge, says, 'It's a very relaxed feel. With one staff member for every three guests, we can be up till four or five in the morning, until the last guest goes to bed. It's a tailor-made environment. Richard [Branson], whether he is staying with us or on Necker Island, likes to come and relax; he likes a homely feeling and to share that with other people. We have groups of business people; family couples with friends; winter skiers; corporate clients... it's a real mix.'

'When you go into some of the larger hotels, it's clear the staff have been taught certain things they have to say; it doesn't come from the heart; and everybody you pass along a corridor or anywhere in the hotel they all say the same things; you just feel they've been taught to say that,' Bea Tollman says. 'I believe my staff genuinely feels pleased to see a guest – hopefully know their name – and feel that they mean what they say.

'Training is everything; and the motivation; to motivate passion into your staff, for them to be proud of working in that hotel or that company,' Tollman adds. 'That's the thing that makes their working life more interesting and they know there's a chance to do better in a company where someone is watching over them, and encouraging them to grow.

'It comes down to knowing the standards of the hotel and having a very critical eye; you should be watching everything,' Bea Tollman says. Nothing should be left half done. If you see something that's not right, you should immediately do it, and be enthusiastic about doing it. You've got to learn and train your eye to notice these things; to put them right; and then to be genuine, be sincere; because hotel management is the same all over the world. Everybody is taught the same things; how to run a department; what you should look for...

'What it amounts to really is the service; and looking for the detail, because it's a detail business. Everybody's got everything and doing the same things today; you read up what your competitors are doing, and you do it. What really counts is your staff: and how you genuinely care about your guests.'

I believe it was the legendary Soichiro Honda who once said that Japanese and Western management was 95 percent the same, 'but different in all important respects.' He meant the software – personal skills that make the difference and provide the competitive edge – especially true in the service industry.

On a recent visit to the Ecole Hoteliere in Lausanne, I was exploring an angle for a story: how and why hotel managers can readily adapt to other management roles but seemingly not the other way round: Perhaps because hotel managers learn an eclectic range of skills having hands-on experience in so many diverse areas of expertise.

Red Carnation has what you might call 'peer-performance' reviews in the form of weekly or monthly meetings at each hotel when all the staff vote for the 'best manager' of each department. They'll also acquire experience of how other departments work by changing positions during the year and functions by changing positions for a time during the year. The doorman might end up as a receptionist; a manager will serve as a doorman; or work in the food and beverage department...

While there seems to be an optimum size for a boutique property, I asked Bea Tollman if there is an 'optimum' size for a personally managed family group such as Red Carnation.

'One wants to be able to grow but not too much that you can't keep up the standards with the input that the higher level of management has to give to the different hotels,' she says. 'You can only spread yourself that thin because you just get busier and busier; standards get higher in the hotels; the things we do take an awful lot of time and effort... How can you keep that spirit up when you've got too many hotels? We've got fifteen operations now, and to look after all of those and to watch what's going on, know what's happening, and encourage them and do the right thing... it takes a tremendous amount of work.

Although I have always assumed that every silver lining has a cloud; I cling to the belief that every cloud has a silver lining. The events of 9/11 precipitated a crisis among world airlines, which went into free fall, with empty seats and canceled services, and large hotel chains suffered falls in occupancy levels, there was a boom in the charter market for business jets (even for trans-Atlantic travel) and boutique hotels reported business almost as normal at a time when fewer people were traveling.

It is easy to understand why. Jet charter (and the growth of scheduled business-only airlines that use business jets) addresses a need for security, discretion and confidentiality. Book a charter and you travel to your own schedule in an unmarked plane with private access at major hubs or convenient small airports, even taken by limo to the steps of the plane. During the flight, you can relax, work or have meetings. And speed by limo (motorcycle escort is optional!) to your office – or boutique hotel.

Business jets (whether chartered or scheduled), along with boutique hotels are 'private' environments compared with the public arena of large hotels and even the premium cabins of conventional airlines. You might call it 'closed circuit' travel, segregated from the madding crowd, and cocooned in your own security blanket. What I would call a true boutique experience. Back to basics, what makes a great hotel? This is a recurring theme that I am often asked to talk about. There is no ideal. People travel in different modes, different frames of mind, with different needs, motivations and prejudices, that can vary from trip to trip, depending on why we're going and where we're headed.

Are we traveling only for business or trying to combine that with a vacation? Do we need to use the room as a high-tech business center? Do we need a prestigious address with facilities to entertain, a high-tech 'command center' to work and keep in touch with the office, or simply a room for the night? How important is location? Are we looking for adventure, new experiences? What is our budget? How much do loyalty and frequent guest programs count? And who is picking up the tab?

Everybody expects a quiet room with high safety standards and service. Add to this your own pet foibles, predilections and prejudices, such as wall-to-wall Muzak, $50 club sandwiches from room service and egregious mini-bar prices. Some people seek recognition, such as being greeted by name by the deputy assistant duty night manager. Others thrive on anonymity. Or 'added value' options, such as early check-in, late check-out, room upgrades, airport transfers, cocktails and canapés, exquisite bed linen, or a luxurious turn-down service with candles and chocolates on the pillow. Small things can make a big difference; a sincere handshake; a misplaced smile; or a gesture beyond the normal call of duty that can make or break the experience. (I once shocked a group of hotel managers by jokingly averring that one of my criteria for judging a hotel was by the quality of the removable wooden coat hangars that I might accidentally take home to add to my collection.)

Hotel experiences (good and bad) stick in the mind like burrs. There was the late night welcome at the Hotel Splendido in Porto Fino with prosciutto and ripe pear and a cold bottle of Chablis; the giant Edwardian bathtubs and lemon-scented soap at the old Hyde Park Hotel in London; the vital telephone call that I took when caught short in the bathroom of the Excelsior Gallia in Milan; and, in a hurry for the airport, losing, for forty fateful minutes, my sole pair of shoes that I had left outside my door to be cleaned at the Plaza Athenée in Paris.

The warmth and sincerity of the welcome and goodbyes I receive at the five-star plus Beau Rivage Palace in Lausanne is truly heart warming, with calls beyond the call of duty. I shall never forget the time when Sylvie, the luminescent head concierge gave my sick wife care beyond the call of duty; and offered us a car to the airport. The Beau Rivage is a rare example of a traditional grand hotel with that authentic boutique feel.

My wife and I once booked into the Westminster Hotel in Nice, a fine rococo building on the Promenade des Anglais. I was on a hard-core business assignment, but we had made arrangements with British Airways' frequent flier miles. We got a lousy room and reception to match: I had to wield my vestigial management skills to change the room and rearrange the attitude.

Flashback to several years ago which shows that a truly grand hotel is still a class act:

I was on a magazine assignment in the south of France with a photographer from New York. We entered the Negresco Hotel in Nice, the grandest of the Belle Epoque palaces almost next door to the Westminster, in pursuit of a room for him – he had not made a reservation.

Nothing strange about that, except that photographers can sometimes look very strange. This one had red suspenders and a purple vest. And I looked strange in a black leather jacket, white pants, espadrilles, no socks, and a mane of windswept hair. But we were received with elaborate courtesy by a liveried voiturier, who took the keys of my 2CV, the doorman and desk clerk.

There was none of the usual: 'How will you be settling your bill, sir?' or, 'Can I take an imprint of your credit card?'

I explained our mission to the manager, congratulating him on the charm and hospitality of his staff. He smiled, 'Ah, yes, Monsieur C, you can never tell who you have in front of you these days!'

Years ago, I always stayed at the same small, somewhat decrepit, hotel in Paris, because of the charm and graciousness of Nicolas, the elderly and erudite White Russian night porter.

I will return to that tatty hotel with a big heart in Avignon, but never to the four-star palace hotel in Nice because of its rude and uncomprehending staff.

Cattle class on one airline can sometimes be a better experience than business class on another. You may have noticed how often two flights on the same airline is like flying with two different airlines. Frequent fliers are able to detect a 'bad' crew from a 'good' crew the moment they board the plane. One hotelier says that he can tell a good hotel from a bad hotel in the first ten minutes.

Welf Eberling, former executive vice president and chief operating officer in New York of Leading Hotels of the World, says, "The perception of luxury today is not gilded moldings or a plasma flat-screen television, but a harmonious blend of product and service. There are certain givens. For example, we don't measure the size of rooms, but how often does room service push in the trolley and there's only one easy chair so the other person has to perch on the corner of the bed?

'Rooms should have three phones with two lines: one by the bed, one on the desk, one in the bathroom. Turn-down service is always a great point of discussion. There's more to it than folding back the top sheet and putting a chocolate on the pillow – it should be full room service, straightening out the bathroom, bringing in new towels. Then, there is the whole spectrum of food and beverage. We are not giving a Michelin star for food it's the service that counts. How is the guest received in the restaurant? Is the waiter attentive, does he pre-empt some of your wishes? In a five-star hotel it should be an experience; like a restaurant.'

Trent Walsh, managing director of Leading Quality Assurance in London, says, 'Leading Hotels' members are inspected twice in a three-year cycle. Our inspectors stay anonymously for 48 hours and score each department against a total of 1,200 quantitative standards and a qualitative scoring – the fuzzy, touchy-feely aspect that is so important in the luxury sector.'

He adds: 'Luxury five-star hotels must fulfill what you would expect: a good bathroom, separate shower, double sinks and quality linen. But only 35 percent of the assessment is based on product; the other 65 percent depends on service, which is much more important. You can have the most wonderful product in the world, but if you don't couple it with a phenomenal service, you are not going to succeed in the luxury hotel market.'

This is why some smaller boutique hotels achieve good scores even if they don't have all the amenities of larger properties. They make up with gains in service.

Andy Thrasyvoulou, founder of myhotelbloomsbury, a four-star boutique hotel in London, claims to have found the right balance between high-tech rooms and comfort. The idea is that the hotel should work to the guest's pace.

'We try to know as much as possible about the guest before he or she arrives,' Thrasyvoulou says. 'Maybe you want to check in at the bar area with a coffee or drink, talk about London with one of our guest service people, or, if you're in a hurry and we know about that, you can sign off quickly.

'One of my frustrations with hotels was that if I wanted something done, you'd have this endless directory of numbers. You ring one up and they say, sorry, it's not us, it's the concierge, or housekeeping. So what we've done is, you ring one number that goes to the guest service pool where they'll have all the information about you. Even if they can't help you immediately, they'll go to talk to housekeeping or whoever and get back to you.'

Thrasyvoulou admits to being influenced by Stuart Scher and J.F. Hofmeyer at Taylor Nelson Sofres, a consultancy in London, who have examined the relationship between customer satisfaction and loyalty.

'There are three elements to customer loyalty and commitment,' Thrasyvoulou says: 'First is reasonable satisfaction, the second is having a compelling reason to use your product or service, the third is being better than your competition.' At least 20 percent of satisfied customers do not stay loyal, he says. The reason may be that competitors have shown them an alternative, which could be as simple as air miles or hotel points.

Mind the gap

2004 International Herald Tribune: CNN Traveller

In my long-ago corporate days, when we were ruled by guilt and anxiety and card-carrying members of Workaholics Anonymous (two-ulcer men in three-ulcer jobs), the notion of a sabbatical, or time out, was a cruel joke. Sabbaticals were for tenured business school professors, or freshly fired vice presidents, floating down to earth on golden parachutes; or the silver-haired rich with time on their hands. Hell, we did not dare take our annual two-week vacation. You were stressed out and got on with it.

Fast-forward to today and news that a new wave of young stressed-out executives in their late twenties to early thirties has joined the 16 to 24 year-olds taking a 'gap year,' the traditional rite of middle-class passage, traveling to foreign lands before or after university.

This is the finding of a survey of 2,013 British executives, aged 26 to 34, carried out by YouGov on behalf of the Bradford & Bingley building society, the second largest in the country.

Nigel Asplin, group general insurance director at Bradford & Bingley, says, 'Traveling has become increasingly popular at an age when life itself has become a "stress zone." People are using extended breaks to relieve work pressure. Having worked for a few years, they feel they deserve it.'

Nearly half of adults (49 percent) believe that the best time to travel is once one has some life experience, rather than during their student years: 46 percent see extended breaks as the chance to review their lifestyle and attitudes.

While this group would obviously have more money than students for travel, half still intend to do it in 'backpacker' style, staying in cheap accommodation and having a daily food budget while still enjoying sports and cultural activities. However, there are some trappings of their affluent lifestyle they wouldn't leave behind: 81 percent would take their digital camera with them, 18 percent their iPOD and 17 percent their PalmPilot. Most popular destinations include Australia and New Zealand, Canada, United States, and South America.

Brett Shepperson, 32, left his job, building a mobile phone network, leveraged his mortgage, and with the £25,000 proceeds took off with his girlfriend for a year traveling around the world, spending an average of four weeks in 13 countries. They scuba dived in the Galapagos Islands, skied in Argentina, and climbed the Cotopaxi mountain in Ecuador. A high point was a Spanish language school in Quito, Ecuador, where they met a rich mix of people, teachers, executives, writers…

'I came back a different person, more confident, more laid-back, a new perspective and mental well-being,' Shepperson says. 'I have a new job now as telecom project manager in Norwich.'

Fiona Smith and Justin Harvey gave up their jobs and a joint income of £60,000 to backpack across South America for six months, traveling through Ecuador, Peru and Bolivia. While they are on a tight budget, they still plan to splurge occasionally. Harvey, who has worked as an IT consultant in London for eight years, looks for respite and 'a different pace of life' for a while.

Visa International, as part of its ongoing research into how people spend their money when overseas, finds that young travelers of today are more financially astute and more resourceful than either their peers who opt to stay at home or the backpackers of 20 years ago. They are likely to be young professionals, students, graduates or young executives on the first steps of their career. This group has thought in great detail about the money they will need and the best ways of handling and accessing it when abroad, either by debit or credit card, or via internet banking.

The research shows that more than a third of 16 to 24 year olds see traveling as a last chance to take time out before starting work or an opportunity to take a break in their career. Dene Harrington, senior relationship manager at Visa International in London, says: 'We find that employers look favorably on people who have taken time out for traveling. They've shown that they are able to organize a trip, look after their security and finances. Experience of different cultures, confidence in meeting people and self-reliance are very important skills in their future career, whatever that may be.

'We were surprised at the number of 30 to 40 year-olds who feel they are far enough ahead in their careers to get out of the rat race, either take a sabbatical or a break between jobs – typically three to four months out.'

That I should be so lucky! I'll settle for a sabbatical long week-end.

Upbeat in the downturn
2010 CNN Business Traveller

I offer no prescient predictions about business travel in the downturn. Or in the upturn as travel rebounds, as it always does. Like economic forecasters, I can only react to events with sapient hindsight and reflect on the past mistakes of others.

But it's an ill wind as they say... And indeed, the economic downturn has been good for business, according to an American Express survey of senior

Roger Collis

UK finance executives over half (58 percent) of whom reveal that decisions made during the downturn have actually improved their firms' long term prospects.

'Business travel spending increases are planned in those areas of travel that are linked to revenue growth,' the survey quotes. And I am betting that these increases are focused on such areas as winning new business; protecting and developing client/customer or partner relationships; and networking at industry conferences and events. At the expense (no pun intended) of corporate get-togethers; internal wheel-spinning ('I must visit Jean-Pierre in Paris to discuss his marketing plan'): And forgoing (just this year anyway) on lubricating that 'essential' economic forum in Monte Carlo. (Let the pundits wallow in the trough of their own confusion.)

Even during these months of tough trading, owners of growing businesses understand the need to travel, not only within their own region, but farther afield. When the going gets tough (especially for small entrepreneurial businesses), the tough get going! Let the bad times roll. My credo has always been … 'what is bad for the travel trade is good for the traveler. And vice versa: although I'm happy to discuss caveats and corollaries.

'Zero-base' planning (aka 'navel-gazing' or sitting on a sharp stone) is a salutary exercise in these lean times.

Road warriors have made travel decisions on a shifting equation of cost, convenience and comfort, depending on where they are headed, and purpose of the trip. But tighter budgets and the sheer hassle of travel today have thrown into sharper focus the need to assess the 'productivity' of a business trip, taking into account the cost of management time rather than cost of travel alone.

So whenever a business interaction is needed, instead of automatically thinking of a trip, even inveterate road warriors now think of other alternatives first, such as videoconferencing in every form – from state-of-the-art virtual reality with eye contact and wrap-around sound to desk-top tele-conferencing; and an old-fashioned telephone call (a 'hot' medium as Canadian media guru Marshall McLuhan once famously said, making one focus entirely on the voice, the spoken word, which makes the phone as confessional as the psychoanalyst's couch; making it easier to deal with intimate or difficult subjects.)

Travel is no longer the first resort to the need for a business meeting. Videoconferencing can be an essential complement to travel. Fly to New York and hold a videoconference with the troops in various cities instead of traipsing around the country to visit them.

'Travel management' has evolved from being essentially a bookkeeping function – travel policy, traveling in the most efficient way, getting the best deals – to 'management' in the management sense. 'Why are we making this trip? What are we going to achieve? Can we do business some other way? How can we achieve better productivity by cutting out unnecessary travel and achieve better productivity for trips that we do make? Companies are reshaping the pattern of their travel. Management productivity has become the new byword for business travel.

Consider a spectrum from what you might call 'hard-core' business travel (a sales trip, or clinching a deal) and internal meetings with associates and partners to 'soft-core' travel (association conferences, exhibitions, seminars and incentive trips).

Videoconferencing has substituted some internal company travel, such as visiting other plants and offices, especially global companies with people having regional responsibilities and large time differences. Not all the troops need to travel to the same place for a monthly update. There is a need to build relationships, but not to meet every time.

Videoconferencing is best used for getting things done rather than building relationships. It can help to accelerate decision-making by letting people interact more often and move things along. It allows for informal and impromptu meetings that would not happen otherwise.

There is also the 'opportunity cost' of traveling somewhere when it might be more productive, going somewhere else, or having somebody fly in to meet you in the office, where you can call other people in when you need them. Or else do you fly to New York and convene a video-conference instead of making a whistle-stop tour around the country. Or do you send Joe? There is always an opportunity to do something else. One has to ask, what's the trade off? It is fairly easy to quantify travel productivity for sales people and line managers; harder for staff people. But that's another challenge.

The 'bottom-line' in travel management is getting other people to visit you.

Five executives in search of a room number
1984 'If my boss calls…'

I'm sure you've heard the story of the salesman who is summoned by his boss to explain an egregious item in his expense account. 'Now see here, Joe. I know you've had a tough month chasing the Fingelstein order up in Niagara Falls. But five hundred dollars for an overcoat; you know there's no way I can allow that. You'd better do these expenses again.'

The next day his boss is furious. 'Joe, I thought I told you to take out that overcoat. These expenses come to the same total as before.'

Joe is unchastened. 'Mel, I know it's the same total. But you find the overcoat.'

This might be one of the chestnuts chuckled over during the happy hour by five wide-bodied executives in their specially adapted wide-bodied airliner. At 30,000 feet the martinis are as steady as the pre-tax profits of their firm, Ocean Opportunities Inc. (Which is not say that both martinis and profits might not hit turbulence at any moment.) But the only hint of disturbance right now is the gastro-intestinal tract of Craig J. Hamstringer Jr, where a recalcitrant ulcer is having pre-prandial tantrums.

While the economy-class passengers are delving into their plastic pails, our portly five are planning their expense accounts for the next monthly reckoning.

The air is rich with creativity as more than overcoats are concealed. Hamstringer is leading the discussion.

'Dave, that Rolex you bought in London, I could hide in the agency dinner we had in Paris if you would let me have the receipt for the car rental.'

Dave Silver frowns. 'I appreciate the offer, Craig, but frankly I can't trade you the Avis receipt, that was a big one. Tell you what, though, we can split the thing down the middle. Or else I take another dinner tab. What do you think guys?'

Barbara Brandywine shunts her generous behind into the spare seat between the two men and squints at the pile of receipts. 'Seems fair enough to me Craig; don't forget Dave lent you his running account at the Windjammer Club last month when it looked like you'd have to dip into your salary for living expenses.'

Hamstringer concedes. 'Okay, Dave, you've got yourself a deal.' Then turning to Manuel: 'You're very quiet Manny, what's with that restaurant you invented in Philadelphia? Are you using it much these days?'

I should explain that it's all the rage among Ocean executives to have fictitious restaurant receipts printed. Manuel Fernandez is a specialist in non-existent establishments of all kinds. He once created not only an entire hotel but a fictitious conference to meet there. It had been so successful that it had only narrowly escaped detection when the president of Ocean wanted to take his wife there on company expenses. That would have caused a moral dilemma twice removed.

Manuel grins. 'The Mexican Beach Club?' It's pretty active; I've had to have more receipts printed. Hey, why don't you invite someone for lunch? We have some very expensive lobsters. They're flown in from the Coast on first-class seats. Very useful if you need to make up a quick coupla hundred bucks at the end of the month.'

George Washington IV, who has nodded off over his second martini, yawns hugely and runs long, black fingers through his executive Afro. 'Hey, man, I've got some crazy airline deal where the brothers and sisters in New York give us ethnic minorities a big discount and bill the company the full fare. How about that?'

Barbara, Manuel and Dave all start speaking at once. Barbara wins. 'I say, Craig's in the minority as being the only non-minority group represented here. Except perhaps Dave, if you just consider New York City,' she adds dubiously. 'Anyway, I definitely think we should go ahead with George's idea. Air travel is where the really big expense account money's going to be made.'

'If that's the way you're going to play it,' Craig says sourly. 'I'm going to form a majority rights movement.'

'Hey, man, don't get uptight,' George says. 'I consider you as an honorary minority member. And don't forget, Ocean's paying for the gig.'

Ocean, of course, as an Equal Opportunity Employer requires our fatal five always to travel together. If they don't always get along, at least they are united on the growing issue of expense account spending rights, the major management issue of the 1980s.

John Kenneth Galbraith's observation about private affluence and public squalor can be paraphrased as expense account affluence and private stinginess. A suite at the Megopolis Hilton when on the company tab and a room without bath at the Hotel de Commerce when on vacation with the wife.

Meanwhile, our five executives are safely ensconced in the bar of the Ritz in Lisbon drinking Dom Perignon. They are relaxed and well disposed to each other after a long, expense-account day. Barbara Brandywine orders another bottle. 'It's my turn, guys,' she says. And reaching to sign the check: 'Craig, I can never remember your room number.'

Safeguarding your digital footprint
2008 International Herald Tribune

Welcome to the surveillance society.

Two-thirds of business travelers have eavesdropped on someone else's confidential conversations; over a third have caught sight of sensitive documents or information on laptops – and over ten percent admit that they have been used this information for their own business purposes, according to a survey of 1,000 frequent travelers in the United States and Britain. The survey, by the Regus Group, a provider of serviced offices and business lounges for travelers around the world, is an ominous reminder of World War 2 posters – 'Walls Have Ears: Careless Talk Costs Lives!'

In these intrusive times, we have all become involuntary eavesdroppers on fellow travelers ranting on cell-phones, or casting an inquisitive glance at a neighbor's open briefcase or laptop screen?

The survey found that 67 percent of British travelers have eavesdropped on someone else business conversation, versus 59 percent of Americans – and 35 percent of British (34 percent of Americans) have caught sight of sensitive company documents; 13 percent of British (19 percent of Americans) have been able to use the information they have overheard in public. More traveling women (71 percent) listen to conversations than men (67 percent); but more men (39 percent) pry at private documents than women (29 percent).

And now reports that the U.S. government has plans to make random border searches of laptops, cell phones, PDAs and Blackberrys and copy or seize data has sent a chill through businesses and civil rights groups. Whether your password protection could prevail is a moot point.

'In today's wired, networked and borderless world, one's office no longer exists within four walls,' says Susan Gurley, executive director of the Association of Corporate Travel Executives. 'Rather, one's office consists of a collection of mobile electronic devices, such as a laptop, a Blackberry, PDA and a cellphone.'

David Porter, head of security and risk at Detica, specialist business consultants (www.detica.com), says, 'The survey points to significant vulnerability in corporate security. I've overheard sensitive conversations in trains, bars, and restaurants – whether lawyers discussing client details or salespeople revealing key contacts. People seem to slip into a very casual security mindset when using laptops and PDAs. They naively think other people will not be interested or aware of what they are doing; in reality this could not be further from the truth.'

'Many companies don't realize the staggering problems people face on the road, and the lengths they go to find a place to work or to have a private conversation.' Says Kurt Mroncz, vice president, global sales at Regus.' The survey shows that half of business travelers resort resorted to working in washrooms, bars and crowded restaurants, even park benches.'

Will Geddes, a security specialist, managing director of ICP Group (www.icpgroup.ltd.uk), offers the following security tips:

– Always have a password and pin number on your phone, so that it will automatically stop after a few minutes of nonuse; 'absolutely critical, otherwise it's like leaving your address book open, with all your passwords and phone numbers.'

– Avoid discussing confidential matters over the phone in a public place – and use code-names for projects and people.

– Make sure that your Memory Stick is password protected as well. You can now get biometric Memory Sticks with thumb print protection.

– Make sure the screen saver on your laptop goes into lock mode after five to 10 minutes, requiring you to enter the password for it to work again.

– Always delete text messages or e-mails on your phone or Blackberry, or get software to forward them to your e-mail back at the office.

– Don't take unnecessary things in your briefcase; only the stuff you really need for that trip; leave all personal things out. And keep documents in covered, unlabeled folders.

– Traveling without a laptop, you can access your office files by logging on to a service such as GoToMyPC (www.gotomypc.com) from any Internet-connected device – even a dumb terminal in a hotel lobby – and pick up work where you left off. The connection is secure, and it feels as though you are sitting in front of your own PC. But you must keep your home computer on, at least in 'sleep mode,' while you are away.

'I go into a VPN – virtual private network – to my office server remotely,' Geddes says. 'A lot of people in the financial services sector do this. It means I'm not holding anything locally, which is a potential risk, if I lose or break the laptop.'

– Consider having a separate laptop (and memory stick) that you use only for trips; and save documents on a Memory Stick rather than on the hard-drive.

– When flying, don't put your laptop or documents in the overhead bin above you, but one diagonal to you. Then when someone rummages in the locker, you can see what is happening. People have had laptops stolen from over their head in business-class cabins.

Safeguarding private data from Big Brother is rather more daunting. Our telephone conversations and e-mails are routinely 'swept' for certain key words or phrases, which may activate a closer surveillance. RFID tags linked with a network of high resolution CCTV panoramic cameras around an airport could be used to track the location of anyone at airports, trains stations, or any public place, with an accuracy of one square meter.

New European Union and U.S. biometric passports carry embedded Radio Frequency Identification (RFID) chips. This not only enables the authorities to check our whereabouts each time we pass unwittingly through a check-point. This puts travelers at risk of identity theft. The chips can be 'read' by anyone with a reader from up to 60 feet away in such places as airports, hotel lobbies, crowds and trains. Hackers could clone the RFID chip, if not the passport.

Worried? You should be. Remember, even a paranoid can have enemies.

Aren't you rather young to be thinking of early retirement?

1984 Chief Executive; 1984 'If my boss calls...'

The patio of George Goodstein's place. The roofs of the village a Cubist painting by Braque or Picasso. Terraced vineyards set among olive and eucalyptus. Pine forests stretching away to a deep blue Mediterranean.

'God, it's magnificent. Quite a change, huh, from Burnt Plains, New Jersey?'

'Yeah, we like it.' George smiles, the deep, comfortable smile of the independent man. 'Hey, what can I get you? The usual, or do you want to try some of the local wine?'

'Thanks, I'd like to a bit later. But I've had a craving for a Goodstein martini since I left London. Is Martha joining us?'

'She's just run down to the village to pick up the papers and get a few supplies. I'm always amused to see how Diamond's doing.'

'Closed at sixty one and an eighth day before yesterday. Pretty nervous.'

'Oh, my interest's strictly academic these days. I unloaded all my stock and options when I pulled out. Well, here's good luck, Tom!'

'Good luck, George. You certainly seem to be getting your fair share of it. Anyway, enough to turn your old colleagues a delicate shade of green. Me included. God, if the chairman could see you now. Or the Welshman.' My laugh sounds a trifle hollow.

'Yeah, we have been lucky, I suppose. Mind you, it didn't just fall off the tree. We did quite a bit of planning, believe it or not.'

'I can imagine. Tell me, George, when did you make the decision to retire?'

'Well, I'd always had this vague, this romantic notion, I guess, of retiring before fifty. But I made the real decision about a year ago. I'd just about had it up to here with Diamond. And a lot of things started to fall into place about the same time. So I guess I beat my target by about five years. Mind you, I don't really call this retirement. Just doing my own thing. I'm kept pretty busy with these wood-burning stoves.'

'But enjoying, huh. Tell me, did you have a rich uncle Henry who left you a great pile of money?

'Listen, if I'd had a rich uncle Henry I wouldn't be working at all, I promise you. I'd probably be in the business of eating and drinking myself to death like some of our expat neighbours here. No, seriously, what I did was to get our priorities in order. First, where did we want to live? We'd always had this thing about the south of France. Okay. So we sold our home in Burnt Plains and bought this place with a bit to spare. Second, how did I ideally want to earn my living? That was a bit more complicated. I'd had or invested 15 good years at Diamond. Vintage years.

'Look at it this way. I'd lost a lot of battles. I'd won a few. I knew as much as I was ever going to know about marketing, let's face it. But I was stuck three-quarters of the way up the corporate ladder. I figured I might make senior vice president of the division. I'd like to have run the British company. But the Mel Geist relationship was going sour and so was I.'

On the Route Nationale a car honked a few bars of Colonel Bogie. 'Bollocks, they make the best meat pies…' George took a long pull from his Gauloise and crumpled the empty pack in his fist in the way he always did at meetings.

'Okay, so I thought whatever I do, I want to be my own man. I vested my pension at Diamond and we had a few grand in savings, not much, but every little helped. Martha was quite keen on buying a small apartment in the Cannes, Juan-les-Pins area and renting it out furnished to holidaymakers. We could have turned over that way. But it wasn't very creative. I thought of consulting, of course. But it's getting harder every day to tell the difference between a consultant and an unemployed executive. I didn't need that kind of identity crisis.

'And the, one day, Mainwaring called and asked if I would be interested in joining a consortium to buy this wood-burning stove company. They're beginning to take off over here in Europe like they have in the States. So I'm now the proud part-owner of the Woodstock Heating Company Limited.'

'George, I'd be careful about getting into anything with Mainwaring. He is an amusing guy but he's got these way-out ideas on the alternative management lifestyle and all that.'

'Mainwaring's all right. He's the ideas man and he usually has at least one of his feet on the ground. As a matter of fact he's led us through the subculture minefield into some excellent promotion. We're just into a new campaign. It has all the ingredients, lifestyle, fuel economy, the whole ecology thing. And we're selling a helluva lot of stoves. No, my problem is keeping the right sort of distance from the new business so that Martha and I can enjoy what we have here. I don't want to risk recreating the Diamond situation. Twelve-hour days, political hassles, no home life.'

'Looking around I wouldn't say there's any danger of that. But you must be traveling quite a bit.'

'I do a three-day commute to London most weeks. I take the morning Air France on Tuesday and come back on Thursday. We're only half an hour from Nice Airport, as you've seen.'

'George, you should have done this years ago.'

'Yeah, but the irony is I couldn't have done it without Diamond. You've got to have had the big company experience. Pretty well any executive can take early retirement and start another career. The thing is that few people are really aware of what they can achieve. I call it the "ladybird can fly syndrome."'

George and I raise our glasses in a silent toast. 'To Diamond Laboratories.'

Roger Collis

Sunday

1966 Town magazine

A pale wet morning in the Windy City. A sibilant river of automobiles congealing in Chicago's down-town anastomosis. And scurrying Sunday people with grave ecumenical smiles. I feel nimble and smooth in blue stepping into the buttery of the Oxford House under a shawl of breakfast smells draped so deliciously over the sidewalk.

Hadn't she said we'd meet up at ten, pass by her den and then maybe take in a cute roadhouse she knows along the lake for barbecued spare-ribs or a steak. I'd said in my brand-new vernacular sure that would be swell. Naturally I could take a spell with her new convertible.

I'm latish but she hasn't arrived and so I sit on a plush bench between Custer's Last Stand and a sign which says Best Damn Gaelic Coffee This Side of Galway Bay. And order plenty of coffee. Mid-west style, Jewish rye-bread and bacon and eggs fried sunny side.

I have a warm nostalgia for the Great American Breakfast. For the times we tucked in side by side at Toffenetti's burnished counters. Or the day we drove up to Grand Rapids from mid-state Indiana on a white April morning. Two hundred miles of whistling turnpike; defying the fat boys in blue to pounce. To Aunt Jemima's Pancake House with hot bilberry waffles and a pretty waitress called Ellen who shyly served us saying she'd always wanted to be a nurse. In this great land of opportunity. Or the stand up breakfasts in shanty pull-ins off the frosty morning highway: clapboard watering places in a hungry concrete desert. And then of course salubrious Sunday brunches on Forty-Second Street replete with jugs of ice-water and flowered dresses. Now shaking the languid cuff for a look at the time and it's well after twelve.

I feel ungallant thoughts beginning to accrue. Perhaps by some mishappenstance she's elected to be waylaid by that third-year student from Northwestern. Or worse still been taken for a ride by the St. Paul's lawyer with a smart apartment near-north side. But I can glean some lean solace in this snug buttery. Having lived vicariously for a number of years.

And I must say we're filling up with some great dishes, albeit sternly escorted by a legion of Frank Sinatras. Not preventing though my intrepid breakfasting on a cool young drawl across the room. Radcliffe I'm almost sure with mommy and daddy always just back from Florida. Phi beta kappa and a boyfriend in zinc. I think how nice it would be to indulge just once in a small felony. For these splendid shanks eating out my heart here in Illinois. They remind me of the ones I used to know all these happy-sad winter months away. Moonlight drives in sweet New Hampshire woods. And philosophical kisses in quilted corners when my accent was an invitation to all the best parties; and I learned to send odd-numbered roses with my bread and butter cards.

Yes life was just one camp-fire song until I moved west and put my pale signature on the streets and bars of Chicago's stern jungle. I expected to see signs everywhere saying Limey Go Home. Thinking there could be no place here for a benign mid-Atlantic man.

But instead they said hey mister spare a nickel for a smoke or something to eat. At the hot dog stand outside the library with its shelves of nourishing books. Where I often browse after dropping some coins as toll into a sad mahogany hand.

Why now they're floating in for cocktails, the smooth upper-crust: men with long flapping overcoats and women with flashing golden knees. For the great American three-martini lunch. All looking with ineffable disdain at my umpteenth coffee cup so delicately poised.

The bartender is all hands and smiles. A croupier dealing in ice and gin. Tucking the olives deftly into place. I wonder would someone come and lace my sad waiting with a smiling word.

Outside the afternoon has pulled the sky down to make a low gun-metal ceiling over the street. The rain has turned into feeble ersatz snow which slops on the windows and forms an arctic plateau on the sill. Fine weather to be cast adrift by a delinquent date. I contemplate whether to reach into my little rag-bag of words to nurture a comely neighbor. Phi beta kappa gets up from her drink and I think bequeaths me a cautious smile.

Food for thought on this rapacious Sunday.

Roger Collis

Land of milk and money

1982 International (Financial Times)

You're not going to believe this, but I'm a tax exile from Switzerland.

I know it may seem like paradise – the land of milk and money – where you can negotiate sweet tax deals and stash your loot in numbered bank accounts. But this is only if you're rich enough not to pay taxes. For the ordinary salaried citizen living in a fiscal glasshouse, it's one of the most rapacious countries on earth. The tax system is a fully-fledged nightmare, not least because Swiss bureaucracy pervades every stitch of the social fabric.. And so uncomfortably efficient is it you have to tread a fine line between what is forbidden and what is compulsory.

In Lausanne, in the canton of Vaud, where I used to live, your tax is computed on your average income over the two preceding years; which is absolutely okay so long as you keep on earning more each year. If you earn less, you're in trouble; there's no adjustment possible until the next two-yearly assessment. Even if you stop work, you still go on paying tax as though you're on full salary.

What's more you pay three taxes – communal, cantonal and federal. The last one is a monster as it comes 'off the top' – no deductions are allowed for the federal tax bill; not even the usual things like paying off former wives and insurance premiums. And God help you if your wife works. Her salary is lumped with yours, so you find you're paying just to keep her out of the house.

There is a brighter side. As Graham Greene once observed, 'Life isn't black and white; it's black and grey.' Tax evasion, as distinct from tax fraud, is a civil rather than a criminal offence. I once 'forgot' to declare some director's fees and the only retribution was a grey-coloured envelope (in Switzerland, buff-coloured envelopes are grey) with a polite note saying, Gotcha! And then simply shoveling the amount on top for next time.

Nonetheless, I'm sure you understand that when I became a full-time writer on half pay, I decided that it was high time to escape from the Swiss treadmill. So I bought myself out of the country and moved to the Côte d'Azur, which I reckoned was a more congenial place to starve.

I find the main difference between the two countries is that the Swiss are often unpleasantly polite and the French are delightfully rude. (Mind you, what appears to be rudeness is very often rudeness.) You might say that the Swiss are policemen manqué while the French are fonctionaires manqués.

The great thing about France, taxwise (and it helps to be wise before the tax), is that you can more or less choose which 'regime' you wish to be taxed under; for example, on the basis of 'real expenses' or 'administrative evaluation.' As an inveterate back-of-the-envelope man, I opted for the latter, which means you don't have to present accounts, and it is available to so-called 'liberal professions.' You simply lump together all the money you've received during the year, whether from fees or reimbursed expenses, deduct 30 percent off the top and that's the income you'll be taxed on. In theory, if you're a 'writer or composer,' such as me, you can deduct another 15 percent, which is all quite civilized.

The important thing is to remain credible with the folk at the tax office: in other words, make sure that your visible income (after laundering expenses) does not egregiously exceed your visible means of support. 'Lifestyle' is an important component of your tax return, and is assessed according to, for example, the tonnage of your yacht, the size and *grandeur* of your country houses, and the age and cubic capacity of your cars. I had a 12-year-old 2CV, which caused my accountant to rub his hands in glee – after which he rubbed them on my cheque-book.

Unfortunately, it hasn't worked out quite as I planned. Madame insisted on buying a new car, and the tax people are finding loopholes in the magic 30 plus 15 percent deductions. I always thought loopholes were a tax-payers prerogative. *Glasnost* is not an option.

But perhaps *perestroika* is. One way to restructure might be to live offshore by not living anywhere, if you follow what I mean. I have friends who are constantly on the move. 'Sorry, old boy, I can't meet you in London I've used up my 90 days,' or whatever it is.

Does one join the Diaspora? What I have done is devise a complex plan for zooming into orbit from a 'non-resident for tax purposes' launch-pad.

Roger Collis

First you write a bestseller; then you create a Liechtenstein trust...

But hell, why should I give all my secrets away? I may be British born and bled, but I'm not about to help the Inland Revenue win the Queen's Award for Export Achievement.

Mind the ion gap!

1986 International Herald Tribune

If you're feeling under the weather on your next business trip, don't blame it all on jet lag, travel fatigue, the recalcitrance of your sparring partners or a subliminal hangover. Put it down to the quality of the air you breathe. There's junk air as well as junk food. You may be suffering from a deficiency of negative ions.

Ions are naturally occurring air molecules that carry a positive or negative charge. The outdoor air concentration varies with the weather, altitude, pollution, time of day and season, but normally consists of 1,000 negative ions and 1,200 positive ions per cubic centimeter. If the air is abnormally high in positive ions, or low in ions of another polarity – which is often the case in aircraft cabins, cars, trains and air-conditioned buildings – you may be prone to headaches, nausea and irritability. On the other hand, air which is rich in negative ions – such as you find in the mountains, besides flowing water and after a thunderstorm – can make you feel good. This is why a growing number of travelers are taking ionizers with them to charge the depleted air in cars and hotel rooms with negative ions.

Weren't ionizers discredited back in the 1950s when the U.S. Food and Drug Administration prohibited their sale for anything other than air-cleaning applications? They were indeed, and for good cause. The notion that ions could influence health and behavior lost credence as a result of dubious research reports and extravagant claims by manufacturers. But recent ion research in the United States, Israel and England is helping to make ionizers scientifically respectable.

At any rate, sales of ionizers are taking off. A British firm, Mountain Breeze, claims to be selling an average of 1,000 ionizers a week. Says marketing director Stephen Cross: 'There's a massive reawakening of interest in ionizers. You should see the testimonials we get; we're doubling our sales every year. In the U.S. you still can't say anything more than that they clean the air. There is empirical evidence that people feel better in an environment which is high in negative ions. We still don't know why, but we're still gradually building up the research base.'

An ionizer is nothing more than a high-voltage circuit which creates a high potential at the tip of a sharp needle, thereby discharging a stream of electrons which collide with air molecules to form negative ions. These then impart a negative charge to dust, pollen, water droplets and cigarette smoke suspended in the air which precipitate out to the nearest grounded surface, such as the floor and walls, by electrolytic action. You can easily test this by placing an ionizer on your desk in a smoke-filled room. The smoke rapidly clears and the ionizer is surrounded by a corona of dust which is easily swept up. If you put your hand close to an ionizer, you can actually feel the stream of electrons on the skin as a slight breeze. And it's sometimes visible in the dark as a faint blue glow. One thing to check if you're buying an ionizer is that it doesn't emit ozone as a byproduct (which many early models did) as this is highly toxic in concentrations of more than a few parts per million.

Few people seriously dispute the air cleaning capacity of ionizers – they are routinely used in offices and some hospitals are installing them to help reduce cross-infection by airborne bacteria and viruses.

Studies carried out in the 1970s at the University of California and at the University of Jerusalem have demonstrated that high levels of positive ions cause the body to react as if it were under stress by stimulating the production of neuro-hormones, such as serotonin – which affects sleep and mood – and adrenalin, as well as histamine, which is associated with hay fever and other allergic reactions; whereas a preponderance of negative ions seems to contribute to a feeling of well-being.

The Jerusalem study examined the effects of the Sharav, a hot, dry wind in Israel which causes up to two thirds of the population to complain of headaches, respiratory discomfort and depression. The Sharav and similar winds, such as the *Fohn* in Switzerland, southern Germany and Austria and the Santa Ana in California, have a high positive ion content which may indeed cause behavioral and clinical symptoms. It has been reported that when the *Fohn* blows, hospitals postpone operations and the traffic accident rate soars. Joan Didion writes of the morbid effects of the Santa Ana when 'every voice seems a scream. It is the season of suicide and divorce and prickly dread, wherever the wind blows.' Raymond Chandler described the hot dry Santa Anas 'that come down through the mountain passes and curl your hair and make your nerves jump and your skin itch.'

More recently, work by Dr Leslie Hawkins, head of the Robens Institute at the University of Surrey in England, has demonstrated that in air-conditioned buildings, where the ion count is low, the incidence of headaches, nausea and lethargy – the 'sick building syndrome' – suffered by occupants is significantly reduced by installing an air ionizer.

Hawkins conducted extensive double-blind occupational studies to determine if positive or negative atmospheric ion levels could influence actual performance levels as well as attitudes among computer operators. He demonstrated that a majority reported feeling more comfortable and alert when the de-ionized environment in which they had been working was replenished with a natural level of negative ions. His studies also revealed that this replenished air increased work efficiency and productivity with a concurrent reduction in reported symptoms of nausea, stress, fatigue and dizziness.

If you fancy doing some research of your own, there's a wide choice of ionizers on the market, including portable ones on the market, including portable ones for hotel rooms and car models that plug into lighter sockets.

Whether or not it makes you feel better, snorting the right sort of ions could be a great way to break the ice at your next meeting.

A Tough Act to Follow
1984 'If my boss calls …'

Scene: A suite in the Intercontinental Hotel in Geneva. Craig J. Hamstringer Jr., pristine vice-president international operations of Ocean Opportunities Inc., is interviewing candidates for the company's new European headquarters. Ocean manufactures a range of health-care products derived from seaweed and microscopic marine life. With their recent acquisition of Kelp Incorporated and Plankton Industries, they have inherited a European network of distributors and agents representing sales of over 100 million dollars.

Evidently this is Hamstringer's first trip outside the United States. A bulky man in his late forties, he is uncomfortably conspicuous in a double-knit plaid suit, trousers flying at half mast over huge white shoes.

Olaf Olafsson, the notorious Icelandic headhunter, to whom Ocean has entrusted this executive search, has regaled our friend with a deliciously lethal lunch at the Plat d'Argent. Hamstringer is suffering from postprandial fatigue potentiated by severe culture shock. He is gratefully clutching a Coca-Cola. The first candidate this afternoon is Jacques Lecouteau, an urbane Frenchman in his mid-fifties.

Hamstringer: Glad to meet you, Mr … ah … Why don't I just call you Jack. I'm Craig by the way. Make yourself comfortable. (*Lecouteau drops into the sofa, which emits an ambiguous hiss. He crosses his legs and exposes a lustrously sheathed calf.*). Jack, why don't we begin by you telling me what you've been doing these last five years.

Lecouteau: Well it's really quite simple, Mr. Hamstringer. For the last ten years in fact I have been secretary general for Laboratories Boulanger in Paris. Well, Neuilly in fact. And well of course I have been responsible for the whole administration of our laboratories.

Hamstringer: I didn't know you worked in a laboratory.

Lecouteau: (*Slight eyebrow movement*) I don't. I work in an office. About fifty square metres, I should say, and a nice view of the park.

Hamstringer: (*Confused*) Okay. Well, what exactly does a secretary…

whatever it was you said ... What does a guy like that do?

Lecouteau: Well, it's quite simple in fact. In my case, I was a kind of *Chef de Cabinet*, if you like to the P.D.G.

Hamstringer: The Pay Day Jay?

Lecouteau: The *Président Directeur-Géneral*. The chief executive in fact.

Hamstringer: Okay, I think I understand. But tell me, Jack, was this a line or a staff position? You are familiar with these terms?

Lecouteau: Perfectly, Mr. Hamstringer. Of course, in a French organization staff and line in the strictly Anglo-Saxon sense have no meaning in fact. I mean staff can merge into line and vice-versa. One needs to establish a kind of dialectical equilibrium. Are you familiar with Descartes, Mr. Hamstringer?

Hamstringer: Yes, I enjoy a game of cards occasionally. But I think we'd better move along. Jack, I see from your resumé that you have quite an impressive background in health care. What is your experience in marine life? Beach life I should say?

Lecouteau: Well, I have a little place in St Tropez. We have some quite attractive beach life I must say. But of course, I do have some quite profound knowledge of the ... how do you say ... with the seaweed extracts.

Hamstringer: Well, Ocean can certainly use that kind of background. I'm not sure about St Tropez though. We have to think of our puritan work ethic. Ha Ha. Jack. The slot we're talking to you about is vice-president administration. You'd not only be responsible for the set-up over here, but also for co-ordination with staff services back home in Broken Springs. You obviously know your way around. But I'd like to explore a little more your organizational experience ... (*Hamstringer is saved by the telephone announcing the next candidate*) Jack, I'll be getting in touch with you for another meeting. Take care now.

The next candidate is a dapper little man in a tightly buttoned grey suit. He has a confident, almost feisty air.

Hamstringer: (*Extracting a large cigar from his mouth and waving it in a circular fashion*) Mr Zurcher, it's good to meet you. Mr Olafsson was most impressed with your qualifications. Looking him up and down.) No small financial skills. Ha Ha. And of course your languages. German, French,

Italian, English. Wow. Do you speak Swiss?

Zurcher: I beg your pardon?

Hamstringer: Of course, you are Swiss! Peter, I'd like to kick off by you telling me something about your present job.

Zurcher: Well, I'm in charge of the accounting department for the past five years. I have eight book-keepers and five clerks, reporting direct to me. Normally we use the typing pool, but I do have a secretary since three months. Naturally, I have excellent banking relations and so on and so forth. They invite me for lunch three or four times a month. That's a thirty percent increase on a year ago. What else ... yes we start at seven thirty in the morning ... we are paid for the 13th month ...

Hamstringer: Thirteen months! So that's how the Swiss do it! Ha Ha. At Ocean we only expect people to work half day. As I always say, 12 hours is enough for anyone. Ha Ha. That's a company joke, Peter. But let's talk concepts for a moment. What do you know about profit centres?

Zurcher: Well of course, we are a very profitable centre. As you must have seen from my resumé, we actually record the profits in my department. We do all the accounting and so on and so forth.

Hamstringer: Sure, but what about the cash flow?

Zurcher: In Switzerland, Mr Hamstringer, the cash flows very quietly. Discreetly is perhaps the better word. But of course, the cash flow doesn't appear on the balance sheet. My department ...

Hamstringer: Peter, I think the jet lag's getting to me. Would you mind if we break for a while? Like a week or so. Mr Olafsson will be in touch. Goodbye now.

Hamstringer tries unsuccessfully to relight his cigar, throws it in the direction of the waste-paper basket and misses. He picks up a resumé from the pile and calls for the next candidate.

It is now late afternoon and Hamstringer is distinctly bent out of shape, as he would say. He must be thinking wistfully of the comfortable business stereotypes back home in Broken Springs. With the aid of an interpreter he orders more Coca-Cola and an ice pack. The next candidate is a Swede by the name of Stig Fussgren. Fussgren is tall, hirsute and gloomy and wears an ancient business suit with open-toed sandals. he exudes a strange organic smell.

Hamstringer: (*With a nervous smile*) Stig, that's a nice easy name to say. Ha Ha. I'm Craig. Now, Stig, let me see ... You've been working in research and development for twelve years. Most of that time in seaweed chemistry. Is that right?

Fussgren: Twelve years and three months, Mr Hamstringer. That's before the devaluation of the Swedish day ...

Hamstringer: The devaluation ...?

Fussgren: Yes, the working day was devalued when the Co-determination of Work Act came into force. We now spend most of our time agreeing what to do with less time for actually doing it. And now with inflation ...

Hamstringer: Okay, Stig, let's get to the chemistry. Now what products have you developed during your tie with Thornqvist-Ericson?

Fussgren: Well, I've been working on the large molecule theory of iodine binding synthetics. I'm sure you're familiar with the diphenyloxymethanone derivatives in globular accretion. In a purely linear sense, of course. (*He shows an elaborate set of yellow teeth.*)

Hamstringer: (*Who has developed a tic in the corner of his left eye.*) We have people back home who understand all that, Stig. What I'd like to explore with you is your experience in actually developing products for the marketplace. The job of our European R & D group will be to work very closely with the marketing team in developing new product concepts.

Fussgren: (*Gloomily*) Well, five years ago I nearly discovered a new vitamin, vitamin Z we would have called it, in kelp extracts. We would have used it to support a skin softening claim in our baby bath-oil. That is, of course, if the vitamin would have had such properties ...

Hamstringer: (*Utterly baffled by this preposterous candidate*) Stig, there must be some questions you'd like to ask about the job. Organisation and operating methods, for example.

Fussgren: There certainly are, Mr Hamstringer. We have a Shoenberg ultra-centrifuge in Stockholm. We use it for kelp extracts and making chocolate mousse for our midsummer office party. Now there's a new model just come out and it would be nice if we could have it. And then there's the question about laundering lab coats. My position has always been ...

Hamstringer (*Grabbing the phone*) Stig, I think this might be a good place to break for today. I must meet our marketing candidate, who's on a very tight schedule A young Dutchman, very aggressive. Er … I am sure you two would hit it off. (He propels Fussgren towards the door) I'll talk to Santa Claus about the centrifuge, Stig. We'll be in touch. Don't call us, we'll call you. Take care now …

Jan van den Werf is a huge bear of a man. Hamstringer greets him like a long lost brother.

Van den Werf: Fantastic to see you again, Craig. (*He attempts a bear hug. Like many Europeans, he misinterprets American informality.*)

Hamstringer: (*Recoiling*) It's nice to have someone who speaks the same language. Han, last time we talked you were telling me about your sales experience – body language and regional dialects – so today I'd like to get into marketing – planning and control, budgeting, media models, market research and that kind of thing. I mean there's more to marketing than sales, as you know.

Van den Werf: (*Composing a complex semaphore with nose and forefinger*) There must be some misunderstanding, Craig. My brother, Hans, and I are applying for this job together. We have always worked as a team. Hans is the marketing expert. In fact he's the intellectual of the family. You know he has a friend who knows someone who has read Wittgenstein. Hans is in Haarlem right now busy polishing a marketing plan which he's been working on for the last five years.

Hamstringer: Harlem! That's a dangerous place to be walking around with a marketing plan. But look, Jan, before this interview degenerates into pure slapstick we'd better get one or two things clear …

(*The phone rings*) Excuse me a moment, will you. Hello. Speaking. Good afternoon, Jackson. I mean, good morning! Ha Ha. Yes, the interviewing is coming along fine. One or two very promising candidates. What's that? You want me to write it up as a sketch for the office party …?

Curtain

Roger Collis

Return to the future for airline passengers?
2010 CNN Traveler

The latest return to the future comes in the form of the patented 'Flex-Seat' from Boston-based Jacob-Innovations – a 'two-storey pod-like design for business-class seating which can be converted to an economy-class set-up on demand' for airlines 'that might want to alter a plane's configuration depending on how many tickets of each class it has sold; and at the same time,'increasing the density of a conventional business class cabin by 50 per cent while providing full reclining' – whatever that means.

The Flex-Seat was presented at the Aircraft Interiors Expo in Hamburg – 'launchpad for cabin programmes that showcase tomorrow's designs'. Check it out at http://jacob-innovations.com/FLEX-SEAT.html. Flex-Seat looks to me like Lego re-invented by the Japanese – pods for bods. Think of it as an accountant's dream for raising the ergonomic stakes of 'cattle-class', or maximising the return on investment of 'premium' passengers – responsible, according to IATA, for 25-30 percent of passenger revenues but only 7-10 percent of numbers.'

Whatever the merits of Flex-Seat, airlines need a *deus ex machina* to extricate them from a dire dilemma: how to reconfigure the expensive real estate of aircraft cabins to conform to a new reality: that all-important premium traffic is declining; and that the class system, as it has evolved over the years, needs to be re-invented.

The statistics are appalling: premium ticket sales continue to fall – they were off 21.3 percent off in June 2009 compared with June 2008, according to the International Air Transport Association Premium Travel Monitor, which should have most airlines in a catatonic tailspin. Premium travel numbers have been in decline for 12 consecutive months.

Even the business travelers that are staying in the front of the plane during the down-turn are doing so at cheaper rates; revenues from premium travel fell even more – 41 percent in the second quarter as airlines slash prices in a frantic attempt to maintain demand.

The effect on the bottom line has been catastrophic. Consider this:

according to IATA, 'Premium passengers are responsible for 25-30 percent of passenger revenues but only 7-10 percent of numbers.' Every percentage loss of travelers in the premium cabins reflects on the yield like a shadow on the wall.

And yet airlines have only themselves to blame. They failed to learn the lessons of the 9/11 crisis, which exquisitely coincided with the cusp of a recession, and sent travel into free fall – precipitating a sea change in the way people view business travel, and view their lives, sharpening their priorities. And they failed to understand that their 'branding,' their class system as it had evolved over the past 40 years had got out of sync with the changing needs of the business traveler. What is more, they have 'debased' the value of their brands through indiscriminate upgrades and cut prices.

Even I am too young to go back to the 1930s with bunk beds on the flying boats and the trans-continental flights between New York (La Guardia and California (Birkbank L.A.) taking two or three days. The opening chapter in Scott Fitzgerald's unfinished novel *The Last Tycoon* has an opening chapter on such a flight. My only surrogate recollection is a photo of a woman fastening her stockings on a bunk bed on a United Airlines flight in the 1930s.

Lillian Hellman wrote about the time on a flight from Los Angeles to New York in the 1950s when Hollywood producer Harry Cohn sent back an invitation for her to join him for lunch, saying that it was much healthier than the "dreck on the plane."

"Two of his younger employees hauled down the largest picnic hamper I have ever seen," Hellman wrote. "It was filled with forty or fifty fine, thin chicken sandwiches, cold white wine, prosciutto wrapped around perfect ripe melon, homemade pickles, large peaches, wonderful walnut cookies."

So what else is new?

When I started traveling on business in the mid-1960s, there were only two classes on the old narrow-body planes and the early jumbos – first and economy. And only three types of fare: first; full (flexible) economy; and 'excursion.'

First class was a golden ghetto for chief honchos and the seriously rich.

Roger Collis

Everyone else flew economy – which wasn't nearly as grand as business class is today: you had to pay for drinks and headsets (with those little plugs that used to bore into your brain) but the food was okay and you had enough space to stretch your legs. Cattle class it was not. And it was democratic. You might find yourself chatting to a lieutenant if not a captain of industry, a diplomat, an aircraft salesman, a honeymoon couple, or perhaps an ambiguous lady of uncertain provenance. There was much scope for social congress.

My fondest memory of those days is of flying back from Chicago to Europe. Staff at the row of airline check-in desks behaved like barkers at a fairground. As most flights left more or less at the same time in the evening, I would move up and down with my flexible ticket and bestow my custom on the airline that would 'guarantee' me four seats across, ideally behind the bulkhead in the non-movie section of the cabin, where I could stretch out and sleep. More creative souls would invoke a last-moment client meeting and upgrade to first class using their Air Travel Cards, swearing blind that there were no seats left in economy.

Life became more complicated when business class emerged as a third cabin in the late 1970s. The idea, you may remember, was to 'reward' business travelers paying the full economy (Y) fare on the new wide-bodied planes with their own exclusive cabin, sequestrating them from backpackers and savvy leisure travelers who might have paid two-thirds or less for their tickets. Comfort and service in most long-haul business class cabins is arguably more comfortable than the old first class, with lie-flat all-singing-all-dancing sleeper seats, and a galaxy of perks and gizmos; but a lot less exclusive.

Piling on frills inevitably piled on the price of the ticket. First class can cost twice the price of business class, which in turn costs up to four times more than a fully flexible economy ticket and 20 times more than the cheapest excursion ticket.

Faced with a blizzard of discounted or 'grey' fares, upgrades, special promotions, such as two-for-one fares, and a maze of frequent flier awards, it's easy to pay a lot more for a lot less – or vice versa.

Virgin Atlantic re-invented the two-class (first/economy) system in 1985 with its Upper Class – billed as first class service and comfort at business-class prices. Upper Class became the concept for the early 1990s as several airlines abandoned first class for a more spacious business class (business class had become a tough act to follow; though there are always people prepared to pay serious money for serious in-flight real estate.)

Continental Airlines was the first carrier to create a combined first/business class, followed by Delta Air Lines, Air Canada, KLM, and many others. Even airlines that have kept first class cabins, only offer them on certain routes.

Premium economy is a successful compromise between the ever-increasing cost of business class and the squalor of cattle class. It attracts and business travelers whose budgets, or corporate travel policies, do not permit them to fly business class; and many leisure, especially older people. The idea is to 'reward' economy passengers paying the full fare, and passengers who could no longer afford business class, with a separate cabin – echoing the rationale for business class 40 years ago.

Perhaps it **is** time to reinvent the wheel.

Games managements play
1994 Business Life

When I shut my eyes these little blocks start drifting down. There are dozens of them: I think they are stored somewhere behind my eyebrows. I can still see them with my eyes open. Gazing at the horizon I slot them into rectangular gaps in apartment buildings. Reading, I rush down the page just ahead of the cascading blocks. My computer screen is invaded by dozens of alien cursors leapfrogging through gaps in the text like a 2CV after lunch in a perched village in Provence. And all the time this relentless bloody music: *Tum Tiddly Um Tiddly Um Tum Tum: Tum Tiddly Um Tiddly Um: Tum Tiddly Um Tiddly Um Tum Tum...* A melody line that makes Three Blind Mice sound like Mozart.

Fellow victims will recognize, with a touch of Schadenfreude that I suffer from Tetris Syndrome in its acute form, contracted from a Nintendo Gameboy. Alexandra, my nine-year old secretary, acquired the thing a few weeks ago. There's a Tetris epidemic at Ecole Saint Marie. Classes have been cancelled. And several teachers have gone down with it. It's what you might call a virus ex machina. My management team has been badly disrupted. Alexandra and Madame are unapproachable for all practical purposes when they are playing Tetris. And the only time I am able to work is when they're playing the damn thing. Don't laugh. Santa may have a little time-bomb with your name waiting in his sack.

Tetris, of course, is nothing new. It has been around on a screen near you since 1987, the invention of one Alexy Pazhitnov, a former programmer at the Moscow Academy of Science. Western Cold War paranoiacs claim that Tetris was a KGB plot to unhinge Western management with this addictive toy. But when Tetris became available with Gameboy – a pocket-sized game console; as they say in the trade – it entered a new and dangerous phase. Now you can travel with Tetris, play it anywhere, on the plane, on the train, in the office, and, most insidiously of all – in the head.

For the uninitiated, Tetris consists of a stream of falling blocks, which the player flips and slides, trying to slot them into even rows. If you make a line, it disappears. Incomplete lines stack up, leaving the next blocks less space to fall, and leaving you with less time to make decisions on where to flip and slide the falling blocks.

Gameboy comes with a dinky little two-by-two inch screen, four-way joystick and four control buttons for select, start, and for rotating the blocks 90 degrees to the left and the right. Plus digital music and sound effects.

It is the most efficient way to waste time so far devised by man.

What makes Tetris so compelling is that it serves as an allegory for well, whatever you want: management, or life in general.

There are seven kinds of block, each made up of four tiny squares: there are twin blocks in the shape of steps, each facing in opposite directions, if you see what I mean. (We call these 'little buggers' because they're so hard to manipulate); a square; twin L-shaped blocks, in both directions; a kind of T-junction; and straight vertical sticks (which we call 'long sods').

Blocks descend in a random sequence from the top of the screen, although I suspect there's some kind of pre-cognition when you're doing well or badly. You get progressive points for completing two or more lines/layers at the same time; four lines is a Tetris, signaled by cybernetic bells. As your score increases, the blocks descend even faster. As they all pile to the top, the music becomes even more frenzied, and the screen clears. *Game Over Please Try Again*. And you do. Time and time again. You can select games of progressive difficulty, for which you are rewarded with little men playing guitars by the Kremlin walls. The ultimate accolade is a space rocket fizzing up and away from its launch pad. *Congratulations!*

You soon develop a strategy which perhaps reflects your management style. You have the bureaucrat who avoids risk by building up the wall line by painful line. But, of course, his score mounts very slowly and he is finally overtaken by a cascade of awkward-shaped blocks.

The entrepreneur takes risk. He builds up a high wall, leaving space in the middle for a single square, in the hope that a 'long sod' will come crashing down to fill it, to the accompaniment of bonus bells and whistles. Murphy's Law is paramount and nothing succeeds like success. But sure as hell, if you're in trouble, you'll get one bad block after another – sometimes five 'little buggers' in a row. While, if you're doing well, there's a marvelous inevitability in the perfect blocks you get (even 'little buggers' have their felicitous moments.

The opportunist never waits for the perfect block, but will plug the gap in the wall with whatever shape comes down. This leaves a few empty spaces; but he may be rewarded with a 'long sod' at the very last moment to send the wall crashing down. Hoorah? The speculator will take a 'position' on such and such a sequence of blocks.

My management team has ordered new games for the next time I pass through Heathrow: such gems as *Balloon Kid; The rescue of Princess Blobette* and *Nintendo World Cup*.

I'm full of ideas for new software. How about *Budget Blaster, Market Forces, Management Buyout*, or perhaps, *Rescue of the Bottom Line?* Let's put fantasy up front where it belongs.

Roger Collis

Madame has suggested that I give up writing and become a full-time Gameboy consultant. It's either that or join the Ecole Saint Marie chapter of Tetris Anonymous.

Power Play

1993 Business Life

Any of you trying to get in touch with me recently is sure to have noticed my new telephone style: I always let the phone ring at least five times instead of snatching it up a micro-second before it rings, and answering with a mildly surprised, 'Hello,?' instead of an unctuously anxious, 'Roger C. here.'

You'll have noticed, too, that my faxes are firmer, more confident, more authoritative (and clearer, thanks to a new cartridge in the printer); the multi-heap filing system on the floor has been partly camouflaged with what the lady at the *Centre d'Agricole* assures me is a Chinese money plant; and that I've replaced the fox-hunting prints with my favorite photograph of Erich von Stroheim in *La Grande Illusion,* along with a sentimental sepia print of me in my last corporate incarnation.

This exemplary change in demeanour stems from a book I've just read called *Power – Creating it, Using it,* by Dr. Helga Drummond, a lecturer at the University of Liverpool. (It's published by Kogan Page at the powerful price of £20.95)

Ask a manager what he most lacks and the answer will be 'power.' Power means being able to get things done by being able to procure resources, being clear about what is expected – knowing what authority exists... Power is all about control; control over people, the Organization, our jobs, ability to spend money. And who doesn't want more control?'

Indeed.

Exhumed in these pages are crucial management realities: how to make someone fall in love with you (*'The surest and simplest technique of seduction is to ask the person questions about themselves. Be patient, as interest develops exponentially.'* I should be so lucky!); how to create luck (*'Luck can be created in perceiving what will be needed and hard work in preparing in readiness* [sic] *for opportunities.'* Yes, but how?); how to create an air of authority (*'Restrict your availability... Aim to cultivate a certain moody impatience.'*); seizing the initiative (*'If you assume control, seldom will anyone stop you.'* Mmm); how to manipulate reality (*'There is no such thing as the facts... the aim of the power seeker is to define reality to your advantage.'* Your reality or mine?); and the art of CYA – the defensive tactic of how to cover your arse (*'What matters is not what you can do but what you can prove you have done.'* Got that?)

As you can see, this is a 'hands-on' book; not a book to be put down lightly, as Dorothy Parker might have said, but to be thrown with great power. Questionnaires appear at the beginning at end of each chapter, with the idea that your score should have improved at the second shot (I must say that mine has deteriorated: how am I supposed to know one is meant to drive to work in a Morgan sports car instead of a Citroen 2CV turbo? Or say, 'I'll sign it' instead of 'our cheque is in the mail' when someone phones to ask about a refund claim. Or send your boss a note after a sticky interview instead of up-dating the resume. (The only one I got right was that one should write the minutes before rather than after the meeting; but Drummond may have got that from me.)

The chapter I like best was 'Acting the Part' – being an *amateur* of style rather than substance: *'Even the way you answer the phone says something about you. Let it ring at least five times, otherwise you give the impression that you are eager to receive a call... Pretending to have forgotten the meeting is a way of signaling how unimportant you regard the other party.'*

Power, it seems to me, is rather like a patent specification – the broader the first claim, the statement of invention, the weaker it is likely to be in terms of validity; the narrower the claim, the stronger the patent, but the less useful it is likely to be. The art of drafting patent specifications is to strike the right balance between validity and the scope of the invention.

'All power relations involve a trade-off between the scope and the intensity of power,' Drummond says. *'People whose power scope is narrow are vulnerable: those possessing extensive power seldom know all that is going on.'* This is why

'*lords of all they survey*' may not, in fact, survey very much. Goodness knows how much power their minions are broking. And it is often specialist staff people, rather than line executives, who wield the serious clout. Power seekers need to recognize and nurture real '*power points*' in an organization. If you're a '*heavy hitter*' on the inside track, you should be concerned with your '*power-weight ratio*' (A Morgan sports car ought to do the trick). Balance of power is concerned with reciprocity: '*The power-holder and the power target are actually influencing one another.*' The boss-secretary relationship, for example.

Power, as far as I'm concerned (not that I'm concerned very far), is having something that people want (or think they want) like money, ideas, knowledge, sex, or contacts. Power is also about making people think you have (or might procure) something they want (or think they want), and so on.

'*Powerlessness,*' Drummond says, '*is a major source of managerial inefficiency, resulting in wasted time, needless conflict, stress, anger and frustration.*'

As Adlai Stevenson once said, 'Power corrupts, but lack of power corrupts absolutely.'

Absolutely.

Topless rules OK

1980, Health & Efficiency; Radio Nova

It was a cultural revolution of sorts. As Mao Tse-Tung might have said: 'Let a million bosoms bloom.'

It started almost as a local event. Legend has it that the first bikini tops came off at Tahiti Plage, near St. Tropez. The year? Most *plagistes* would settle for 1970, give or take a season or two either way.

Take in the scene.

An unremarkable summer day with a faint breeze coming in off the sea, rustling the palm tree, setting the beach boys to work tightening the parasols, and wafting the first pungent smells of the *plat du jour* – mmmm, *l'epaule d'agneau aux herbes* — across the patio to the serried rows of baking bodies on the sand. Monsieur Felix is starting on his rounds with a sheaf of menus. Fingers are snapping to order aperitifs. The beach is coming to life after a gloriously somnolent morning.

But what's this? That agreeable strawberry blonde in the white bathing suit is sitting up at the windbreak. Without her bikini top? According to Tony, she's a Swedish-speaking Finn, although what that has to do with it I'm not sure. Of course, we'd all noticed her undoing her top when she turned over on her front an hour or so ago. And, of course, several of the girls do that. Still. And look, there's another a few yards away. And another. Why, it's our very own Martine! And Jean-Pierre doesn't seem in the least concerned, quite smug in fact. As well he might; what a figure! And there's another. This is incredible. It's almost as though there had been a pre-arranged signal for all tops to be peeled off.

Within a few minutes, right along the far row of *matelas* a dozen pairs of bare bosoms are wagging saucily. Under the benign auspices of Monsieur Felix, who looks as though he's seen it all, and more besides. To be sure, a few tongues are wagging as well. But no bolts of lightning from the scandalized gods, no screaming police sirens. Just a few venturesome *Tropeziennes* quietly starting a new fashion along the Cote d'Azur. A fashion? More like an institution. The shape of things to come.

Before long, at neighboring beaches along the peninsula, at Pampelonne, at Plage des Salins, at Plage de la Briand, at Plage de l'Escalet, at Plage des Graniers, and, of course, at the famous poolside of the Hotel Byblos at St. Tropez, there was an effulgent, but cautious, flowering of bare breasts.

Aficionados reported four distinct phases in going topless. Women would start, with understandable hesitation, lying on their fronts with their bare breasts nuzzling the sand. Then, they would experiment with lying on the backs exposing their breasts to the sun. Then, they would progress to sitting up, and finally would graduate to swimming, and walking around the beach topless.

At the end of that first lustrous topless season, 'Seins' Tropez, the capital of summer chic, had become the Mecca of the MLS — the redoubtable

Roger Collis

'*Mouvement de Liberation des Seins*,' an offshoot of Women's Lib, infiltrated, one suspects, by a number of self-serving men. By the end of the summer of 1971, within a dozen kilometers of St. Tropez, bikini marks had become almost as rare as parking spaces in the Place de la Republique. Topless sunbathing was here to stay.

But for the next couple of seasons, 'going topless' remained the almost exclusive phenomenon of the sybaritic peninsula. It was written about, talked about, indulged in, and awesomely photographed, gushed over, and deplored. But it seemed to be just another local event, another St Tropez self-indulgence, condoned by tolerant authorities. Elsewhere was more staid. A far cry from bathing machines, to be sure, but at most private and public beaches along the coast, bikini tops remained, more or less firmly fastened. It was a quiet revolution, so far.

Until Thursday, June 14, 1973, the day that *Nice-Matin* splashed, 'Nice has been invaded by the bare bosoms of St. Tropez.' The beachhead for this assault was the irreproachable Ruhl Plage on the Promenade des Anglais, in front of the Hotel Negresco, that rococo home-from-home of the bourgeois chic, and to be designated in 1974 as a *monument historique*. Under a photo of three topless beauties, the paper laconically avowed that, the scenery of Nice is none the worse for a few discarded bikini tops.' One expected the earth to fall in, or at least a *tremblement de terre* of force five on the Richter scale. But Monsieur Malacarne, who, with son Bob and daughter Claudie, runs Ruhl Plage with a genial but firm hand, was curiously unfazed. Claudie was reported chatting to one of the topless denizens, Sandra, who predictably came from St. Tropez. A neat bit of PR.

Other beaches along the front were quick to follow; the Opera Plage, the Forum, the Bains de la Plage. The latter was managed by Monsieur Jo Burdin, president of the *Syndicat des Plagistes des Alpes-Maritimes*, who offered a Gallic shrug. 'I'm not aware of any municipal or prefectorial regulations forbidding topless sunbathing.'

But the very next day, June 15, Nice-Matin soberly declares that while indeed there were no specific provisions in the law, the penal code could be invoked under the catch-all clause of 'public order and decency.' Adding,

'There may have been an armistice at St. Tropez, but we may have a war on our hands in Nice.'

And war it seemed to be. There were ugly scenes on the Promenades des Anglais in front of Ruhl Plage and other beaches. The police, always impeccably buttoned-up, turned out in force to take the names and addressed of topless sunbathers. Jeering crowds gathered. A reporter from Radio Monte Carlo was photographed interviewing a topless girl, who had covered her face to avoid prosecution. A real revolution was in the air.

Finally, French pragmatism prevailed. On June 17, 1973, Nice-Matin quoted the then mayor of Nice, Jacques Medecin: 'I think that the topless fashion is now an established part of our social life. In no way, does topless sunbathing represent an affront to public decency. And I am delighted that our pretty girls are exploiting their natural advantages in this way. The police have more serious matters to attend to...'

An armistice was tacitly declared, and all was fairly quiet on the topless front until August 2, 1976, when Nice-Matin observed that topless sunbathing had become so commonplace that nobody really took any notice. Well, not quite true, perhaps. Men, it seemed, were either 'discreetly interested,' or 'falsely indifferent,' the wide variety of bare bosoms having presumably invited more aesthetic discrimination. Aesthetic became an issue; should freedom to go topless extend to the old or blemished, as well as the nubile? The thought of topless harridans sending putative shivers down male chauvinist spines. There was discussion about the harmful effect on children of seeing their mothers baring their breasts in public. But children, when interviewed, appeared to be unconcerned. 'Bof!' was the universal Gallic rejoinder. So much for that. Even the most conservative commentators agreed that all the unleashed pulchritude was not exactly rending the fabric of society.

From then on it was pretty plain sailing. The topless debate became more technical, turning to matters of health and beauty. It was generally agreed that for certain women with heavy or pear-shaped breasts, a bra is to be recommended during vigorous exercise, in order to avoid the 'breaking down of the elastic mammary fibers,' and the consequent 'falling' of the breasts. New cosmetics proliferated; nipple oils and 'specially formulated' sun-screens and 'nutrients.' Topless sunbathing was applauded as a major factor in the 'psychological liberation' of women, 'freeing them from the straitjackets of their puritan upbringings,' and 'enabling them to come to terms with their physical limitations.'

You've come a long way, baby!

All the way, in fact, to 'Miss Seins Nus' competitions at beaches all along the coast; 1979 was a record year for 'Miss' elections, the great event of the season being 'Miss France Nue' who was elected on August 23 at St. Maxime, just across the Golfe de St. Tropez from the resort of resorts that started it all. Florence Satizelle, the 19-year-old Parisienne, who won the title, will put her charms to the test once again in Canada next spring in the 'Miss Nude World' elections.

At Tahiti Plage, it's business as usual. A casual eye is kept open for parasol pirates. A Chriscraft gurgling at the jetty is unloading a bevy of topless beauties for lunch. Monsieur Felix, perennially distinguished, is making his rounds with the menus. The *plat du jour* chalked up on the board on the big palm tree is 'rouget a la nicoise.' An unremarkable day.

But what's this? A couple of very pretty girls are walking across the patio to the restaurant. Wearing bikini tops!? Heads are turning. A faint ripple of amusement. Ah, well we're a cosmopolitan crowd. After all, the topless revolution is over. We can afford to be tolerant.

Going up in smoke

1996 Resident Abroad; 1994 Business World

I knew this was the big one when Madame dragged me along to the doctor to see about this ghastly bronchitis. After all, even a hypochondriac can get sick. I joke that a massive coronary would be a better way to go. And provided they don't get to you in time, it doesn't have to be expensive.

Madame gives me one of her special looks. A hard, professional look from my practitioner, perhaps not altogether disinterested at the prospect of PPP coughing up (sorry about that). I should be able to buy a bit of time with the equivalent of one million francs on the 'International Plan.'

French surgeons often demand cash under the table before they'll embark on an operation under the Social Security. But if you're a private patient it's cash over the table. And plenty of it, please. And while you're dispensing, let's spread some bread to all my pals to whom I'll be referring you for special tests.

I'd already seen a doctor in London a few weeks before. What you might call the holistic approach. Tap, tap. 'Well, yes, everything seems okay. Quite a bit of tension here, in the neck, top of the shoulders. Lucky I just came back from a course in manipulation. Try to relax… Tap, tap, loosen this up a bit. I can see you were active when you were young. Don't worry, we all drink too much. You know the definition of an alcoholic is someone who drinks more than their doctor. Ha, ha. What you really have to worry about is if you're voice changes suddenly, becomes hoarse, go to a doctor at once. No, I don't think we need any blood. Yes, a cheque will be fine.' Slightly less rapacious than my solicitor ('Shall we say five hundred pounds on account, Mr. C?').

The French approach was more brutal, to say the least. Didn't I know that I was in the very highest high risk group for lung cancer (a highly profitable disease), heart attacks and strokes? Well, yes, I did know. The chap seemed less than chuffed when he found my blood pressure was way down. Yes, no exercise; two, okay, three packs of Gauloises a day. *Sans filtre!* Far too much to drink, overweight. Miracle I'm still alive.

'Don't laugh, monsieur, I had a patient who dropped dead right outside this door.'

I didn't like to ask him whether this was before or after the consultation. Perhaps only in France are you presumed doomed until you have proved yourself healthy. After proving yourself solvent, that is.

At the *Polyclinque Jeanne d'Arc* in Juan les Pins where I went for a *lavage bronchique*, bravado seeps away. All I need to hear is Roy Schneider singing 'By, bye, life, bye, bye, happiness' on the Muzak, as I go under the anaesthetic. Instead, 'Money, money, money, it's a rich man's world.' No, I'm kidding: all I hear is the clacking of computer keys, tuned no doubt to Lotus 1-2-3. The receptionist promised they wouldn't cash my cheque guarantee for a month to give time for my insurance to come through. They cashed it after three days, as it turned out. Joan of Arc's revenge, Madame said.

I waited a week for the test results. I switched on the computer and created the file, DEATH. A kind of lachrymose debriefing. The play I would never write now... the unfinished autobiography... eleventh hour attempt to become a real writer, whack out a couple of stories before the final deadline in the sky.

If I do survive, is there a life after tobacco? 'I smoke 10 to 14 cigars a day,' said George Burns. Pause while he exhales the punch line: 'At my age I have to hold on to something.'

Look for omens and you're going to find them. Everyone I talk to seems to know someone who has just got something dreadful or unmentionable. 'But they do marvelous things these days, old chap. You might live for weeks, months even.' Charming.

Then, early one morning, after a bout of coughing my voice changed. I sounded like an aged actress who had lived on gin for the last hundred years.

'Do you think my voice seems different?' I kept asking people on the phone. 'No, sounds the same to me. Perhaps a bit husky though.' I ran through my repertoire. I could just do my World Service voice: '*This is the end of the world news.*' But I couldn't get my larynx round '*Run Rabbit, Run,*' like Flanagan and Allen, or do a proper cock-a-doodle-doo for Alexandra, my nine-year-old secretary. This was the cruelest blow. I vowed I'd never let them operate. Not on my voice box. Better to parlay these fugitive chords as station ID's on local radio. Driver, follow that voice!

'Well, monsieur, you 'ave just bought yourself a new life,' the doctor said, as I wrote him another cheque. He didn't suggest what I should do with the old one.

A pack of Gauloises lies on my desk, haunting me. It contains 17 cigarettes. I smell them from time to time. Perhaps I should put the pack with Alexandra's first pair of shoes on top of the bookcase. Or maybe have it set in Perspex with a plaque in valuable brass; a kind of time capsule – 'A lifetime talking point.'

The problem with being a born-again non-smoker is my unfamiliarity with the moral high ground occupied by a growing army of anti-smoking crusaders. I never liked running with the crowd.

'I'd prefer it if you didn't.' 'Here, why don't you use this for an ashtray?' 'Do you mind me eating while you smoke?' And so on.

Madame says the next step is to give up drinking and lose some weight. But with the present exchange rate, wine is about the only thing I can afford.

Still, I can tell you that living is a lot cheaper than dying in the South of France.

It's an ill wind…

1997 Financial Gazette

I am a currency speculator. Not quite in the same league as George Soros, I admit. Nor a very successful one, I might add. But every day I make awesome monetary decisions. Do we do a big shop at Champion, our local supermarket, in Antibes, with a Credit Lyonnais cheque or my Lloyds Visa card? Or change the last of my dollar bills?

Do we deposit the cheque for £275 that arrived this morning in the Credit Lyonnais and suffer the 200 franc rip-off charge because we desperately need the money here? Or do we mail it to Lloyds in London to keep the overdraft within bounds and hope that a larger cheque will arrive soon from that late-paying magazine publisher? Or do we deposit a much larger personal cheque here and hope to God that the money from my newspaper column has been credited to the account, which it normally should have been if the secretary in Paris hasn't got on holiday again before paying the contributors? Or do we feel flush enough to whack it into the holiday fund at the Union de Banques Suisses in Lausanne?

The bottom line, you see, is that I earn in pounds and dollars and spend in French francs. Then there's the question of tax. But I think we'll leave that for another time – which is the way I prefer to deal with tax.

Roger Collis

You'll have gathered that our financial arrangements are complex if not well-ordered. But as an expatriate writer of a certain age and uncertain future rubbing along in Antibes with a management team (Madame and Alexandra, my 12-year-old secretary) to support, ordering up optimum spondulicks involves a shifting equation of cash flow and the exchange rate between the pound and the dollar and the French franc, the pound and the dollar, the dollar and the French franc; and the exchange rate between all three currencies and the French lamb chop. Plus, of course, the time dimension.

Whether to take a short or a long position against the French franc is a daily dilemma – a quixotic second-guessing of the Bundesbank, Threadneedle Street and George Soros, although being frequently short in cash-flow terms, my position, you might say, is inevitably self-selecting. ('What is your position, Monsieur C?' Precarious.) I spend so much time these days worrying about the roundabouts and swings of currency markets that currency speculation is threatening to take over my day job instead of just my lying awake at night.

First thing in the morning, while Madame is brewing a nice pot of high-grown Darjeeling (sterling-based from Whittards of Chelsea) and preparing toast and Marmite (franc-based at a usurious mark-up from the English ship chandlers in the port), and Alexandra is starting her homework she has just remembered before going to school, I nip round the corner for yesterday's *Guardian*.

I am perforce an involuntary addict of headlines such as STRENGTH IN BRITAIN LIFTS THE POUND; DOLLAR RISES IN LIGHT TRADING; DOLLAR IS DOWN AND LOSING STATUS; and INFLATION COULD STILL SPOIL IT ALL. But first I search frantically for the little box, TOURIST RATES – BANK SELLS. Then I check the cross-rates in the *International Herald Tribune*, which you never get unless you're George Soros; but it does give me some idea of where to bung the cheque from New Zealand. I then check my Alzheimer's with the *Guardian* Quick Crossword.

The last few months I've been cautiously optimistic, if not buoyant, at the rise of the pound. Sterling's ignominious scuttle from the ERM in 1992, which cut my income by a third overnight, left me with an exchange rate of around 7.2 at the nadir. Large sterling cheques would vaporize when they hit the Credit Lyonnais. Yesterday, I got a miraculous 10.1. Mind you, I can remember when it was the right side of 12.

I don't expect it to last. After all, an optimist is simply a pessimist who is badly informed. But I can do without hysterical commentaries by pundits in the British press screaming for a *cheaper* pound. All that culminated in a *Guardian* leader the other day, headed TAKING A POUNDING; INDUSTRY MUST BE RESCUED NOW. Followed a couple of days later with a triumphant POUND COMES OFF THE BOIL.

I remember when a strong pound used to be a matter of national pride. What humiliation we felt when Harold Wilson was forced to devalue in the 1960s. The pound fell from 12 to 10 Swiss francs! Since then a succession of governments has managed to debase the currency through inflation and further devaluations.

Euros are something I could live with – if I had enough of them. But in true British tradition, they'll probably turn out to be the wrong kind.

Soros strikes again

1998 Financial Gazette

George Soros strikes again. Having delivered the *coup de grace* to sterling in 1992 – which cut my income by a third overnight, you may remember (and what a sleepless night it was) – George is now betting £6 billion or thereabouts (what's a billion or two between enemies?) for a repeat performance.

We were cruising along quite nicely, with the pound nudging 10 francs (almost par for the Micawber Index), when I saw George's bespectacled little face smiling benignly at me from the Guardian's finance page. A thought struck me: why not stick it on the bulletin board in the electronic shoebox here in Antibes? After all, Montgomery had a picture of Rommel in his caravan at el Alemain.

Now the pound's down to 9.34 on the tourist rate and weakening – as the weather people say – while we tread the dangerous edge of my overdraft limit. And news just in that nuclear warheads may not 'provide a viable deterrent' to the eventuality of an asteroid hitting the earth around 2030 and 'ending civilization as we know it.'

I know I shouldn't have thrown away that 'good luck' chain letter which promised me bad luck if I didn't send it off to six more people within 36 hours. Sure enough, there was a complacent headline this morning in yesterday's Guardian – POUND FALLS TO SIX-MONTH LOW – 'to the relief of exporters' (what about expatriates?) and 'this is good news for Eddie George and George Soros.'

Fahcrissake. Who's in charge of monetary policy? George Eddie, Eddie Soros, Eddie Brown, George Soros, George Brown or Gordon Brown? The next thing we'll be told is that governments are still running things.

If proof were needed that they are not, there on the next page was a picture of the saturnine Rupert Murdoch emerging from 10 Downing Street after his daily briefing to George Blair. You don't have to buy politicians these days; they sell themselves. Thank heavens Bill Gates is speculating in cyberspace.

Here's a last sub-emotional appeal to Eddie Soros to get off my back and have a go at the French franc for a change. Or perhaps the rouble. RUSSIA PUTS ALL INTO FIGHT TO SAVE FIRM ROUBLE is a headline in tomorrow's (I mean today's) Guardian – a sure sign that Boris Yeltsin's vodkanomics is still on track. But on third thoughts, a run on the franc in the run-up to the euro on 1st January 1999 might put the skids under the euro. The concomitant rise of sterling (and the dollar) would be a great blessing for expatriates, if not exports.

The idea may not be entirely fanciful. While researching a story the other day for the New York Times on how the euro might affect the business traveler, I playfully suggested to Henry Ruff, Head of Euro (no less) at Visa International, whether there might not be a 'window of opportunity' for unscrupulous speculators to derail European Monetary Union before the eleven first-wave countries irrevocably lock the exchange rates of their national currencies against the euro on 1st January 1999.

'That would be a disaster scenario where the market differentiated between what we call a national currency unit and the euro,' Ruff said. 'The next few months would be the only time that somebody like George Soros could move in. It would shake the foundations of the euro in the market. But obviously, all the central banks are queuing up to make sure that doesn't happen. Otherwise, the whole thing could be blown out of the water.'

The euro will not – as my French neighbor still insists – mean that all prices will be the same across 'Euroland.' All euros will be equal but some will be more equal than others. But price transparency will make it easier to compare prices from one country to another.

This may lead us to greater price uniformity across Europe and may ultimately bring prices down through greater cross-border competition. But don't hold your breath.

We're also likely to see wider swings in exchange rates between the euro, the pound and the dollar and other currencies on the grounds that the strengths and weaknesses of the constituent euro-economies will influence the single currency behind the scenes, as it were, given that the euro is more a political than an economic confection. The ghosts of the former currencies – deutschemarks, francs, pesetas and escudos – will shadow the euro for some time to come – cursed by the Maastricht convergence criteria.

I don't know about your convergence criteria. Mine are unlikely to carry much weight with Lloyds and Credit Lyonnais. But the prevailing advice is to start thinking in euros and dealing in them when that becomes possible for electronic and credit-card transactions next year. Friends are saying that I should open an offshore euro account.

But I'm waiting for George.

Roger Collis

A Dog's Life in America

1984 'If my boss calls ...'

In a climate rife with reform and sociological in-fighting the dogs of America, along with astronauts and Wall Street security analysts, are fast emerging as the number one privileged caste. And if a controversial Canine Desegregation Bill gets through Congress it will only remain for the powerful dog lobby to win the right for dogs to be admitted to the nation's restaurants without discrimination against either colour or breed. Already restaurant owners are required by law to 'prominently display and encourage' the use of 'doggy bags,' the contents of which are subject to random checks by Federal inspectors to ensure the require quality of victuals.

In fact it is the scope and application of the food laws that most fully recognises the ethnic superiority of dogs. The law states that no less than thirty-five percent of supermarket shelf-space shall be set aside for the burgeoning varieties of dog food products. (This compares with an additional fifteen percent for dogs' cosmetic and toiletry items).

A huge proportion of network TV airtime is devoted to effulgent advertisements for fortified marrow bones and tempting doggy TV dinners rich with esoteric nutrients. the hilarious comedy show, 'It's a Dog's Life,' on prime weekend time, has been top of the Nielsen ratings for several months. And a spokesman for Canine Cable News has announced a new dog series for later this year. Madison Avenue has responded to the challenge of a rapacious dog-food market by some supreme creative efforts. A striking new commercial, 'Dog's Dinner,' is tipped to win a *Lion d'Or* at the Cannes Festival. A number of advertising agencies have appointed well-known dogs to their board of directors. An all-dog agency is being mooted from a carefully guarded suite at the Waldorf Towers.

Not surprisingly, the regulations prescribing the quality and range of dog-food ingredients are far more exacting than for human products. Every dog food must contain 'all the essential minerals and vitamins needed for normal growth and maintenance.' And ingredients must be set out in exhaustive detail on the can or packet. Even the precise chemical nature of the artificial preservatives must be shown.

Consequently, many housewives, especially from the lower income groups, have been buying the more tempting dog foods in the heartbreaking attempt to give their families a balanced diet. There were riots last week when it was announced that dog licences would now need to be shown at check-out counters to prove bona fide dog ownership. A number of old ladies were arrested and several people taken to hospital with umbrella wounds. Dog breeders have already cornered the lucrative black market and the more enterprising car-hire firms are offering a 'Rentadog' service for people doing their weekly shopping.

Considering that elections are still over the horizon there is unusual concern in Washington. I have it from a reliable source on Capitol Hill that the next director of the FDA (that's the Federal Dogfood Administration) will be a youngish German shepherd, Chester C. Peenemunde, a suave mid-Atlantic animal with a New England owner of impeccable pedigree. Time magazine has featured Peenemunde an unprecedented five times on its cover. In his Brooks Brothers collar he has become a familiar figure on the Washington cocktail circuit.

Although Peenemunde has been tainted with liberalism he is widely expected to adopt a tough law'n'order stance. What is certain is that millions of Americans this year will be reduced to eating food only fit for human consumption.

Banking woes
1998 Financial Gazette

I like to think of myself as radical, even revolutionary, viewing the world with a rakish, satirical eye. But when it comes to banks and matters pertaining, I am deeply conservative, even to the point of hiding unopened letters under the mattress. And spreading the message (if not the bread) to each bank that one has serious funds elsewhere ('This is my main account,' you assure them disingenuously, and, of course, you'll 'top up' the account when the exchange rates between the franc/dollar/pound hit whatever ...

So that when the lady from the Credit Lyonnais phones to remind us ever so politely that we are 3,000 francs or so overdrawn, I can thank her effusively along the lines that alas, Madame has been far too busy (forgotten) to balance the cheque-book and of course we'll deposit a sterling cheque from Lloyds the very next time we're in town (optimum currency rates permitting), having kited a cheque from Lloyds as collateral. It's all down to mutual confidence.

Not that the banks have always reciprocated my trust. I once had an account with the First Bank of Elkhart Indiana, which was suddenly taken over by some other bank and disappeared along with my account. I only had a few dollars left, but still. On the advice of a seemingly well-heeled French friend, we opened an account at something called the Banque de France et Sudmeris, which suddenly became the Banca Commercile Italiana (France), and was then snapped up by the Banque Populaire.

During the course of this last takeover, we had several thousand francs worth of cheques from Lloyds blocked in the system for several nail-biting weeks. We now bank with the Credit Lyonnais, dubbed the 'Debit Lyonnais' because of its gigantic losses, cantilevered by the French government, which, in a perverse way, seems more reassuring.

Banking efficiency – or at least, transparency – seems to be inversely proportional to the ubiquitous use of personal cheques. Monthly statements from the Union des Banques Suisses in Lausanne arrive (in plain grey envelopes) at least a week before those from Credit Lyonnais and are far more lucid. As you'd expect, they show a running balance of transactions so that you can see where you are – and where you were – on any day of the month.

The same for Lloyds. Whereas the Credit Lyonnais (along with the Banque Populaire and its predecessors) simply gives a list of sums debited (often in no particular order) and right at the end cheques or transfers credited, and the final balance. Ask for a statement halfway through the month, and you get an incoherent list of transactions which you have to try to balance for yourself. The Cartesian approach to single-entry book-keeping?

Yet France is an obsessive cheque society: the French pay for practically everything, even trivial sums, by cheque – petrol, books of stamps, beach parasols... you are rarely asked for a *carte d'identité*. Whereas in Switzerland, cheques are viewed with grave suspicion. This is a cash society, and plenty of it, please. Invoices come with standard green slips for cash payment at the post office, for which you get a stamped counterfoil as a receipt.

Cheques work in the United States for payments by post, but not for face-to-face transactions. When I presented a store in Rahway, New Jersey, with a cheque drawn on the First Bank of Elkhart, Indiana, the reaction was Batemanesque. I thought they were going to call the police. Worse still would have been to offer cash, the poor man's credit card.

Even in Britain, my expatriate reflexes are affronted by demands by mini-cab drivers to show a cheque 'guarantee card.' When I was an officer and 'temporary' gentlemen (as National Service types were called), it was unthinkable for trades people to query one's cheque. Second Lieutenant His Nibs of the 17th/21st Foot and Mouth would write cheques for £3 or more with impunity at emporia in Yeovil High Street. Passing a bad cheque was almost a court martial offence. But that's another story.

Meanwhile, French banks have taken to the euro with gusto. Last month's statement from the Banque Populaire cited the balance in euros as well as francs, assuming a going-in exchange rate of 6.50 francs at midnight on January 1st 1999, when the euro will be officially extant. There will then be a three-year transition or 'familiarization' phase, during which transactions will be quoted in both francs and euros, until Big Bang day, January 1st 2002, when euro banknotes and coins will start circulating, gradually replacing the franc until July 1st 2002 when the euro will reign supreme. Credit Lyonnais will offer customers a 'dedicated' pocket calculator for converting euros to francs and vice versa.

[Ten years later, French bank statements, and card receipts, still show the franc equivalent next to the euro total, helpful for folk like me who still think in francs.]

I can see problems on the euro horizon. The French sides of the one and two euro coins illustrated in the Credit Lyonnais booklets are sure to be confused with the real and counterfeit 10- and 20-franc pieces currently in circulation. And there is sure to be misunderstanding about the new currency. For heaven's sake, The French are still talking in old francs, especially when it comes to real estate. ('You should be able to get an apartment for 10 million.') And an elderly neighbor insists that one franc will equal one euro. 'Otherwise, what's the point?' he says. He may well have a point. Eat your heart out, all you franc, lire and drachma zillionaires.

But we're not there yet. The euro still has to contend with the millennium bug.

Paradise redeemed

1993 The Times Magazine

'Nice-Cote d'Azur is a business airport and we're giving it all the business facilities,' says the chap from the *Chambre de Commerce*. 'It's not a tourist airport; half our passengers are traveling on business.'

Standing in a sweaty arrivals line you might wonder which half you should be cursing – the boisterous conventioneers or the bucket-and-spade brigade. What you decide may depend on the role you are playing – if you have worked it out, that is. Even hard-core business people are tempted to build a holiday on the back of a business trip. Or vice versa.

Ten years ago, Nice used to be the most attractive airport in Europe. You came in over the sea to land, touching down on the edge of the runway to palm trees, flowers and a fragrant breeze. You could be off and away in five minutes, breezing through passport control and customs to the car park in front of the terminal.

You still come in over the sea, but inevitably, I suppose, it's not quite as user-friendly. The original building has been subsumed in a canopy of steel and glass. And the airport is surrounded by a clutter of aesthetically challenged office buildings, hotels and spaghetti junctions – part of the building boom that threatens to engulf the Cote d'Azur in an anarchic wave of concrete. I think they're hoping to have the whole coast concreted over by the end of the decade – with Monte Carlo perhaps as the third terminal of Nice airport. Six million passengers this year; 10 million by the end of the decade, and maybe 20 million by 2010. 'We have 48 scheduled airlines operating here; consider us a French Manchester.' Let us hope that Manchester stays where it is.

The Cote d'Azur region is home to one million people, half of whom live in Nice. The coexistence of this resident population and eight million visitors (half of them French) has led to a giant step down in both taste and standards.

The hinterland is scarred by crass developments – far-flung hypermarkets, giant furniture showrooms and concrete factories. The urbanized coastal strip eastward from Nice owes little to Coney Island – except that the fast food isn't as good. Traffic all year round is hell. But it's still a good spot to come for a change of pollution.

August is the cruellest month, when it can suffer the full frontal invasion from Paris, with oppressive heat and nightmare crowds. But there are peak periods all year round. Those with the means flee to their *résidences secondaires* in the mountains. Those without stay and suffer.

April and September are my favourite months. Beaches are still alive – although it can be too cold to swim – and you can sit outside on the terraces of cafes and restaurants. April and May are the only months when it is possible to lie on the beach and then zoom up to the ski slopes at Auron or Isola 2000 – about an hour's drive away. Spring is a season of promise and fulfilment, with high summer still a distant threat. There is a sprinkling of tourists – just enough to remind you that this is not such a bad place to live after all – with a favourable tourist/denizen ratio. Nothing is more infuriating for the professional expatriate than to be taken for a tourist.

'What's the weather like?' everyone asks when they call from Paris or London. Chances are that it's fine. You can make their day by saying it's pouring with rain. Or tell them you're out on the patio with a tall *pastis*. Or feed them the yin and yang bit. 'God, it's a gorgeous day; the sea is a deep blue and I can see the coast as far as Bordighera. Trouble is I'm stuck here at my computer screen. I haven't even been out on the terrace this morning.' It all depends what kind of 'statement' you want to make.

Even if it is raining, they know it is much warmer than where they are. And you are sure to be dressed for the part: informal chic (no shorts) is de rigueur, save for very formal meetings. (I know one businessman who never wears socks all year round.)

The bad news is crime. The sun and money have attracted drifters and small-time hoodlums (though organized crime rules okay). Mugging is now a way of life. You read every day in *Nice-Matin* of jewellery heists in shops and villas — a new breed of road pirates terrorize motorists, even in broad daylight. Car theft is endemic; and the smashed wing in the car park is routine. Summer nights are pierced by the wail of *pompiers* on their way to an accident, an ear-splitting buzz of delinquent motor bikes, police sirens, and the blasting exhausts of loutish Porsches.

And yet, and yet. The sea is still blue (albeit covered with a shimmering sheen of suntan oil), the sun shines a lot of the time, and much of the coast is still beautiful. You can find tranquility in the medieval perched villages of the *arrière pays*, their roofs a Cubist painting by Braque or Picasso, terraced vineyards set among ancient olive trees and eucalyptus with pine forests stretching down to the sea. There is a feast of music, opera and ballet, countless museums and exhibitions, and half a dozen fine golf courses minutes away from the urban blight.

I have found that rediscovering the Cote d'Azur is the best revenge. Which all comes down to finding your very own kind of refuge from the sleaze.

On Friday evenings at Nice airport, crowd-watching can be good value when the shuttle flights from Paris arrive. There are groupies and weekend wives, dowagers waving vintage arms, a gaggle of executives on their way to lubricate a conference in Monaco, machos in designer dungarees, and ambiguous ladies with impatient poodles. On Monday mornings, the first flight to Paris is filled with sun-tanned executives who seem not quite to have decided whether they are on business or pleasure.

I could live with that kind of identity crisis.

Conference chic

1995-1996 Business Life/Resident Abroad

Now here's a management problem. Madame took Mr. Wong's 36-hour Hong Kong suit to the express cleaners (*Le Pressing Pour Les Gens Pressés*) yesterday afternoon and now the lady says it won't be ready for the conference in Monte Carlo tomorrow. Alexandra, my nine-year-old secretary, crinkles her eyes in mock concern and says something in playground French that I'm not sure I want to understand. Madame says it's not her fault, and I should have stayed in Hong Kong for another 36-hours or asked Mr. Wong to fax me another suit. Do I detect a touch of Schadenfreude among my management team? This is not a time for levity and recrimination, I point out sternly, but for kindred reflection and quiet panic.

If this were any old conference I'd get Madame to ring up and say I was *hors de combat* or simply wear my leather jacket and jeans and go as a photographer. What makes it so vital is that nine o'clock tomorrow I'm expected to give a keynote address to something called the International Association of Professional Meeting Planners. And here I am, suitless. Perhaps I could start with, 'Mr., er, Madame Chairperson, ladies and gentlemen, unsuited as I am…'

Now come on, I can hear you murmuring, don't try and kid us that even you only possess one suit. And you'd be right. I'm not exactly a closet Beau Brummel, but I have a wardrobe full of suits, cascading down the styles of the ages. But none of them fit.

I take one girth-stricken look. There are suits for the thin man trying to get out, and for the fat man trying to get in. But nothing I can get into right now. I have pin-stripes, chalk-stripes, discreet herringbone and a splendid, creamy-beige summer job, the absurdly over-sanguine consequence of The Drinking Man's Diet 100 years ago. I only have to pull the trousers up to my knees and I know it's not going to work.

Flicking nostalgically through the collection, I feel like some kind of sartorial geologist. We have some well-preserved specimens from the paleo-double-breasted period along with some rare single-button curiosities from the early to mid-Pleistocene. Double-breasted are back again, I see. Not like the old George Raft look: more like a cross between the Mikado and a dressing gown in a Noel Coward play.

Ties – I can do you ties – from very wide to very thin. And shoes, from what used to be called Chukker boots to some rather fine dress shoes from Bally, an excruciating half-size too small, which by the end of the morning force me to walk with what I can only describe as a Talmudic shuffle. (Useful in the right circles.) And I can do 'casual chic:' lots of white cotton trousers and short-sleeved shirts which don't need to do up at the neck, which they can't do anyway. The nearest we get to conference chic is an ancient Pierre Cardin double-breasted blazer, now suffering from designer fatigue, and a tired grey Brooks Brothers number: the jacket is okay, but the trousers are unreliable in the seat. Perhaps if they could arrange a wheelchair…

In its day, the Brooks Brothers had a fair amount of success. It has 'natural shoulders' (or the 'just-stepped-off-a-long-haul-flight' look) with trousers that are still sitting down when you stand up. But with the right haberdashery – oxford button-down shirts, fake old-school tie, and Florsheim wing-tip shoes (brogues), it was just the ticket in my mid-corporate period.

Conferences – like companies – develop their own cultures, and dress codes play a crucial part. Sometimes this is spelled out, sometimes not. I don't know which is worse; turning up in an all-purpose business suit, or trying to imagine what is meant by 'smart casual.' Dressing up and dressing down is the game delegates play.

What amazed me at a recent conference in Orlando was the amount of gear that people brought along. I was always being wrong-footed. 'Smart casual' at the plenary sessions meant open-necked floral shirts, maroon golfing-trousers. And those ridiculous designer trainers. But the heavy hitters came dressed to the nines, as though they were just off for a meeting with the New York security analysts. So I was more or less okay, except that Mr. Wong's suit looked a bit jet-lagged. Still on Hong Kong time, probably.

You may be relieved to know that Mr. Wong's suit has just turned up at the cleaners, so we're on for tomorrow. Pending my next trip to Hong Kong, I'm thinking of having Mr. Wong's suit copied in Savile Row.

How I never met Graham Greene

1991 'Roger and Out,' Business Life

Since Graham Greene died in April [1991] the question arises: who is now the most distinguished British resident in Antibes? Monsieur Grom Grin, as he was affectionately called by the locals, is a tough act to follow.

Not that I'd presume to push myself forward, you understand. It's just that my credibility back home depends on knowing who it is I'm now assumed to know.

For the past ten years I've dined out on the awkward assumption that Monsieur Grin and I were close friends. The sad truth is that I never actually met the great man.

'Ah you live in Antibes! You must know Graham Greene,' people said.

'Yes, we are, ah, neighbors, of course.' Well what would you say?

To play the part, I had to bone up on Monsieur Grin. I don't mean exploring the moral agony of Scobie in *The Heart of the Matter*, but sussing out his daily habits and haunts; what you might call *The Human Factor*. True detail is the heart of the bogus anecdote.

I did my homework with the local *commercants*. (*'Yes, we 'ave another English writer comes 'ere – Grom Grin. Per'aps you know 'im?'* Ahem.)

'Yes, he always starts work before he gets up... before he has a bath or anything,' I confide. *'He has a gin and tonic mid-morning, then a martini as an aperitif... and for lunch, a bowl of mussels with a bottle of white wine... He's quite fond of veal as well. Always starts work straight after breakfast.'*

Stuff like that.

Every day, Greene left his three-room apartment in the Residence des Fleurs to walk the length of the marina, through the arch in the ramparts to the old town, dodging between the anarchic drivers and the dog shit (*merde de pays*) like everyone else. (The dangerous edge of things?) He'd pick up *Nice Matin* and *The Times* from the *tabac* on the corner then dodge across the road to Chez Felix, said to be his favourite restaurant, for lunch.

Over his veal or fish, he would mark up passages or make notes. He would often be accompanied by his 'great friend,' Madame Cloetta, a striking white-haired woman, quite a bit younger. This was 'HHK' (Healthy, Happy, Kitten) to whom he had dedicated *Travels with my Aunt* in 1969. She was also the 'Y' of many other dedications.

The restaurant was a source of inspiration for Greene. He wrote: 'Since 1959, Chez Felix was a home-from-home. I found short stories served to me with my meal.' He mentions it in the short story collection, *May We Borrow Your Husband?* And in every interview I have read.

Friends in London were always saying to me, 'Let's go to Chez Felix in search of inspiration when we next come down.' Fearful of bumping into Grom Grin, I always managed to head them off. (*'Juliette, I can't introduce you now. You see that bald bloke with him? That's Sol Bloomgarden, the movie producer.*)

By the way, if you're thinking of making a pilgrimage to Chez Felix, I advise you to think again. Madame and I had a memorable meal there about four years ago – so memorable we very nearly complained to the *Office du Tourisme*. Not that they could care less. A much better bet is the Auberge Provencale, round the corner in the Place Nationale. Here we saw Grom Grin with another tall man and a stunning girl (Y's daughter?). But what can you do, apart from stare? Send over a bottle of champagne with your card? There used to be a restaurant in Helsinki with phones at each table, so you could ring up folk you fancied (actually, I think it was a nightclub.) Nowadays, Alexandra, my six-year-old secretary, makes all the tricky introductions.

I suppose I could have phoned Grom Grin at home. But, as you'd expect, he was ex-directory. Even if I had known his number, what could I have said to Grom Grin?

'Hullo, Grom Grin? I'm 'Roger and Out.' You don't know me, but I've read all your books, so could we please meet for a cup of tea?'

'I'm pleased to say you've got the wrong number.'

Not much reflected glory in that.

I thought of writing Grin a note (I prefer a script, even if it is my own) and asking Monsieur Martin, *patron* of the Auberge Provencale, to hand it to M. Grin when he next came in, but that seemed pretty futile.

The best chance would have been for a distinguished editor to send me along to do an interview. But apparently, Greene didn't like talking about his work (and especially about his private life – which he considered a form of trespass) – and anyway, didn't suffer reporters gladly, unless, presumably, they had serious literary credentials. Naturally, this included me out.

Perhaps with my talent for the trivial and inopportune, I might have scored by persuading the great man to 'free-associate' about business travel – getting the corporate rate at hotels, or perhaps the sticky matter of airport congestion and other passionately boring subjects.

'Mr. Grin, ah, Greene, you often send your characters to faraway, exotic places. Did you conceive this as an unconscious desire for incentive travel?' Could have been gold.

But back to the core problem. The penny dropped a moment ago as I was flicking through some old magazines in search of something to plagiarize. I came across a story by Gay Talese, the American writer, in Esquire, in which he tells how he was sent to Los Angeles to interview Frank Sinatra, but couldn't get to see him. So he interviewed everyone around Sinatra instead. The story was called, *'How I Never met Frank Sinatra.'*

I have now decided I *don't* want to know the most distinguished foreign resident in Antibes, whoever he or she may be. I'm going to dine out on *not* having met Graham Greene. At least it has the ring of truthful deception.

As the saying goes: 'It's a wise man who knows how to quit when he's behind.'

Loose connections
1994 Resident Abroad; 1994 'Roger and Out,' Business Life

Two-forty in the morning is no time for a modem to go on the blink, especially when you're desperate to transmit your column to Paris for Friday's paper.

'As long as we can call it up on the screen when we arrive in the office,' my editor had said. I could feel the portcullis crashing down. I'd get short shrift if I rang in to say I was nursing a sick modem. Perhaps I could fax it? Perhaps not. Even if they found the fax, someone would have to type the stuff into the system. It was file by modem, or nothing. Long gone are the days when you had a chap to take down your stuff on Mr. Bell's electric telephone.

Actually, it wasn't the modem itself that was out of action, but the cable that connects my Tandy 200 laptop to the phone socket. I don't want to get too technical but the wires inside had somehow worked loose and so every time I used it I needed to spend several agonizing minutes jiggling it around to get a connection.

There'd be a dreadful crackling on the telephone before I could get the dialling tone. Jiggle-jiggle, twist-twist, until I finally got a connection and could whack my timeless prose down the wire.

The modem cable causing me such grief had been bodged up five years ago by the lad in charge of my local Tandy shop from a cable I'd brought back from London to the electronic shoe-box in Antibes. It was all very clandestine because the dreaded France Telecom had not seen fit to 'approve' it. My handy Tandyman did a spot of anarchic wiring. He had long since disappeared, however, and his wiring had finally come adrift.

But never mind. Make it work this time, and buy a new cable in the morning. Should be no problem. After all, we now have a harmonized, homogenized, bureaucratized Single Market in modems and competition in cross-border cables.

They say that an optimist is a pessimist who is badly informed. By ten o'clock next morning, I knew that I had a full-scale Euro-problem on my hands.

My local Tandy shop in Nice did not want to know. 'M'sieur, you 'ave a problem,' the man said with satisfaction. 'France Telecom 'as not approved a modem cable for your machine. What you 'ave done until now is forbidden. There is nothing more to do.' You could almost see the Gallic shrug. I thought he was going to report me to the French anti-modem squad.

So I rang a friendly Tandy shop in Finchley Road where I get most of my computer supplies. What relief to have Watkinson on the line! He may not have an answer, but at least we seem to be on the same side. He gets briskly to the point. 'Do you have a box?'

A box? 'Yes, a box about two inches square that you stick on the wall. All our phones have a box. With a capacitor inside. If we sell a phone to someone who's going to the Continent, they attach the box to their local phone system. In your case, you wire the box into the line and then just plug in the UK cable.'

Watkinson, you're a genius. Can you please courier a box and cable?

'Well, the quickest way would be to order one from our warehouse in Birmingham. I'll give them a bell. Can you call me back?'

When I rang back, Watkinson had talked things over with the customer services manager, who suggested it might be better for me to check out a Belgian cable ('The only thing that changes is the wall socket') before ordering a UK cable and box from Brum. I now had two key contacts: Neil in Mail Order, Birmingham, and a Monsieur Toussaint at Tandy in Brussels.

I thought it wise to apply a touch of 'belt and braces' management at this crucial stage (I couldn't quite visualize how this 'box' fitted in. That's the trouble with talking to computer people. You are clinging desperately to shreds of meaning which vanish as soon as you put the phone down.) I ordered a box and cable right away from Neil and then I rang Brussels.

Monsieur Toussaint wasn't there, but Monsieur Thomas was reassuring. 'In Belgium we are 100 percent homologue with France,' he said with pride. 'All that you do is exchange the Belgian PTT wall plug for a French one. You'll find it much simpler than an English cable, where we must modify the two wires in the plug for the modem jack in the computer.'

If you say so, mate! But by now I was up against another deadline. So I got down to some contingency DIY. Ever so carefully, I opened the wonky plug and found two semi-naked wires, a white and a red, which looked as if they were crossed. I uncrossed them and stuck them with super-glue to where they were probably meant to be. Jiggle-jiggle, crackle-crackle, and got a connection.

The Belgian cable arrived four days later. The problem was that the wiring in the French and Belgian phone plugs seemed to have little in common. Better wait for Birmingham.

Ten days (and four phone calls) later, it arrived. The cable had a very modern-looking plug, but not one destined to fit any socket I could find.

My marine engineer chap finally took pity on me – sucking in his breath at the sight of my stricken cable's super-glued connections. 'Short-circuit,' he said with gravity. 'You could have blown up the phone lines!'

I imagined white lightning flashing through France Telecom's wires, perhaps blasting Monsieur *le directeur* out of his chair in Draguinan. Paris blacked out. Brussels cut off... the Gendarmerie beating on the door of the electronic shoe-box.

But in half an hour, I was safely rewired.

All I can say is welcome to the Single Market.

Le coeur de filet de boeuf s'il vous plait, and not a moment to lose

1995 'Roger and Out,' Business Life; 1996 Resident Abroad

'We're looking at a middle-of-the-book feature called *How to Afford the Cote d'Azur*. Would you be interested?' says the editor of this glossy magazine on the line from New York.

How to afford the Cote d'Azur. Something I've never been able to afford to find out.

But the fee – even in dollars – would stretch to a case or two of supermarket Beaujolais as well as more shirts from Mr. Wong in Hong Kong. I could almost hear the hook being baited.

'This is by no means a budget article. We want you to stay and eat in all the places you recommend: about 20 hotels and restaurants, I'd say. We pay expenses – I'll get you an advance right away. Shall we say two thousand? You'll probably need twice that again. And, ah, the deadline is January 5th. Which, ah, gives you five weeks? Okay? Listen, we're delighted. I'm going to courier a 12-page assignment letter...'

Well, yes. What can I say when you approach me in the aftermath of lunch? Can I have a cooling-off period? Until three o'clock in the morning. When all my deadlines come home to roost. Talk about spreading bread on troubled waters...

Five weeks. Let's see, if I do one hotel and one restaurant every day for the next 40 days – and drop everything else... No, I won't make it. I need to eat in two restaurants a day and stay in two hotels a night... Or we could work *en famille*. Madame and I sleeping in different beds together, as it were, and meeting for meals. Yes, the whole thing's coming together. Alexandra can look after the kiddies' menus and help with desserts. Only problem now is writing the damn thing.

I'd done some of this when we first came down to live here about 15 years ago. Would you believe I used to update the 'Riviera' chapter for something called 'Get 'em and Go' guides in New York?

Well, perhaps you would. You know the kind of thing. You first set the scene: 'A cornucopia of sun-drenched beaches, picturesque coves, harbo(u)rs packed with pleasure craft, jet set resorts, wooded hills, tranquil villages rife with history and legend, the French Riviera has something for everyone to enjoy... A magical playground blah, blah,' a world of 'breathtaking/awesome views/vistas/panoramas with mountains plunging into the shimmering sea,' and 'fabulous enamels /ceramics/hand-painted murals/century of your choice' in museums and 'sensitively restored' churches set in 'ancient olive groves.' (You'd see the same stuff in different guides – everyone copied from everyone else.) Restaurants would offer 'gourmet cuisine' (that's American for real food).

This was strictly desk research. I was never given the wherewithal to visit any of these places.

It came down to checking phone numbers, prices, and whether the chef still recommended the *aiguillettes de canard de Challons aux sang* or was now flogging his *Charlotte de St Pierre* (a 'fish fantasy'), moved on with his two Michelin stars, or gone into public relations full time. The whole thing was no more than culinary tyre-kicking.

Last Sunday we took to the *arrière pays* in search of the first address on my list: the Auberge la Vignette Haute in Auribeau-sur-Siagne, between Cannes and Grasse – fortified by the prospect of a free lunch.

Roger Collis

Half and hour, the man said. But it took more than an hour (in spite of, or because of, the large-scale Michelin green map and two back-seat drivers) to find the place, a 17th century bergerie over-restored with impressive vulgarity, complete with suits of armor, high-kitsch pewter-clad glasses, plates and candlesticks, mock distressed-leather menu holders. The Muzak distributed Strauss (Johann) as you went in. The view of the Massif de Tanneron was authentic. As were the pre-prandial snorts inside. Eating professionally is a hard business.

But I was fortified by a fine review by Kingsley Amis of lunch at Simpson's-in-the-Strand (his favorite restaurant, it seems), which I saw the other day in Harpers & Queen. Amis was eloquent about a concoction of quail's eggs with haddock and cheese, followed by Lancashire Hot Pot and treacle tart with custard, all washed down with red sparkling burgundy, rounded off with a glass of vintage port. 'Two of you can have the full treatment for £70 including wine and VAT.' I thought, if Amis can do it, so can I.

The full treatment at the Auberge for Madame, Alexandra and me took three hours and came to about 96 quid. Expensive when you're trying to afford the Cote d'Azur, but tremendous value all the same.

The cost of the meal is determined by your choice of main course. (*Mignon de porcau pruneaux* comes in at 290 francs; *le pavé de saumon grille, sa sauce a l'huile d'olive vierge extra et vinaigre de balsamique* comes in at 350 francs; *le coeur de filet de boeuf grille avec ses trois sauces* is 390 francs; and *la fricassée de queues de homard, son jus de crustaces au Sauternes et raviolis d'artichauts* will set you back 490 francs and *gibier de saison* will set you back 430 francs. You pay about 100 francs less for lunch on weekdays.)

Now here's the clever part: everything else is included: *le panier de crudités* (masses of raw vegetables, umpteen sauces, pâtés, smoked saucisson, olives, pickled mushrooms), a gigantic cheeseboard, and a copious selection of sorbets, fruit and nuts, and all the house wine (white, red, rose) you can drink (a fragrant little Côte de Provence). You were allowed to pay for wine off the list (I spotted a Pouilly fumé Ladoucette 1987 for 143 francs: try that for price in London). Our only extras were orange juice for Alexandra, who grazed free of charge, and a 30-franc tip (although service is included) as an investment for next time.

But there's no time for next time. The idea is to try somewhere else each Sunday. And inaugurate a syndicated food review ('800 words, old boy. Make a meal of it.') to fund the whole thing. How about 'Restaurant/auberge/bistrot of the Month/Week?' Or 'Gourmet Corner?' Or 'Lunching Out on the Côte d'Azur?' No? Okay, 'Roger and Out and About.'

The Archimedean moment came while peeing to martial music in the gents. I thought. Why not start a restaurant where you can eat just one course; starters, say or dessert? Why subject people to the sequential tyranny, and expense, of course after course? Price the fare at a fair price and you're in business.

After some lateral thinking I'm back in the writing game. You have wine critics; why not starter critics? Or pudding critics? 'Hullo again. Our first guest this evening is that distinguished free-loader, Roger and Out from the Côte d'Azur, who is going to talk about an apocryphal ha-ha spotted dick…'

I'm not alone in the market. Peter Millar, deputy editor of *The European*, also serves as 'soup correspondent.' (Obviously trying to pre-empt my work in progress; Food and the Single Man – recipes for survival and seduction.) So if you've any (printable) ideas, please let me know.

But not for the next few weeks. I've got far too much eating and drinking to do. Life's too short for fast food.

Don't confuse me with the fax

1994 International Herald Tribune/Resident Abroad; Business Life.

Well, we've finally joined the low-tech revolution and got a fax. The electronic shoe-box is now in the business of shoveling paper around the world, like everyone else.

Put it down to market forces. We'd held out so long in the futile hope that we'd be able to up-load, down-load, and generally off-load on an electronic screen. But in fact, the only time I use the modem on the Tandy is to file my weekly column to Paris.

And the local fax service now charges four quid per page *received*! Just one more 100-page press release and I'd have been wiped out. So move over, please. It's my turn to run out of paper, cut it off in fulsome flood, or scramble (the latest faxes have a special control which randomly squeezes lines to unreadability or else expands them into a supermarket bar-code – somewhat similar to the 'garbled' function on the erstwhile Telex machines. Look out for the new three-dimensional fax. Any time soon they'll be able to fax you a pizza.

The installation was not without drama. Our marine engineer chap who wires everything up at our place, was working on a super-yacht in Cannes and didn't turn up until early evening. (Sun over the yard arm in Cannes and sun-drenched traffic jam in Juan-les-Pins.) The next hour was spent translating Korean English into more or less English English.

And then where to put the blasted thing? I don't want to get into tactical geography, but what with its super-short power cable and its extra-long phone cable, the optimal spot was the lavatory. Good lateral thinking. But on third thoughts, let's put it in the *salon*, pro tem, until our chap can re-wire the office socket.

Socket and see! Meanwhile, the fax has become a family affair as we sit around after supper waiting for something to happen. Certainly beats watching French television. Alexandra, my nine-year-old secretary, has inaugurated a voluminous exchange of drawings with her cousins in Germany. And Madame seems to relish her role as gatekeeper of the written word. Let's hope I can get the thing moved to the electronic shoe-box proper fairly smartish.

But let's not get too carried away. The sober truth is that the ubiquitous fax is a retrograde step on our way to the paperless office. While the fax makes use of all the latest technology in digitalized fibre optic networks, it is intrinsically low tech; let's face it, the fax starts and ends with paper. The fax is simply the most efficient way of moving paper from one office to another.

What makes faxing so seductive is that a fax is a soft option for a hard phone call. But there are times when the only way to make a cold call is, well, to make a cold call. Getting past Essex/Knightsbridge/Mayfair girl, not to mention Manhattan girl, can require really hard chat.

On the other hand, a factitious fax may be just the ticket for dealing with those primeval questions: 'Does he know you?' 'What's it concerning?' Either way, as a self-respecting sit down comedian, I prefer a script, even if it is my own. A well-directed fax can breach the most scrupulous switchboard. Or hit them on their mobile.

The expert knows how to use the fax in conjunction with a phone call. Phone now, fax later. Or vice versa. 'Howard, I'll fax it right away so you'll have something in writing.' Or, 'Hello, Mrs. Whitstable. Did he get my fax?' Yes, about my proposal. Ah, well, it is a bit complicated. I'd just like to go over a couple of points...'

At least half the faxes one receives are dirty and unreadable – or missing a page. At least in the old days, you used to get a fairly legible typescript that you could type in.

But even an unreadable or dirty fax is better than nothing. At least you know that somebody is trying to fax you. A major problem with faxes is that you can never be sure that they've arrived. I've spent a lot of time fruitlessly faxing a wrong number or a machine that has either broken down without telling anyone or else run out of paper. The best approach is either to scatter your faxes to several numbers in the hope that one will have been well received. The question, 'Did you get my fax?' is far from rhetorical. It usually elicits a slight pause followed by the ominous words, 'Look, I'm going to give you another number...'

This reminds me of my first office about a hundred years ago as an upwardly mobile Bob Cratchit in the Dickensian offices of Messrs. Boult, Wade & Tennant, chartered patent agents, in the City, when we sent out letters by airmail, with a confirmatory copy by sea mail. ('I'll send you a fax confirming my fax.')

I suppose the fax achieved critical mass when people stopped asking 'Do you have a fax?' People are aggrieved if you dare to demur. Nobody now believes that you haven't got a fax in the office and at home. The way I've handled this solecism is either to try and make out that I am unlisted, or permanently out of paper. ('Don't fax me, I'll fax you.') Another ploy is to ask if you can send the stuff directly to their PC. Should they call your bluff, tell them you have a sick modem.

'Fax now, think later' is a specious catchword, responsible for heaven knows how many zillion acres of gratuitous junk. The telex (remember the telex?) was never such a paper tiger because somebody had to type the stuff into the machine. So a telex was mercifully short, if not to the point. In the hands of an expert, the telex (taking its cue from the cablegram) became an art form – brevity was brought to the very edge of ambiguity. Remember Cary Grant's apocryphal reply to an agent who cabled: 'HOW OLD CARY GRANT?' with 'OLD CARY GRANT FINE STOP HOW YOU?'

And there's nothing to compare with the *frisson* of getting back to the hotel after a hard day in the field to find the following telex: 'URGENT YOU CALL ME 6.30AM YOUR TIME. CHARLES REQUIRES... GARBLED... GARBLED... YOUR MARKETS. REGARDS GREENWALD.'

The shortest telex I ever received was from my boss: 'NO. REGARDS JOE.' Which reminds me of the classic cable from the newspaper proprietor to the dilatory foreign correspondent: 'UP-PULL SOCKS QUICKMOST OR UNJOB.'

Getting fired by fax isn't nearly as stylish.

You can even telex into a computer at the other end, which you can't do with the fax. Yes, I know about scanners which are supposed to be able to 'read' hard copy into the computer. So why is it that editors always ask for a nice clean typescript instead of a fax, please? Welcome back to the Stone Age.

But the great fallacy with the fax is to assume that it is desirable just because it is possible. The system has become more important than the quality of what is communicated – a medium without a message. 'I fax, therefore I am: I am, therefore I fax.

Response to a fax is measured by the Fax Conversion Factor (FCF) ranging from a deafening silence (you can never be sure whether a fax has been received or simply ignored); a letter; a fax; or a phone call. Score top marks for a peak-time phone call from Hong Kong.

And, of course, you can bung off faxes at night on cheap rates. I can dispatch a week's faxes on Sunday mornings. The only problem is finding other people's fax numbers engaged as they try to fax you. (Telecoms will soon get wise to this and start charging 'peak off-peak' rates.

I've often thought of connecting the fax directly to the paper-shredder, on the principle we applied to top-secret documents in the army – 'destroy before reading.'

The great fallacy with the fax is to assume that it is desirable just because it is there – the case with a lot of new technology. The system has become more important than the quality of what is communicated – a medium without a message. 'I fax, therefore I am: I am, therefore I fax.'

Faxes like mine which prints on thermal paper, should carry a 'best read before date' as faxes have a nasty way of self-destructing (like Mr. Wong's 36-hour Hong Kong suit) after a few months. I was going through my files in search of something important the other day, when I came across a letterhead squatting above a faded sheet. Well, perhaps it wasn't important anyway. Hence the immortal adage: 'I've made up my mind; don't confuse me with the fax.'

All the help I can get

1995 Business Life; 1996 Resident Abroad

The *feng shui* talisman I brought back from Hong Kong is placed according to the instructions of my proxy geomancer in the top right-hand drawer of my desk, modestly covered by a few papers of a literary nature which I shall rotate with some tricky stuff from the tax people.

Warding off negative *chih* is my latest obsession.

My talisman (for want of a proper name) looks like a gift-wrapped scarf for Aunt Vera – a rectangle of bright red paper with Chinese writing, 18 inches by 12 inches, enclosed in a cellophane sleeve. Taking it out just now, I notice a few grains of rice and leaves of what could be breakfast tea trapped in the envelope. Artefacts of some ceremonial meal? Or deliberately placed there to placate angry dragons? I mean no disrespect. I feel I have had good *chih* since I got back to Antibes two weeks ago. Or it might have been a *post hoc propter hoc* phenomenon. Only *feng shui* will tell.

Feng shui, Cantonese for wind and water, is the ancient art of geomancy which seeks harmony between buildings and nature. Failure to achieve it can harm not only individuals but entire corporations.

The Chinese believe that the Earth and the Heavens are intelligent beings shot through with positive and negative currents of energy. Positive currents are known as 'dragon lines.' They carry good *chih*, or 'life force.' The job of a geomancer – a *feng shui* master – is to make certain, with the help of a compass, that a building, a room, even a piece of furniture, is aligned to a dragon line and shielded from dangerous cross-currents. No building goes up in Hong Kong without the advice of a *feng shui* master, who advises, not only on the site, design, decoration and furnishing, but on the most auspicious time to move in or to open a hotel or office. Easy to mock, until you think how the rules of *feng shui* correspond to the ideas of those seeking to preserve the beauty of our surroundings. Makers of the Chinese landscape, in which houses and towns are sited in harmony with trees, hills and rivers, seem to have got it right. We could do with a spot of *feng shui* on the Cote d'Azur.

Feng shui explains the position of the bronze lions in front of the Hong Kong & Shanghai Bank, the shape of the Standard Charter Bank's brand new headquarters and the glass façade of the Regent Hotel's lobby (to ensure that the Kowloon dragon's route to the sea is not blocked). It's also why the insouciant triangular edges of the Bank of China building are viewed with deep unease and suspicion.

But it was the powerful vibes from the Hong Kong Electric Company building, and bad influences coming from a sharp edge of the nearby Far East Finance Tower, that were held responsible for the headaches of Dario Regazzoni, general manager of the Hotel Conrad.

'For about a month before our opening I was popping aspirin from morning till night,' he says. Our *feng shui* master told me to give up my view of the Peak and move my bookcase to block half the window. You must think I'm crazy, but since then I've felt fine and the business is great.'

Regazzoni opened the blinds to show me the view he was missing and then closed them hurriedly. 'Listen, I don't think about *feng shui* every day; I've got other things to worry about.' But you can be sure that the goldfish bowl and potted palm are not for decoration alone.

On *feng shui* advice the Conrad has a fountain in front to deflect malign influences from the Finance Tower. Palm trees have been carefully planted around a carved stone to ward off ill-effects from it being out of alignment with the entrance.

Two minutes away at the headquarters of the Peninsula Group, I had planned to talk about 'The Asian Decade' with David Katemopoulos, director of sales and marketing – a slightly-built Hong Kong Chinese of great charm and persuasion. How Katemopoulos acquired a Greek name is a long and involved story. We spent the rest of the time talking about the group's *feng shui* master. Apart from determining where filing cabinets and desk diaries should be positioned, he also does personal consultations among the staff.

'One of our purchasing managers at the Peninsula Hotel had two daughters: his wife was two months pregnant and they wanted a boy,' Katemopolous says. 'So he tested the *feng shui* master by asking: "Teacher, how many children do I have?" He said: "Right now you have two girls and your wife is pregnant." Okay, can you tell me whether it's going to be a girl or a boy? If you are right, I will come to your office and thank you with many gifts. The master said, "You're going to have a boy." And sure enough they did. Our guy called to make an appointment to see the master as he had promised. But the secretary said, "That's nice, but you'll have to wait two years to see him!"'

'Nothing about the future that you can't tell from the past,' I venture archly.

'That's right,' Katemopoulos says, glancing at his watch. 'I'd like to offer you this talisman which our *feng shui* master gave to the staff. We have a few spares. Place it in the top right-hand drawer of your desk. Inside is this handwritten Buddhist text but you're not supposed to open it.'

I believe my talisman survived the journey home. I squeezed it reverently into my briefcase, worried by the Sony sticking up underneath and the sharp edges of the cassettes. Would Customs ask me to open it up? Could the talisman contain an unlawful substance? 'Are you resident in this country, sir? A silk scarf for Aunt Vera? Would you mind if we have a look, sir?' *Feng shui!* 'There's no need for that, sir. Would you mind stepping this way..?'

No bad dragons today. Home and dry with positive *chi* and more auspicious scenarios. And a new set of problems on the horizon.

Literally. From where I sit at my computer I can see the sharp contours of the Corniche and the coast as far as Bordighera. How do I cope with the malign glitter of the sea? Are the neighbors reflecting bad *chi* from their new pool or glass curtain-wall? A few days of rain might drive angry dragons back to where they belong. Since all good *chi* comes from landward, should I spend more time at my desk? Is this why I always seem to have my best ideas over there, which disappear the moment I leap across to the keyboard? On the other hand, my desk is closer to the bathroom, and I've heard about running water representing money flowing away. A Confucian concept of cash-flow? Will Mr. Wong's 36-hour Hong Kong suit self-destruct at next week's conference in Monte Carlo? Should I move my desk over to block out the view? Where should I put the goldfish?

Ask a stupid question! Still, at my age and stage, I need all the help I can get.

Writing well is the best revenge

1995 The Author (Society of Authors)

Not a bad day as Fridays go. A couple of cheques in the mail and my column safely away. I am looking forward to a nice soft-focus weekend in the bosom of my family and some 'unstructured time' exploring the siesta for fugitive ideas. Meanwhile, a quiet introspective pastis with lots of ice should hit the spot.

After all these years my radar might have warned me. I should have been on red alert. An optimist, they say, is simply a pessimist who is badly informed. The roof falls in around 7pm when my editor at the *International Herald Tribune* rings from Paris.

'Roger? I am shocked. Someone on the financial desk has just shown me a story of yours in the *European*! The *European* is one of our direct competitors. I don't know what John [the editor-in-chief] is going to say... I am shocked.' This is from an editor I had once respected, of exemplary judgment and integrity.

Shocked! I am devastated. My *IHT* column has been at the centre of my life since we started it eleven years ago (back in 1985). I have served you loyally through feast and famine. I have been proud to be promoted as part of the editorial team. I believe I've been a good ambassador and have never knowingly betrayed or compromised the paper. However, as a freelance I have to make a living. Especially with the dollar sliding into the vortex. Loyalty surely is a two-way street.

Obviously, you don't want to see my name in direct competitors like the *Wall Street Journal* or *USA Today*. I have been approached by one, choosing to stay with the *IHT*. Competition, it seems, is in the eye of the editor – or more likely that of the suits in the advertising department.

I write for the *Daily Telegraph*. Is this a problem? The 'Witch of Neuilly' did not say. I write two columns a month for a *Financial Times* magazine; what if I were to write a similar column for the *FT*? Is this a problem? Where does 'competition' begin and end?

No joy in remonstrating. My editor is wholly sincere. Which shocks me even more.

A week or so later, a softer, more subtle but potentially more dangerous threat arrives in the form of a letter from *Resident Abroad* magazine to freelance contributors asking us to assign the entire copyright for all past and future articles to Pearson Professional for use in all other media – throughout the world – and that 'as the author of the Material I irrevocably and unconditionally waive all moral rights in the Material...' Pearson Professional is 'the new subsidiary of Pearson plc which has operational responsibility for FT magazines.'

'We realize that you might like to clarify one or two minor details, or indeed raise one or two small questions before signing the form. If so, it would facilitate enormously if you could write to me, so that I can pass your letters to the Legal Department and they can provide enlightenment.' (Kafka, thou shouldst be living at this hour!)

This is not an ironic signal from the beloved editor. (I have received three similar demands/threats from major publishers in the last three months – all of which I chucked out: no thunderbolts so far.) Time to take a stand. *Resident Abroad* shall receive a full forensic salvo.

Topped and tailed with affectionate salutations to 'The *RA* Headquarters Team,' here is the gist of my reply:

My position is clear: I decline to assign copyright for the following reasons:

(1) As a freelance I am not subject to the 'master and servant' case law which Pearson employees 'enjoy.' There surely has to be some *quid pro quo* for the insecurity of being self-employed! My implied contract with *RA* is to grant 'first serial rights' – in other words, a licence to publish – in return for a fee. This applies both to commissioned and on spec work.

(2) [My monthly] 'The Professional Expatriate' column contains some of my best creative writing: I propose collecting some of this for a new book. I also need to be able to sue it elsewhere following publication in *RA*. This material may represent serious future income. Some of the humorous pieces have sold many times around the world in print and on radio. It's pretty clear that I'm not going to hand over the copyright.

(3) I have signed a contract with the *New York Times* Syndicate who distribute my business travel columns. This would clearly conflict with a copyright assignment to Pearson International.

(4) The Assignment Form seeks to capture retrospective copyright for previously unpublished stuff. This is high chutzpah. And impracticable. Even a first-year law student could see that.

(5) The second paragraph of your letter ('The Legal Department's initiative...' is disingenuous gobbledegook. Pearson does not need copyright to 'expand the range of media in which content is delivered to our customer

base' but simply a licence to republish.

I am prepared to grant Pearson a licence to republish my *RA* stuff – for an appropriate consideration. Wow! I'm getting into the style of this.

You say that [The] Legal Department believes that getting contributors to send out this form is a way to make our lives easier.' The lives of whom? I attach an editorial from the Summer 1995 issue of *The Author*, which makes our professional position plain. I hope that the Legal Department can 'provide enlightenment.'

These two tales illustrate a double-whammy for freelances: newspaper and magazine publishers not only want our exclusive services but to own our contributions as well. They like, when it suits them, to consider us as surrogate staff – but without salary and benefits. Of course. But always with the subliminal threat 'If you don't want the work, chum, there are plenty more like you...' In these dire times, it's sometimes hard to tell the difference between a freelance and an unemployed journalist. Or between a consultant and an unemployed executive for that matter. Put it down to market forces.

Which means one needs to be pragmatic. There's no sense in needlessly sticking one's head above the parapet. One needs to strike a dialectical balance between honour and self-destruction.

One strategy is to establish a 'power base' with a publication before starting to spread your stuff around – although selling the stuff many times over by syndicating is one of the few ways of making money in this game. There's no harm in being 'owned' ('Bind me with chains of gold,' is how a successful friend of mine puts it) as long as they don't own your copyright; focus your efforts and later sign a syndication deal for worldwide distribution – the idea that if you become a big media 'name' they cannot afford to let you go. Well, yes. 'Up to a point, Lord Copper.'

Another strategy, of course, is to use a pseudonym for competitive publications. But you may get short-changed. 'You have to understand, old boy, we thought we were paying for Joe Bloggs.' On the other hand, you may find yourself being headhunted under your pseudonym, (Here's one for paranoiacs: the stand-in on the business desk gets muddled – he sticks your real name on the story and your pseudonym on the cheque.)

Paradoxically, it's often celebrity or specialist writers who encounter most constraints. Not that I'd presume to push myself forward, you understand, but I do answer to a 'niche' reputation in business travel and corporate satire. The point is that I'd have saved myself no end of grief with the *IHT* if I'd started writing a gardening column in the *European* instead of on business travel.

Publishers cheat and dissemble. One doesn't have to be a professional cynic to realize that they sell copyright material which is not their property. Refuse to sign (which you should) their wretched copyright assignment form and they'll probably go ahead and use your stuff regardless. How are you to know?

One device is for newspapers and magazines to establish 'lift-off' rights with other publishers for a 'global' fee. It has happened to me time and time again suddenly to find a story of mine gratuitously republished in another paper – sometimes to my grave embarrassment having legitimately sold the same story to the editor of a competitive publication to that of the one carrying the 'pirated' piece.

Newspapers often put the muscle on freelancers to prevent them working for other publications. ('Tom, I expect to be commissioning in the next few days for the Motor Show supplement. I'd prefer not to see your name in the *Telegraph*.) Fair enough. Tom's probably happy enough to get a chunk of work from his regular stable. But still.

You won't score by being narrowly legalistic. Be sensible (and sensitive) about 'competitive' publications. But don't let them push you around, using whatever moral, legal, and commercial coinage you can garner. Getting your stuff syndicated is one road to independence and self-respect. And should everything fall apart, show your mettle as a true freelance by getting a good story out of it.

Writing well is the best revenge.

Cold comfort calls

1994 Resident Abroad; Business Life

Chutzpah is practiced every day from the electronic shoebox. Sometimes it may stretch to *lèse majesté*. Here I am in white cotton trousers, tee shirt announcing 'I love mankind it's people I hate,' a tall pastis sweating a ring of ink on my notes, with Alexandra, my nine-year-old secretary, threatening to pull the phone off the desk by tugging the cord of the listening-in thingummy as she listens in to this conversation with a Captain of Industry, whom I met for the first time (and probably last) time six and a half minutes ago. Welcome to the Cold Call.

It usually starts with a desperate germ of an idea for a deadline you are about to miss and a scribbled name and phone number from someone with whom you're still on speaking terms after what you wrote last time. ('Ah, William, I wonder if you know anyone at Nirvana Cruises...You know the chairman? Fantastic! May I mention your name?') Then you're off, networking your way from one cold call to another. Necessity is the mother of friendship. Until you reach pay dirt.

The coldest of cold calls is when all you have is a phone number. Never ask for the 'chairman': you won't get past the switchboard. It's better to ask for 'the Chairman's office' and 'confide' in his secretary. Assume a warm, dissembling manner: 'Hullo, I'm Roger C. No, we haven't actually met, but he probably knows my name. Of course! What time's that likely to be? Okay, I'll try and keep my line free. Thanks so much. Bye-bye.' Getting someone you don't know to call you back is the ultimate in cold call professionalism – unless of course, they are trying to sell you something.)

Pretending to be familiar with personal habits provides verisimilitude. Ah, I see, he's out of the office till Monday. No, I don't want to bother him at home over the weekend; so would you be kind enough...''He's not back from lunch? Ah, yes, I expect he's out with Bill.' And, of course, never ask to speak to 'Mr' Jones: a professional cold caller will say, 'Ah, is John, ah, (a regimental pause of two three) ah, John Jones available? Establish a vicarious first name relationship.

After announcing yourself, you may be asked – in a North Circular accent (after which you may be shunted around the North Circular) – 'What company is that?' Or even ruder, 'Of…?' Of course, if you can say, 'Doncaster Strip Mining,' so much the better. But this annoys me almost as much as 'Does he know you?' What I do is just repeat, 'This is Roger C speaking' with a harder edge; emphasis on the 'c'. It depends whether you are buying or selling. But you can have a bit of fun from time to time. 'London Graphite?' says North Circular. 'Yes, London. You know, that little place outside Golders Green?'

Unfortunately – or fortunately – I don't enjoy the clout of the strip-mining or graphite people. So I say, 'Hullo' (with the warm confidence of a chat show host), 'this is Roger C' (emphasis on the 'is' – the idea being to make people think they should, must, know that name, that voice, when they don't have the foggiest). And then the punchline: 'calling from Antibes.' (If North Circular thinks I'm phoning from Wales, I disabuse her with a sharp, 'in France!' – which usually gets me through.) The location is the message, you might say.

Then your party is supposed to say, 'Antibes! Some people have it made. What's the weather like?' You can make their day by saying it's pouring down. Or tell them you're out on the terrace and you're just taking them into the shade. Or feed them the yin and yang bit. 'Ah, it's a glorious day; the sea is deep purple. And I can see the coast as far as Bordighera. Trouble is I've been stuck all morning at my computer screen. Accompanied by the urgent rasping of the printer. It depends on the kind of 'statement you want to make. We all need a daily dose of *Schadenfreude*. The object is to prompt a warm chuckle, followed by the magic words: 'What can I do for you?'

My life is pretty well ordained by the one-hour time difference between England and the Continent. This may sound ridiculous to folk who have daily business with Japan or the U.S.

But GMT plus one in the winter and plus two in the summer can be subtly disrupting, leading to a kind of sedentary jet lag. The phone will ring from London just as I'm sitting down to lunch. If I'm waiting for an important call, I choose a dish that can't wait: a nice Spanish omelette is ideal.

Conversely, phoning London, you are limited to a 'window' of say two hours in the morning, and two in the afternoon (a maximum of four hours per working day). Well, you can't reach many honchos much before 9.30 their time (10.30 my time); between two and four they're at lunch; by six they've left for Tunbridge Wells. One trick is to make a pre-emptive call while they're at lunch. 'Of course, I'd forgotten you're an hour behind. Would you asking him/her to call me back?'

(Of course, if you have their mobile number, you can theoretically reach them, or leave a message, any time. But like direct line numbers, unless you know them well (and even if you know them well), this may not always be a good strategy.)

Time spent in psyching yourself up for cold calls is seldom wasted (to corrupt an old military maxim). This may even involve dressing for the part. I've never gone so far as to hire a top hat and tails. But I frequently wear a tie, decent trousers and even shoes (well, espadrilles), and drink something more appropriate – a decent breakfast wine or Bombay gin instead of *pastis*. I might even shave. And for a particular editorial call, I have in mind to call out Mr Wong's 36-hour Hong Kong suit along with my old Florsheim telephone boots.

I'm sorry, I'm not in today
1994 'Roger and Out,' Business Life; 1996 Resident Abroad

Roger and out indeed! Well, yes, I was off the air for a while (discourtesy of France Telecom). If you've had no reply, it's because my answering machine is on the blink and I'm still shopping around for a new one. (Goodness knows how many important sales calls and wrong numbers I've missed.)

Not an easy task, these days, with so many high-tech options. Working in one and a half languages I need to reply in French and English. But which should be first? And should I use my own voice or a famous sound-alike? Such as Le Grand Charles (*"Non! Monsieur, il est absent"*), Richard Nixon

Roger Collis

(instant erasure), Ronald Reagan, Michael Jackson or Tweety Pie. Maybe different voices for pre-selected names. Then I'll need crossed-line babble for tricky calls. And a *force de frappe* to confound the disingenuous. Just slide this rheostat lever so, and the other party gets a blast of the prelude to *Lohengrin*. Beats Vivaldi for repelling boarders.

John Hatt, a delightfully eccentric friend of mine, who founded Eland Books, a publishing house in London specialising in vintage travel titles, is celebrated for both the excellence of his list and playing hard to get. Phone Hatt at his home-cum-office and you'll hear this message on the answering machine: "This machine is not taking messages. If you want to contact Eland Books, please send a postcard which will be dealt with at once. Letters will be forwarded and not dealt with for some time."

I was at John's place one afternoon and the phone was ringing all the time. Once he picked it up after three rings. Some sort of code. Manic laughter. "God I've been absolutely longing to talk to you." And to me: "I try not to give out codes. This person was so desperate she tried an old one. Pathetic, isn't it? It's now after 5.30. Now, whatever happens, I do not answer the phone till Monday. I can work with it ringing. It doesn't bother me." Better to call him at *Harpers & Queen* – where he is travel editor – and leave a message. He may or may not call you back. Great if you can get away with it.

I know I couldn't. In fact my life is pretty much ordained by the one-hour time difference between England and the Continent. This may sound ridiculous to folk who have daily business with Japan or the US.

But then you know where you are. You know, for example, that a nice long lunch in London will give you time to field an early morning call from New York. And that Tokyo will have to work overtime to catch you coming in late in the morning.

GMT plus one in the winter and plus two in the summer is subtly disrupting, leading to a kind of sedentary jet lag. (When in London, I always keep my watch on French time, which gives me an excuse for a precocious drink and helps me not to be too late for meetings.)

The phone will ring from London just as I'm about to sit down to lunch (if I'm expecting an important call, I have an early lunch or something that will spoil (omelettes are ideal) or leaving for the airport.

Conversely, phoning London, you are limited to a "window" of, say, two hours in the morning, and two in the afternoon (a maximum four hours per working day). On non-hangover days I am at my desk by 8 am, 7 am London time. Well, you can't reach many top honchos much before 9.30 (10.30 my time), between two and four they're at lunch, by six they have left for Tunbridge Wells. (One trick is to make a pre-emptive call when you can be sure they're not there. "Of course, I'd forgotten you're an hour behind. No, just tell him I rang would you please, Mrs Whitstable?" (The art of freelancing is to get them to call you.) Newspaper folk are harder to reach: you can write off the morning altogether. The answer might be to follow Harold Geneen (late of ITT), who is said to have arrogantly stayed on New York time wherever he was.

But this would disrupt my nocturnal affair with the BBC World Service, which sticks to GMT all year round: it's hard enough as it is working out whether I'm one or two hours ahead – especially when you're half asleep.

The World Service is a lifeline for expats. It is not just radio: it is The Wireless. A cornucopia of entertainment and erudition. Tuning in when I go to bed, I'm sure to be kept awake half the night with the promise of programmes to come – hard core news on the hour, jazz from Humphrey Lyttleton, reviews of new books ... Waking up at three o'clock - Scott Fitzgerald's "dark night of the soul" – I'm sure to be refreshed with a Bartok recital or a lucubration on soya bean futures or the plight of the rain forest. Reveille is usually 5.30 (GMT for Financial News and *Words of Faith* (often interchangeable). It's often hard to tell whether I've dreamed something, heard it during the night or dredged it up from the sub-conscious.

I listen during the night when the local FM English-language radio station in Monte Carlo shuts off its own trash presented by adenoidal antipodean DJs and relays the World Service from around midnight to 6am. Short-wave doesn't really work on my little Sony. I suppose I ought to get a satellite dish, but then I'd never get any work done in the electronic shoe-box during the day.

Tuning in when I go to bed with the Sony tucked close to my ear, I'm sure to be kept awake half the night with the promise of programs to come: hard-core news on the hour; 'People and Politics;' 'Jazz for the Asking;' 'Farming World,' with crucial updates on tilth or irrigation or a lucubration on the perils of global warming; the plight of the rain forests or regional elections in Equador... drifting in and out of sleep.

Suddenly awake at three o'clock, I am sure to be refreshed by a Bartok quartet, or Edward Greenstreet playing a vintage recording of that glorious aria from the Barber of Seville in which Tito Gobbi informs Maria Callas that his master fancies her. Then I'll drift asleep and wake once again half way through Alastair Cooke's Letter from America. I place the machine I use for interviews next to the radio to record fugitive gems. Sometimes I find I've captured a concerto for solo snore and orchestra, or that both sets of batteries have drained.

Reveille is 05.30 GMT (07.30 my time) for Business News and *Words of Faith* (often interchangeable). 'Dollar weak in slack trading.' Catch me at breakfast and I'm sure to have the price of copper bouncing around fruitlessly in my mind.

It's often hard to tell whether I've dreamed something, heard it during the night or dredged it up from the subconscious. But I must say that 'sleeping on it' often produces the goods.

"The Big Idea always comes from the unconscious mind. Nobody ever arrives at a very big idea through a conscious, rational thought process;" is what I think I heard David Ogilvy, the veteran adman say in a recent programme called *Keys to Creativity*. "I was doing a campaign once and I couldn't think of a big idea. I was desperate and the night before I had to show something, I had a dream. I woke up at two o'clock and for once in my life I wrote it down. I went into the office and had that dream put into a TV commercial that is still running 30 years later.

"One reason that so few people have big ideas is that they're incap-able of unhooking their unconscious mind. First you have to brief your unconscious, so that it will give you ideas that are relevant. Then you have to switch off your thought process and wait for your unconscious to ring you up on the phone and say, 'I've got a good idea!'

"Ways to do that? Lots of people find taking long hot baths produces good ideas. Or long walks in the country. I've always found wine produces good ideas: the better the wine the better the idea. I said that at a press conference and somebody sent me a case of Chateau Lafitte. So I had to produce."

I'm afraid the best I can run to is the Mouton-Cadet Baron Philippe 1987 or the Chateauneuf du Pape 1988 which sells in my supermarket for 51 francs. Going down the scale is a Vin de pays du Var, which produces tolerable ideas for 8.65 francs a bottle. (First let it wheeze.) Then you have various forms of Chateau Vinaigre (Monday was a good year) and a convenient little rosé for seven francs the one-and-a-half litre plastic bottle with a picture of jovial friars toiling in the vineyards. A wine appreciated by the winos of the Place Nationale, where I pass for a daily dose of reassurance.

I'm tempted to make a late-late mid life career change and go back into the agency game. But to quote President Bush: "I don't want to make the wrong mistake."

Lightening the load with 'Live Luggage'
CNN Traveler 2010

Traveling light these days doesn't necessarily mean traveling with just hand baggage. It means investing in a new generation of 'power assisted' or 'zero-gravity' suitcases. Linked to a telescopic handle, the frailest of high-powered corporate damsels can whiz along to the departure gate, mobile phone clamped to her ear, tripping up fellow travelers with a flick of the wrist. Not to mention tired old road warriors like me – getting tripped up I mean. Live Luggage (www.liveluggage.com) claims its motorized suitcase, replete with 'anti-gravity' handle and powered by a 12 volt battery, 'transfers 85 percent of the weight to the wheels.' When you pull the case to angles between 15 and 35 degrees, power kicks in to help move the case more easily. 'Sensors fitted within the handle assess the type of ground and upward slopes.' You may think all this is a snitch for $1,300. But let's hope you don't need to drag it too far. A full charge keeps the motors going for a paltry 1.75 miles – zilch in modern airports. Still, could be a resort in a storm.

I wonder it took so long for Traveling Man to reinvent the wheel. Motorized or not, the wheeled suitcase has enfranchised the humble and weak – and introduced us to 'suitcase rage.' Personal space has increased by at least six feet. Lining up at airport security I walked into the trailing suitcase of the person in front. I cursed: the person turned round: I gave my eyes the run of the ceiling. Survival in the new airport jungle means playing the suitcase, not the person.

Then there's the problem of terminal wobble. Pulling my new black pin-striped designer suitcase too fast the other day, it started swaying alarmingly from side to side – like the Millennium Bridge across the Thames when it first opened – threatening to turn the damn thing over as I raced to the gate. So get a suitcase with 'stabilizers,' whatever they are.

Samsonite – which has been making luggage since 1910 – launched its first suitcase on wheels, the Silhouette, in 1974. Samsonite pioneered lightweight materials, magnesium and thermoplastics, culminating in the 'lightest ever B-Lite – weighing 2.2kg compared to the 10.2kg trunks made by us in the beginning.'

Say that again! Even I am too young to remember the days of steamer trunks. But I do have a heroic leather suitcase in the loft with tags and labels and two great straps and buckles. Even empty, this mother would weigh in over the excess baggage limit of many carriers.

I can hardly manage to lift it off the ground. ('Porter!' Now those were the days.)

Remember Schlep's Law: 'The weight of hand baggage increases exponentially with the walking distance to the gate.'

In the 1960s and 1970s, Samsonite briefcases were de rigueur for young executives: they came in stippled gray plastic with magnesium bindings and locks in various widths, from six to two inches wide: tough but heavy by today's standards.

I soon decamped to leather briefcases – and ultimately, to PVC shopping bags with 'executive' zip pockets and outré designs, like pigs, fruit and poppies...

Airline rules can be capricious (and rapacious) as to how many pieces you are allowed to check, or how much weight per piece, or total weight, you are allowed under airline 'a la carte' pricing. Time is luggage as the man said. Now even hand baggage has wheels.

The other day I saw an Amazonian woman straight out of Djuna Barnes ('a woman of great strength and military beauty') trailing a tiny bag, which was getting in everyone's way. It was like a toy poodle on wheels.

'Hybrid' baggage: where you attach a smaller bag (or bags) on top of a wheeled suitcase, detach this, clip on that. Mix and match; build your own suitcase. 'So, how many pieces of baggage are you checking in, sir?' 'Good question.'

Tony Benn, veteran Socialist firebrand and former minister of technology has invented a 'seat-case' – a suitcase with a fold-out stool on which to sit out long queues at the airport.

My dream suitcase would be remotely controlled with two 'intelligent' motorized wheels, and helium inflated, that can propel itself to the doors of the plane, and lift itself up to the overhead rack.

Meanwhile, look out for suitcases with wheels fitted with blades, like Boadicea's chariot, ideal for close combat in the concourse.

Some of my best friends are strangers

1990 Highlife; 1993 The Times Magazine; 2002 'The Survivor's Guide to Business Travel'

Slot me into an airline seat next to an interesting-looking neighbor, with a gin and tonic and a back-up copy of *War and Peace*, and I'll surrender to serendipity. After all these years and goodness knows how many expense-account miles, my think-bubble still fills with anticipatory asterisks and exclamation marks at the prospect of meeting someone new. I remain an unreconstructed Walter Mitty who has not accepted that the most interesting person on the plane is sure to be sitting two rows in front of me. Human contact – however inhuman – is probably the last adventure left in air travel.

Not that Fate has always given me an even hand. Sartre knew what he was talking about when he said: "Hell is other people." There was the man who spent six excruciating hours trying to sell me a corporate jet; the woman I spent six delightful hours trying to seduce, only to have the cool dry handshake after touchdown. "No, I'm OK, thanks, my husband's meeting me." And the long-distance life story: "You're a writer! My life has been so interesting. I'll tell you my story, you write it up and we'll split the proceeds."

(Even worse was boasting about being a writer, only to meet a real novelist on a promotion tour for his new book – the kind where the author's name is three times as big as the title.)

But why do people have this urge to tell you their life story? And why are instant friendships forgotten as soon as the wheels touch down? The truth is that nobody wants to remember. As Groucho famously said, "I never forget a face, but in your case I'll make an exception."

My theory is that the relationship between passengers sitting next to one another in a plane has a confessional element to it. Relaxed by food and drink and the prospect of never meeting your captive companion again, you can unburden your soul without trIn the old days, before seats were assigned, you had to target a seatmate in the departure lounge, follow him or her up the steps into the plane, and fling your briefcase on to the adjacent seat with a disingenuous smile.

Nowadays, you're left to the mercy of the check-in clerk. On long flights I ask for an aisle seat so that I can escape from my seatmate or adopt a custodial stance as circumstances demand. "Shall we share a central table?" or perhaps a more risque, "Your armrest or mine?" are useful gambits when the drinks come round.

People who complain about getting shanghaied by in-flight bores often have themselves to blame. Simple stratagems like putting on the headset, fiddling with your laptop or pretending to read (or write) *A Brief History of Time* should do the trick. The ultimate conversation killer is to answer

"What do you do?" with: "I'm in deep-sea sewage."

One way to attract attention is to delve into a crowded briefcase (people can't resist squinting at someone else's belongings). You can lubricate the gambit with a conversation piece, like bundles of $100 bills or a stuffed boa constrictor.

But don't make the same mistake as a former colleague of mine on a flight home from India. He showed a necklace he had bought for his wife (this is a true story) to the woman he'd been chatting up – which she graciously accepted.

Invest in an upgrade if you really want to meet a better class of person. Downgrade if you want to be alone. Four seats across in economy is the ultimate refuge.

Concorde is the ultimate upgrade – probably the best way to meet the high and the mighty. "The 9:30 A. M. Concorde from New York to London is the most valuable flight in the world," says an investment banker. It may be the only time in your life you will get to meet folks like Michelle Pfeiffer or Lord Hanson, Britain's top corporate raider. "You rub shoulders with rich and powerful people on the Concorde," says Robert Heller, the business author, "and if you rub long enough, some of the gold dust may come off on your shoulders."

One idea might be to allow us to change seats halfway through a flight so everybody gets the chance to meet. After all, on a long-haul flight you may be in the air for up to 16 hours. That's almost long enough to get married, start a family and get divorced, although not necessarily in that order. (No, I have not, is the answer to your question.) The new Airbus A380 600-seat super jumbo is like an airborne village with infinite scope for social congress, should we so desire.

Meanwhile, I think airlines should offer more latitude (not to mention longitude) in choosing in-flight companions. One idea might be to use the reservations computer for a spot of computer dating. They would simply punch in your high-altitude likes and dislikes and match you with a suitable seatmate.

We might even see appeals like the following in the personal column of the

Roger Collis

New York Review of Books:

"Sales executive, 35 (can pass for 34), attractive management style, into white-water canoeing, Indian artefacts, client lunches, seeks upwardly nubile flight companion for meaningful business-class relationship, view sharing seat-back videos, tall stories. Sincere replies only, please."

But if you find, as I do, that most fruitful in-flight encounters take place in the mind, beware of the "snore syndrome" – floating off into a Mittyesque trance, and waking up to dusty looks from your neighbors.

DO'S & DON'T'S

*Do invest in an upgrade – you may meet a better class of person. Downgrade if you want to be alone: four seats across in cattle class is the ultimate refuge.

*Do avoid the middle seat at all costs. Yes, you have a choice of two neighbors but it's hard to escape. The aisle seat offers strategic flexibility.

*Do avoid children (they're usually up front of every cabin) – unless you want advice on the latest computer software.

*Do take plenty of reading material for emergencies. If you don't have *War and Peace*, pretend you're writing it.

*Don't go overboard eating and drinking everything in sight; you never know who may be sitting beside you. Wrap-around magenta shades and mineral water with a musical score or screenplay invite more scrupulous attention.

*Don't say to a celebrity: "I've seen your face before. Give me a second…"

*Don't boast or make indiscreet remarks until you've positively identified your neighbor. He or she may know your boss/client/auditor/husband/wife.

*Don't hand out someone else's business card – unless that is the statement you really want to make.

My empty handshake

1968 The Guardian; 1984 If my boss calls …

I once dreamed of being a big tycoon. With sharp shark-skin suits and a fat Mercedes to take me everywhere. The diamond in my tie would flash as I made awesome decisions. And I thought how great to have a country place for unwinding at weekends. Maybe along that part of the river they call the Gold coast. With bedrooms softly quilted and a private harbour for powerboats bringing friends. On summer nights we'd sit gratefully outside and summon drinks with a little bell across the fragrant lawns.

I tried so hard for success. Even managing to arrive each morning sprightly at nine in the gleaming shrine hewn from a cliff of aluminium and glass. Where with the other pilgrims I'd join in solemn meditation upon the fortunes of fizzy tablets and terrible ailments which the advertising men devised. For I was a smooth regulation man cultivating the firm handshake and the quiet senatorial smile. My demeanour was deployed with total discretion. And naturally I kept my memoranda cool using all the latest expressions from the business magazines. Evenings I would stay late knowing how important it is to work dramatic hours. High up in my little glass cage composing lofty reports in a smooth euphemistic prose.

Of course I knew all the time they were plotting to get rid of me. Grey flannel faces would button up tightly at my approach albeit delivering some specious words of praise. But I could see through these chameleonic ways. I was wary and nimble holding my fire until I could see the whites of their manicured smiles. My radar was tuned in at meetings and cocktail parties. And soon my pocketbook was full of innuendoes. But I thought what a laugh for them to try their little jungle games. As though I hadn't heard of infra red cameras and transistorized martini olives.

So I came and went stealthily on corrugated rubber soles. With uppers in distinguished blue suede. I kept my prayer-wheel oiled and carefully tended my tobacco plant never knowing when I might need the camouflage. Each evening after work I retreated to my little apartment which looked out portentously on to the blind wall of a cigarette factory. With a crate of eggs, a catering-size can of beans and several yards of Polish sausage I enjoyed a fragile security. Always having the television warmed up to smother approaching angst. But most nights I would sit up with my fabulous collection of business magazines plotting a dizzy trajectory for my career. Having regretfully postponed the gentle distraction. A slender companion to share my lonely success. I dreamed of waking to tousled flaxen hair and the smell of fresh rashers. Instead so sad to slide uncherished into those grey mornings.

But work went well until that savage day. When I arrived in the office to find my telephone spirited away and my secretary dabbing her eyes saying she had been reassigned. I was moved to find such rare compassion in those slender fingers which had typed so many proud symphonies for me. Now pointing to the long envelope marked personal and confidential tucked into my lonely blotter. Asking me if would have the courtesy to step by this morning for a word on future policy.

There was no mistaking the iron fist behind that velvet idiom. And for a moment my stomach muscles stood to attention as the adrenalin flowed. But I soon bounced back off the ropes and years of jungle training went into my stance. The brisk handkerchief and a well chosen smile. Walking past serried rows of eyes that look up knowingly from behind the thudding typewriters. And along dark corridors where the sound of executions is muffled by rich carpets. A soft tap at the door and into the august presence. Coiling cigar smoke and the hiss of air-conditioning. On the wall I spied two modern masters no doubt of solid investment value. No philistine here. And behind the desk such a grave profile with just the right amount of silver grey at the temples and a hint of impending dewlaps. Turning to me with a smile as fragile as fine porcelain. Head exquisitely tilted to dispense regret. This reorganization Mr C. I know you'll appreciate the necessity. I've enjoyed reading some of your reports but feel you've been getting a little stale of late. Perhaps you need a complete break. Really for your own sake it might be best if we said goodbye. Of course I shall be personally sorry to have you leave us Mr C.

I was grieved by these hard words but thought it prudent not to demur. Knowing how important it is on a hostile shore to ebb decorously. I thought of silver linings and the cool professionals I'd read about who do the rounds bidding remunerative farewells. I gathered myself to murmur thanks at joining such exclusive ranks. And I shot out an expectant cuff. But alas there was no gold in that cold handshake. And outside with a premonitory snap of winter in the air no fat Mercedes to take me anywhere.

Even 'masters of the universe' can have enemies

Nov/Dec 2008 CNN Traveller

It's the kind of nightmare you wake up from to find it is really happening. You are about to join the swelling ranks of the 'empty-deskers,' bemusedly toting their boxes from the cathedrals of steel and glass at Canary Wharf, and all the points west (and east). Welcome to the wide world of, 'Don't call us: we'll call you.'

Kafka, thou shouldst be living at this hour/the City hath need of thee/She is a fen of stagnant waters…

At least the bastards *forewarned* you (if not forearmed you).

('I hear that Tom's leaving Diamond Securities.' 'Really! Does Tom know yet?') Perhaps Tom is already on gardening leave, planting out new hedge-funds; or toying with derivatives in the woodshed.

Yes, they told you to clear your desk 'of personal effects' by lunchtime; which should allow time (allowing for a late lunch) to retrieve the framed set of hunting prints, golf clubs, fishing gear and your remote-controlled toy Lamborghini…

By their possessions shall ye know them.

Ah, the dangers of the gilded Blackberry – it has turned traitor in your hour of need. You enter the password into your office PC to retrieve precious files and a message comes up: 'Access Denied.' And they've already blocked your all-singing-all-dancing PDA – which contains thousands of precious addresses – along with your platinum corporate credit card.

Suddenly, your PC is no longer your PC. In the (good) old days, you would just pick up your Rolodex (remember the Rolodex?), or Filofax, and head for the woods. There is a lot to be said, even today (especially today), for the Little Black Book.

'Everything in your life is with the company,' lamented one Lehman Bros employee fresh from the firing line recently. Talk about *The Naked Ape*. You have become The Naked Manager.

So much for the information age, when data can so easily dissolve before the eyes. Unless you have had the prescience to back up the data on your very own laptop or memory sticks with as much corporate stuff as you can download. And perhaps a few recordings of meetings that you made with a tie-clip microphone on your Olympus LS-10 digital recorder. Strictly for insurance (or re-assurance) purposes you understand.

Mind you, it needn't be so bad. You may leave carefree, without a backward glance as you head for 'early retirement' in the Cayman Islands: 'In order to spend more time with my money.' More productive, surely, than moving on to wreck another financial institution.

Then again, it could be a lot worse. You could be a middle-management road warrior, without a pension, your savings stashed under the mattress, hearing of your imminent exodus in the course of an already stressful business trip.

A major cause (and effect) of executive stress is insecurity. Not necessarily fear of losing your job, but the fact that the higher up you are in the hierarchy, the more dependent you are on administrative and/or political skills you have acquired in that corporate culture. The danger is that you can lose your 'trade skills' and with them your flexibility.

Security is something we all crave. But it means different things to different people – a golden parachute, or an account in the Cayman Islands. For me it means flexibility, to have what I call, 'portable skills' that can be employed pretty well anywhere. If it's an illusion, it's a comforting one. This is why the consultant often feels more secure than the corporate. It's good to have several strings to your bow; even if there's a chance they will all break at once.

Survival is about keeping your data bank up to date, developing your contacts, and sharpening your portable skills.

ALSO BY ROGER COLLIS

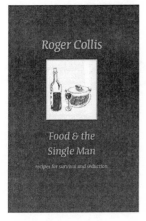

An antidote to conventional cook books

Food and the Single Man
Recipes for Survival and Seduction - ebook
Second edition
'Fast food does not need to be junk food: food can be junk at any speed.'
Here is the second edition of a small book of cheering advice for any man (or woman, or working couple), who has ever stared gloomily into the fridge late at night.

Served up with wit, panache and the occasional weird spice combination, this engaging book, part memoir and part cookery book, distils a life-time's experience into 110 pages. Here are tasty soups, stews, puddings and many inventive ways with leftovers. There is even a chapter on creative 'grazing.'

A life spent 'on the road' as a corporate executive and journalist, has given Roger a wealth of culinary experience, good and bad. In this sharp, timely little book, Roger urges his readers to 'trust the taste buds' in their heads.

He shows how, with a little intuition and fresh ingredients to hand, anyone can create satisfying, healthy and nourishing nosh simply and quickly while avoiding the temptation of processed food and microwave bung-ins.

'Like politics, and writing a newspaper column, cooking is the art of the possible. This means making do with whatever you have available in the fridge or store cupboard. (It doesn't have to be baked beans on toast – although this is a great comfort food with memories of students' dorms and bed-sitter days) as long as you have staples, such as, pasta; rice; potatoes; bread; olive oil; butter; eggs; a tin of sardines or smoked oysters or mussels, you can always put together a tasty something.) There is an exquisite dialectic between a purist and a realist.'

'Cooking for oneself is an act of self-respect; cooking for others is sharing a passion. Be humble; be proud; enjoy. And always remember: Eating well is the best revenge.'

The 2nd edition is available on Amazon, and the major on-line publishers.

Roger Collis is probably best known for his weekly column, 'The Frequent Traveler,' every Friday for 23 years (1985-2008), in the *International Herald Tribune*; and as a contributing travel columnist for the *New York Times*.' He wrote a bi- monthly column for CNN 'Traveller' magazine for 20 years, and contributes to publications on both sides of the Atlantic.

Roger was educated at Liverpool University, where he was president of the Dramatic Society; he is a member of the International Alumni Association of IMD Business School in Lausanne.

He moved to Switzerland in 1961 to run a 'creative boutique' in Lausanne for the largest British international advertising agency at the time, Colman Prentis & Varley; then became head of European marketing for Miles Laboratories, an emerging U.S. multinational, before being headhunted to become a group vice president at Cederroth International, a family-held Swedish health care company headquartered in Geneva. His last corporate job was marketing and sales director for the British subsidiary of the international pharmaceuticals giant Merck Inc. of Rahway, New Jersey.

In 1980, he made a long anticipated career change, moving to Antibes in the South of France, where he spent more than 20 years reinventing himself as a writer and newspaper/magazine journalist, contributing to local radio and to the BBC World Service, before moving back to England in 2001.

The second edition of Roger's bestselling book, *The Survivor's Guide to Business Travel*, was described by the London Times as 'the best source of independent travel advice on the market.' He is also the author of *If My Boss Calls, Make Sure you Get His Name*, a collection of columns satirizing the corporate life. He won a special award in the Carlson Wagonlit 2004 press awards for the Business Travel industry.

Roger has recently published an e-book, *Food and the Single Man – recipes for survival and seduction*.

He is a versatile voice artist and narrator: his latest venture is a 62-minute CD of 29 readings from the King James Bible, with interludes on the Celtic Harp.